TO ALL THE
WHISTLEBLOWERS,
AND ALL OF THOSE
WHO PUT THEMSELVES
AT RISK BY TELLING
THE TRUTH.

TATIANA BAZZICHELLI (ED.)

WHISTLEBLOWING FOR CHANGE

EXPOSING SYSTEMS OF POWER AND INJUSTICE

Author and Editor: Tatiana Bazzichelli
Editorial Coordinator and Project Manager: Elena Veljanovska
Graphic Design, Cover and Layout: Jonas Frankki
Copy Editing: Alannah Travers, Rebeka Veljanovska
Proofreading: Nada Bakr, Tatiana Bazzichelli, Lieke Ploeger, Elena Veljanovska
Administration: Lieke Ploeger
Legal Adviser: Lorin Decarli

Printed by Majuskel
Medienproduktion GmbH, Wetzlar
Print-ISBN 978-3-8376-5793-7
PDF-ISBN 978-3-8394-5793-1
EPUB-ISBN 978-3-7328-5793-7

https://doi.org/10.14361/9783839457931
ISSN of series: 2702-8852
eISSN of series: 2702-8860
Printed on permanent acid-free text paper.

Bibliographic information published by the Deutsche Nationalbibliothek

The Deutsche Nationalbibliothek lists this publication in the Deutsche National-
bibliografie; detailed bibliographic data are available in the Internet at
http://dnb.d-nb.de.

The book is funded by The Reva and David Logan Foundation (grant provided by NEO
Philanthropy) and the Rudolf Augstein Foundation. Supported [in part] by a grant from
the Open Society Initiative for Europe within the Open Society Foundations. Part of
Re-Imagine Europe co-funded by the Creative Europe Programme of the European
Union.

This open access publication has been enabled by the support of
POLLUX (Fachinformationsdienst Politikwissenschaft)

and a collaborative network of academic libraries for the promotion of the Open Access
transformation in the Social Sciences and Humanities (transcript Open Library Politikwissenschaft 2021).

This publication is compliant with the "Recommendations on quality standards for the
open access provision of books", Nationaler Open Access Kontaktpunkt 2018 (https://
pub.uni-bielefeld.de/record/2932189)

Main Sponsor: Staats- und Universitäts-
bibliothek Bremen (POLLUX –
Informationsdienst Politikwissenschaft)
Full Sponsorship: Universitätsbibliothek
Bayreuth | Universitätsbibliothek
der Humboldt-Universität zu
Berlin | Freie Universität Berlin -
Universitätsbibliothek | Staatsbibliothek
zu Berlin | Universitätsbibliothek
Bielefeld | Universitätsbibliothek der
Ruhr-Universität Bochum (RUB) |
Universitäts- und Landesbib-liothek
Bonn | Vorarlberger Landesbibliothek |
Universitätsbibliothek der Technischen
Universität Chemnitz | Universitäts- und
Landesbibliothek Universitätsbibliothek
Göttingen | Universitätsbibliothek
Greifswald | Universitätsbibliothek
der FernUniversität in Hagen | Staats-
und Universitätsbibliothek Carl von
Ossietzky, Hamburg | TIB – Leibniz-
Informationszentrum Technik und
Naturwissenschaften und Darmstadt
| Sächsische Landesbibliothek Staats-
und Universitätsbibliothek Dresden
(SLUB) | Universitätsbibliothek
Duisburg-Essen | Universitäts- und
Landesbibliothek Düsseldorf |
Universitätsbibliothek Erlangen-Nürnberg
| Universitätsbibliothek Frankfurt/M.
| Niedersächsische Staats- und
Universitätsbibliothek | Gottfried Wilhelm
Leibniz Bibliothek - Niedersächsische
Landesbibliothek | Universitätsbibliothek
Heidelberg | Universitätsbibliothek Kassel
| Universitätsbibliothek Kiel (CAU) |
Universitätsbibliothek Koblenz · Landau
| Universitäts- und Stadtbibliothek
Köln | Universitätsbibliothek Leipzig
| Zentral- und Hochschulbibliothek
Luzern | Universitätsbibliothek Otto-
von-Guericke-Universität Magdeburg
| Universitätsbiblio-thek Marburg |
Max Planck Digital Library (MPDL) |
Universitäts- und Landesbibliothek
Münster | Universitätsbibliothek
der Carl von Ossietzky-Universität,
Oldenburg | Universitätsbibliothek
Osnabrück | Universitätsbibliothek
Passau | Universitätsbibliothek
St. Gallen | Universitätsbibliothek
Vechta | Universitätsbibliothek Wien
| Universitätsbibliothek Wuppertal |
Zentralbibliothek Zürich
Sponsoring Light: Bundesministerium
der Verteidigung | Landesbibliothek
Oldenburg
Micro Sponsorship: Stiftung
Wissenschaft und Politik (SWP) -
Deutsches Institut für Internationale
Politik und Sicherheit | Leibniz-Institut
für Europäische Geschichte, Mainz

WHISTLEBLOWING FOR CHANGE

EXPOSING SYSTEMS OF POWER AND INJUSTICE

ACKNOWLEDGEMENTS

This book is a result of offline and online personal encounters, networked experiences, struggles and dreams. It would have not been possible without those who have blown the whistle in the past decades. My first and deepest thanks go therefore to the whistleblowers. Additionally, I would like to thank all the people who are continuing to put themselves at risk by telling the truth, supporting whistleblowers, advocating for whistleblowing, and informing about whistleblowing. There is still an enormous amount of work to be done legally, politically, technologically, and culturally, and I hope that this book will contribute to making their work more understood.

I would like to thank deeply all the people that wrote and were interviewed in this book, in alphabetical order: Magnus Ag, Barrett Brown, Brandon Bryant, Daryl Davis, Suelette Dreyfus, Naomi Colvin, Daniel Hale, Delphine Halgand-Mishra, Os Keyes, John Kiriakou, Simona Levi, Lisa Ling, Lauri Love, Annie Machon, Joana Moll, Anna Myers, Frederik Obermaier, Bastian Obermayer, Trevor Paglen, Lieke Ploeger, Laura Poitras, Denis "Jaromil" Roio, Robert Trafford, Christoph Trautvetter, Pelin Ünker, Charlotte Webb, Cian Westmoreland, Billie Winner-Davis, and Theresa Züger. It is a privilege to have had the chance to get closer to their work and their lives.

To this list I would also add Chelsea Manning, Edward Snowden, Julian Assange and the team of WikiLeaks, whose determination in exposing systems of power has been an important inspiration for many in this field.

My deepest thanks go to my colleagues at the Disruption Network Lab, and in particular to Elena Veljanovska, who worked closely with me to make this book come to life. We spent a lot of time together reflecting on the subjects, carefully checking sentences, and running against time to be able to deliver this book according to plan. Her work as editorial coordinator was irreplaceable. Thank you from the depths of my heart also to Lieke Ploeger, with whom I share the adventure of running the Disruption Network Lab, who supported our work dealing with important matters of the Lab while we were too busy with our writing, and for her contribution in the final readings. A special thank you to Alannah Travers and Rebeka Veljanovska for their impeccable work of copy editing and proofreading, and to Jonas Frankki for his visionary graphic and unique work on the layout (and, on a personal note, for supporting me greatly in moments of doubt and through difficulties during the realisation of this book).

Thank you also to the other wonderful colleagues of the Disruption Network Lab: first of all Nada Bakr, working with her positive spirit and competences as project manager since 2017 and also contributing to the reading of the chapters of this book before going to print; Lorin Decarli, who has been advising us on legal matters; all the past and present team members of the Disruption Network Lab, who shaped its current state, especially Daniela Silvestrin, Kim Voss, Claudia Dorfmüller and Monti Harmony.

It is difficult to thank all the people that contributed to making this book possible—therefore I apologise in advance for any of them missing in these pages. However, I feel the need to specifically thank some of them, because they contributed with their activities directly and indirectly, and have been central for the development of the networks of trust around the Disruption Network Lab for many years: Jacob Appelbaum, who understood the deep aims of my work since the first time we met in 2009, and shared with me both his great knowledge in the field and his friends—some of whom are also part of this book—and stimulated me to perfect my analytic work on this book; Renata Avila, who offered her help and skills in many situations through her ability to understand who is the right person for the right work in critical moments; Mustafa Al-Bassam, Serena Tinari, the Wau Holland Foundation, the Chelsea Manning Initiative Berlin, for similar reasons that they know; Mauro Mondello because we shared the curation of important conferences of the Disruption Network Lab, among them the most sensitive we ever organised, and probably many other difficult ones that will follow; Chantal Meloni, John Goetz and Laura Lucchini, because we shaped the contents of the first Disruption Network Lab conference in 2015; Tonje Hessen Schei and Gabriella Coleman, because they shared with me their networks of trust during the events they took part in; the staff of Transparency International, in particular Michael Hornsby and Eka Rostomashvili, for the long lasting cooperation with the Disruption Network Lab events since 2019; Annegret Falter and the Whistleblower-Netzwerk e.V. for their important work in Germany and the exchange we had at the beginning of our programme; Stefania Maurizi, Giovanni Pellerano, Rima Sghaier, and all the team of GlobaLeaks, Priscilla Robledo and Federico Anghelé of The Good Lobby Italia, for their knowledgeable partnership and the crucial work they do in the field of whistleblowing in Italy.

Last but not least, thank you to the team of transcript Verlag and all funders that believed in this book project: the Reva and David Logan Foundation; the Rudolf Augstein Foundation; the Open Society Initiative for Europe within the Open Society Foundations; Re-Imagine Europe co-funded by the Creative Europe Programme of the European Union.

Finally, thank you to all the people that will read this book and will contribute to shaping its future dissemination, by speaking about it or being inspired by it.

TATIANA BAZZICHELLI

Tatiana Bazzichelli is founding board member and programme director of the Disruptio
Her focus of work is hacktivism, network culture, art, and whistleblowing. In 2011–2014 s
at transmediale art & digital culture festival, where she developed the year-round progra
transmedial culture Berlin", and curated several conference events and workshops. She w
the Transparency International Anti-Corruption Award Committee 2020. From 2019 to 2
pointed jury member for the Hauptstadtkulturfonds (Capital Cultural Fund) by the Germ
ernment together with the State of Berlin, and from 2020 jury member for the Kulturlich
award for digital cultural education by the German Federal Government. She received a
Information and Media Studies at the Faculty of Arts of Aarhus University in 2011, and she
post-doctoral research at the Centre for Digital Cultures, Leuphana University of Lünebu
search, *Networked Disruption: Rethinking Oppositions in Art, Hacktivism and the Business of So*
was the result of her 2009 visiting scholarship at the H-STAR Institute of Stanford Unive
the book *Networking: The Net as Artwork* (2006) and co-edited *Disrupting Business: Art and A*
of Financial Crisis (2013). She has taught classes on whistleblowing, hacktivism, art, and d
many institutions, including the Department of Cultural Practice at the Potsdam Unive

INTRODUCTION

TATIANA BAZZICHELLI

WHISTLEBLOWING FOR CHANGE

DISRUPTION FROM WITHIN

WHISTLEBLOWING FOR CHANGE presents a critical perspective on both how to challenge power dynamics and how to expose societal injustices and wrongdoing. This book is an examination of the practice of whistleblowing in relation to cultural and artistic creation, which is a vital resource of inspiration for interventions that can generate political change.

The anthology is based on a conceptual connection between the stories of whistleblowers, investigative journalists, members of the hacker community, political activists and researchers, artists and critical thinkers in the field of information technology, politics and society. It presents multiple theoretical perspectives and direct experiences in crucial fields of investigation, thanks to diverse contributions from writers who have been central in inspiring and developing the activities of the Disruption Network Lab. By symbolically appropriating the term "disruption"—a notion traditionally used as a strategy of generating economic innovation—and bringing it into the context of political criticism, this book opens a new terrain of investigation into the framework of whistleblowing. Whistleblowing is presented as an act of "disruption", which is able to provoke the unexpected within closed systems.

To make the idea of *Whistleblowing for Change* more accessible for readers, I will conceptually connect the beginning of this collective journey with my personal story, as many authors will do over the following pages.[1] Consequently, I will connect my individual perspective to the collaborative notion of whistleblowing, which is seen in this anthology as an act that is able to have an impact in and across cultures, politics, and societies, encouraging a mindset of exposing systems of power and injustice.

The theoretical reflections that follow come from my situated analysis of political and technological resistance in today's information society. They do not necessary represent the view on whistleblowing and societal matters of the individual authors of this book, who have very diverse backgrounds and experiences. However, my aim is to examine this growing phenomenon, to offer interdisciplinary pathways to empower the public by investigating whistleblowing as a developing political practice that has the ability to provoke change from within.

Is Another World Possible?

Exactly twenty years ago, in the summer of 2001, I was highly engaged in the so-called hacker movement in Italy, and specifically in the underground culture in Rome. I was part of a collective group, AvANa (Avvisi Ai Naviganti), a former BBS-Bulletin Board System active since 1994 within the Social Centre "Forte Prenestino", which was (and still is) a very important squatted community space for experimentation at the intersection of music, culture, political antagonism, social interventions, self-organisation and Do-It-Yourself production, but also art and hacking. Together with many people in the grassroots scene in Rome, and with the Strano Network group from Tuscany, I sought to connect the discourse of hacking with artistic practices, as a form of critical reinvention of technology and culture.

In 2001, while we were all politically active, socialising knowledge around free software, cyber-rights, and a collective dimension of hacking, our activities intertwined with the so-called no-global movement—although we considered ourselves to be global. We wanted to fight the new course that global capitalism was taking, often using highly creative methods. It was an important time for local and international grassroots media, with the creation of many independent radios, self-organised TVs, and online media, including Indymedia Italy, which shared the idea of providing information by ourselves and for ourselves. In 2001, there were intense discussions about creating a form of political opposition that was effective, because it was a moment of change, not only in terms of technology and society, but also in politics. It was also the time in which we all experienced something very difficult.

In July 2021, a large international event in Genoa and many local events in different cities commemorated the three days of protests that occurred over July 19–21, 2001 during the 27th G8 Summit, which was exactly twenty years ago. For three days in 2001, across Genoa, the movement suffered a great repression from the Italian police and "carabinieri". Protester Carlo Giuliani was shot in Piazza Alimonda by a paramilitary police officer, and a brutal assault occurred inside the Pascoli-Diaz-Pertini school complex, where special unit Italian police irrupted and violently beat up many of the demonstrators who had been using the buildings as a dormitory and media centre. Around ninety of them were arrested and, after being transferred to the temporary Bolzaneto detention facility, many were tortured.[2] The issue of whether this was torture or not has been debated for years—in Italy at that time, torture was not recognised as a crime, and the investigations suffered a huge delay. It was not until April 2015 that the European Court of Human Rights ruled that Italy had violated the European Convention on Human Rights during the G8 Summit of Genoa, with Italy passing a law making torture a crime in 2017, although the law's definition of torture appears to still be too narrow.[3]

During the July 2001 G8 Summit I was not in Genoa, but in Florence with the Strano Network group. We were running an independent radio programme which informed the public about the demonstrations from a public square in Florence, connected live with Radio GAP (Global Audio Project), an independent network based at the Media Centre at the Diaz School, where other grassroots media platforms and the Genoa Social Forum were also temporarily housed.

We were working in collaboration with many other independent local radios in Italy, with the shared aim of documenting the G8 protests in Genoa. During the police irruption inside the Diaz School, we were connected live with Radio GAP. Thus, we experienced the police raid live, and it was a real shock. As soon as the police entered the building, the radio was forced to cut the live connection. There was a sense of hopelessness; we understood what was happening, we knew that it was a moment of violent repression and innocent people were suffering, and it was very difficult to cope with.[4]

In the days that followed, there was much discussion inside the Italian movement, while the press focused on the agenda of violence, on the sterile dichotomy of "good and bad protesters", with the important points that brought us together in the fight becoming secondary. The consequences of the repression were hard to forget; trials went on for years, and many people left the movement. The impact was so strong that many groups decided to stop. But it was only an apparent end. Many others continued, and projects were created anew, inventing new tactics to think about politics and activism.

After the three days of Genoa, as we called them, I started an important reflection of my own. I moved to Berlin in 2003, and became part of the city's hacker and queer scene, trying to understand how to imagine a form of political opposition that was not just frontal, but more fluid. I was reflecting on how to confront the enemy in a way that was not merely oppositional, how to not become the victim of it, and how to avoid ending up in situations from which there was no escape.

This is what happened in Genoa; the repression was orchestrated in a way that trapped the movement in a situation we could not escape from. We needed to find new strategies.

From Opposition to Disruption

In 2006, I wrote the book *Networking: The Net as Artwork*, related to the history of Italian hacking and media art, tracing a connection with the grassroots activities of social centres and activists. As a consequence of what I experienced in 2001, and the repression of Genoa, I started researching the concept of disruption as an art form. In 2008, as a PhD researcher at Aarhus University in Denmark, and later, as a Visiting Scholar at Stanford University, I came to rethink opposition in art activism, and in the business of social networking.

During these years, I also experienced another situation that totally changed my point of view, coinciding with the establishment of the so-called "social networking." From the 1990s until today, I have considered the idea of networking to be creating a context for open interactions among people, and one in which people can experiment and create artworks by developing this context independently.

From the middle of the 2000s, networking became a business and the core interest of the network economy, transforming the idea of social relations into a commodity. The consequence of this was the progressive commercialisation of openness, Do-It-Yourself and hacker ethics by social media platforms and networking enterprises. Sharing values and business development became intertwined, generating a feedback loop that was instrumental to the development of users' attention-based capitalism, despite the opposite intentions of many actors who had contributed to building up a free and open internet from the start. I felt that if we were just going to reject the business of social networking, we were going to fail. We had already failed many times before, in trying to oppose something that was clearly more powerful than us, with more resources and reach. My perspective became to imagine a critique that was not just a frontal opposition, but one that aimed to understand the inner logics of business, trying to change it from within. The outcome was the notion of Networked Disruption.

In the book *Networked Disruption: Rethinking Oppositions in Art, Hacktivism and the Business of Social Networking* (Aarhus University, 2013), I analysed the concept of disruption from a socio-political perspective, in relation to art and hacktivism.[5] The notion of disruption is appropriated from business culture to reflect on different modalities of producing criticism and, in a sense, to dismantle the constant process of appropriation that we experience (i.e. the counter-culture is taken over by businesses, the DIY culture is taken over by the network economy, a radical form of political criticism is appropriated by the opponents who adopt the same language but change its meaning, etc.).

It is a feedback loop of constant appropriation, but how do we break this loop? In my theory of Networked Disruption (2011), I proposed to analyse critical practices that occurred *through* radical disruption of business logic instead of in opposition to it.

In the business world, disruption happens when an unexpected innovation is introduced into a market, displacing an earlier technology and producing new business values and behavioural tendencies.[6] Disruption is a concept that comes from business studies. It means to introduce something into the market that the market does not expect, and to provoke a perturbation inside a closed system.

Transferring the idea of business disruption to the field of art and activism, I imagined a speculative approach where disruption became a means to generate unexpected practices and interventions, which play within the business models of the media industry, and bend their limits. This conceptual shift arose from the need to find new activist strategies that are harder to appropriate and that go beyond the mere act of opposition, which might become a trap that reinforces power hierarchies.

Through a feedback-loop-model based on the co-existence of art, business development and their disruption, I proposed to bypass the classic power/contra-power dichotomy which often serves to indirectly legitimise the adversary, instead imagining new radical routes based on the act of *provoking* disruptive and subversive interventions from the inside of the media industry as an art and activist form.[7]

An earlier example of this concept could be the experience of Luther Blissett, a multiple-use name that was shared among various individuals between 1994 and 1999—first in Italy and then internationally. The "collective name" was created to expose how media businesses, and the construction of media stories, worked. The people involved in the Luther Blissett Project created fakes, media hoaxes, and unexpected events, to later reveal societal misconduct that needed to be exposed. The idea of subversion of the status quo through "collective situations" was central, even if Luther Blissett was never openly political; it was an experiment of *applying the myth of a common cause*. There was always a moment of realisation, questioning the meaning of the truth—and claiming responsibility under the name of Luther Blissett as a conclusion of the intervention. Later, we could conceptually connect the same discourse to the tactics adopted during the early phase of Anonymous. Anonymous represented the concept of disruption quite accurately, because it revealed the hidden logic and misconduct within society and the media industry and, at the same time, played with the concept of anonymity for facts that needed to be exposed.

Networked Disruption addresses both a methodology of business innovation (disruption as an economic model) and a methodology of generating criticism (disruption as a creative act of dissent). What these methodologies have in common is that they provoke a change from within. However, they operate within two different layers and have opposing scopes; the former feeds the business machine, and the latter deconstructs it to expose its limits.[8]

Following this speculative thread, Disrupting Business becomes a theoretical framework for artistic and hacktivist criticism to operate, and a media tactic where the logics of economic, political and technological systems are exposed. This is possible by first understanding how such systems work, and consequently stretching them to their limits, by imagining possible bugs and zones of intervention that function to provoke awareness, and to reveal malfunctions—a method of criticism that has been applied in the hacker scene for decades.

Networked Disruption can happen in the context of art, but also through political and social actions and other fields of technological experimentation. Instead of radically confronting business from an outside perspective that rarely exists, contributing to fuelling innovation through acts of dissent that are promptly appropriated, the scope becomes to analyse a disruptive feedback loop of innovation and its criticism, by studying its inner logics, identifying its contradictions, and subverting it from within.[9]

By further operating a symbolic appropriation of the term disruption as the radical act of generating criticism within closed systems, and transferring it to the contexts of whistleblowing and truth-telling, a new terrain of investigation and experimentation opens up. Disruption becomes a tactic to expose systems of power and injustice.

Whistleblowing: A Disruption from Within

Around 2012 in Berlin, many people who were concerned with media culture, privacy, and social justice were beginning to become interested in whistleblowing. In 2013, we heard for the first time about Edward Snowden's disclosures. Before then, we had read about the case of Chelsea Manning. And of course, we were following the WikiLeaks releases and discussing new methods of publishing stories as a collaborative and open effort.

For me, the encounter with this scene was crucial. In 2011, I started to work as a curator at the transmediale festival in Berlin and I was applying the analysis of artistic disruption as an experiment to shape part of the festival programme—combining the idea of curating and networking as a methodology for practice-based research.

If disruption is a form of criticism that works inside closed systems and tries to bring the unexpected from within the systems themselves, as well as aiming to change them, this is pretty much what a whistleblower does. Whistleblowing is a disruption that comes from within closed systems with the aim to open them up and to provoke a change. Usually, whistleblowers are deeply part of these systems; they work inside these structures, and very often they contribute to making them

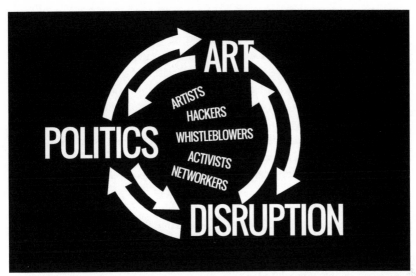

A second version of the *Disruptive Loop Diagram* (2019) displays the idea of a feedback loop that intertwines layers of interventions between art, politics and disruption. Graphic: Jonas Frankki

possible. But after witnessing wrongdoing and abuses, they decide to operate a radical mind change, and blow the whistle.

When I was working at transmediale as curator for the 2014 festival edition, I created a conference stream that was specifically about whistleblowing, and the connection between art and evidence—as described in my following chapter, and the interviews with Laura Poitras and Trevor Paglen. Before getting close to the whistleblowing scene, I had been looking at how to imagine art as a form of disruption that can interfere with business, and how we can imagine business as a form of disruption that can interfere with art. In the second phase of my research, which also connects to the foundation of the Disruption Network Lab in 2014, I applied the concept of disruption to whistleblowing.

How can we speak about disruption as a form of politics, both informing art and creating social change? How can we create a change that does not come from the outside, but from within the systems that we are dealing with? How can we analyse practices based on this co-existence of opposition, from one side belonging to the systems and from the other side undermining them?

The focus is on practices by artists, hackers, activists, networkers and whistleblowers that create disruption within politically closed systems, and at the same time generate a change. By adopting a comparative approach conceptually (researching the mutual interferences between whistleblowing, information technology and disruption), but also shedding light on practices that generate unexpected consequences inside social, political and economic systems, we propose to analyse critical strategies in the framework of whistleblowing.

The objective becomes to explore the current transformation of political and technological opposition in times of increasing geopolitical surveillance, introducing disruptive methods of intervention. Disruption opens up a possibility of interfering with systems politically, technologically and artistically. This speculative theoretical approach is what informs this anthology and unites conceptually whistleblowers, hackers, artists, activists, advocates, journalists, and researchers. The goal is to encourage the exploration of critical models of thinking and understanding, and to analyse the wider effects of whistleblowing as an act of dissent on politics, society, and the arts.

Coming back to the first question I started with: is criticism only possible through opposition?

Is today's populism co-opting the practice of disruption? Or can we respond critically to chaos and misinformation, generating disruption as a political strategy?

Disruption becomes a multifaceted concept to understanding how whistleblowing could inform social change.[10]

Exposing Systems of Power and Injustice

This anthology presents contributions about political, artistic and technological issues directly experienced and inspired by whistleblowers in order to open up a debate about whistleblowing to a broader public. As the challenge lies in exposing facts and wrongdoings that are hidden and non-accessible to the general public, whistleblowing is presented as a concrete act of change—a form of creative resistance from within systems—producing new forms of action as well as short-term and long-term effects in political, technological and cultural contexts.

Whistleblowing for Change is based on a conceptual montage of contributions by whistleblowers, investigative journalists, and members of the hacker and tech community, political activists, researchers, artists, and critical thinkers. It is a journey through multiple individual stories, practical and theoretical perspectives from writers and speakers who have been crucial in inspiring and developing the activities of the Disruption Network Lab. The majority of the writers have actively been part of the Disruption Network Lab's programme, and some of them have even been in contact with me before April 2015, when the first conference of the Disruption Network Lab, "Drones: Eyes From a Distance", took place in Berlin at Kunstquartier Bethanien.[11] Other contributors were suggested to me by some of the speakers that I initially approached, following an invisible line of mutual trust that goes back over ten years. As we will read in the short texts introducing the following thematic chapters, the association between the different contributions is speculative. It follows my specific theoretical perspective that connects a diversity of practices and approaches to explore new courses of action and investigation, as described in the chapter about the Disruption Network Lab's methodology of building networks of trust.

It is very difficult to understand the deep meaning of whistleblowing without getting to personally know the people who have blown the whistle, or the wider community of activists, journalists, advocates, and researchers who work in this field. Although whistleblowing is often part of a dry and technical discourse, it relates intimately to the lives of the people who experience it, or work on it. This book seeks to bring these lives and this work closer to the readers and, therefore, many contributions are written as personal reflections or direct interviews.[12]

Whistleblowing for Change is also an opportunity to *expose systems of power and injustice*, which is our core motto at the Disruption Network Lab. The anthology offers a tentative proposal that whistleblowing is a source of change, connecting it with the idea of *disruption from within*—and imagining that, despite the fact that we are dealing with pervasive systems of power, change is still possible, and it depends upon the actions of us all. For this reason, *Whistleblowing for Change* brings together a montage of different approaches, about and by whistleblowers, but also by researchers, journalists, and activists that want to open closed systems.

In some contexts of law, politics, and society, whistleblowing is still targeted as a form of treason. This is seen not only in the context of releasing classified information, but also in the mindset that stigmatises such acts as something deplorable. The consequence is that in our society, whistleblowers are persecuted, disregarded, isolated, and strong measures are taken against them.

On the contrary, this anthology aims to make readers reflect on the importance of such a gesture. Exposing misconduct by speaking out against it is seen as a form of action that can improve our culture and society. In the book there are contributions from whistleblowers, but also from journalists working to expose misconduct and wrongdoing, alongside artists, researchers, and activists who share a similar approach in various fields of expertise. The challenge is to reflect on the impact of whistleblowing at a broader level, as a practice that can help to shape a better world.

I believe that whistleblowing should become a civil right. My hope is that by conceptually expanding this act to a various set of practices, it will contribute to making people who are heavily persecuted for speaking out more supported. Many of the authors who have been invited to take part in this collective work contribute to *exposing systems of power and injustice*, and often pay a high price for revealing the truth.

This anthology is a forum for creative inspiration on understanding how to make a difference in society. It is an invitation to dig deeper and keep fighting.

Notes

1. This chapter elaborates upon the topics of previous workshops and lectures I gave across universities and institutions in the past years, and in particular expands on the transcription of my seminar: *Tactics of Disruption Between Art, Hacktivism & Whistleblowing*, which took place online at "The Horizontal Reading Group", Akademie Schloss Solitude, on 12.5.2021. A special thanks goes to Alannah Travers for the first transcription of the seminar and to the Akademie Schloss Solitude for providing the video recording of my talk. A further version of this talk was prepared for the Interdisciplinary Summer School 2021, Trinity College Dublin, under the title *Digital Culture & Digital Justice*, on 1.7.2021, which contributed to deepen my most recent reflections on the interconnections between oppositional practices, disruption, and whistleblowing.

2. For a detailed reconstruction of the police violence and brutality during the 2001 G8 Summit in Genoa and the legal investigations related to it, check the website: https://www.supportolegale.org.

3. See: https://www.reuters.com/article/us-italy-torture-idUSKBN19Q2SQ, retrieved August 3, 2021.

4. See the website (in Italian) where around midnight on July 21, 2001, Radio GAP documented the raid on the Diaz school live: https://processig8.net/Radio/radio_GAP.html.

5. Bazzichelli, Tatiana, *Networked Disruption: Rethinking Oppositions in Art, Hacktivism and the Business of Social Networking*, (Aarhus: DARC Press, 2013), available online for free at https://networkingart.eu/2015/03/networked-disruption.

6. For a business analysis of disruptive innovation see the 1997 book by Clayton M. Christensen: *The Innovator's Dilemma: When new technologies cause great firms to fail*, Boston, Massachusetts, USA: Harvard Business School Press. The book was inspired by the concept of the paradigm shift, introduced by philosopher of science Thomas Khun in his 1962 book *Structure of Scientific Revolutions*, Chicago: Chicago University Press, and then developed further by management consultant Dick Foster in his 1986 book *Innovation: The Attacker's Advantage*, Mono, Ontario, Canada: Summit Books.

7. See the graphic model in the introduction of the book, Bazzichelli, Tatiana, *Networked Disruption: Rethinking Oppositions in Art, Hacktivism and the Business of Social Networking*, (Aarhus: DARC Press, 2013), 10, also visible at https://www.disruptionlab.org/research.

8. This conceptual model is based on the mutual interferences and feedback loops between art/activism, disruption and its criticism, rather than on the analysis of cyclical phases of appropriation and destruction operated by capitalism. It differs therefore from the Joseph Schumpeter's 1942 "creative destruction", readapted from the economy theory of Karl Marx and Friedrich Engels in *The Communist Manifesto*, where capitalism is cyclically revolutionising the means of production, by provoking a *creative destruction* of previous economic systems. In my analysis, disruption is not destruction, but an internal perturbation coming from the inside of closed systems.

9. For a deeper analysis of disrupting business as a material of reinvention, see the book: Cox Geoff, Bazzichelli Tatiana, eds., *Disrupting Business: Art & Activism in Times of Financial Crisis*, New York: DATA browser 05, Autonomedia, 2013.

10. To read more about the *Disruptive Loop Diagram*, and how disruption connects with the practice of whistleblowing, see also the interview with Lieke Ploeger and me, "Exposing Systems of Power and Injustice" by Bianca Herlo and Daniel Irrgang, in the context of the conference "Practicing Sovereignty" at the Weizenbaum Institute in Berlin: https://sovereignty. weizenbaum-institut.de/resources/an-interview-with-the-disruption-network-lab.

11. The complete list of the Disruption Network Lab conference programme from April 2015 to today is available online at https://www.disruptionlab. org/conferences. The video documentation of the whole Disruption Network Lab's events is available at https://www.youtube.com/c/DisruptionNetworkLab/videos.

12. To preserve the personal style, background stories and experiences of the writers, the editorial decision for this anthology is to maintain the original (American or British) English spelling of the authors. We decided to uniform the book in British English but kept the original spelling for the American writers, if normally used in their writing. It is not an irrelevant choice for this book, if we consider the case of GCHQ whistleblower Katharine Gun in 2003, and the problem of the British English spelling correction at *The Observer* by a young journalist who, by turning the leaked top-secret memo from American to British English, almost undermined Gun's act of whistleblowing about an illegal spying operation ordered by the US National Security Agency (as described in this article from the person at the centre of this "incident": https://www.theguardian.com/film/2019/jul/27/international-incident-work-mistake-official-secrets-film). On a personal note, we also want to show solidarity with the person who committed the mistake, and make clear that mistakes in this field are something to learn from; therefore we also need to value them and take care not to repeat them.

Keep Fighting by the Free Chelsea Manning Initiative Berlin, at the Disruption Network Lab conference "Stunts: Distributed, Playful and Disruptive", December 12, 2015, Berlin. Photo by Nadine Nelken.

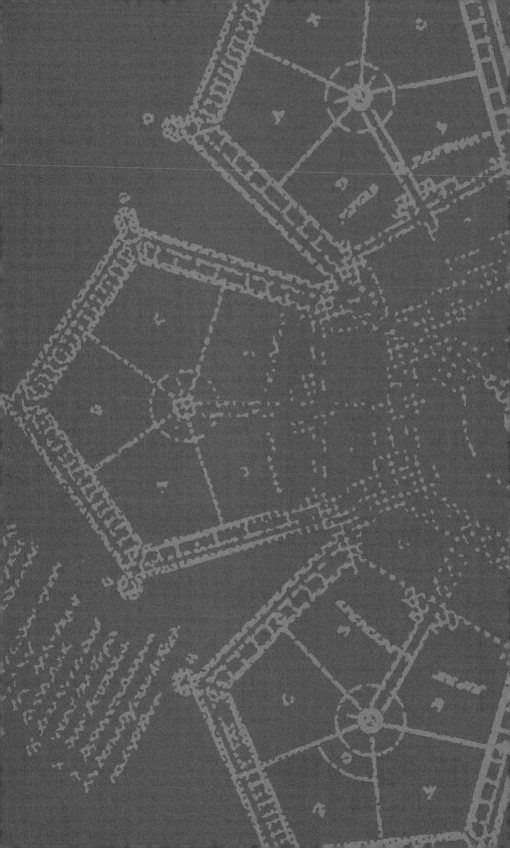

1

WHISTLE-BLOWING

THE IMPACT OF SPEAKING OUT

BILLIE JEAN WINNER-DAVIS
JOHN KIRIAKOU
BRANDON BRYANT
ANNIE MACHON

THIS BOOK STARTS with the personal story of Billie Jean Winner-Davis, who writes about her youngest daughter Reality Winner, a former contractor at the NSA who was arrested in 2017. Reality was charged under the Espionage Act for leaking a top-secret document to alert the public about the Russian GRU efforts to infiltrate voting systems in US. While Billie Winner-Davis was writing this piece seeking justice, Reality was still imprisoned in Texas, and was later transferred to a halfway housing facility. Billie Winner-Davis's contribution is followed by the personal reflections on the effects of national security whistleblowing by the CIA anti-torture whistleblower John Kiriakou, the first US intelligence officer to reveal information about the US intelligence's use of torture techniques on al-Qaeda prisoners. Putting an emphasis on the motivations and consequences for blowing the whistle, Brandon Bryant writes about his experience as the first drone operator to speak out publicly about the conditions of the US Air Force Predator programme, which was responsible for several drone strikes and attacks overseas. He deals with questions of power, technology and ethics, and how they shape our life when we enter into contact with warfare using remotely controlled technologies. The section ends with the piece by Annie Machon, a former intelligence officer for the UK's Security Service MI5, who helped blow the whistle on the misconducts of the British spy agencies. She deals with the reasons why, despite being faced with high risks and repercussions, whistleblowers choose to speak out, introducing the stories of some of the most impactful whistleblowers of the past years.

BILLIE JEAN WINNER-DAVIS

Billie Jean Winner-Davis is the mother of Reality Winner and Brittany Winner. Prior to June 3, 2017, Billie was a social worker enjoying her lifelong (26+ years) career with Child Protective Services in South Texas. On June 3, 2017, when her youngest daughter Reality Leigh Winner was arrested and charged under the Espionage Act, Billie's entire life changed and she became a mother with a mission: to advocate for her daughter Reality and ensure that the public heard their side and that her daughter was not forgotten. Since Reality Winner's arrest, Billie has utilised social media, has written to numerous organisations, congressional leaders, and media outlets; doing anything she could think of to build awareness and support. She has worked with a small number of supporters to develop a non-profit organisation—Stand With Reality, as well as other whistleblower and veteran's support groups. Most importantly, she has been an advocate for her daughter within the system, communicating with her for support and communicating with the jail and prison officials to ensure Reality's needs were met and that she was treated fairly and is safe.

BILLIE JEAN WINNER-DAVIS
THE CASE OF REALITY WINNER
A MOTHER'S VIEW

MY NAME is Billie Jean Winner-Davis. On June 3, 2017 my daughter Reality Leigh Winner called my husband, Gary, and told him that she was in trouble. She was in the custody of FBI agents at her home in Augusta, Georgia, and was being taken to jail. Our family nightmare was just beginning. Today, nearly 4 years to the date of her arrest and jailing, my daughter is still in the custody of the United States Bureau of Prisons. This piece is my story of this nightmare and how the country I once believed in turned its back on me and persecuted my baby girl.

Reality Leigh and her older sister Brittany were both born and raised in South Texas in a very rural area. Both girls were extremely smart and each talented in their own ways. Reality was a straight A student and top 10 of her high school class. She was in the National Honor Society, was an extremely talented artist, and played soccer and tennis. She never associated with the popular crowd and didn't follow trends. She was extremely critical of anyone who didn't strive to be their best and had "rules" for her boyfriends to follow if they wanted to continue to date her. She would assign them homework and reading assignments and would monitor their grades. She became interested in languages, art, and religion at a young age, and with her goal of being an Air Force linguist in mind, taught herself to speak and read Arabic during her senior year of high school. Reality enlisted in the Air Force's delayed entry program before her high school graduation, and as she stepped onto the bus taking her off to basic training, she shared that she had turned down a full ride scholarship for engineering at the local Texas A&M University. She wanted to experience being an adult and didn't want to spend her time in a classroom or collecting what she described as "a thousand-dollar piece of paper" (degree). I was extremely proud of her and her decision to join the Air Force. Two months later, we attended her graduation from basic training and I was amazed to see the transformation in her. She was a soldier. She was a fierce young person who had taken an oath to defend and protect her country.

Reality served in the United States Air Force as a linguist and an analyst for 6 years. She was trained at the Defensive Language Institute in Monterrey California, and is fluent in Farsi, Dari, and Pashto. For Reality, just learning the language was not enough. She immersed herself in the history and culture of Persia and Afghanistan and fell in love with this new world she had found. She read everything she could about the Middle East and watched newscasts for a deeper understanding about the war and its origins. Due to her commitment and diligence, Reality was awarded a medal of commendation, for outstanding service. Her commendation medal (given to me and my husband for Christmas by Reality) outlines her outstanding accomplishments. Reality was responsible for geo-locating 120 enemy combatants during 734 airborne sorties and facilitating 816 intelligence missions, producing 3,236 time sensitive reports which assisted with the identification and protection from more than 100 enemies in the battlefield. The commendation goes on to state that while deployed, Airman Winner was appointed as the lead deployment language analyst, producing 2,500 reports, aiding in 650 enemy captures, 600 enemies killed in action, and identifying 900 high value targets. My daughter was also commended for providing fitness courses to her fellow soldiers, ensuring wellness and health to 2,500 fellow wingmen. Prior to receiving and reading the commendation, I had very little understanding of what my daughter did in the Air Force. I knew she worked at the NSA, as she took me for a tour once when I visited her, but I did not know what she did while she was there. Reading the words on the commendation on Christmas Eve 2016, I was in awe of my daughter and what she had done for her country. What she had done for us. I was also quite fearful about the emotional toll her involvement in the war would have on her. Although she had just accepted a job as an analyst with a private company at the NSA in Augusta, Georgia, Reality talked about wanting to go to Iran or Afghanistan to help the people. For the first time I understood why she wanted to do this. Why she supported the White Helmets and urged me to donate to them as she did. It was because she had seen the devastation up close on her computer monitor. Because she had been involved in identifying targets and contributing to their fate. Because she had been responsible for some of the damage caused.

In addition to being an outstanding Airman, my daughter Reality Leigh devoted her free time to volunteerism. She worked with the Samaritan's Purse each year to promote and provide "Shoe Box" gifts for children across the world and also ran as a "Wingman" for a program in Maryland called "Athletes Serving Athletes", where she would run marathon races pushing youth with severe disabilities across finish lines. She fostered and adopted rescue animals and fed the homeless. Reality is and has always been a selfless and compassionate person, who believes in helping and doing the right thing. She adopted a vegan lifestyle, in order to stay true to her beliefs in helping to prevent climate change and stop the abuse of animals for human consumption. She also trained and was certified as both a spinning instructor and a yoga instructor, believing that fitness and mediation could heal.

In January 2017, Reality left our house and traveled to Augusta, GA, where she would begin her work as a contractor at the NSA on Fort Gordon. Reality had been deployed to Augusta, GA for a special assignment while in the Air Force and had fallen in love with the town. She had friends there and was also employed at a yoga studio and was eager to rejoin her cross-fit crew. She had her whole future in front of her and had so many things to look forward to. She quickly became involved with a dog rescue and began fostering a neglected and special needs collie mix, Mickey. She began weightlifting, on top of teaching spinning and yoga and doing her cross-fit routine, and was scheduled for her first weightlifting competition. She followed her father's dream and took a weekend trip to Belize in his honor, as it was somewhere he had always talked about taking her. She met a new guy and was excited about an upcoming date that was never to occur. She was 25 years old and had a bright and adventurous future in front of her. She could achieve anything.

On June 3, 2017, as she returned home from her weekly grocery shopping trip, Reality was met by 11 FBI agents, all male, 9 of them armed. They explained that they had a warrant for her house, car, phone and person. They took her keys and phone and coaxed her into the back room of her home, where she had already told them she felt uncomfortable. They coerced a confession from her, using friendly interviewing tactics and violating her Miranda rights, never once telling her she had the right to remain silent and the right to request an attorney be present for the interrogation. In the United States, the Miranda warning is a required notification that law enforcement and criminal investigators must provide when interrogating a person in a criminal investigation. The Miranda warning lets the subject know, very clearly, that they have the right to remain silent and they have the right to call an attorney. Reality was never advised of these rights, and due to her military and employment experience, would not have known that she had the right to refuse to answer questions without an attorney present.

Reality admitted during this interrogation to printing a top-secret document detailing the Russian GRU efforts to infiltrate voting systems in 21 states. She admitted to folding the document and hiding it in her pantyhose, taking out of the NSA and mailing it anonymously to *The Intercept*. Reality was swiftly arrested and transferred to a county jail in rural Lincoln County, Georgia, where she would wait for a release that never came.

The following Monday, Reality was charged with willful retention and transmission of national defense information under the 1917 Espionage act for the release of a classified document to a news source, *The Intercept*. Although I do not understand the information or content of the document printed by *The Intercept*, I have been told that the document contained summarized information from the national intelligence agencies, of an attempt, by the GRU in Russia, to infiltrate the voting systems just days before the 2016 election.[1]

The document allegedly detailed a Russian government spear-phishing e-mail campaign directed at the voting systems in 21 states around the time of the 2016 US Presidential election. People have explained to me that the document contained information as to how the Russians attempted to get inside voting software systems in order to change voter registration and vote information. As per news articles I read about this, the information in this document was being kept classified and was not even released to the states that were targeted. The Federal Election Committee was also kept in the dark until the unauthorized release to *The Intercept*. The FEC was the first agency to speak out on social media about this important information and they were the very first to use the hashtag #RealityWinner. During the week that Reality printed and mailed this document anonymously to *The Intercept*, then President Trump was telling Americans that the investigation into Russian interference in the 2016 election was a hoax. Trump pressured then FBI Director James Comey to end the inquiry into the Russia investigation, and when Comey refused to do so, he fired Comey. Trump was reported to tell Russian diplomats during a meeting in the Oval Office that he fired Comey, putting an end to the investigation. This is when my daughter decided to act. She had nothing to gain, mailing the document anonymously, and was only acting in our country's best interest, yet they persecuted her like a spy.

Since her arrest, many have asked if she has expressed her motives for releasing the document. I tell people, in all honesty, that we have never had a conversation about the document, her release, or her motives. Every single conversation that I have had with my daughter, whether it be during a jail visit, a phone call, or through e-mail or letters has been monitored closely by the United States government. The only clues I have into her motives for releasing the information to the public are found in the FBI interrogation transcript, where she verbalized that she felt helpless and questioned why, when everything else was being leaked, this information was not getting out there. At the time of the release, the Russian interference in our elections via social media campaigns was known, but prior to the publishing of Reality's leaked document, there was no information about the Russian attacks on our actual voting software or systems. This information seemed to be new. Prior to *The Intercept's* publishing, and the news of my daughter's arrest and charge for leaking this information, I am told that America had never been provided with irrefutable intelligence information about a Russian attack on our voting systems during the 2016 election. In my opinion, Russia had acted to interfere with our democracy, and my daughter believed Americans had the right to know. My daughter told the FBI agents honestly, "Why do I have this job if I'm just going to sit back and be helpless", "I felt really hopeless and, uhm, seeing that information that had been contested back and forth back and forth in the public domain for so long, trying to figure out, like, with everything else that keeps getting released and keeps getting leaked why isn't this getting—why isn't this out there? Why can't this be public?" Those are Reality's words, typed and recorded on the official FBI transcript from their interrogation with Reality Winner at her home in Augusta, Georgia on June 3, 2017.

Reality was denied bail, as the government claimed she was a danger and a flight risk. They utilized private messages between her and her sister, hyperbole between 2 very witty and sarcastic young sisters who had no idea the government would fish around in their private sister conversations for anything incriminating. The government weaponized her military service, stating that because Reality was an expert in Middle Eastern languages, and had had access to classified information during her Air Force term, she could be recruited by another country. Her $30,000.00 savings was also used to show that she had means to flee.

The Intercept, the online media outlet known for publishing whistleblower reports mishandled the classified document anonymously mailed to them by my daughter, making it easier for the FBI to quickly identify Reality as the source of the leaked information. The document provided to *The Intercept* and shown to the FBI contained printer marks that were unique to the very printer the NSA used. Because of the mistakes identified, First Look Media and the Press Freedom Defense Fund quickly acted to assemble a legal team to join the small Augusta, GA firm of Bell and Brigham and paid for the very expensive legal defense. The legal team filed repeatedly for bail or pre-trial release for Reality, but she was denied by the court and appellate court, and remained trapped inside the substandard jail in Lincolnton, GA for over 1 year before finally breaking and accepting a plea deal that would give her a record breaking and award-winning sentence. During their fight for pre-trial bail, the legal team argued that when compared to any other case of the same nature in the US, the treatment of my daughter Reality Winner was incongruent and harsh. The legal team compared Reality's case with those against Thomas Drake, General Petraeus, John Kiriakou, Jeffery Sterling, Stephen Jin-Woo Kim, and Weissman. The defense pointed out that the allegations against Reality were not different "except that she is accused of far less serious conduct: disclosing only a single document, a single time, to a single source", yet her treatment and denial of bail was so much harsher and unexplainable. To me, the denial of bail was an effective tactic—the government knew what they were doing. They knew that Reality (anyone not accustomed to or exposed to jail conditions) would not be able to withstand the torturous conditions and that eventually, she would break, she would agree to anything to get moved on to a more humane environment.

In June 2018, Reality changed her not-guilty plea to guilty and accepted a plea deal. The plea deal offered up by the Government followed a series of court rulings that went against my daughter, ignoring her petition to throw out her confession based on the violation of Miranda Warning rights, and denying her 40 out of 41 witnesses to subpoena for her trial. Being new to anything related to criminal courts, it appeared the plea deal was the best that could be hoped for, however, in retrospect, the plea deal the government coerced Reality into accepting was extremely harsh. I believe direction for this harsh deal came from Washington, DC, as an act of vengeance against Reality for revealing the truth. The plea deal conditions are as follows: Reality agreed to a prison term of 63 months (her time in Lincoln County Jail was counted as time served toward her sentence), with a 3 year supervised release period following incarceration. Reality would forfeit all rights to benefit in any way due to her case and is under a gag order for the rest of her life. According to the plea deal, which is available in court documents and on the *Stand With Reality* website court documents, Reality will never be able to speak about her work with the Air Force or NSA, and cannot write a book, memoir, or publish anything related to her work or case without pre-approval from the United States Government. The government even went so far as to include family, future family members, and associates in the plea deal, prohibiting any persons connected to Reality presently or in the future from benefiting financially from any endeavors related to Reality and her case. The sentence for Reality was a record-breaking sentence, especially considering that she was convicted of far less serious conduct than any other national security whistleblower, in that she released a single document, one time, to a single media outlet. The government officials involved in the prosecution of Reality Winner have actually been given awards for their work in securing the harshest sentence ever in a civilian criminal case of this kind. I will never forgive anyone involved in her persecution. I witnessed the attorneys for the government gleefully destroying my daughter's character and life. It was painful for me, as Reality's mother, to experience this and I never imagined that this happened in the United States of America.

During the past 4 years the media's resistance to spotlighting Reality's prosecution and case has been, in my opinion, a severe handicap for her. When she was first arrested, media swarmed all over my husband and me, wanting to know all about Reality and wanting access to her. The media had been provided with a press release by the Department of Justice, that painted Reality as a threat to America and my husband and I quickly realized that we were the only ones to defend her to the public, and to provide another narrative about who Reality is. Her denial of bail and continued jailing and a gag order imposed by the court shut down media avenues to report anything sensational, and even though I have tried to keep her case and story alive in the news, the coverage for her has been minimal. I can only offer my own guesses and opinions as to why media dropped coverage of Reality and her case. One reason I think has to do with the strict gag order imposed by the court forbidding any involved parties from media involvement or discussion of the case as well as the jailing of Reality herself, making it impossible for anyone to access her. Another reason I offer for Reality Winner being lost is due to the crazy news cycles during the Trump administration. Media outlets struggled to get out headline news fast enough due to the flood of news every day. Without sensational events, interviews, and court drama, Reality Winner's case, in my view, was not worth the time and expense to cover. I tried everything I could think of to make my daughter newsworthy, to make it worth the while of a reporter or outlet to cover and report on what was happening to her, but more often than not, I could only gain the interest of local news personnel and agencies. I can only look back and offer that had mainstream media continued to report the treatment of Reality, to include the denial of bail, the violation of her Miranda rights, the abuse and neglect she suffered in jail, and the tactics used by the Federal government to secure the harsh sentence, I believe things would have turned out differently for Reality. I believe that there would have been public outrage and pressure to ensure fair treatment. At least I would hope that there would be. What little media reports and social media attention I have managed to secure, never seems to be enough, never seems to be at the right time, and has not yet successfully gained the attention of the White House or the Office of the Pardon Attorney for the United States.

Going through this experience with Reality, my youngest daughter, has been extremely painful. Anyone with a close family member incarcerated will tell you that in a sense, when one is imprisoned, the family and those who love the person jailed are also in prison; trapped and abused by a cruel system. Having my daughter charged and convicted of espionage is also painful for me and a source of bitter anger. What my daughter did for America, for our democracy, in my opinion, was absolutely not espionage, in fact, in my opinion, her actions are the complete opposite of what one would describe as espionage.

Prior to Reality's arrest, charge and conviction for releasing this document, I had no exposure to whistleblowers or the world of classified information. I lived in a world where the names Edward Snowden and Chelsea Manning were just names, and I had no knowledge of their lives or cases. I didn't even know the term "whistleblower". When I learned about the charges against Reality and the document she released, my very first thought was that it could not have been her, as her work did not involve Russia in any way, and my very next thought was why was this information a secret? Why was our government keeping this vital information from us? Why was our president lying to us and trying to cover this up? The mere fact that they would arrest someone for revealing such valuable information to the American people, who had every right to know, was baffling to me. I was taught throughout school and growing up that the United States of America was a country built on a democracy, that "We The People" governed ourselves. If "We The People" govern ourselves, then how can this government be keeping secrets from "We The People"? What else are they hiding from us? Who gets to decide what is secret, what "We The People" are not allowed to know? As reporting on my daughter and the document she released started surfacing, I learned that other agencies, such as the Federal Election Committee, the state election personnel, and our own elected officials in congress were not made aware of the attack on our voting systems. Later, the document released by my daughter was used in congressional hearings, even though elected officials made sure to state that they strongly condemned the person who leaked the document. If my daughter had not decided to act and release this document when she did, would we have ever known the truth? Would then President Trump have ever authorized the release of this information when he was doing everything he could to suppress the truth?

What I have learned through this experience is the importance of whistleblowers in our world. Whistleblowers give us the truth, expose what our corrupt leaders and governments are hiding from us, and they keep us safe. I would guess that about 98% of Americans live in their own bubbles, never questioning information being told to them and not caring about what lies underneath or behind the systems that govern them. Most Americans live their lives day to day, trusting that everything being told to them is the truth and although there is always corruption, our democratic government is still functioning in our best interest. I say this because prior to June 3, 2017, I was one of these people. I believed that our government was truly a democratic system and that we the people governed ourselves. I believed that if a person acted to do the right thing everything would be considered and they would be treated fairly. The persecution of my daughter, Reality Winner, for her release of the truth, has destroyed my belief in the American system. Her torturous treatment and the way in which my elected representatives and systems have turned their backs on her have deeply scarred me forever. I cannot imagine the damage inflicted on Reality herself and what it will take, once she is finally released and able to breathe freely, to heal the wounds inflicted upon her by the United States of America.

Author's Afternote:

This piece was written while my daughter, Reality Leigh Winner was still imprisoned at a federal prison in Fort Worth, Texas. On June 2, 2021 Reality was released from the prison and placed in a halfway house facility in South Texas. On Wednesday June 9, 2021 Reality was released to our home, where she will serve out the remainder of her prison term on "home confinement". Reality is still confined and is not yet free, but she is now in a better place, where she will receive love, support, and any and all assistance we can give her. Reality was not granted a compassionate release or clemency; she earned this release by her exemplary behavior in prison. I am still bitter knowing that my government and everyone who was supposed to represent democracy turned their backs on Reality and my pleas for her. I still fight for clemency, as, like I have stated, she is not yet free. I still fight for a pardon as well, as I believe she deserves to be forgiven and for all of her rights to be restored. I am forever grateful to every single person who provided support, love, and prayers for Reality and our family, this was a great source of strength for me and for Reality.

Notes

1. See: Matthew Cole, Richard Esposito, Sam Biddle, Ryan Grim, "Top-Secret NSA Report Details Russian Hacking Effort Days Before 2016 Election" *The Intercept*, published June 5, 2017, https://theintercept.com/2017/06/05/top-secret-nsa-report-details-russian-hacking-effort-days-before-2016-election.

...IRIAKOU

...s a former CIA officer, former senior investigator for the Senate Foreign ...
...mer counterterrorism consultant for *ABC News*. He was responsible for th...
...of Abu Zubaydah, believed to be the third-ranking official in al-Qaeda. In ...
...e on the CIA's torture program, saying that the CIA tortured prisoners, t...
...ernment policy, and that the policy had been approved by then-President G...
...sixth whistleblower indicted by the Obama administration under the Espio...
...ish spies. He served 22 months in prison as a result of the ...lation...

JOHN KIRIAKOU
NATIONAL SECURITY WHISTLEBLOWING
TORTURE AND ITS AFTERMATH

I WAS VERY FORTUNATE to have spent 15 years at the CIA. The first half of my career was as a Middle East analyst. The second half was in counterterrorism operations. It was a dangerous and difficult job, but it was the most fun I've ever had in my life. I travelled to 65 countries with the CIA, and for a long time I felt like I was truly serving the American people and helping to keep them safe.

The September 11 attacks changed all of that. Things suddenly became deadly serious. For the first time in my career, I had to think about the danger that I was heading into, rather than the fun I would have on my overseas missions. But like everybody else in the building on September 11, I volunteered to go to Afghanistan to do whatever was asked of me. It was harder than I had expected to get to Afghanistan. My Arabic was excellent, and I had assumed that the CIA would send me there as a translator in the interrogations that I thought certainly were taking place. As it turned out, the CIA was interested in capturing al-Qaeda fighters in those early days. But it was more interested in killing them, so there weren't any interrogations that required a translator. Finally, in January 2002, I was sent to Pakistan as the CIA's chief of counterterrorist operations. It was the most challenging—and rewarding—position I had at the CIA.

Within about six weeks of my arrival in Pakistan, we received word that Abu Zubaydah was somewhere in Pakistan and we had to capture him. We thought at the time that Abu Zubaydah was the number three-ranking official in al-Qaeda. That turned out to not be true, but he was still a very bad man. It was Abu Zubaydah, for example, who founded al-Qaeda's "House of Martyrs" safehouse in Peshawar, Pakistan, where new recruits to the terrorist group waited before being sent to Afghanistan for training. It was Abu Zubaydah who created and managed al-Qaeda's two training camps in southern Afghanistan, where recruits were taught how to use weapons, how to make bombs, how to engage in urban warfare, and hand-to-hand combat, and how to carry out clandestine terrorist attacks. And Abu Zubaydah also played a role in al-Qaeda's logistics. If you were an al-Qaeda fighter and you were tired of jihad, it was Abu Zubaydah who would get you a fake passport and transport back to your home country.

The first problem I encountered was the fact that Pakistan is the size of Texas and it has nearly 200 million people in it. To say, "He's somewhere in Pakistan. Go and catch him" is simply a non-starter. Over the next two weeks, I came up with several bad ideas that got us no closer to locating Abu Zubaydah than we were when we had first heard about his presence in the country. I finally told CIA Headquarters that I needed the help of a targeting analyst. A targeting analyst is someone who pours through vast amounts of data, sometimes millions of pieces of information, in order to locate someone whom we have been tasked with capturing.

A few days after my request, a targeting analyst arrived and began going through the information that we had. After two weeks he came to me and said, "I just simply can't narrow his possible locations down to fewer than 14". That was a lot. We had never raided more than two sites before in a single night in our search for al-Qaeda fighters. We would need an enormous team.

I had to ask Headquarters for a lot more help. Just 24 hours later, they flew in a team of several dozen CIA officers and FBI agents, as well as pallets of weapons, equipment, night-vision goggles, ammunition, battering rams, secure communications, and cash. I rented two safehouses, divided up the teams, liaised with our Pakistani counterparts, and within just 48 hours, got everybody into place for the biggest counterterrorist raid in the CIA's history. On the night of March 22, 2002, we broke down the doors of 14 al-Qaeda safehouses simultaneously and we arrested dozens upon dozens of al-Qaeda fighters.

One of the fighters we caught that night was Abu Zubaydah. When our officers began breaking down the door of his safehouse, he and two compatriots climbed to the roof of their safehouse and tried to escape by jumping to the roof of the neighboring house. A Pakistani policeman on the ground shot Abu Zubaydah three times as he jumped from the roof, hitting him in the thigh, the groin, and the stomach with an AK-47.

We identified Abu Zubaydah by comparing his ear with that from a six-year-old passport photo and, realizing that it was indeed him, we rushed him to a hospital for emergency surgery to stop the bleeding. Word, though, had gotten around the al-Qaeda community that we had found him, and so al-Qaeda fighters whom we had not located began driving by the hospital and opening fire on it. I said to my Pakistani colleague, "If they realize that we're unarmed, we're dead. Can you get a helicopter in here?" He said that he could, and 20 minutes later, a Pakistani military helicopter landed in the hospital parking lot. I walked into the operating room and told the doctor to "sew him up. We have to go". Another half hour later, we landed at a Pakistani military base about 50 miles away. Abu Zubaydah remained unconscious for another 24 hours.

A Pakistani military medical team began immediately to work on Abu Zubaydah to finish the job that the hospital team had begun. Once the doctors finished the emergency operation, one came up to me and said, "I have to tell you the truth. I've been doing this for a long time and I've never seen injuries so severe where the patient lived. Keep your fingers crossed, but I don't think he's going to make it".

In the meantime, CIA Director George Tenet told me that my orders were "24/7 CIA eyes on. Do not leave his bedside". Once Abu Zubaydah came out of surgery, I was afraid that I might fall asleep and that he might escape. Perhaps he wasn't as severely wounded as the doctor had believed. Perhaps the doctor was secretly al-Qaeda. I didn't know whom to trust, so I decided to trust nobody. I tore up a sheet and tied Abu Zubaydah to the bed by his wrists and ankles. About 24 hours later, he began to stir, and he motioned for me to go next to his bed. I moved his oxygen mask away from his mouth and asked him in Arabic, "What is your name?" He shook his head and said to me in English, "I will not speak to you in God's language". I said, "That's ok, Abu Zubaydah. We know who you are". He then began to cry and said, "Please, brother. Kill me. Take the pillow and kill me". I said, "Nobody is going to kill you. We've been looking for you for a long time. You're going to get the best medical care that the American government can provide. But I'm going to give you a piece of advice. It's that you have to cooperate. I am the nicest guy that you're going to meet in this experience. My colleagues are not nice like I am. So if there's one thing that you should do, it's that you must cooperate". He responded, "You seem like a nice man, but you're the enemy. And I'll never cooperate".

Another 24 hours later, a private jet flew into the base and a team of CIA officers, clad completely in black with black hoods and masks, and heavily armed, got off the plane. Three FBI agents and I carried Abu Zubaydah out to the plane on a gurney, we tied him down to the luggage rack at the back of the plane, he squeezed my hand, and I bent over and said, "Remember, you have to cooperate". I wished him luck, the plane took off a few minutes later, and I never saw him again.

Two months later I was back at CIA Headquarters. I was in the cafeteria getting lunch when a senior counterterrorism officer approached me. He said very casually, "I'm glad I ran into you. Do you want to be trained in the use of "Enhanced Interrogation Techniques?" I had never heard the term before, so I asked what it meant. My colleague said very excitedly, "We're going to start getting rough with these guys". I asked again what that meant, and he described ten different techniques that to me constituted a torture program. He protested that they were not part of a torture program. "The President and the Justice Department have approved them", he said. "It's not torture".

I told my colleague that I thought he was insane, but that I would take an hour to think about it. I went up to the CIA's 7th floor, the executive floor, to talk to a very senior officer for whom I had worked in the Middle East a decade earlier. I knocked on his door and told him about my encounter in the cafeteria. "What do you think?" I asked. His advice was clear: "First, let's call a spade a spade. This is a torture program. They can use whatever euphemism they want. But it's torture. Second, you know how these people are. Somebody is going to go too far and they're going to kill a prisoner. There's going to be a Congressional investigation, then there's going to be a Justice Department investigation, and somebody is going to go to prison. Do you want to go to prison?" I went back to my counterterrorism colleague and said, "This is a torture program and I don't want any part of it". As it turned out, 14 officers were asked if they wanted to take part in the torture program. I'm sorry to say that I was the only one who declined. What was especially painful to me was that I knew these men. Some of them were friends of mine. We had dinner at each other's houses. Our wives were friends. I had no idea that they had had it in their hearts to mercilessly torture another human being. I was as angry as they were about the September 11 attacks. I was as sickened as they were over the loss of 3,000 American lives that day. But I didn't even know it was possible to sell one's soul to sate the desire for revenge.

The torture of Abu Zubaydah began at a secret prison on August 1, 2002. Of the 10 torture techniques that had been approved by the White House and the Justice Department, waterboarding was supposed to be the ultimate technique. It was supposed to be a technique of last resort, used only if a prisoner refused to cooperate and had actionable intelligence that could prevent another terrorist attack and save American lives. In fact, CIA officers *began* torturing Abu Zubaydah by waterboarding him. He was waterboarded 83 times and he never gave any actionable intelligence to his torturers. The FBI, on the other hand, which had been interrogating Abu Zubaydah before the CIA took over, collected a great deal of intelligence simply by treating him kindly. The CIA method was an abject failure.

The question of whether to torture went back and forth in Washington for months. The FBI argued against torture while the CIA argued in favor. When the FBI was in charge, Abu Zubaydah and subsequent prisoners provided actionable intelligence. When the CIA was in charge, the prisoners went silent. But the CIA was lying to policymakers in Washington and was promising them that the program was working.

I objected to the torture program internally at the CIA and I was ignored. Indeed, I was branded as "the human rights guy" and I was passed over for promotion because of what my boss called "a shocking lack of commitment to counterterrorism". I had just captured one of the most wanted terrorists in the world! But because I didn't want to torture him to within an inch of his life, I lacked "commitment" to counterterrorism.

My internal objections did nothing to stop or even to slow the program. I waited for somebody else to say something. There had to be one person involved in the program who was willing to go public. But nobody said a word. I realized that the

CIA had turned into something that I no longer recognized. It wasn't an organization that "recruited spies to steal secrets", as the Deputy Director for Operations used to repeat as a mantra. It wasn't an organization that analyzed those stolen secrets to allow Washington's policymakers to make the best-informed policy possible. Instead, it had become a paramilitary organization, one for which there were no rules, one for which there was no accountability. I didn't want any part of it. So in March 2004 I resigned and accepted a job in the private sector.

I honestly believed that when I left the CIA I had put that life behind me. I declined the CIA's offer to keep my security clearance. I wanted a clean break. I had no intention of ever going back, so I didn't want the security clearance or any continuing ties to the organization. I did keep up on the news, though. And I continued to wait for somebody to say something publicly about the torture program. I was heartened when somebody—it has never been clear whom—leaked to *The Washington Post* the fact that the CIA had been running an archipelago of secret prisons around the world. I was also happy to see that Amnesty International, Human Rights Watch, and the International Committee of the Red Cross reported that the CIA was carrying out torture. The media, however, didn't seem to be interested. They were waiting for somebody from inside the CIA to confirm the information. They didn't want speculation from the outside.

By December 2007, things had come to a head for me. Brian Ross, a famed journalist for *ABC News*, called me and said that he had a source who had told him that I had tortured Abu Zubaydah. That was absolutely untrue, I said. "Your source is either misinformed or lying. I was the only person who was kind to Abu Zubaydah". In the meantime, President George W. Bush, during the first week of that month, looked directly into a camera and said at a press conference, "We do not torture". I knew that was a lie. A few days later, while on his way to Camp David for the weekend, he told a reporter in response to a shouted question, "There is no torture. If there is, it's the result of a rogue CIA officer". I decided that I had had enough. I would agree to an interview with Brian Ross and no matter what he asked me, I would tell the truth.

In the interview that followed, I said three things that changed the course of the rest of my life. I said that the CIA was torturing its prisoners; I said that torture was official US government policy; and I said that the policy had been personally approved by the President. As you can imagine, those statements utterly changed the course of the rest of my life. Within 24 hours, the CIA filed something called a "crimes report" against me with the FBI, alleging that I had revealed classified information in the interview. The FBI investigated me for a full year, from December 2007 to December 2008. And then, to my very pleasant surprise, they determined that I had not committed a crime. The Justice Department went so far as to send my attorneys a "declination letter", declining to prosecute me. They said, simply, that they had found that I had revealed no classified information. The truth was that even if the torture program had been secret, it was the worst kept secret in Washington.

Three weeks later, Barrack Obama was inaugurated as President of the United States, and he named a former boss and nemesis of mine, John Brennan, as the deputy national security advisor. What I did not know was that Brennan then asked the Justice Department to secretly reopen the case against me. I had no idea that for the next three years my phones were tapped, my emails were being intercepted, and teams of FBI agents were following me everywhere I went, even into restaurants and to church with my family. In January 2012, four years after I blew the whistle on the CIA's torture program, I was arrested and charged with five felonies, including three counts of espionage, all coming out of that interview. Espionage is one of the gravest crimes with which an American can be charged, and it often carries the death penalty. In my case, the Justice Department immediately offered me a deal—take a plea to an espionage charge and do 45 years in prison. One prosecutor said, "Take a plea now and you might live to meet your grandchildren, Mr. Kiriakou".

One of the things that I learned very quickly in the criminal justice system is that the deck is stacked—always—against the defendant. I learned that the government engages in two different practices, called venue shopping and charge stacking, that make it nearly impossible for you to defend yourself or to get a fair trial. Venue shopping is where the Justice Department seeks to charge you in the federal district where you are most likely to be convicted and where you are most likely to get the longest sentence. Charge stacking is where they charge you with a myriad of felonies, they wait until you go bankrupt, and then they offer to drop all the charges but one if you agree to plead guilty. And I learned that, according to *ProPublica*, the federal government wins 98.2 percent of its cases[1], almost all of which are a result of a plea bargain. That's not justice.

I had a few things in my favor. First of all, torture is a crime. The US as long ago as 1946 outlawed exactly those techniques used by the CIA[2], and the United States is a signatory to the United Nations Convention Against Torture and Other Cruel, Inhuman, and Degrading Treatment or Punishment.[3] More importantly, it is illegal in the United States to classify a crime. That is, it is illegal to classify a program that is illegal solely for the purpose of preventing its illegality from being made public. The problem for me was that, even if torture was illegal, I would have to make that argument *after* my conviction and incarceration. Secondly, I might have been able to use something called "graymail" to my advantage. This is not blackmail, it is not illegal, but it might force the Justice Department to the negotiating table. Graymail was this: "I have decided to plead 'not guilty' and I will go to trial to defend myself. In the course of that defense, I might reveal some of the things I've learned over 15 years in the CIA. I might reveal some of the war crimes and crimes against humanity that I have witnessed over the course of my career. Do you really want to go down that road?"

The Justice Department came back on a Monday and said, "Take a guilty plea to an espionage charge and do 10 years". I told them that I wouldn't do 10 minutes. On Wednesday, they came back with an offer of eight years. And on Friday they dropped their offer to five years. My lead attorney told me, "In 52 years as an attorney in Washington, I've never seen them come down in time. In every other case, if they offer you 10 years and you decline, their next offer is 12 years, and the next is 15 years". I asked why they would come down in time with every offer. My attorney's response was direct: "It's because they have a shit case and they know it's shit. We're going to trial".

Ten months later, just as had been predicted, I went bankrupt. I owed my attorneys $1.15 million dollars. That was in addition to everything I had already paid them. The Justice Department came back with what they called their "best and final offer. If I pled guilty to violating an obscure law, the Intelligence Identities Protection Act of 1982, they would drop all the other charges, I would be sentenced to 30 months in prison, and I would do 23 months". My wife and I stayed up all night discussing the offer. At 7:00 the next morning, I called my attorneys and told them that I would turn the offer down. I was confident that I hadn't done anything wrong. It was the CIA's torture program that was wrong. I wanted to go to trial. The response from the attorneys was immediate. "Put on a pot of coffee", they said. "We're on our way over".

Three of my 11 attorneys arrived a few minutes later. The one with 52 years of experience was the most direct. "You stupid sonofabitch", he said. "Take the deal". The other two were more subtle. They reminded me that the jury consultant we had hired had told me that, "In any other district in America we would win this thing. But in the Eastern District of Virginia? Forget it. Your jury will be made up of employees and family members of employees of the CIA, the FBI, the Defense Department, the Department of Homeland Security, and Intelligence Community contractors. You don't have a chance". The attorney whom I liked and trusted the most said, "If you were my own brother, I would beg you to take the deal. This thing can be a blip in your life or it can be the defining event in your life. Make it the blip". I took the deal.

In the end, it was the right decision. I have five children who, at the time, were between the ages of one and 18. It was better to just get it over with. But to quote one of my outstanding attorneys, "This case was far bigger than John Kiriakou. This case was about transparency. It was about honesty and integrity in government".

It was then that my education about whistleblowing began. I learned several important things, things that have allowed me to advise other would-be whistleblowers. First, there is a legal definition of whistleblowing. It is "bringing to light any evidence of waste, fraud, abuse, illegality, or threats to the public health or public safety".[4] Motivation is irrelevant. Whistleblowers are sentinels of the public trust. Without them, chaos, corruption, and subterfuge rein. Second, I learned that whistleblowers have a very clearly defined sense of right and wrong—far more clearly defined than the general public. This is usually a result of having been raised in a strong nuclear family, often one with a religious background. And third, studies have shown that most whistleblowers never make a personal, professional, or financial comeback after their whistleblowing. Most lose their jobs and are not able to ever work in their fields again. Most have friends and family members walk away from them. And most have to work until the day they die because of the personal financial cost of their whistleblowing.[5] Still, it is extremely rare for a whistleblower to say that he or she would choose to not blow the whistle in retrospect.

In my own case, most of my CIA friends walked away from me. One said, "Never attempt to contact me again". Not surprisingly, he was instrumental in conceiving of and carrying out the CIA's torture program. It was no loss. But several family members with whom I had been close also cut off contact with me. My wife chose to end our marriage. I was unable to find gainful employment for six years after my release from prison.

Still, I would do it all again. Just four weeks before I was released from prison, Senator John McCain stood on the floor of the Senate and said that the American people owed me a debt of gratitude.[6] He said that had I not blown the whistle on the CIA's torture program, the American people would have had no idea what their government was doing in their name. My Congressman, James Moran, gave the same message from the floor of the House of Representatives.[7] He asked President Barrack Obama to pardon me.

And as for the CIA, successive directors have said under oath before the intelligence oversight committees that the law of the land now prevails. There is no torture program. And the secret prisons where torture took place apparently no longer exist. In her own confirmation hearings to be director of the CIA, Gina Haspel told Senate Intelligence Committee members that the torture program has been abandoned. It was a mistake. It did not result in the development of any actionable intelligence. It did not save any American lives. And it bankrupted the CIA morally and ethically.[8] I call that a victory.

I did make one mistake, and I advise all potential whistleblowers to not make the same mistake I made. If you are considering blowing the whistle to expose waste, fraud, abuse, illegality, or threats to the public health or public safety, hire an attorney first. And hire an attorney who specializes in whistleblower protection. Few attorneys, even famous A-list attorneys, understand or have backgrounds in the intricacies of whistleblowing. Whistleblowers often know that they're breaking the law when making their revelations. But they do that because sometimes laws need to be broken. When that happens, the only defense is an affirmative one. The whistleblower must be able to explain why he did what he did. He must be able to say that what he did was in the public service.

Isn't that what public service is all about? On my very first day at the CIA I raised my right hand and took an oath to "protect the Constitution of the United States against all enemies domestic and foreign". It took me a long time to realize that of the 300 people in the room that day, I was the only one who took that oath seriously. The price has been high, certainly. But I have no regrets. Somebody had to stand up for the rule of law. Somebody had to be willing to take on the centers of power. Somebody had to work for the common good. I was glad to do it.

Notes

1. Dafna Linzer, "Obama Has Granted Clemency More Rarely Than Any Modern President", *ProPublica*, published Nov. 2, 2012, accessed February 27, 2021, https://www.propublica.org/article/obama-has-granted-clemency-more-rarely-than-any-modern-president.

2. *18 U.S. Code CHAPTER 113C— TORTURE*, 2000, https://www.law.cornell.edu/uscode/text/18/part-I/chapter-113C, accessed February 27, 2021.

3. *Convention against Torture and Other Cruel, Inhuman or Degrading Treatment or Punishment*, New York, 10 December, 1984, accessed February 27, 2021, https://treaties.un.org/doc/Treaties/1987/06/19870626%2002-38%20AM/Ch_IV_9p.pdf.

4. *One Hundred Twelfth Congress of the United States of America*, accessed February 27, 2021, https://www.govinfo.gov/content/pkg/BILLS-112s743enr/pdf/BILLS-112s743enr.pdf.

5. Press, Eyal. *Beautiful Souls: The Courage and Conscience of Ordinary People in Extraordinary Times*. Picador Books, 2012.

6. "Shining a light on the past", *The Economist*, published December 13, 2014, accessed February 27, 2021, https://www.economist.com/united-states/2014/12/11/shining-a-light-on-the-past.

7. "Presidential Pardon for John Kiriakou", *Congressional Record Volume 160, no. 140*, November 17, 2014, accessed February 27, 2021, https://fas.org/irp/congress/2014_cr/kiriakou.html.

8. Ken Dilanian, "CIA nominee Gina Haspel now says agency shouldn't have tortured terror suspects", *NBC News*, published May 15, 2018, accessed February 27, 2021, https://www.nbcnews.com/politics/congress/cia-nominee-gina-haspel-now-agency-shouldn-t-have-tortured-n874296.

BRANDON BRYANT

Photo by Nadine Nelken

Brandon Bryant joined the US Air Force in 2005, started training for the drone program April 12th of 2006, flew his first mission on December 3rd of that year, and fired his first hellfire shot on January 26th the following year. After leaving active duty on April 17th of 2011, he was the first drone operator to publicly speak out about the realities of the program. Seen on *Democracy Now, CNN, Fox*, published in *GQ*, *Time Magazine*, and collaborating on the first article by *The Intercept*, Brandon seeks to answer all questions and get as much information to the public as possible. In 2015 the Vereinigung Deutscher Wissenschaftler and the German section of the International Association of Lawyers against Nuclear Arms awarded Bryant with the Whistleblower Award. He was a part of Robert Greenwald's documentary *Unmanned* and in Tonje Hessen Schei's documentary *Drone*. He has spoken in front of the Security Council, and schools and par-

BRANDON BRYANT

THE ART OF WAR, THE MORAL LAW AND THE ART OF WHISTLEBLOWING

IN 2013 GQ published an interview with me titled "Confessions of a Drone Warrior". As someone who has studied warrior cultures, philosophies and codes of honor my whole life, I felt offended being called a Warrior. From Sun Tzu's *The Art of War*, to Japanese *Bushido* and the European *Chivalry* of the Middle Ages, the role of the warrior is to understand the nature of violence and war, to adhere to strict codes of honor in order to *prevent* war or at least contain its spread and effects.

Historically however, war always gets out of hand, and codes of conduct are used as propaganda to make war seem more civilized. But we need to discuss the mechanisms of war, to analyze its justifications and see through the hypocrisies. The drone war does the opposite of preventing and containing war. It removes the understanding and judgement of the warrior. And as a drone operator, my role was to push a button, to execute targets outside of combat, targets labelled as suspicious without further justification, explanation, or evidence. It is the most cowardly form of war.

I was in the Air Force for eight years from 2005 until 2013. I joined the drone program on April 12th of 2006, and I left April 17th of 2011. I had four years and 360 days of interacting with this type of technology and I've had a lot of time to think about it. I don't really think I have to explain again the danger of what's going on with the surveillance and the lack of privacy that this type of technology brings to the forefront, but I think that it is necessary to say what it meant from my perspective.

While I was in the training to be a drone operator, I freely expressed my discomfort in the actions that we were taking and my doubt upon whether or not I would be able to follow through with the act of killing. I never joined the military to kill, though I knew that was happening. In my defense, the poverty draft is a real thing, and the prize of an education was, at the time, worth the price of indentured servitude to the State.

I wanted to be a hero growing up and do something good with my life, but when I was in the drone program I felt like a coward. We were 10,000 miles away, and me and the pilot were pulling the trigger. We were not feeling any sort of physical reaction to what was going on. It was just a click of a button. What's more cowardly than that? What's more cowardly than being able to kill someone half a world away and have no skin in the game? American media excuse it by saying we're not putting our troops in, we're not hurting our own monetary value. By utilizing this technology we're killing them before they can come and kill us. That mentality is wrong because you're all of a sudden not giving respect to the other person's struggle. You're not giving respect to their ability to live their lives there. That's what this technology does when it's not used with responsibility.

You are on the opposite side of the world viewing entire people's lives in the comfort of your own home, being able to get off a shift, go home, eat a hamburger and play with your kids, pet your dog, go to sleep in your own bed. Then you do the same thing the next day and you're able to kill someone and witness the effect that your act has on those people that are on the ground. For some reason, the people that created this type of technology thought that because the disconnect was so big it wouldn't be an issue. But you've got people who are doing this job day in and day out, having to deal with the stressors of normal everyday life.

You're as intimate as a sniper without the excessive training. You're a low class sniper at the bottom of the rung. No one respects you in the military because they think that your job is easy. They're jealous of you because you don't have to do the hard stuff. But you're also given this responsibility to take people's lives. If you look at it even further, we're not even given the information that we need to really truly know what's going on. When I expressed my doubt, I was told to "shut up and color" and that should I disobey I would be handed a dishonorable discharge for failure to obey a direct order. Those who are served a dishonorable discharge are treated worse than felons who are convicted with rape and murder.

As Sun Tzu states in his opening to *The Art of War*, the art of war is of vital importance to the State. It is of my own mind that I bring this into the forefront of this written piece because those in leadership command in the US have forgotten it and have thus doomed us all to pick up their mess. Sun Tzu describes four other constant factors of war, but I will limit my discussion here to the Moral Law, as in our modern day contingencies, this one is the most violated and must be addressed before the others can be recognized. Although war is the epitome of evil one living being can do towards another, we need to do all we can to make sure it is contained within rigid boundaries.

To discuss the Moral Law, I will use the analogy of the wrestling mat and the actions that differentiate between winning and losing. Myomoto Musashi says that if you fight 1 or 10,000 it is the same, so I am bringing the complexities of 10,000 down to the simplicity of 1. In sports competitions, the rules are laid out and known to the athletes and coaches, but are enforced by a third party of referees which hold fair play in a manner sacred akin to an active priesthood. When that sacredness is violated, it's recognized by everyone involved, and undermines the whole organization's trustworthiness. In these instances, corruption must be addressed in order to appease fans and competitors alike, or failure is guaranteed.

On the wrestling mat, the contestants are contained within a circle, a predetermined boundary, and if the contestants break that agreement, a referee will blow the whistle in order to reset the match within time constraints. Each contestant has a specialty set of abilities that they practice towards achieving perfection in movement to break through any hindrance that the opponent might have. When two equal powers go against one another, all it takes is a single error and a split second to determine the winner in a bout.

On the mat, the Moral Law is determined by who has practiced the hardest, who listens to his coach, and who has worked with his fellow teammates along the same path of supreme technical mastery as he treads. In war and whistleblowing, the Moral Law is determined by what is in alignment with the people and the sovereign, regardless of the outcome of their lives and the danger inherent in action.

As a drone operator you are both on the other side of the world, and at the same time incredibly intimate with your target. You are more distant than a pilot dropping the bombs on Dresden, and closer than the closest combat. You don't know who they are, but you watch them for days on end. You know their favorite tea shop where they meet their friends. You see them hugging their wives or playing soccer with their kids. Then you are told to execute them. I had to execute people for carrying weapons. Officially this is not what we do. I am sure I have seen children running into a building I was supposed to blow up. My superiors told me I had not seen any children. They make you kill indiscriminately. It was the worst feeling that I ever had, like if my soul was being ripped out of me. Your country makes you into a murderer.

This is the most cowardly method of warfare that has ever been created in the entirety of human history. We watch human beings who live in a completely different culture than what we've experienced. What we need to do as people is to reach out to them. If America is the greatest country in the world, we are given the responsibility to not abuse this type of technology.

Where can we go in order to find those with the power to halt these violations and tell us the truth of what is happening? These acts of war in this modern age are leading us directly into what can only be described as a living hell, and if we have not already made it there, we are sitting at the doorstep waiting for the devil himself to open the portal from which there is no return. The organizations created in order to act as referees have no power to enforce the rules. Those that enforce the law do so at the discretion of those that profit from breaking those societal rules. Those who play the game and do so in the name of honor and fairness are punished when blowing the whistle themselves. Within the current dynamic of the modern world there is no accountability for any action, only punishment for truth.

It cannot come from State Players, who are strictly adhering to another of Sun Tzu's principles, that war is deception, for the State is at war with everyone, including itself. We cannot rely on the wealthy who directly profit from the deception of the People and the deaths of proclaimed enemies. We cannot rely on the media, who are stuck on 6 second soundbites, and run a theater of distraction for the people through emotional and mental manipulation. We cannot rely on our "allies" because they are just as far into this that they fall for the sunk cost fallacy. It can't even come from our enemies who know that whatever allegations they bring against us we can bring those same allegations to them, thus we are confined in a never ending blame game.

In my own path I have struggled mightily to find the answer to this problem. I have read every sacred scripture from every world religion I could get my eyes on. I have directly confronted people from the United Nations security council, down to my own peers whom should share my sentiments, and everyone in between. Nowhere have I found anyone worthy enough to solve this problem or anyone who doesn't have their hand in the honey pot of profits.

Today, I am still fighting to expose corruption, wrongdoings, and power asymmetries. In the US privileges and prevarication appear to be pervasive and incorrigible at the expense of the people. The corrupt have infiltrated every level of the American life and continue to get away with their wrongs. It is infuriating. From my experience as a soldier and whistleblower, I have come up with a lucid opposition to systems that feed on conflicts and inequality, as the pivot of a spiritual and political struggle aimed at holding powerful accountable and placing individuals at the center.

It has been nearly a year since the global pandemic of the coronavirus disrupted society at the time of this writing. The wealthy have stolen more money from the average person than ever before. War is tearing up the world, and famine threatens our already precarious health concerns. Those in leadership positions have blatantly ignored the science and hard facts in front of their face for the dancing dollar, leading more people in the US to die than the entirety of 9/11 and the conflicts that have arisen from it. We have polluted the world through our policing, and have destroyed democracy in everything but name, placing its facsimile in front of a fascist regime. The play between "left and right" or "democrat and republican" is a meaningless shadow meant to disarm and distract from the real problems facing our world and the imminent death to us all that will come should we continue to ignore them.

All political leadership have shown themselves to be in the pocket of the wealthy, worshiping Mammon while proclaiming loyalty to the Christian god to appease the mindless masses who cannot make their own decisions. It is here we see that the modern "Church" isn't in line with their Christ's message, but has been taken over in order to make capitalism more appealing to those that are being capitalized upon. We have a man who sits upon a Gold throne with an upside down cross telling us we need to give more to the poor as needy snake oil salesmen sell spiritual remedies while flying on private jets and living in multi-million dollar homes.

Donald J. Trump, former President of the United States, has been acquitted of treason by his very same followers and has doomed the United States of America into following the fate of Rome and every fallen empire in history. A man that the Christian Conservative believes has been sent by their god to bring about America's Salvation. A con-man and a scoundrel who sought to declare himself a living god and the first American Emperor. The completely anonymous "Q" has led even more people astray through his false predictions and prophecies. Those desperate to believe in something will find the strangest thing to believe in. As a trained Intelligence Analyst, it breaks my mind trying to twist this Rubik's Cube of a problem into anything that makes a lick of sense.

Where is Truth in our world and where are those that can enforce fair play for the masses?

In my own journey, I have found that the truth can only be found within the self, and can only be expressed as a part of one's self. The Moral Law doesn't give way to either the individual or the masses, but finds a balance between both, as we are individuals living upon the reliance of the whole. If we look at Heaven, it is found in the cycles of the moon, the rising and setting of the sun, and the seasons and the tides. It is reliable and unaffected by human interference. If we look at Earth, it is all those temporary things that ultimately lead into the cycle of life and death, also reliable and ultimately unaffected by human interference. I have yet to find a commander worthy enough of my own personal loyalty outside the works of fiction, so I have modeled myself after what I admire most of their characteristics, leading with the prime examples given to me by my great-grandfather and my mother. It is through my searching through religious and philosophical texts that I have found the method & discipline in order to continue walking the path that I have chosen in my own way.

Adhering to the Moral Law is the only thing that has ultimately saved me, regardless of the hurt and rage that I have experienced. Finding the truth of what I have been able to endure when I was unsure of my own capabilities, searching for internal peace instead of giving into external conflict, and making sure that I act in accordance to my own code of conduct. These are the things that will allow me to live even after my body has died.

Never did I think that I would experience the world in the way that I have. Fifteen years ago, I started this journey, mostly to get my soul right with whatever deity presides over the souls of the dead and the damned. I didn't do it for fame, for who wants to be famous for being a party to crimes against humanity? I didn't want any wealth, for why should I place myself into a corruptible position? While I ultimately did do it for my own self, I sacrificed everything I had hoped and dreamed of to do it.

When I left the drone program on April 17th of 2011 I never wanted to hear the word *drone* ever again. I wanted to get away from drones and technology completely. I was living with the fact that I had killed 13 people, and when I had gotten out I felt I had succeeded in surviving the machinations of the industrial military complex. I was a whole and healthy person who might have this burden on his soul but was going to go forward to try to do something good in the world. I got into the Survival Program of the United States Air Force, where I met the best people I have ever met in the military. They wanted to do it right, they wanted to help people, and to make sure people came home safe, to *return with honor.*

Even though I was in this program, trying to make my way and doing really good, it was still very hard. It felt like walking up a raging river. I was trying to make my way doing really good, and then I was injured and hospitalized, and the river swept me along. When I was in the hospital bed I wondered if there was anything out there that I could do to make this right.

Three years later I became a whistleblower.

I had been trying to run away and to escape my responsibilities, but watching the news I could see how much information was missing, and how Obama was telling everyone how awesome drones are. At a certain point I couldn't stay silent anymore. I knew that there were wrong things going on in the world, and that no one else was going to talk about them. I've talked to people and media that desperately needed the insider's point of view in order to get the whole picture. People in power were avoiding accountability simply because of the nature of the machine. I needed to tell people what was going on, to ultimately hold those in power accountable.

I always felt that if there's something out there that bothers you or that you feel needs to be righted and you don't do it with anything other than love and compassion, you're a traitor to yourself and all of us. That's a lesson that I had to learn really intimately. It was a really hard lesson to learn, but at the time I got a lot of encouragement from people.

Over the course of time, after doing my duty and blowing the whistle, I have suffered violent repercussions on both my private life and my public persona. I faced situations in which I feared for my life, I became a target of smear campaigns that attempted to get me to do foolish things so they could entrap me, and I experienced attempts to annihilate me physically and psychologically.[1] Today, I am a disillusioned man, someone who does not trust anyone, and I would honestly encourage the same attitude of detachment to those who seek the greater truth.

If there are no referees to make sure that the game is played fairly, we must empower each individual to do what I have been able to do. There must not be an organization that is more than temporary, very vocal, and very public. Mankind cannot afford to ignore this and expect to live on this planet for 20 more years. We are at that point where if we do not act against the principalities and powers which have governed us into the grave, then we have failed our ancestors and any future generation that had hoped to live a wonderful and prosperous life. Instead of using our technologies to kill indiscriminately and immorally, completely removing the Moral Law from the Art of War, we must create diplomats who can utilize both technology and wisdom, we must reclaim the role of the Warrior as those who prevent and contain war, be it whistleblowers, activists or hackers.

If we continue to punish those that wish to give us truth, then nothing will get better. We must remember Julian Assange, Edward Snowden, and Chelsea Manning, as well as Daniel Hale and Reality Winner. We must acknowledge the sacrifices that they have given to the greater humanity in the attempt to lead us from falling off a cliff towards our collective destruction. We must take every word, both true and false, very seriously in order to discriminate between right and wrong.

This is the essence of the Moral Law and the events happening in the world in our modern age that we need to confront.

Notes

1. Kevin Gosztola, "How a Drone Whistleblower in Montana Survived a Political Prosecution", *The Dissenter*, published on August 18, 2021, https://thedissenter.org/how-drone-whistleblower-montana-survived-political-prosecution.

ANNIE MACHON

Annie Machon was an intelligence officer for the UK's Security Service, MI5, before resigning to help blow the whistle on the crimes and incompetence of the British spies. She is now a writer, media pundit, and international public speaker on a wide variety of geopolitical issues, including the wars on terrorism, whistleblowers, drugs, and the internet. In 2021 she was awarded the SA Award for Integrity in Intelligence by the Sam Adams Associates, a global group of intelligence, diplomatic and military whistleblowers. She served four years as the European Director of Law Enforcement Action Partnership and remains a member of the European Board, is a director of the World Ethical Data Foundation (https://worldethicaldata.org), and is an advisory board member of the Good Technology Collective and the Courage Foundation. Annie has an MA (Hons) in Classics from Cambridge University.

ANNIE MACHON
THE REGULATORS OF LAST RESORT

WAY BACK in the late 1990s I was involved in a UK intelligence whistleblowing case with my former partner and colleague, David Shayler. As intelligence officers working for the UK domestic Security Service, MI5, we had witnessed so many problematic events that we resigned to blow the whistle, thereby facing arrest and prosecution for daring to speak out about deep state crimes. The whole case dragged on for over seven years and included two high profile court cases, one in France when the British government failed to have Shayler extradited back to the UK in 1998, and another when he was prosecuted and convicted after he had voluntarily returned to the UK in 2000 to "face the music" for a breach of the draconian Official Secrets Act.

During those years I learned a lot about the legal and political machinations behind the scenes, the way that the media can be manipulated, and the vital need for personal privacy. Drawing on these experiences, over the last twenty years I have tried to help and support other subsequent whistleblowers, mainly those emerging from government and intelligence circles, but also those from other sectors which are equally important, such as the health sector and finance. All are equally vital in holding power to account and I salute them. However, my focus here will be on those emerging from government and intelligence circles as they are the ones who are not only most likely to witness the most heinous issues up to and including war crimes, but also who stand to lose their professional life, reputations, and potentially their liberty, for merely speaking truth to power.

Whistleblowers You May Know

To begin with, let us play a game of word association. I write "Edward Snowden"—what is the first thought to leap into your mind? Hero? Traitor? Who?

Or might it be whistleblower?

The controversial issue of whistleblowing was firmly thrust into the global public consciousness over the last decade with the ongoing saga of WikiLeaks and with high profile cases such as that of Chelsea Manning and, of course, Snowden himself, who is probably the most famous whistleblower in the world.

Often whistleblowers can get a bad rap in the media, deemed to be traitors, grasses or snitches. Or they are set on such a heroic pedestal that their example can actually be discouraging, making you consider whether you would ever take such a risk, often with the depressing conclusion that it would be impossible for a whole range of practical reasons—professional reputation, job security, family safety, even liberty. However, you have to ask yourself why, when faced with these risks and repercussions, individuals do indeed speak out; why they still do consider the risks worth taking? Particularly those emerging from the world of intelligence, the military or the diplomatic corps who face the most grievous penalties. The UK spy community is the most legally protected and least accountable of any Western democracy, but the USA and EU countries are catching up fast. So, as a result of such entrenched governmental secrecy across these areas, whistleblowing is realistically the only available avenue to alert your fellow citizens to abuses carried out secretly in their name.

From personal experience, I have a nodding acquaintance with the process. In the 1990s I worked as an intelligence officer for the UK domestic Security Service, generally known as MI5, before resigning to help my former partner and colleague David Shayler blow the whistle on a catalogue of incompetence and crime. As a result, we had to go on the run around Europe, lived in hiding and exile in France for 3 years, and saw our friends, family and journalists arrested around us. I was also arrested, although never charged with any crime, and David went to prison twice for exposing the crimes of the spies. It was a heavy price to pay. However, it could all have been so different if the UK government had agreed to take his evidence of spy crimes, undertake to investigate them thoroughly, and apply the necessary reforms. This would have saved us a lot of heartache, and could potentially have improved the work of the spies. But the government's instinctive response is always to protect the spies and prosecute the whistleblower, while the mistakes and crimes go uninvestigated and unresolved. It even, it often appears, rewards the malefactors with promotions and honours.

The draconian Official Secrets Act (1989) imposes a blanket ban on any disclosure whatsoever. As a result, we the citizens have to take it on trust that our spies work with integrity. There is no meaningful oversight and no real accountability. In the UK, many good people do indeed sign up to MI5, MI6 and GCHQ, as they want a job that can make a difference and potentially save lives. However, once on the inside, they are told to keep quiet about any ethical concerns: "don't rock the boat, and just follow orders". In such an environment there is no ventilation, no accountability, and no staff federation, and this inevitably leads to a general consensus—a bullying "group think" mentality. This in turn can lead to mistakes being covered up rather than lessons learned, and can then potentially go down a dangerous moral slide. As a result, over the last 20 years we have seen scandal heaped upon intelligence scandal, as the spies allowed their fake and politicised information to be used to make a false case for an illegal war in Iraq; we have seen them descend into a spiral of extraordinary rendition (i.e. kidnapping) and torture, for which they are now being sued if not prosecuted; and we have seen that they facilitate dodgy deals in the deserts with dictators.

Since the Shayler case in the late 1990s, other UK whistleblowers have hit the headlines: GCHQ's Katharine Gun, who exposed illegal spying on our so-called allies in the run-up to the Iraq war in 2003. She managed to avoid prosecution because of a possible legal defence of necessity that resulted from Shayler's case. Or Ambassador Craig Murray, who exposed the torture of political dissidents in Uzbekistan—and when I say torture, I mean the boiling alive of political opponents of the regime, with the photographs to prove it. Murray was not prosecuted, but he lost his career and was traduced with tawdry slurs about his personal life across the British media.

The USA is little better. Since 2001, many intelligence whistleblowers there have faced a grim fate. Ex-CIA officer John Kiriakou, who exposed the CIA's torture programme, languished for almost two years in prison while the torturers remain free; Bill Binney, Ed Loomis, and Kirk Wiebe of the NSA were hounded and narrowly escaped prosecution for exposing NSA malfeasance; a colleague, Tom Drake, faced a 35-year prison sentence, despite having gone through all the approved, official channels; and in 2013 a kangaroo court was held to try Chelsea Manning for her exposure of US war crimes. Inevitably, it is the whistleblower Manning who was sentenced to a 35 year stretch in prison, not the war criminals. President Obama used and abused the 1917 US Espionage Act against whistleblowers during his years in the White House more times than all his predecessors put together, while at the same time allowing a bona fide spy ring—the Russian illegals including Anna Chapman—to return home in 2010. This paranoid hunt for the "insider threat"—the whistleblower—has been going on since at least 2008, as we know from documents leaked, ironically, to WikiLeaks in 2010.

Against this background, fully aware of the hideous risks he was taking and the prospect of the rest of his life behind bars, in 2013 a young man stepped forward—Edward Snowden. He was clear then about his motivation and he remains clear now in the interviews he has done since: what he had seen on the inside of the NSA caused him huge concern. The American intelligence infrastructure, along with its partner agencies across the world, was constructing a global surveillance network that not only threatens the constitution of the United States, but also erodes the privacy of all the world's citizens. Even against such a background of other brave whistleblowers, Snowden stands out for me for three key reasons: his personal and conscious courage at such a time, the sheer scale of his disclosures, and the continuing, global impact of what he exposed.

Unfortunately, while whistleblowers understand the legal risks they are taking when they emerge from the intelligence world or the diplomatic corps, they are often media virgins and are eternally surprised by the treatment meted out to them. Until the turn of the millennium, intelligence whistleblowers had no choice but to entrust themselves to the established media. Some, like "Deep Throat", the source of the Watergate scandal in 1970s America, were distrustful and remained in the shadows. Others, such as Daniel Ellsberg who released the Pentagon Papers in 1971, or the UK's Clive Ponting who in 1982 released information about the sinking of the General Belgrano ship during the Falklands War, were fortunate to work with campaigning journalists who fought both for their sources and the principle of press freedom. Even when Shayler went public in the late 1990s, he had no option but to work with the established media.

From personal experience, I can attest to the fact that this is not always a painless experience. With a few honourable exceptions, most of the journalists will just asset-strip their whistleblowers for information. They make their careers, while the whistleblower breaks theirs. Plus, there are many ways our soi-disant free press can be manipulated and controlled by the spies. The soft power involves inducting journalists to be agents of influence within their organisation, or cosy chats between editors and spies, or proprietors and top spies—that is how stories can be spun or erased. The hard power is extensive too—the application of laws such as libel, counter-terrorism laws, injunctions, and also the use of the secrecy laws against journalists themselves. Or even blatant intimidation and theatre, as happened after *The Guardian* newspaper in the UK published the early Snowden disclosures—the spooks went in and physically smashed up the hard drives containing his information.

All this casts that well known chilling effect on the freedom of the press and the free-flow of information from the government to the governed, which is so vital for an informed and participatory citizenry. Which brings me back to WikiLeaks. Established in 2007, this provides a secure and high-tech conduit for whistleblowers that gives them more control and securely stores the documents to prove their allegations. This is also why the US government saw it as such a threat and has pursued it in such a draconian and punitive way over the years since the first big revelations in 2010. Ironically, this is also partly why much of the traditional media turned on WikiLeaks—it threatened the old media business model. But from a whistleblower's perspective, WikiLeaks and its successors offer a brave new world. The technological genie is well and truly out of the bottle.

There is, of course, another possible path. The intelligence agencies could establish meaningful channels for ventilation of staff concerns, where the evidence is properly investigated and reforms are made as necessary. Having such a sound procedure in place to address concerns strikes me as a win-win scenario for staff efficiency and morale, the organisation's operational capability and reputation, and potentially the wider public safety too. However, unless and until secretive governmental organisations institute such legitimate and effective avenues for potential whistleblowers to go down, embarrassing disclosures will continue. Nobody sets out to be a whistleblower, but, absent effective reforms, they will remain our regulators of last resort.

The Edward Snowden Disclosures

In 2013 I stumbled across a story[1] about a worrying new surveillance programme developed by the NSA: Prism.[2] While nobody was identified as the source of the disclosure, I was awestruck by the bravery of this unknown person. At that time, the Obama administration had been waging an aggressive war on whistleblowers. Obama had used and abused the 1917 US Espionage Act against whistleblowers during his years in the White House more times than all his predecessors put together. Against this background, four days after the initial Prism disclosure, Edward Snowden announced to the world[3] that he was the source of the story and many more to come. He was clear then about his motivation and he remains clear now: what he had seen on the inside of the NSA caused him huge concern. The American intelligence infrastructure, along with its equivalent agencies across the world, was constructing a global surveillance network that not only threatened the constitution of the United States, but also eroded the privacy of all the world's citizens.

The global surveillance state wanted to "master the internet",[4] as another disclosure proved, and the UK's GCHQ stepped up to the plate. As increasing numbers of us conduct aspects of our lives over the internet (be it banking, health, social lives, organisations, activism, relationships)—and indeed now have to in the COVID-19 lock down era—this growing lack of privacy strikes at the very root of democracy. Privacy was enshrined as a basic human right in the UN Declaration in 1948 precisely because without it we are vulnerable to the encroachments and abuses of the state. What Snowden has disclosed would be the East Germany's Stasi's wet dream and goes far beyond the dystopic horrors of George Orwell's novel *1984*.

So, what did Snowden disclose? Prism was only the start, and that was bad enough—a programme to scoop up all our metadata: whom we're in contact with, for how long, what we're reading, what we're viewing. NSA apologists say that this is not invasive, it is not looking at the contents of communications. I can assure you that metadata is intelligence gold dust. It can provide a far more detailed contextual overview of a person's life than any individual communication often can. But it gets worse. Then came Tempora[5] and associated documents that disclosed that the UK's GCHQ was mainlining information from the transatlantic fibre optic cables, which affected all European and North American citizens, as well as displaying how GCHQ was prostituting itself[6] to the NSA for money and putting American NSA objectives above the priorities of the UK government. And then came XKeyscore,[7] enthusiastically used by Germany's BND,[8] presumably without the knowledge of its political masters. There have been many more: Brazil's Petrobras[9] oil company, the French telephone network,[10] charities,[11] the Muscular[12] access point and the massive Fascia[13] database, which contains trillions of device-location records… Where to stop?

By 2013 Britain's Joint Threat Research Intelligence Group[14] was using Squeaky Dolphin's[15] real-time monitoring of social media networks, and the bulk collection of private webcam images via the Optic Nerve[16] programme. This last example most grimly does away with the "done nothing wrong, nothing to hide" argument. In this era of COVID-19, of families living in different countries and long-distance relationships, video calls are increasingly used to stay in contact with loved ones. And this contact can be somewhat intimate and explicit at times between adult, consensual couples. Anyone who has ever used video calls over the internet for such purposes must surely be feeling violated, even though they are doing nothing wrong?

Out of this morass of spying came moments of personal annoyance for western politicians, not least the information that German Chancellor Angela Merkel's mobile phone was also being tapped,[17] as were those of numerous other politicians.[18] Which rather blows out of the water the much-abused argument that all this surveillance is to stop terrorists. On what planet would the NSA spooks need to live to seriously think that Merkel could be deemed a terrorist? All these disclosures are of the gravest public interest. Yet how have western politicians reacted? In the usual way—shoot the messenger. All the standard li(n)es have been trotted out by the spies: Snowden was too junior to know what he was talking about and was "just" a contracted systems administrator (this line says more about the ignorance of the politicians regarding all things tech than anything about Snowden's job); Snowden was a traitor for fleeing to Russia, when in fact he was trapped there by the USA withdrawing his passport while in transit to Latin America; Snowden should "man up"[19] and return to the US to stand trial. There were even apparently calls from the spies[20] for him to be extrajudicially murdered. Despite this, his disclosures have resulted in European Parliamentary hearings and congressional hearings in the US, where senior spooks have been caught out lying[21] about the efficacy of these spy programmes. A US federal judge has declared[22] the NSA's activities unconstitutional, and minor reforms are underway to protect the rights of US citizens within their own country. Which is a start. However, that still leaves the rest of us living under the baleful gaze of the NSA and its vassals.

The British response has been largely muted, with politicians immediately assuring the grateful citizens of the UK that everything done by the spies was legal and proportionate,[23] when in fact it was manifestly not. Indeed, they then rushed through a new law called the Investigatory Powers Act (2016) that retrospectively made legal all the bulk hacking the spies had been doing illegally for the previous 15 years. Nor is this any consolation for the rest of Europe's citizens—after all, why should the British Foreign Secretary be able to take it upon himself to authorise intercept programmes such as Tempora that sweep up the communications of an entire continent? Press discussion of Snowden's disclosures in the UK has been largely muted because of a censorship notice slapped on the media[24], while *The Guardian* newspaper that helped to break the story had its hard disks smashed up[25] by GCHQ.

Other countries have displayed a more robust response; Brazil is planning to build its own transatlantic cables to Europe to avoid the Tempora programme, while in Germany people have been demanding[26] that the constitution be upheld and privacy ensured against the American surveillance behemoth. The European parliamentary Civil Liberties, Justice and Home Affairs (LIBE) committee has held months-long hearings[27] with evidence from tech experts, whistleblowers and campaigners about what it should do to protect EU citizens from the predations of the US. Edward Snowden himself gave a statement[28] at these hearings. This is all well and good, but it would be more helpful if they could give Snowden asylum in Europe and also put in place some meaningful measures to protect our rights—in fact, all they would need to do is enact the provisions of the European parliament's own July 2001 report into the Echelon fiasco[29], which recommended that the EU break away from its dependency on US developed tech hardware. Echelon[30], some of you may remember, was a global proto-surveillance network, where the intelligence agencies of the US, UK, New Zealand, Australia, and Canada (now called Five Eyes) could all share products and subvert democratic oversight measures in each others' countries. In 2001 the EU recommended that Europe develop its own internet infrastructure and move away from its dependency on US corporate proprietary software. All good suggestions, but all too soon forgotten after 9/11 and the rush to the "war on terror".

Almost eight years on from Snowden I would still suggest that these measures should indeed be implemented. The European Parliament needs to take action now and show its 430 million citizens that it is serious about protecting their rights rather than pandering to the demands of the US government and its corporate sponsors. I want to salute the bravery of Edward Snowden. His conscious courage has given us all a fighting chance against a corporate-industrial-intelligence complex that is running amok across the world. I hope that we can all find within us an answering courage to do what is right and indeed take back our rights. His bravery and sacrifice must not be in vain.

WikiLeaks

No chapter about whistleblowers would be complete without a comment on WikiLeaks. I am painfully aware that, as I write, its founder, Julian Assange, still languishes in the UK's high-security prison Belmarsh, even though his extradition to the USA on trumped-up espionage charges was turned down recently by a UK court. Therefore, I shall restrict myself to a few key points. Here we have an award-winning journalist[31] and publisher, Julian Assange, whose organisation WikiLeaks has never been found to report anything factually incorrect in 15 years, being told that if he were to be extradited from the UK to face the full wrath of a vengeful American establishment, he is not entitled to claim protection of the First Amendment because he is an Australian citizen, not an American.

It has been an open secret for years that the US government has installed a secret Grand Jury[32] in Virginia (the home of the CIA) to investigate Assange and bring him to "justice" for publishing embarrassing US government documents as well as evidence of war crimes.[33] There have been calls[34] from US politicians for the death sentence, life in prison without parole, and even assassination. The US has been scrambling around for years to try to find any charge it could potentially throw at him, and now they are using the Espionage Act as if he were a whistleblower. Except he is not. He is an editor running a high-tech publishing outfit that has protected global whistleblowers and thereby caused embarrassment to governments and corporations around the world, not just America. If he can be prosecuted for publishing information very much in the public interest, then all the legacy media feeding off the WikiLeaks hydrant of information are equally vulnerable.[35]

Another key point that needs to be raised is that non-Americans can indeed be accorded First Amendment rights in the USA. Just look at the case of former UK MI6 intelligence officer, Christopher Steele. Steele is a British intelligence officer of pretty much my vintage. According to what is available publicly,[36] he worked for MI6, the British overseas intelligence gathering agency, for 22 years, serving in Russia in the early 90s and in Paris at the end of that decade—around the time that MI5 whistleblower, David Shayler, was imprisoned[37] in that city pending a failed extradition case to the UK. It is probable that Steele would have been monitoring us then. After being outed[38] as an MI6 officer in 1999 by his former colleague, Richard Tomlinson, he was pretty much desk-bound in London until he resigned in 2009 to set up, in the inimitable way of so many former spooks, a private consultancy that can provide plausibly deniable services to corporations and perhaps their former employers. Steele established just such a mercenary spy outfit, Orbis Business Intelligence,[39] with another ex-colleague, Chris Burrows, in 2009. Orbis made its name in exposing corruption at the heart of FIFA[40] in 2015 and was thereafter approached as an out-sourced partner by Fusion GPS—the company initially hired to dig dirt[41] on presidential candidate Donald Trump in 2016 by one of his Republican rivals and which then went on to dig up dirt on behalf of Hillary Clinton's DNC.

The result is what has become known as the "Dirty Dossier",[42] a grubby collection of prurient gossip with no real evidence or properly sourced information. Despite all this, Steele has won a legal case[43] in the USA, where he had been sued by three Russian oligarchs who claimed that the Dirty Dossier traduced their reputations. And he won on the basis that his report was protected by First Amendment rights under the constitution of the USA, which guarantees US citizens the right to freedom of expression. Despite the fact that Steele is British.

But Judge Anthony Epstein disagreed, writing in his judgment that "advocacy on issues of public interest has the capacity to inform public debate, and thereby furthers the purposes of the First Amendment, regardless of the citizenship or residency of the speakers".

This is the nub of the issue: Steele, a former official UK intelligence officer and current mercenary spy-for-hire, is granted legal protection by the American courts for digging up and subsequently leaking what appears to be controversial and defamatory information about the last President as well as various Russians, all paid for by Trump's political opponents. And Steele is given the full protection of the US legal system. This being the case, surely Julian Assange of all people also requires the protection of the First Amendment in the USA? Otherwise the concept that free media around the world can hold power to account is surely dead?

In Conclusion

Having lived through a long drawn-out whistleblowing case with my former partner, and having worked with many other whistleblowers over the last 20 years, I have seen the personal toll, persecution, and sacrifice. For societal, as well as individual reasons, it is unconscionable that we allow this to continue. These are people trying to protect others, right wrongs, and benefit us all. Yet the process often destroys the individual, and the vested interests roll on untouched. It is time to recalibrate the system. Those of conscience need to be able to speak out and speak up with safety rather than punishment. This will work to all our benefit. Whistleblowers need to be protected and valued, not persecuted and prosecuted.

Notes

1. Glenn Greenwald and Ewen MacAskill, "NSA Prism program taps in to user data of Apple, Google and others", *The Guardian*, published June 7, 2013, https://www.theguardian.com/world/2013/jun/06/us-tech-giants-nsa-data.

2. "PRISM (surveillance program)", *Wikipedia*, last modified April 16, 2021, https://en.wikipedia.org/wiki/PRISM_(surveillance_program).

3. Glenn Greenwald, Ewen MacAskill, and Laura Poitras, "Edward Snowden: the whistleblower behind the NSA surveillance revelations", *The Guardian*, published June 11, 2013, https://www.theguardian.com/world/2013/jun/09/edward-snowden-nsa-whistleblower-surveillance.

4. Ewen MacAskill, Julian Borger, Nick Hopkins, Nick Davies and James Ball, "GCHQ taps fibre-optic cables for secret access to world's communications", *The Guardian*, published June 21, 2013, https://www.theguardian.com/uk/2013/jun/21/gchq-cables-secret-world-communications-nsa.

5. Kadhim Shubber, "A simple guide to GCHQ's internet surveillance programme Tempora", *Wired*, published June 24, 2013, https://www.wired.co.uk/article/gchq-tempora-101.

6. Nick Hopkins and Julian Borger, "Exclusive: NSA pays £100m in secret funding for GCHQ", *The Guardian*, published August 1, 2013, https://www.theguardian.com/uk-news/2013/aug/01/nsa-paid-gchq-spying-edward-snowden.

7. Glenn Greenwald, "XKeyscore: NSA tool collects 'nearly everything a user does on the internet'", *The Guardian*, published July 31, 2013, https://www.theguardian.com/world/2013/jul/31/nsa-top-secret-program-online-data.

8. "XKeyscore" *Wikipedia*, last modified March 21, 2021, https://en.wikipedia.org/wiki/XKeyscore.

9. Jonathan Watts, "NSA accused of spying on Brazilian oil company Petrobras", *The Guardian*, published September 9, 2013, https://www.theguardian.com/world/2013/sep/09/nsa-spying-brazil-oil-petrobras.

10. "US spy agency 'taped millions of French calls'", *The Local*, published October 21, 2013, https://www.thelocal.fr/20131021/us-snooped-on-70-million-phone-calls-in-france.

11. James Ball and Nick Hopkins, "GCHQ and NSA targeted charities, Germans, Israeli PM and EU chief", *The Guardian*, published December 20, 2013, https://www.theguardian.com/uk-news/2013/dec/20/gchq-targeted-aid-agencies-german-government-eu-commissioner.

12. "MUSCULAR (surveillance program)", *Wikipedia*, last modified January 24, 2021,

https://en.wikipedia.org/wiki/MUSCULAR_(surveillance_program).

13. "FASCIA (database)", *Wikipedia*, last modified September 25, 2020, https://en.wikipedia.org/wiki/FASCIA_(database).

14. "Joint Threat Research Intelligence Group", *Wikipedia*, last modified February 5, 2021, https://en.wikipedia.org/wiki/Joint_Threat_Research_Intelligence_Group.

15. "Squeaky Dolphin", *Wikipedia*, last modified August 21, 2020, https://en.wikipedia.org/wiki/Squeaky_Dolphin.

16. "Optic Nerve (GCHQ)", *Wikipedia*, last modified December 21, 2020, https://en.wikipedia.org/wiki/Optic_Nerve_(GCHQ).

17. "German prosecutors to probe NSA tapping of Merkel's mobile?", *DW*, published June 4, 2014, https://www.dw.com/en/german-prosecutors-to-probe-nsa-tapping-of-merkels-mobile/a-17681026.

18. James Ball, "NSA monitored calls of 35 world leaders after US official handed over contacts", *The Guardian*, published October 25, 2013, https://www.theguardian.com/world/2013/oct/24/nsa-surveillance-world-leaders-calls.

19. Michael J. Glennon, "Is Snowden Obliged to Accept Punishment?", *Just Security*, published June 7, 2014, https://www.justsecurity.org/11068/guest-post-snowden-obliged-accept-punishment/#more-11068.

20. Benny Johnson, "America's Spies Want Edward Snowden Dead", *BuzzFeed News*, published January 16, 2014, https://www.buzzfeednews.com/article/bennyjohnson/americas-spies-want-edward-snowden-dead.

21. Shaun Waterman, "NSA chief's admission of misleading numbers adds to Obama administration blunders", *The Washington Post*, published October 2, 2013, https://www.washingtontimes.com/news/2013/oct/2/nsa-chief-figures-foiled-terror-plots-misleading.

22. Spencer Ackerman and Dan Roberts, "NSA phone surveillance program likely unconstitutional, federal judge rules", *The Guardian*, published December 16, 2013, https://www.theguardian.com/world/2013/dec/16/nsa-phone-surveillance-likely-unconstitutional-judge.

23. "William Hague: Public should not fear GCHQ systems", *BBC*, published June 9, 2013, https://www.bbc.com/news/av/uk-politics-22832051.

24. Josh Halliday, "MoD serves news outlets with D notice over surveillance leaks", *The Guardian*, published June 17, 2013, https://www.theguardian.com/world/2013/jun/17/defence-d-bbc-media-censor-surveillance-security.

25. Kim Zetter, "U.K. Ordered Guardian to Destroy Snowden Files Because Its Servers Weren't Secure", *Wired*, published August 20, 2013, https://www.wired.com/2013/08/guardian-snowden-files-destroyed.

26. Hilmar Schmundt and Gerald Traufetter, "NSA Scandal Boosts German Tech Industry", *Spiegel International*, published February 4, 2014, https://www.spiegel.de/international/business/german-it-industry-looks-for-boom-from-snowden-revelations-a-950786.html.

27. Annie Machon, "European Parliament LIBE Inquiry on Electronic Mass Surveillance of EU Citizens", *Using Our Intelligence* (blog), September 30, 2013, https://anniemachon.ch/annie_machon/2013/09/european-parliament-libe-inquiry-on-electronic-mass-surveillance.html.

28. Glyn Moody, "Snowden Gives Testimony To European Parliament Inquiry Into Mass Surveillance, Asks For EU Asylum", *Techdirt*, published March 7, 2014, https://www.techdirt.com/articles/20140307/05485226476/snowden-gives-testimony-to-european-parliament-inquiry-into-mass-surveillance-asks-eu-asylum.shtml.

29. "European Parliament resolution on the existence of a global system for the interception of private and commercial communications (ECHELON interception system) (2001/2098 (INI))", *European Parliament*, published April 24, 2001, p. 36, https://www.europarl.europa.eu/sides/getDoc.do?pubRef=-//EP//TEXT+REPORT+A5-2001-0264+0+DOC+XML+V0//EN#title2.

30. "Echelon", *Wikipedia*, last modified April 7, 2021, https://en.wikipedia.org/wiki/ECHELON.

31. Jason Deans, "Julian Assange wins Martha Gellhorn journalism prize", *The Guardian*, published June 2, 2011, https://www.theguardian.com/media/2011/jun/02/julian-assange-martha-gelhorn-prize.

32. The CNN Wire Staff, "Assange attorney: Secret grand jury meeting in Virginia on WikiLeaks", *CNN*, published December 13, 2010, http://edition.cnn.com/2010/CRIME/12/13/wikileaks.investigation/index.html.

33. "Collateral Murder", *WikiLeaks*, published April 5, 2015, https://collateralmurder.wikileaks.org.

34. Nick Collins, "WikiLeaks guilty parties should face death penalty", *The Telegraph*, published December 1, 2010, https://www.telegraph.co.uk/news/worldnews/wikileaks/8172916/WikiLeaks-guilty-parties-should-face-death-penalty.html.

35. Dan Kennedy, "WikiLeaks and the first amendment", *The Guardian*, published December 16, 2010, https://www.theguardian.com/commentisfree/cifamerica/2010/dec/16/julian-assange-wikileaks-eric-holder.

36. "Christopher Steele", *Wikipedia*, last modified April 13, 2021, https://en.wikipedia.org/wiki/Christopher_Steele.

37. Kathy Marks, "Jailed Shayler vows to fight extradition", *Independent*, published August 2, 1998, https://www.independent.co.uk/news/jailed-shayler-vows-to-fight-extradition-1169270.html.

38. Bodie and Doyle, "List of MI6 Agents", Indymedia UK, published August 8, 2003, https://www.indymedia.org.uk/en/2003/08/275809.html.

39. *Orbis*, https://orbisbi.com.

40. Owen Gibson and Damien Gayle, "Fifa officials arrested on corruption charges as World Cup inquiry launched", *The Guardian*, published May 27, 2015, https://www.theguardian.com/football/2015/may/27/several-top-fifa-officials-arrested.

41. Kenneth P. Vogel ,"The Trump Dossier: What We Know and Who Paid for It", *The New York Times*, published October 25, 2017, https://www.nytimes.com/2017/10/25/us/politics/steele-dossier-trump-expained.html.

42. "Clinton team and Democrats 'bankrolled' Trump dirty dossier", *BBC*, published October 25, 2017, https://www.bbc.com/news/world-us-canada-41752908.

43. "Defamation case against Christopher Steele dismissed", *BBC*, published August 21, 2018, https://www.bbc.com/news/world-us-canada-45251255.

2

ART AS EVIDENCE

WHEN ART MEETS WHISTLEBLOWING

TATIANA BAZZICHELLI
LAURA POITRAS
TREVOR PAGLEN
ROBERT TRAFFORD

ART AS EVIDENCE

encourages the creation of art through critical models of thinking and understanding, as well as stresses the role of artistic creation to investigate issues and translate information. The contributions of this section, in the format of theoretical reflections, newspaper articles and interviews, engage with the artistic potential of revealing facts, exposing misconduct and wrongdoings, and promoting awareness about social, political and technological matters.

The 2013 debate on the PRISM, XKeyscore and TEMPORA internet surveillance programmes, based on the NSA documents Edward Snowden disclosed to journalists, symbolised an increasing geopolitical control. New identities emerged: whistleblowers, cyberpunks, hacktivists and individuals that brought attention to abuses of government and large corporations, making the act of leaking a central part of their strategy.

This section deals with the effects of this debate on art and culture, presenting the concept of Art as Evidence, a notion suggested by Laura Poitras in 2013.

The first chapter traces the background of the concept of Art as Evidence, and the effects of whistleblowing on art and culture, covering the time frame from the early WikiLeaks projects to the impact of the Snowden disclosures. Afterwards, Academy Award-winning filmmaker and journalist Laura Poitras, artist and geographer Trevor Paglen and research coordinator at Forensic Architecture Robert Trafford reflect critically on the role of art and evidence in the context of post-9/11 politics and society. They use multiple disciplines and methodologies to understand ground truths and to present them in a variety of contexts, addressing the production of evidence as a collaborative act by civil society.

#DefendWikiLeaks

#NoWitnessTorture

#FreeAssangeNOW   #WISEUpAction

FREE SPEECH ON TRIAL

On 24th Feb Julian Assange will go on trial in Belmarsh prison because of his publications.

By exposing war crimes, political corruption and the pernicious security and surveillance state Assange could face extradition and up to 175 years in a U.S. prison. The war on **whistleblowers** is a back door war on journalists and freedom of speech. The detention of **Wikileakers** Assange, Chelsea Manning and Jeremy Hammond is therefore a violation of human rights and a serious attack to democracy.

© ★ HOGRE

Free Speech on Trial, Designed by Hogre, January 20
Free download from https://stealthisposter

TATIANA BAZZICHELLI
INTRODUCING ART AS EVIDENCE
THE ARTISTIC RESPONSE TO WHISTLEBLOWING

A New Form of Cultural Resistance

THE TIME FRAME
from 2009 to 2016 was a crucial period of collective experiences towards the formulation of artistic practices in relation to whistleblowing. In this period of time, close networks of trust were established around this topic, rooted in WikiLeaks' activities which pushed the boundaries of what is correct to publish, and what could count as art.

In November 2009, WikiLeaks published 570,000 confidential 9/11 pager messages, documenting over 24-hours in real time of the period surrounding the September 11, 2001 attacks in New York and Washington. The archive showed US national text pager intercepts of official exchanges at the Pentagon, FBI, FEMA and New York Police Department, and from computers reporting faults at investment banks inside the World Trade Centre.[1]

In 2010, the publication of *Collateral Murder* and the Afghan War Diary, anonymously disclosed by Chelsea Manning to WikiLeaks, as well as the WikiLeaks release of top-secret State Department cables from US embassies around the world, signed the start of a specific period of time in which artists, hackers, activists, researchers, and critical thinkers engaged extensively with the formulation of new forms of technological resistances and artistic critique.[2]

Three years later, Edward Snowden's disclosures of National Security Agency documents have changed our perception of surveillance and control in the information society. The debate over abuses of government and large corporations has reached a broad audience, encouraging reflection on new tactics and strategies of resistance. Whistleblowing, leaking, and disclosing have opened up new terrains of struggle.

What is the artistic and activist response to this process? How is it possible to transfer the surveillance and whistleblowing debate into a cultural and artistic framework, to reach and empower both experts and non-experts?

The objective of this chapter is to introduce the concept of Art as Evidence as a framework to describe artistic and hacktivist practices able to reveal hidden facts, to expose misconducts and wrongdoings of institutions and corporations, to produce awareness about social, political and technological matters that need public exposure, and in general, to inform the reality we live in. Art becomes a means to sensibilise about sensitive issues, generating an in-depth analysis within the framework of social and political action, as well as hacktivism, post-digital culture, and network practices.

The framework of Art as Evidence is presented in this essay as a context of artistic exploration, in which the issues under scrutiny are investigated in their imaginative artistic potential by questioning the concept of evidence itself. The main tactics are not only the disclosure of information and provoking of awareness through artistic interventions, but also encouraging the imagining of alternative models of thinking and understanding which lead to the creation of new imaginaries by playing with the "unexpected", a methodology that has been at the core of artistic experimentation since the Avant-garde, which introduced the use of shock and estrangement as artistic practice.

This chapter follows a situated perspective, based on the networks of trust I established in the course of the last ten years in this field, and the personal sharing with some of the key people that contributed to the development of the debate around art and whistleblowing. The concept of Art as Evidence was inspired by an exchange between Academy Award-winning filmmaker and journalist Laura Poitras, artist, academic researcher, and investigative journalist Jacob Appelbaum, artist and geographer Trevor Paglen, and myself. As described in the following interview with Laura Poitras, in the fall of 2013 she suggested the framework of Art as Evidence for our keynote event at the transmediale festival in Berlin, to describe this common artistic perspective, and a conceptual zone to investigate artistic practices that speak and inform about reality, as well as provoke a reaction about it.[3]

According to Laura Poitras, connecting art with evidence means to reflect on "the tools and mediums we can use to translate evidence or information beyond simply revealing the facts, [and] how people experience that information differently—not just intellectually, but emotionally or conceptually."[4] Following this perspective, art becomes not only a way to translate information, but also an entry point to investigate sensitive issues, and to explore and experience them by sharing them with an audience.

In Laura Poitras' words: "The work that I've been trying to do is to find ways to communicate about what is a really horrible chapter in American history. We can do a reminder that Guantanamo opened in 2002 and there are people there who have never been charged with anything, but where's the international pressure? [...] It isn't enough to change the reality, but it's also not enough to say what it means. It's actually incomprehensible to imagine being in prison and never be charged with anything. I feel like art is a way to express something about the real world. As artists we're not separate from political realities, we're responding to them and communicating about them."[5]

In this context, the act of leaking and provoking awareness through whistleblowing and truth-telling becomes a central part of the strategy of media criticism, by bringing attention to abuses of governments, institutions, and corporations. The objective is to reflect on interventions that work within the systems under scrutiny, and increase awareness on sensitive subjects by exposing misconduct, misinformation and wrongdoing in the framework of politics and society. This means interlinking the act of disclosing with that of creating art, shifting the debate from the initial intentions of whistleblowers to inform the public, to another level where whistleblowing becomes a source of creative experimentation and social change.

The concept of whistleblowing in this essay is presented as something concrete and accessible to a broader public—something that everyone can experience and expand into the framework of artistic and activist interventions. Furthermore, the meaning of "evidence" itself is expressed in different ways, and expanded into a context of imaginary experimentation, which the artistic form allows.

Resisting the Normalisation of Surveillance

As Glenn Greenwald points out in his book *No Place to Hide*, reflecting on the harm of surveillance in society, "Only when we believe that nobody else is watching us do we feel free—safe—to truly experiment, to test boundaries, to explore new ways of thinking and being, to explore what it means to be ourselves. What made the internet so appealing was precisely that it afforded the ability to speak and act anonymously, which is so vital to individual exploration. For that reason, it is in the realm of privacy where creativity, dissent, and challenges to orthodoxy germinate."[6]

This point is crucial to sensibilising people on the use of codes and software for protecting privacy, improving tools of counter-surveillance and anonymity. However, if we assume that today there is "No Place to Hide", as proven by the global surveillance disclosures of Edward Snowden and other acts of whistleblowing described in this book, how can we imagine tactics of criticism and artistic experimentation that happen within a context of freedom of expression?

On one side, the perception of constant surveillance might be a limitation to imagination. On the other side, if the idea of being surveilled became normalised, we could start imagining how to produce artistic explorations that come from *within* systems of monitoring and oppression.

There is an obvious risk in living with the perception of being monitored through pervasive surveillance. As Greenwald himself suggests, reconnecting his reflections with the ones of Michael Foucault in *Discipline and Punish*, "those who believe they are watched will instinctively choose to do that which is wanted of them without even realizing that they are being controlled."[7] In the context of debate over disclosures about state surveillance networks that function globally, the challenge becomes to find terrains of struggles and interventions, assuming we are all potentially watched.

As the hacktivist and researcher Jaromil writes in his abstract for the talk *Demilitarize technology: An insider's critique of contemporary hacker politics*, "On a subjective level, while we constantly risk becoming obsessed by revelations about the global surveillance *panopticon* and the military-industrial complex, we are also exposed to mass-deceiving propaganda and media manipulations, while even interpersonal communication becomes a field for the expanding narrative of total war."[8]

What he advocates is to circumvent the shared "grim aura" of fear and individualism through our capacity to imagine a better society, enhancing "the possibility for a hacker subject to maintain integrity and seek a positive constituency for her relations" by growing socially oriented networks of trust. This implies a reflection on collective empowerment, opening up the discourse of whistleblowing to a broader community of people.

In a panel at the Disruption Network Lab's 2015 conference event *SAMIZDATA: Evidence of Conspiracy*, Jacob Appelbaum observed that surveillance forces you to do things that you are asked to do. By normalising surveillance, we legitimise systemic power structures and asymmetries in society. As is widely known, Appelbaum has been in self-exile in Germany for the past eight years, unwilling to submit himself to harassment from the US authorities for his previous involvement with WikiLeaks and his refusal to testify against Julian Assange in the context of the Grand Jury investigation against him. He points out that surveillance is only an aspect of a broader political structure, whilst the challenge is to work on liberating each other, provoking systemic changes: "Whistleblowing is a tactic but it is not a whole strategy, it is not enough on its own. We should find terrains of struggles in the information society."[9]

On the same panel, speaking about information asymmetry, researcher on civil disobedience Theresa Züger pointed out that state and corporations gather information about us, but we don't have information about how much we are surveilled: "Whistleblowing is breaking this, by directly intervening within politics, and changing what we know. It is not only a symbolic gesture of disobedience, but people have taken enormous risks."[10]

This debate relates to the necessity of collective empowerment and simultaneously lowering risks, distributing the potential punishment and sharing information that only relatively few people have access to, as was pointed out in the early days of the debate on the Snowden Files.

The models of disclosing information we have witnessed over the past decade are diverse, from leaking the information to specific organisations, as whistleblower Chelsea Manning did in 2010, passing her material to WikiLeaks; to appointing specific people to filter information, as Edward Snowden chose to do in 2013, by trusting Glenn Greenwald and Laura Poitras to receive and have access to the NSA documents; to leaking large information via BitTorrent and Mega, as happened in the 2015 case of the hack of the Hacker Team data by Phineas Fisher, and the reporting of evidence by Citizen Lab on the targeting of human rights activists via the surveillance software provided by the Hacking Team company; to the collaborative model adopted in the 2015-2016 Panama Papers investigation by *Süddeutsche Zeitung* journalists Bastian Obermayer and Frederik Obermaier, connecting with the International Consortium of Investigative Journalists to analyse the law firm documents, involving a multitude of journalists from more than one hundred media organisations in around eighty countries.

In the case of the Snowden Files, the Berlin-based journalist and curator Krystian Woznicki started a public debate in July 2014 with his article, "Open the Snowden Files! Raising New Issues of Public Interest", attracting a significant amount of comments on the *Berliner Gazette* website.[11] Woznicki argued that "the access to the documents of the NSA-Gate remains closed" and "this blocks the democratic potential of the Snowden disclosures."[12] Laura Poitras, referring to her activity of reporting the Snowden disclosures and her contact with the source, pointed out that "it is a very justified criticism just in terms of how to scale the reporting, and it certainty has been a challenge, but it is also about how you build this kind of relationship and networks of trust, and they have been hard to balance"—an issue that we have discussed further in the context of our recent interview for this book.[13]

In the chapter on the role of political media, "The Fourth Estate", in his book *No Place to Hide*, Glenn Greenwald describes the power dynamics at stake when media subservient to government try to discredit him for reporting on sensitive issues and working with a source that disclosed classified information. Many parallel issues play a role: the trust of the source seeking to coordinate the reporting via specific journalists, the clear risk of punishment from the powers of government, and the sensitive choice of deciding what is appropriate to report and what is not. At the end of his book, he writes:

The prevailing institutions seem too powerful to challenge; orthodoxies feel too entrenched to uproot; there are always many parties with a vested interest in maintaining the status quo. But it is human beings collectively, not a small number of elites working in secret who can decide what kind of world we want to live in. Promoting the human capacity to reason and make decisions: that is the purpose of whistleblowing, of activism, of political journalism. And that's what is happening now, thanks to the revelations brought about by Edward Snowden.[14]

Between the end of the 1990s and beginning of the 2000s, in the so-called media art scene, the debate about the collectivisation of media tactics was central. Today, the challenge is to imagine a distributed range of practices able to bring back a shared perception of power, which should not only rely on the traditional mass media system, but also reflect on strategies of collective actions and interventions—providing solutions, which are political and not merely technological.

Artistic Practice as Evidence of Reality

In April 2012, Laura Poitras held a surveillance teach-in at the Whitney Museum of American Art in New York. It was an artistic and practical commentary on living in the contemporary Panopticon. For this programme, NSA whistleblower William Binney and Jacob Appelbaum joined her to discuss state surveillance, civil right to privacy, and how technological innovations are legitimating pervasive access to private information.[15] The event took place in the context of Laura Poitras' work, which had previously chronicled post-9/11 America with her films *My Country, My Country* (2006), *The Oath* (2010), and before the release of *Citizenfour*, her 2014 Academy Award winning documentary on the surveillance state and Edward Snowden's disclosures.

As stated in our 2013 interview (included in this publication), describing her artistic practice, Laura Poitras stated: "I don't want the audience to think that it's some other reality that they have no connection with. I want to emotionally implicate the audience—especially US audiences—in the events they are seeing."[16] Her solo show at the Whitney Museum of American Art, *Astro Noise* (February 5 to May 1, 2016), expanded this perspective; she created installations of immersive environments combining various material, from footage to information around NSA surveillance and post-9/11 America.

Connecting to this line of imagining art as a means to speak about reality, in February 2014 I curated a panel at the transmediale festival in Berlin involving Laura Poitras, Jacob Appelbaum and Trevor Paglen. On this specific occasion, the filmmaking work of Poitras was combined with the secret geographies of Trevor Paglen and the colour infrared photography of Jacob Appelbaum. The concept of surveillance was translated and explored through concrete artistic examples, interlinking various areas of expertise. We discussed how art could become functional in creating evidence and informing about our society; a scope that is clear in the work of Laura Poitras, and her films and exhibitions that show how art can be used to transfer information, and to expose misconduct and wrongdoing. This approach is also relevant in the work of Trevor Paglen, bringing misconduct and systems of powers into the light. He does this through his photography, and through other artistic projects investigating hidden mechanisms of artificial intelligence, facial recognition, and machine learning, as we can read in the interview that follows in this publication.

In the 2010 photographic monograph *Invisible: Covert Operations and Classified Landscapes*, Trevor Paglen explored the secret activities of the US military and intelligence agencies, creating photos of top-secret sites that are not accessible, but that can be mapped and brought to evidence. As we discuss in the interview, photography becomes a means of truth-telling, revealing to the public the existence of secret operations, depicting both what can and cannot be seen. High-end optical systems are used to document government locations, and classified spacecrafts in Earth's orbit are photographed by tracking the data of amateur satellite watchers. In Paglen's series of drone photography, we see an apparently normal landscape, but only when the photo is exposed to its maximum resolution are we are able to disclose drones in the sky, and therefore have an idea of the clandestine military activities that are happening on the American landscape.

During our panel at the transmediale festival, the notion of Art as Evidence was also related with the colour infrared photographic work by Jacob Appelbaum, based on a Kodak EIR colour infrared film, medium format. The following 2015 solo show *SAMIZDATA: Evidence of Conspiracy* that I curated at the NOME Gallery in Berlin presented six cibachrome prints (a fully analogue positive slide printing technique), portraying Bill Binney, Laura Poitras, Glenn Greenwald, David Miranda, Julian Assange, Sarah Harrison and Ai Weiwei, as well as two installations: *P2P (Panda-to-Panda)*, and the necklace piece *Schuld, Scham & Angst (Guilt, Shame & Fear)*.

Appelbaum shot the photos using colour infrared films, previously adopted to expose hidden details during aerial surveillance, to portray people under surveillance who have themselves worked to report on governmental misconducts and exposed crimes against civil society. According to him, "it is beautiful irony and conceptually strong to use surveillance film to critique surveillance culture. In a world of digital surveillance, re-purposing analogue aerial agricultural surveillance film for the portraiture of peoples who are exposed to and who work to expose surveillance seemed the appropriate medium."[17]

The photos, given as a gift by Appelbaum to the people that are portrayed, were also the evidence of a personal network of trust, where grassroots collaboration between trusted people who share passions, ideals and political views were documented. In the context of the interconnected network of artistic evidence, the installation *P2P (Panda-to-Panda)*, created in collaboration with Ai Weiwei, was a stuffed panda with Snowden materials and other classified documents saved in an SD card, exemplifying a peer-to-peer network of trusted individuals that got the panda as gift for their struggle for social justice. The project *Schuld, Scham & Angst (Guilt, Shame & Fear)* was a piece of one hundred necklaces, each containing shredded unreleased documents, journalistic notes, and other classified documents from the previous two years of reporting on the Snowden files, thought to be pieces of evidence carried around by people, symbolising the shame and guilt of shredding sensitive documents, as society often demands.[18]

Another project resulting from the collaboration between Jacob Appelbaum and Trevor Paglen is the *Autonomy Cube* sculpture (exhibited at the Edith-Russ-Haus for Media Art, Oldenburg, from October 22, 2015 to January 3, 2016). The cube, which worked as a node in the Tor network, gave visitors access to the Tor network along with a copy of the Tor programme, turning the museum into a space for free speech and autonomy. By making the cube enter into a cultural context, the exhibition allowed "art institutions to actually be part of a worldwide network of things such as opening up lines of communication, securing people's fundamental right to anonymity, to free speech, and thus to human rights."[19] Paglen and Appelbaum have built around a dozen cubes in total, that have often been activated at the same time, building and improving the Tor network.

Blowing the Whistle, Questioning Evidence

In 2016, I was asked by Akademie Schloss Solitude and ZKM Center for Art and Media to curate a call that I named "Blowing the Whistle, Questioning Evidence", which was announced in February 2017.[20] I was trying to bring together multiple perspectives: from one side, to imagine art as an source of exposing misconduct, reflecting on the impact and consequences of whistleblowing; from the other side, I wanted to question the discourse of providing evidence. What does it mean to produce art as evidence of our society? Is there only one single truth, or are there many? This question opens up a crucial debate in the artistic field, because it can result in the deconstruction of a linear form of understanding, proposing the idea that truth (and evidence) is always multiple. Whistleblowers often work on exposing hidden evidence of crimes, but what if the truth could be varied, and how do we then work with the consequent discourse of providing social justice? This double-sided perspective becomes an occasion to speak about power mechanisms and different forces of powers that are usually at stake.

In relation to the concept of art as evidence, I proposed to open up a field of artistic research and practice where the fight against surveillance and for the protection of civil rights and social justice becomes a terrain of intervention by understanding the inner logic of systems of power and questioning them: questioning government agencies, private enterprises and corporations that base their profit on the collection of meta-data, as well as intelligence services that base their business on tracking and surveilling people.

What normally motivates whistleblowers is informing the public, and many whistleblowers would not compare themselves with artists. However, following a speculative perspective, I would argue that whistleblowers are able to provoke the unexpected, operate a disruption of closed systems from within, and investigate hidden sides of reality. They experience in their personal life a radical change of perspective, a sort of *détournement of belief* that contributes to generating societal transformations. Although their risks and mindsets are not equal, artists are able to encourage different modes of thinking by investigating hidden sides of power and society, and, at the same time, provoke a reflection on the meaning and limits of evidence itself.

Conceptually interlinking the act of whistleblowing to artistic practices, focusing on the function of generating awareness by producing as well as questioning evidence, would allow for the opening up of the meaning of whistleblowing more widely. If we see the act of whistleblowing as a cultural perspective able to provoke change, with the strength to radically construct a different point of view, it is possible to find such a mindset in the activities of many artists, activists, journalists, researchers and people in general. Obviously, the consequences of an act of whistleblowing and the creation of an artistic project are not the same, at least in countries where artistic expression is not persecuted as a crime. But I consider it very important to engage in this speculative comparison, to better understand the aim of whistleblowing, to decriminalise it, to open up a wider debate on what this practice is in the first place, as well as to stretch the boundaries of what art might be. The following experiences which lie at the crossing between generating social awareness, providing public knowledge, and sharing the tools for producing evidence, are a good example of how whistleblowing could inform activist practices and inspire artistic projects.

More than thirty years ago, Norwegian researcher and journalist Jørgen Johansen exposed the sites of secret NATO military bases in Norway, combining and analysing public records, freely accessible to everyone. The government considered his publications to be the disclosure of classified information and prosecuted him with espionage charges, although he had collected and analysed information that anyone could have found. In an interview in September 2015, he points out: "If you are a person who thinks the world should be better, you must act in a way that gives the opposition movements around the world the possibility to do their jobs. If you're just an obedient consumer or an obedient citizen, you're letting surveillance continue on those who really have something to hide because they are the state's opposition."[21]

Following the opening up of the practice of whistleblowing among wider society, German artist collective Peng! launched their campaign *Intelexit* in September 2015, inviting people inside the secret services, as well as intelligence agencies, to blow the whistle and make a stand (www.intelexit.org). This initiative promoted whistleblowing as a common practice, by building up a support structure and safety network to enable whistleblowing, taking into account the risks. The campaign used disruptive methods to intervene with intelligence systems, for example placing unexpected billboards in front of the offices of intelligence services and distributing flyers via drones flying over NSA bases. As usual for the interventions by the Peng! collective, the project served also as a provocation to open up a debate about the issues of surveillance and truth-telling, as well as the importance of sources' protection.[22]

The act of speaking out as a tactic of resistance and societal change is nothing new, but it deserves an in-depth analysis, especially today, with the debate about surveillance and big data involving an increasing audience. In recent years, more artists and groups have been dealing with the topics of art and evidence, and many have stressed the importance of investigative aesthetics as an artistic practice.

To mention a few: James Bridle, who focused his practice on the concept of the New Aesthetics (2012), researching drones, military technologies and asylum seeker deportation, among other topics; the !Mediengruppe Bitnik, that work critically on online and offline systems of control, and in early 2013 developed the project "Delivery for Mr. Assange", tracking the journey of a parcel sent to the Ecuadorian Embassy; Paolo Cirio, who explored the concept of Evidentiary Realism (2017) and related artistic works, scrutinising and revealing the hidden systems of social reality, intersecting documentary, forensic, and investigative practices; Joana Moll, tracing the connection between hidden interfaces, data exploitation, corporate business models, free labour, media surveillance, CO_2 exploitation and domesticated electricity as also highlighted in this publication; Adam Harvey, researching privacy, surveillance, and computer vision, developing camouflage techniques for subverting face detection, thermal imaging, and location tracking; Ingrid Burrington and her work focusing on mapping, documenting, and identifying elements of network infrastructure, exposing the hidden landscapes of the internet; the artistic duo UBERMORGEN, net.art pioneers and media hackers that research data and create polarising social experiments, who have been creatively working with the concept of truth-telling since the 1990s; and of course the long lasting investigative work of Forensic Architecture, based on the collaborative concept of Horizontal Verification and the Socialised Production of Evidence, applying an open-source counter-forensic practice for the production of evidence—a strategy well described in the following contribution in this book by Robert Trafford.[23]

This essay is an invitation to discuss, reflect and develop new artistic practices that take inspiration from, but also go beyond, whistleblowing, to open up the fight against surveillance to a broader community. Art as Evidence therefore means, in this context, to explore the current transformation of political and technological criticism in times of increased geopolitical surveillance, analysing methods and artistic practices to question and produce evidence.

Artistic works of evidence and about evidence become therefore not only a challenge to expose facts and wrongdoings that are hidden and not accessible to the general public, but also an opportunity to collectively question the concept of evidence itself, and to reflect on which speculative forms of artistic research and practice might arise from its analysis.

Notes

1. WikiLeaks' "9/11 tragedy pager intercepts" is visible at https://911.wikileaks.org. The project is rebroadcast in real time on subsequent 9/11s. Read more in the article: Declan McCullagh, "Egads! Confidential 9/11 Pager Messages Disclosed", *CBS News*, November 25, 2009, https://www.cbsnews.com/news/egads-confidential-9-11-pager-messages-disclosed.

2. In May 2013, in the context of the yearly programme "reSource" that I was curating at the transmediale festival, I organised with Diani Barreto and with the support of the (later named) Chelsea Manning Initiative Berlin, the panel "The Medium of Treason. The Bradley Manning Case: Agency or Misconduct in a Digital Society?" at the Urban Spree Gallery in Berlin. This event revisited the making of the Collateral Murder video and discussed the "United States v. Bradley Manning" trial on June 3, 2013. The video of the panel with Andy Müller Maguhn, John Goetz and Birgitta Jónsdóttir is available at: https://archive.transmediale.de/content/resource-005-the-medium-of-treason.

3. This happened during the process of our sharing for the organisation of the keynote "Art as Evidence", about art and the NSA surveillance at the transmediale festival at the Haus der Kulturen der Welt in Berlin on January 30, 2014, https://archive.

transmediale.de/content/keynote-art-as-evidence, which is described in depth in the following interview with Laura Poitras in this book. After this transmediale festival edition, I again connected the topic of art and whistleblowing curating the exhibition "Networked Disruption: Rethinking Oppositions in Art, Hacktivism and Business", which opened in March 2015 at the ŠKUC Gallery, in Ljubljana, Slovenia, expanding the subject of my previous book (*Networked Disruption*, 2013) into the practices of whistleblowing and truth-telling: https://aksioma.org/networked.disruption.

4. Bazzichelli, Tatiana, "The Art of Disclosure: Interview with Laura Poitras", initially published in *The Afterglow* transmediale magazine, 2, Berlin, (2014): 16-18, and expanded for this anthology. The quote is taken from the actualised version of the interview, following this chapter.

5. See the video documentation of the panel: "SAMIZDATA: Evidence of Conspiracy", with Jacob Appelbaum, Laura Poitras and Theresa Züger, moderated by Tatiana Bazzichelli, Disruption Network Lab, Kunstquartier Bethanien, Berlin, September 11, 2015, https://www.youtube.com/watch?v=XyZAYanzMKw, retrieved July 27, 2021.

6. Greenwald, Glenn, "No Place to Hide: Edward Snowden, the NSA, and the Surveillance State", (London: Penguin Books, 2015), 174.

7. Ibid, p. 176.

8. Abstract sent by Jaromil to me by personal email for the preparation of the conference event "SAMIZDATA: Tactics and Strategies for Resistance", Disruption Network Lab at Kunstquartier Bethanien, September 11–12, 2015, https://www.disruptionlab.org/samizdata.

9. In September 2015, our theoretical and practical exchange over the concept of Art as Evidence was taken up further in the context of the exhibition "SAMIZDATA: Evidence of Conspiracy", a solo show in Germany of Jacob Appelbaum, that I curated at the NOME Gallery in Berlin (https://nomegallery.com/exhibitions/samizdata-evidence-of-conspiracy), and in the conference event "SAMIZDATA: Tactics and Strategies for Resistance" (see link in the note above).

10. Ibid: video documentation of the panel: SAMIZDATA.

11. See the "Open the Snowden Files" dossier in the Berliner Gazette: http://berlinergazette.de/open-the-snowden-files.

12. Woznicki, Krystian, "Open the Snowden Files! Raising New Issues of Public Interest", Berliner Gazette, July 2014, http://berlinergazette.de/wp-content/uploads/Open-the-Snowden-Files_KW_E.pdf, retrieved October 8, 2015.

13. Ibid: video documentation of the panel: "SAMIZDATA: Evidence of Conspiracy", with Jacob Appelbaum, Laura Poitras and Theresa Züger.

14. Ibid, p. 259.

15. Video documentation of the surveillance teach-in panel with Laura Poitras, Jacob Appelbaum and Bill Binney on April 20, 2012 at the Whitney Biennial: https://www.praxisfilms.org/exhibitions/whitney-biennial. This event also featured a clandestine portrait intervention in the Whitney Museum, where two photos portraying Julian Assange were installed. Furthermore, NSA interception point addresses were handed out in the audience.

16. Bazzichelli, Tatiana, "The Art of Disclosure: Interview with Laura Poitras", first published in The Afterglow transmediale magazine, 2, Berlin, 2014, 16-18.

17. Bazzichelli, Tatiana, "Interview with Jacob Appelbaum", August 18, 2015, published in the catalogue of the exhibition: SAMIZDATA: Evidence of Conspiracy, Jacob Appelbaum, September 11–October 31, 2015, curated by Tatiana Bazzichelli, NOME, Berlin, p. 7. Online catalogue at: https://nomegallery.com/wp-content/uploads/2017/02/SAMIZDATA-by-Jacob-Appelbaum.pdf.

18. Visit the artworks on "SAMIZDATA: Evidence of Conspiracy", solo show in Germany of Jacob Appelbaum, NOME Gallery, Berlin, September 11–October 31, 2015 (https://nomegallery.com/exhibitions/samizdata-evidence-of-conspiracy).

19. Ibid, 13.

20. See the website dedicated to the call and project "Blowing the Whistle, Questioning Evidence", which resulted in four web residencies awarded to Adam Harvey (SkyLift: Low-Cost Geo-Location Spoofing Device), Hang Do Thi Duc (Me And My Facebook Data), Joana Moll (Algorithms Allowed), and Marloes de Valk (How to Escape Reality in 10 Simple Steps), and ten shortlisted projects available at: https://www.akademie-solitude.de/en/project/web-residencies-en/calls-2017-en/blowing-the-whistle-questioning-evidence-en/ (Akademie Schloss Solitude and ZKM Center for Art and Media, retrieved July 30, 2021).

21. Interview in ExBerliner magazine: "A Norwegian whistleblower in Berlin" by Dyllan Furness, September 8, 2015, http://www.exberliner.com/features/people/open-secrets/, retrieved July 27, 2021. To know more about the story of Jørgen Johansen, watch also the panel "SAMIZDATA: Strategies for Resistance", with Jørgen Johansen, Jaromil and Sophie Toupin, moderated by Valie Djordjevic, September 12, 2015, Disruption Network Lab, Kunstquartier Bethanien, Berlin, https://www.youtube.com/watch?v=nf7u8b2FKTY.

22. The highlights of the Intelexit campaign from 2015 and the plans for 2016 were presented by Gloria Spindle of the Peng! collective at the 32C3 Chaos Communication Congress on December 29, 2015. The video is available at: https://www.youtube.com/watch?v=NomUeEBfYNo.

23. To know more about the above mentioned artists and projects visit: James Bridle, https://jamesbridle.com and https://new-aesthetic.tumblr.com; !Mediengruppe Bitnik: https://bitnik.org; Paolo Cirio, https://paolocirio.net and https://www.evidentiaryrealism.net; Joana Moll, http://www.janavirgin.com; Adam Harvey, https://ahprojects.com; Ingrid Burrington, http://lifewinning.com; UBERMORGEN: https://www.ubermorgen.com; Forensic Architecture, https://forensic-architecture.org. To provide more references, in the context of the exhibition "Whistleblower & Vigilanten. Figuren des digitalen Widerstands/Whistleblowers & Vigilantes. Figures of Digital Resistance" artists, experts on whistleblowing, and whistleblowers were connected to reflect critically on forms of surveillance and control (curated by Inke Arns at the Dortmunder U, Dortmund, in 2016: https://www.dortmunder-u.de/veranstaltung/whistleblower-vigilanten-figuren-des-digitalen-widerstands). Furthermore, our Disruption Network Lab conference "Truth-Tellers: The Impact of Speaking Out" in November 2016 questioned the issues of truth and evidence in a conceptual way, by analysing concretely the effects of disclosures, the work of the sources, and the conscious understanding of the consequences of speaking out (https://www.disruptionlab.org/truth-tellers).

LAURA POITRAS

Photo by Jan Stürmann

Laura Poitras is a filmmaker, journalist, and artist. *Citizenfour*, the third instalment of her post-9/11 trilogy, won an Academy Award for Best Documentary, along with awards from the British Film Academy, Independent Spirit Awards, Director's Guild of America, and the German Filmpreis. Part one of the trilogy, Academy Award-nominated *My Country, My Country*, about the US occupation of Iraq, premiered at the Berlinale. Part two, *The Oath*, on Guantanamo Bay Prison and the war on terror, also screened at the Berlinale and was nominated for two Emmy awards. Poitras' reporting on NSA mass surveillance received a Pulitzer Prize for Public Service, along with many other journalism awards. Poitras was placed on a US government secret watchlist in 2006. In 2015, she filed a successful lawsuit to obtain her classified FBI

LAURA POITRAS
THE ART OF DISCLOSURE
TWO INTERVIEWS BY TATIANA BAZZICHELLI, 2013–2021

THE FIRST interview with Laura Poitras was conducted in person in Berlin on November 28, 2013, and by email, in the context of our preparation for Laura Poitras' keynote, "Art as Evidence", at the transmediale festival edition "Afterglow", which took place at the Haus der Kulturen der Welt in Berlin from January 29 to February 2, 2014.

The keynote opened the conference stream "Hashes to Ashes" on January 30. The aim of the conference stream was to highlight the pervasive process of silencing—and metaphorically reducing to ashes—activities that exposed misconducts in political, technological and economic systems, as well as to reflect on what burned underneath such processes, and to advocate for a different scenario. A shorter version of this interview was published in the transmediale magazine in January 2014.

The second interview was conducted in person in Berlin on June 16, 2021.

Tatiana Bazzichelli: By working on your documentaries about America post-9/11 and as a journalist exposing the NSA's surveillance programs you have taken many risks, especially reporting on the lives of other people at risk. How do you deal with being both a subject and an observer in your work?

Laura Poitras: How I navigate being both an observer and a participant is different with each film. In the first film I made in Iraq, *My Country, My Country*, when I started working on post-9/11 issues, I am not in the film. That was a conscious decision because I didn't want it to be a film about a reporter in a dangerous place. I wanted the sympathy to be for the Iraqis. It was a very deliberate rejection of mainstream coverage of the war. If people come away from the film and say: "Wow, this is what Iraqis are going through, and this family is really similar to my family", then I succeeded. But how I handle my position has changed over time. In 2006, after I released my film about the occupation of Iraq, I became a target of the US government, placed on a terrorist watchlist, and started being detained at the US border, so I have been pushed into the story more and more.

With *The Oath*, the question was different. In that case I was editing with Jonathan Oppenheim, and we put together a rough cut of the film where I was not in it. We were doing test screenings and we realized that there was something that the viewers were really disturbed by—they were questioning the access. Rather than drawing them into the film, it was distracting them. Jonathan realized that we had to introduce me in the narrative and acknowledge the camera. There is a wonderful scene in the taxicab with Abu Jandal driving, and at one point his passenger asks: "What's the camera for?" Abu Jandal gives this fantastic lie. This scene acknowledges the presence of the camera, the filmmaker, and we also learn that he is a really good liar.

Now I am working on a documentary about NSA surveillance and the Edward Snowden disclosures, and I will acknowledge my presence in the story because I have many different roles: I am the filmmaker; I am the person who Snowden contacted to share his disclosures, along with Glenn Greenwald; I am documenting the process of the reporting; and I am reporting on the disclosures. There is no way I can pretend I am not part of the story.

In terms of risk, the people I have filmed put their lives on the line. That was the case in Iraq, Yemen, and certainly now with Snowden's disclosures. Snowden, William Binney, Thomas Drake, Jacob Appelbaum, Julian Assange, Sarah Harrison, and Glenn. Each of them is taking huge risks to expose the scope of NSA's global surveillance. There are definitely risks I take in making these films, but they are lesser risks than the people that I have documented take.

TB: The previous films you directed tell us that history is a puzzle of events, and it is impossible to combine them without accessing pieces hidden by powerful forces. Do you think your films reached the objectives you wanted to communicate?

LP: Doing this work on America post-9/11, I'm interested in documenting how America exerts power in the world. I'm against the documentary tradition of just going to the "third world" and filming people suffering outside of context. I don't want the audience to think that it's some other reality that they have no connection with. I want to emotionally implicate the audience—especially US audiences—in the events they are seeing. In terms of if my films reach their "objectives", I think people assume because I make films with political content that I'm interested in political messages. That they are a means to an end, or a form of activism. But the success or failure of the films has to do with whether they succeed as films. Are they truthful? Do they take the audience on a journey, do they inform, do they challenge, and connect emotionally? Etc. I make films to discover things and challenge myself, and the audience.

Of course I want my work to have impact and reach wide audiences. To do that, I think they must work as art and as cinema. I made a film about the occupation of Iraq, but it didn't end the Iraq war. Does that make it a failure? The NSA surveillance film will have more impact than my previous films, because of the magnitude of Snowden's disclosures, but those disclosures are somewhat outside the documentary. Documentaries don't exist to break news; they need to provide more lasting qualities to stand up over time. The issues in the film are about government surveillance and abuses of power, the loss of privacy and threat to the free Internet in the twenty-first century, etc., but the core of the film is about what happens when a few people take enormous risks to expose power and wrongdoing.

TB: Your films cannot be compared with news because news is always somehow distant, instead you get to know the people you are speaking about well, and you really see their point of view. It's about their life, that they decide to share with you, so your role is different, and so are the roles of the people you're filming.

LP: It's different, for better or for worse. Documentaries take longer to complete, and some things need to be public immediately. You don't want to hold back reporting on something like the Abu Ghraib photos. At the moment I am in a push/pull situation of reporting on the NSA documents and also editing the documentary. Whatever outcome there will be from these disclosures, the documentary will record that people took risks to disclose and report what the NSA is doing.

TB: What can we do as people working in the arts to help such a process of information disclosure, contributing to rewriting pieces of collective culture?

LP: I think of someone like Trevor Paglen, because he works on so many different levels. He works on an aesthetic level, and his secret geographies are also pieces of evidence that he's trying to uncover. He combines them in this really beautiful way where you get both documentary evidence of places that we're not supposed to see, and really spectacular images. I love that dialectical tension.

No artist, writer, or reporter works in a political vacuum; you're always working in a political context, even if the subject of your work is not political issues. I guess I would say what I find the least interesting is art that references political realities, but there's no real risk taking on the part of the art making, either on the structural form, or in the content of the work. It's more like appropriation, where politics becomes appropriated by the art world's trends. Any piece of work needs to work on its own terms, that's the most important relevance it has, rather than any political relevance, and I think that that can be as profound or meaningful, like something that's incredibly minimalist, that makes the viewer think in a different kind of way, and ignites your imagination. This is also a very political thing to do, although it's not about war or politics.

TB: I am thinking about *O' Say Can You See*, your short movie about the Twin Towers and Ground Zero. There have been a lot of films about that, but I found it so interesting that you were not filming Ground Zero, but the people looking at it. For me that's a clear artistic perspective.

LP: My education is in art and I have a social theory background—both inform my work. Every time you take on an issue or topic that you want to represent, it presents certain challenges and possibilities. At Ground Zero, people were looking at something that was gone and difficult to comprehend, but the emotions were so profound that we could represent what had happened in the absence of showing. There are limits to representation. Imagining what people were seeing was more powerful than showing it.

TB: Why did you start working on your trilogy about America post-9/11? How did such topics change your way of seeing society and politics?

LP: I was in New York on 9/11, and the days after you really felt that the world could go in so many different directions. In the aftermath of 9/11, and particularly in the build-up to the Iraq war, I felt that I had skills that can be used to understand and document what was happening. The US press totally failed the public after 9/11, becoming cheerleaders for the Iraq war. So I decided to go to Iraq and document the occupation on the ground. What are the human consequences of what the US is doing, and not just for Iraqis but also for the military that were asked to undertake this really flawed and horrific policy?

When I started that film, I didn't think I was making a series of films about America post-9/11. I was naive and thought the US would at least pretend to respect the rule of law. Of course, America is built on a history of violence pre-9/11, but legalizing torture was something I never thought would happen in my lifetime. Justifying torture in legal memos, or creating the Guantanamo Bay Prison where people are held indefinitely without charge, that is a new chapter.

As a US citizen, these policies are done in my name. I have a certain platform and protection as a US citizen that allows me to address and expose these issues with less risk than others. Glenn and I have talked about this—about the obligation we have to investigate these policies because we are US citizens.

TB: Were you imagining this kind of parable would be touching people in their daily lives, like what's happening with ethical resisters and whistleblowers?

LP: I never imagined there would be this kind of attacks on whistleblowers and journalists. Look at the resources the US has used in the post-9/11 era—and for what? More people now hate us. I have seen that first-hand. It's baffling how the priorities have been calculated. I was placed on a government terrorist watchlist for making a documentary about the occupation of Iraq. That is an attack on the press.

I think we are in a new era where in the name of national security everything can be transgressed. The United States is doing things that I think if you had imagined it thirteen years ago you would be shocked. Like drone assassinations. How did we become a country that assassinates people based on SIM cards and phone numbers? Is that what you think of when you think of a democracy? Is that the world we want to live in?

TB: What is the last part of the trilogy teaching you, and how is this new experience adding meaning to the others described in the previous movies? What is coming next?

LP: The world that Snowden's disclosures have opened is terrifying. I have worked in war zones, but doing this reporting is so much scarier. How this power operates and how it can strip citizens of the fundamental right to communicate and associate freely. The scope of the surveillance is so vast. It gets inside your head. It is violence.

About what's next, I imagine that I will work on the issue of surveillance beyond the film. The scope of it goes beyond any one film.

TB: The fact that you are a woman dealing with sensitive subjects, traveling alone filming across off-limit countries, and developing technical skills to protect your data makes you very unique. How do you see such experiences from a woman/gender perspective?

LP: Speaking about technology, I do not think it is gender specific. I think that if you perceive the state as dangerous or a threat, which I do as a journalist who needs to protect sources, you have an obligation to learn how to use these tools to protect source material. Once you understand that a phone has a GPS device in it, you understand that it is geo-locating you and that potentially is dangerous, so you turn it off, or you stop carrying a phone. I do not think this is gender specific.

In terms of being a woman doing work in the field, overall it has made the work easier. In the Iraqi context, to be a woman allowed me more access because it is a very gender segregated society. If I was a man, I would have not been able to live in the same house as Dr. Riyadh and his family. I was able to film with the women and also film with men. Being a woman allowed me to have a certain kind of access that I would not have otherwise.

I also get access because often I work without a crew. When I was filming in Iraq, I remember I was inside the Green Zone and Richard Armitage gave the speech to the State Department. There wasn't supposed to be any press there, but I just had a small camera and I started filming. He gave a speech where he said, "we are going change the face of the Middle East". He was speaking to a group of people from the US State Department inside the Green Zone and he would have never said that if he thought that there was anyone from the press there.

TB: In my own writing I claim that networking is an artwork. The point is not to produce artistic objects, but to generate contexts of connectivity among people that are often unpredictable. Do you think that entering in connection with Snowden contributed to the production of an artwork in the form of ethical resistance?

LP: I feel that this film, or the experience of working on this film, has spilled outside of the filmmaking. In addition to making the film, many other things have emerged. Connections and relationships have been built. But all those kinds of things, and this network, happened because I was branching out of a more linear storytelling, because while I was working on the film, I was also doing a surveillance teach-in at Whitney with Jacob Appelbaum and William Binney, then a short film about Binney's disclosures, and then when Snowden contacted me, that changed everything.

TB: Why do you think Snowden trusted you?

LP: I think he felt that if these disclosures are going to make an impact, that he wanted to reach out to people who were going to do it in a way that wasn't going to be shut down by the US government. Ed had read that I was on a government watchlist and so he knew I understood the threat of surveillance. Glenn and I have both been outspoken on the topic of surveillance, US imperialism, and we had a track record of not being easily intimidated.

TB: I found it a really mature gesture that he decided to come out because he was afraid that other people could have been incriminated.

LP: When I received the email in which Ed told me I want you to put a target on my back, I was in shock for days. I thought my role as a journalist in this context was to protect his identity, and then he said, "What I'm asking you is not to protect my identity, but the opposite, to expose it". And then he explained his reasons about how he didn't want to cause harm to others, and that in the end it would lead back to him. He was incredibly brave. It still makes my heart skip a beat.

TB: I suppose you were also really shocked that Snowden is a really young guy.

LP: I was completely shocked when I met Snowden, and I saw how young he was. Glenn was too. We literally could not believe it—it took us a moment to adjust our expectations. I assumed he would be somebody much older, someone in the latter part of his career and life. I never imagined someone so young would risk so much. In retrospect, I understand it.

One of the most moving things that Snowden said when we were interviewing him in Hong Kong was that he remembers the internet before it was surveilled. He said that mankind has never created anything like it—a tool where people of all ages and cultures can communicate and engage in dialogue. It took someone with such love for the potential of the internet, to risk so much.

TB: You are part of transmediale 2014 with Jacob Appelbaum and Trevor Paglen in the keynote event 'Art as Evidence'. How can art be evidence, and how do you put such a concept into practice via your work?

LP: What we're doing in the talk is thinking about what tools and mediums we can use to translate evidence or information beyond simply revealing the facts, how people can experience that information differently, not just intellectually but emotionally or conceptually. Art allows so many ways to enter into a dialogue with an audience, and that's a practice titalichat I have done in my work, and that Trevor does with mapping secret geographies, and that Jake does with his photography focusing often on dissidents. We engage with the world in some kind of factual way, but we're also translating information that we're confronted with and sharing it with an audience. What we're going to try to do at Art as Evidence is to explore those concepts and give examples of that.

We will combine each of our areas of interest and expertise. I think one of the topics we might discuss is space and surveillance. Trevor has been filming spy satellites. We have some other ideas. I don't want to say too much.

ON JUNE 16, 2021, I met Laura Poitras again at Neuer Berliner Kunstverein (n.b.k.) gallery in Berlin, two days before the opening of her first European solo-show *Circles*. We decided to expand on the previous interview, to reflect on the facts and experiences that have been taking place since the release of the documentary film *Citizenfour* in November 2014 to the present.

Tatiana Bazzichelli: After almost eight years from the time of our first interview many things changed. You and Glenn Greenwald left First Look Media, the organization that you co-founded in 2013. First Look's publication, *The Intercept*, decided to shut down access to the Snowden Archive and dismissed the research team overseeing its security. Snowden is still in asylum in Moscow because of his act of whistleblowing. What does the closure of the Snowden Archive mean for the possibilities of further investigations of the material, and for holding the NSA accountable?

Laura Poitras: I was fired from First Look Media. I didn't just leave; I was terminated after speaking to the New York Times about *The Intercept's* failure to protect whistleblower Reality Winner, and the lack of internal accountability and the cover-up that followed. This malpractice was a betrayal of the organization, which was founded by journalists to protect sources and whistleblowers and hold the powerful accountable. It is a scandal that an organization with such vast financial resources and digital security expertise made so many egregious mistakes, and then didn't apply its own founding principles to itself.

The most shocking thing was that the Editor-in-Chief, Betsy Reed, took an active role in the investigation, which was investigating herself. This, and the many source-protection failures, were so scandalous that I felt a need to speak out about them.

If you allow a culture of impunity to persist, it endangers future sources and whistleblowers, so I spoke out, and I was fired a few weeks later. Glenn (Greenwald) resigned over many reasons, including the Reality Winner scandal.

What transpired in terms of the Snowden Archive was another devastating betrayal of the organization's founding principles. People put their lives on the line to reveal this information; Ed (Edward Snowden) put his life on the line, I put my life on the line, Glenn put his life on the line.

I am still shocked that *The Intercept* and Betsy Reed terminated the staff who oversaw the Snowden Archive's security and destroyed the infrastructure built to provide secure access to the Archive for journalists at *The Intercept* and third-party journalists and international news organizations. This was not a budget decision. The Archive staff made up a miniscule 1.5% of *The Intercept*'s budget. It was a purging—the staff who were terminated were outspoken critics of leadership at *The Intercept*, especially their source protection failures. The challenge with the Archive is how to scale the reporting, while also protecting the Archive from an unauthorized disclosure, leak, or theft. This requires systems of trust, technical expertise, and compartmentalization.

This is a very well-known security phrase: "privacy by design, not by trust". That is what I mean by "compartmentalization"—essentially making it impossible for any one person to steal the archive, while also enabling many people to research it. *The Intercept* flushed it all down the toilet. I wrote to the Board of Directors to try and stop this from happening, but Betsy Reed and CEO Michael Bloom said the Snowden Archive was no longer of journalistic value to *The Intercept*. I should stress that the Snowden Archive still exists, and there is still more to report. What *The Intercept* did was shut down its access and the secure infrastructure that enabled journalists at *The Intercept* and other newsrooms to access it.

This was a real betrayal of Ed and the many people who put so much effort into creating a secure infrastructure. If I were to reflect on my biggest regret in the NSA reporting knowing what I know now, it is joining *The Intercept* and First Look *Media* in 2014 instead of continuing to work with other news organizations.

TB: Is it possible to maintain secure regulated access to these kinds of leaks, years after the interest from news organizations has dissipated? What does the closure of the Snowden Archive tell us about how to deal with leaks in the future?

LP: I think we all learn from each other. There were certain things that we really did do right, and there were certain mistakes we made in these large leaks. I believe there will be future whistleblowers who will come forward, so I think we have to learn from the things that people did right and the things that people did wrong. One of the brilliant things that Julian Assange and WikiLeaks did was to work with multiple international news organizations. It allows for the scaling of information and limits the possibility for the US government to put pressure on *The Times* or *The Washington Post*, for example, as it's harder if *The Guardian* and *Der Spiegel* and *Le Monde* are going ahead and publishing anyway. When you have a massive archive, this is a brilliant partnership model for working with multiple people, and is something we should absolutely carry forward. We also learned of the importance of using encryption from WikiLeaks, and that journalists cannot do their jobs if they don't understand how to protect their sources; they have a responsibility and duty of care.

If you look at the case of the unredacted leak of all the State Department cables, this wasn't the fault of WikiLeaks, it was the fault of their partners at *The Guardian* who didn't protect passwords. The unauthorized disclosure happened because a journalist published a password for an encrypted file.

In retrospect, if I were to get to redo 2014, I would have continued reporting with *Der Spiegel* and other news organizations. My former colleagues at *The Intercept* and First Look have said that all the important things in the Archive have been reported. That is not accurate. There is a vast amount of information that hasn't been reported of enormous contemporary and historical significance. The Snowden Archive contains a history of the Iraq war, the rise of the surveillance state, the global infrastructure of the US empire, etc.

TB: If you wanted to, could you access the archives and keep reporting?

LP: Yes. But no single person could ever fully report or grasp the scale of the information; it requires so many different skill sets, especially highly technical knowledge like crypto, etc.

TB: Your termination at *The Intercept* came two months after you spoke to the press about *The Intercept*'s failure to protect Reality Winner, and the lack of accountability that followed. You wrote that Winner was arrested before the story was even published, denying the crucial window of time for the focus to be on the information she revealed to the public. She is still detained at the moment, your contract at First Look was terminated, and very few people are following up on what she risked herself for. How can we guarantee an adequate protection for whistleblowers if they reach the press? How can we make possible that what she revealed still has an impact on society?

LP: That's part of the tragedy with Reality Winner: the FBI arrested her before the story was even published. She had no opportunity to seek legal advice, and she had no opportunity to see the impact of the story or communicate why she made the choices she did. She was also denied the ability to mount a defense because of all the evidence *The Intercept* provided the US government. This is because of the failures of *The Intercept*. They handed the document she leaked back to the government, they published metadata showing when and where the document was printed, and the reporter disclosed the city from which it was postmarked to a government contractor.

Imagine how different the outcome would have been in the case of Edward Snowden, had I gone to the US government and shared documents with them. Imagine how different the NSA story and Ed's life would have been if he had been arrested and imprisoned before the stories were published? The public would never have heard his motivation, and it would have allowed the government to write its own narrative.

If the government had its way, I'd be in prison, and so would Ed. If I had made similar errors to those made at *The Intercept*, Ed would be in prison, and the public would not know his motivations. This crucial window of time changes outcomes.

The tragic thing about this is that *The Intercept* had so much money and digital security expertise, and they completely failed to protect Reality Winner. Furthermore, there was zero accountability for these failures: nobody was re-assigned or even lost a single day's pay. We are talking about people's lives.

The Intercept was so lazy and reckless, and then they covered it up. To date, two people have been terminated after raising objections about *The Intercept*'s failure to protect Reality Winner: myself and the former head of research, Lynn Dombek.

TB: Would the model that was used for the Panama Papers work?

LP: I wasn't in the room or part of the reporting, though I did work on a film about the Panama Papers. From an outside perspective, it is the kind of model you need: one that brings a sense of scale to the information and also protects sources.

TB: The Espionage Act has been abused by the US government with many whistleblowers, including Reality Winner and Julian Assange. You worked on the film *Risk* (2017) that reported on the Assange Case. Julian Assange is risking extradition, although he is not a whistleblower but a publisher. The silence of the media about Assange is also a worrying signal in the framework of freedom of the press. Did you imagine these consequences of his work while making *Risk*?

LP: First of all, the indictment of Julian Assange under the Espionage Act is one of the gravest threats to press freedom that we've ever had, and a threat to First Amendment in the US. He's a publisher. He's not even a US citizen. And the fact that he's been indicted is absolutely terrifying. I wrote an op-ed in *The New York Times* in defense of Julian, saying that if he is guilty of violating the Espionage Act then so am I, arguing that it is used selectively against people who the government wants to silence and criminalize.

In terms of Julian's situation, the US should absolutely drop the case. The judge in the UK denied the US government's extradition request. The Department of Justice should drop the appeal. The charges go back a decade to 2010 and 2011. To put that into perspective, this case sets a precedent where the US government can go after any international journalist or publisher for things they published more than a decade ago.

When I was making *Risk*, I never had any doubt about the seriousness of the US government's efforts to go after WikiLeaks. I'd also never imagined that Ecuador would withdraw his political asylum—it was clearly justified and based on documented facts. The right of asylum is something that's recognized internationally. If the subtext of the question is about the more critical aspects of Julian in the film, then I can address those too. There were scenes in the film Julian was unhappy with, where he's talking about the women who made the accusations. What is in the film are his own words. I didn't make the film because I was interested in those accusations, but I needed to address them in the film.

I have complete solidarity with Julian as a publisher. Julian has changed the landscape of journalism; the world is better for it and I defend it. But that doesn't mean that there's no room for criticism. He transformed journalism, exposed US war crimes and is absolutely being punished for it. This is a threat to every journalist in the world, and the lack of coverage is shocking.

TB: What happened to Julian Assange is a serious attempt in silencing the press, and setting a precedent that can be used against other journalists. It could apply to many others, including you. What are the risks for you, Glenn Greenwald and other journalists and news organizations who received and reported on the Snowden files and other leaks?

LP: This is all about the selective use of Espionage Act. If you read the Espionage Act literally, the US government could choose to indict any national security journalist with exactly the same type of language that they're using to indict Julian. What's really staggering about Julian, however, is that he's not even a US citizen. The Espionage Act has been abused consistently by Obama, Trump, and now Biden, to go after whistleblowers, journalists, and publishers. It should absolutely be abolished. This is why citizens and the press need to take a stand in defense of Julian Assange and press freedom.

TB: Coming back to the concept of Art as Evidence, the title of our keynote event at transmediale 2014, in the following year you worked on your first solo museum exhibition, *Astro Noise*, exhibited at the Whitney Museum of American Art in 2016. The exhibition was a conceptual road map to understanding and navigating the landscape of total surveillance and the "war on terror". How did the exhibition contribute to producing evidence?

LP: Today we're sitting at n.b.k. in Berlin showing new work which falls into that category. The collaboration that I'm doing with Sean Vegezzi is called *Edgelands* (2021—ongoing), and we've been documenting landscapes in New York using our skills as filmmakers and journalists to bring forth information to the public.

As a non-fiction filmmaker, I work with primary documents and documentary footage which in some cases can be evidence, such as the Snowden Archive. These primary materials then translate into ways in which you can communicate both what they reveal as information or evidence, and in terms of expressing larger issues, such as the dangers of surveillance. For instance, one of the pieces here is called ANARCHIST, which consists of images from the Snowden Archive and intercepts of signals communication that visualize the UK Government Communications Headquarters (GCHQ) and the US National Security Agency

(NSA) hacking into Israeli drones that flew over the occupied territory of Gaza and the West Bank.

In one image, a drone is shown to be armed. So this is evidence hanging as a picture in a gallery space revealing armed drones which Israel has been consistently refusing to admit the existence of.

This is an example of art as evidence. The goal in my art is to make work that is truthful to the facts, but that also has emotional meaning. If you don't feel something, then I have failed. The primary material feeds into how to work with it, and how it can be expressed.

TB: Are you still of the same opinion today as in 2014 about art being functional in revealing truths and misconducts? You are currently collaborating with Forensic Architecture for the exhibition *Investigative Commons* at the Haus der Kulturen der Welt in Berlin, and you are opening your new solo-show this Friday...

LP: I've worked with Forensic Architecture on two projects. I'm really excited about the work that they do. They use multiple disciplines and methodologies to understand ground truths and to present that in multiple contexts or forums. Their information is used in courtroom settings, because of the forensic nature of their work, and it's also exhibited in museum spaces, providing counter-narratives to government narratives. We share an interest in ground truths, and making work using primary documents and deep dive analysis.

The *Investigative Commons* is a kind of laboratory. The idea is to bring together people who have similarities in methodologies, but also do different things, and to see how that might allow for generative conversations and new types of work. The collaboration I've done with them most recently is about the NSO Group, an Israeli cyber-weapons manufacturer, and their malware Pegasus, which has been used to target human rights defenders and journalists and is linked to the assassination of Jamal Khashoggi, because his close collaborator was targeted with Pegasus.

This is an investigation that Forensic Architecture undertook, and invited me to participate in. I participated in the interviewing of people who've been targeted by Pegasus. I made a film about Forensic Architecture's process, and their investigation of the NSO as they map incidences of Pegasus infections to understand the connections between digital violence and physical violence. Forensic Architecture recently opened an office in Berlin and is partnering with the European Center for Constitutional and Human Rights (ECCHR), whose Founder, Wolfgang Kaleck, I've known for many years, and who was essential to my reporting around the Snowden work and who also represents Edward Snowden.

Regarding the n.b.k. exhibition, there are three main works: *Edgelands*, a collaboration with Sean Vegezzi, which is on three screens documenting locations in New York City that are linked by themes, including surveillance, state power, and incarceration, interconnected by the waterways of New York City. The collaboration with Forensic Architecture, also on three screens, includes my documentary about the investigation, on another screen is FA's investigation into the corporate structure of NSO group, and finally a collaboration between Forensic Architecture and Brian Eno. In this project, Brian was asked to work with Forensic Architecture's database of Pegasus infections and make a sonic representation of it.

The show is titled *Circles*; named after one of the subsidiaries of the NSO Group also called *Circles*, but it has other meanings about networks of collaborators and returning to Berlin.

TREVOR PAGLEN

Trevor Paglen is an artist whose work spans image-making, sculpture, investigative journalism, writing and engineering. Paglen's work has had one-person exhibitions at the Smithsonian Museum of American Art, Washington D.C.; Carnegie Museum of Art, Pittsburgh; Fondazione Prada, Milan; the Barbican Centre, London; Vienna Secession, Vienna; and Protocinema, Istanbul. His work has featured in group exhibitions at the Metropolitan Museum of Art, the San Francisco Museum of Modern Art, the Tate Modern, and numerous other venues. Paglen has launched an artwork into distant orbit around Earth in collaboration with Creative Time and MIT, has contributed research and cinematography to the Academy Award-winning film *Citizenfour*, and created a radioactive public sculpture for the exclusion zone in Fukushima, Japan. Paglen is the author of several books and numerous articles on subjects including experimental geography, artificial intelligence, state secrecy, military symbology, photography, and visuality. Paglen's work has been profiled in *The New York Times*, *The New Yorker*, *The Wall Street Journal*, *Wired*, *The Financial Times*, *Art Forum*, and *Aperture*. In 2014, he received the Electronic Frontier Foundation's Pioneer Award and, in 2016, he won the Deutsche Börse Photography Prize. Paglen was named a MacArthur Fellow in 2017. Paglen holds a B.A. and a Ph.D. in Geography from U.C. Berkeley and an MFA from the Institute

TREVOR PAGLEN

TURNKEY TYRANNY, SURVEILLANCE AND THE TERROR STATE

This article by Trevor Paglen was originally published in *Guernica Mag* on June 25, 2013. By arrangement with Creative Time Reports, we include it here to contextualise the debate which followed Edward Snowden's disclosures of the NSA surveillance programme.

Trevor Paglen, *They Watch the Moon*, 2010. Image courtesy of Metro Pictures, Altman Siegel and Galerie Thomas Zander.

BY EXPOSING NSA programs like PRISM and Boundless Informant, Edward Snowden has revealed that we are not moving toward a surveillance state: we live in the heart of one. The 30-year-old whistleblower told *The Guardian*'s Glenn Greenwald that the NSA's data collection created the possibility of a "turnkey tyranny", whereby a malevolent future government could create an authoritarian state with the flick of a switch. The truth is actually worse. Within the context of current economic, political and environmental trends, the existence of a surveillance state doesn't just create a theoretical possibility of tyranny with the turn of a key—it virtually guarantees it.

For more than a decade, we've seen the rise of what we might call a "Terror State", of which the NSA's surveillance capabilities represent just one part. Its rise occurs at a historical moment when state agencies and programs designed to enable social mobility, provide economic security and enhance civic life have been targeted for significant cuts. The last three decades, in fact, have seen serious and consistent attacks on social security, food assistance programs, unemployment benefits and education and health programs. As the social safety net has shrunk, the prison system has grown. The United States now imprisons its own citizens at a higher rate than any other country in the world.

While civic parts of the state have been in retreat, institutions of the Terror State have grown dramatically. In the name of an amorphous and never-ending "war on terror", the Department of Homeland Security was created, while institutions such as the CIA, FBI and NSA, and darker parts of the military like the Joint Special Operations Command (JSOC) have expanded considerably in size and political influence. The world has become a battlefield—a stage for extra-legal renditions, indefinite detentions without trial, drone assassination programs and cyberwarfare. We have entered an era of secret laws, classified interpretations of laws and the retroactive "legalization" of classified programs that were clearly illegal when they began. Funding for the secret parts of the state comes from a "black budget" hidden from Congress—not to mention the people—that now tops $100 billion annually. Finally, to ensure that only government-approved "leaks" appear in the media, the Terror State has waged an unprecedented war on whistleblowers, leakers and journalists. All of these state programs and capacities would have been considered aberrant only a short time ago. Now, they are the norm.

Politicians claim that the Terror State is necessary to defend democratic institutions from the threat of terrorism. But there is a deep irony to this rhetoric. Terrorism does not pose, has never posed and never will pose an existential threat to the United States. Terrorists will never have the capacity to "take away our freedom". Terrorist outfits have no armies with which to invade, and no means to impose martial law. They do not have their hands on supra-national power levers like the World Bank and the International Monetary Fund. They cannot force nations into brutal austerity programs and other forms of economic subjugation. But while terrorism cannot pose an existential threat to the United States, the institutions of a Terror State absolutely can. Indeed, their continued expansion poses a serious threat to principles of democracy and equality.

At its most spectacular, terrorism works by instilling so much fear in a society that the society begins to collapse on itself. The effects of persistent mass surveillance provide one example of such disintegration. Most obviously, surveillance represents a searing breach of personal privacy, as became clear when NSA analysts passed around phone-sex recordings of overseas troops and their stateside spouses. And while surveillance inhibits the exercise of civil liberties for all, it inevitably targets racial, religious and political minorities. Witness the Department of Homeland Security's surveillance of Occupy activists, the NYPD's monitoring of Muslim Americans, the FBI's ruthless entrapment of young Muslim men and the use of anti-terror statutes against environmental activists. Moreover, mass surveillance also has a deep effect on culture, encouraging conformity to a narrow range of "acceptable" ideas by frightening people away from non-mainstream thought. If the government keeps a record of every library book you read, you might be disinclined to check out *The Anarchist Cookbook* today; tomorrow you might think twice before borrowing Lenin's *Imperialism*.

Looking past whatever threats may or may not exist from overseas terrorists, the next few decades will be decades of crisis. Left unchecked, systemic instability caused by growing economic inequality and impending environmental disaster will produce widespread insecurity. On the economic side, we are facing an increasingly acute crisis of capitalism and a growing disparity between the "haves" and "have-nots", both nationally and globally. For several decades, the vast majority of economic gains have gone to the wealthiest segments of society, while the middle and working classes have seen incomes stagnate and decline. Paul Krugman has dubbed this phenomenon the "Great Divergence".

A few statistics are telling: between 1992 and 2007, the income of the 400 wealthiest people in the United States rose by 392 percent. Their tax rate fell by 37 percent. Since 1979, productivity has risen by more than 80 percent, but the median worker's wage has only gone up by 10 percent. This is not an accident. The evisceration of the American middle and working class has everything to do with an all-out assault on unions; the rewriting of the laws governing bankruptcy, student loans, credit card debt, predatory lending and financial trading; and the transfer of public wealth to private hands through deregulation, privatization and reduced taxes on the wealthy. The Great Divergence is, to put it bluntly, the effect of a class war waged by the rich against the rest of society, and there are no signs of it letting up.

All the while, we are on a collision course with nature. Mega-storms, tornadoes, wildfires, floods and erratic weather patterns are gradually becoming the rule rather than the exception. There are no signs of any serious efforts to reduce greenhouse emissions at levels anywhere near those required to avert the worst climate-change scenarios. According to the most robust climate models, global carbon emissions between now and mid-century must be kept below 565 gigatons to meet the Copenhagen Accord's target of limiting global warming to a two-degree Celsius increase. Meanwhile, as Bill McKibben has noted, the world's energy companies currently hold in reserve 2,795 gigatons of carbon, which they plan to release in the coming decades. Clearly, they have bet that world governments will fail to significantly regulate greenhouse emissions. The plan is to keep burning fossil fuels, no matter the environmental consequences.

While right-wing politicians write off climate change as a global conspiracy among scientists, the Pentagon has identified it as a significant threat to national security. After a decade of studies and war games involving climate-change scenarios, the Department of Defense's 2010 Quadrennial Review (the main public document outlining American military doctrine) explains that "climate-related changes are already being observed in every region of the world", and that they "could have significant geopolitical impacts around the world, contributing to poverty, environmental degradation, and the further weakening of fragile governments. Climate change will contribute to food and water scarcity, will increase the spread of disease, and may spur or exacerbate mass migration". Nationally and internationally, the effects of climate change will be felt unevenly. Whether it's rising water levels or skyrocketing prices for foods due to irregular weather, the effects of a tumultuous climate will disproportionately impact society's most precarious populations.

Thus, the effects of climate change will exacerbate already existing trends toward greater economic inequality, leading to widespread humanitarian crises and social unrest. The coming decades will bring Occupy-like protests on ever-larger scales as high unemployment and economic strife, particularly among youth, becomes a "new normal". Moreover, the effects of climate change will produce new populations of displaced people and refugees. Economic and environmental insecurity represent the future for vast swaths of the world's population. One way or another, governments will be forced to respond.

As future governments face these intensifying crises, the decline of the state's civic capacities virtually guarantees that they will meet any unrest with the authoritarian levers of the Terror State. It won't matter whether a "liberal" or "conservative" government is in place; faced with an immediate crisis, the state will use whatever means are available to end said crisis. When the most robust levers available are tools of mass surveillance and coercion, then those tools will be used. What's more, laws like the National Defense Authorization Act, which provides for the indefinite detention of American citizens, indicate that military and intelligence programs originally crafted for combating overseas terrorists will be applied domestically.

The larger, longer-term scandal of Snowden's revelations is that, together with other political trends, the NSA's programs do not merely provide the capacity for "turnkey tyranny"—they render any other future all but impossible.

TREVOR PAGLEN
CHARTING THE INVISIBLE
INTERVIEW BY TATIANA BAZZICHELLI

This interview was conducted on April 15, 2021.

Tatiana Bazzichelli: This anthology aims to reflect upon the impact of whistle-blowing on culture, politics, and society. What impact has whistleblowing had on your work, and how were you able to contribute to the debate around it with your photography?

Trevor Paglen: For a very long time, I have dealt with materials that are often hidden in one way or another, whether that is because they're secret—quite literally in terms of military or intelligence—or because they are internal corporate tools or documents. Much of the work I have done in my career has been made of this. Having said that, I have not worked with whistleblowers that much. Obviously, I was involved in some of the work around Edward Snowden, a very central whistle-blower. More often, however, the work that I've done has been taking information from different places where one person might have a tiny bit of information that might not look by itself to be particularly important. When you combine it with a piece of information over here and a piece of information over here, however, you start to develop an image and tell a story. In my own work, that figure of the whistleblower can come from many different places; it can be from a person, like Edward Snowden, or it can come from court documents, in the case of a lawsuit. I would find the paperwork and look at it, or business filings, and try to understand how a company was put together, or who the people were that were putting it together and trying to use that as a piece of information. Sometimes this has come in the form of records of airplane flights or maintenance records; sometimes that's come in the form of documents, such as a credit report about somebody. In terms of how I use these documents, some organizations like Bellingcat or Forensic Architecture really try to put together disparate kinds of information in order to make a true statement about the world or to create evidence that could be used in a legal framework. What I try to do is a little bit different, in the sense that I don't aspire to create evidence that can be used in a court of law, so much as trying to create images and cultural reflections that help us see the world around us. That brings into visibility aspects of the things going on and helps us to articulate them. Once we can articulate them, we can think about what to do about them. Photography is a big part of that, absolutely.

TB: Your footage of National Security Agency bases was included in Poitras' film *Citizenfour*, but you have been photographing hidden military bases, secret air sites, undersea network cables, and offshore prisons for years before the Snowden disclosures. Tracing a line connecting these projects, could you reflect on what brings them together?

TP: My earliest projects were actually looking at prisons in California, in the 1990s. As this so called 'war on terror' began in the early 2000s, I was looking at it through the framework of thinking about prisons and thinking about incarceration and the relationship between those in the US, and colonialism and frontiers. I did not think it was a coincidence that the central institution of the 'war on terror' was a prison at Guantanamo Bay. At that time, I thought a lot about the relationship between secrecy, imperialism, violence, and politics. I tried to identify where secret prisons were around the world—we knew at that time that the CIA was running a network of secret prisons—and I was trying to find them and go to places like Afghanistan to photograph them and talk to people who had been in these prisons. I tried to dissect the legal structures that were created to enable these secret projects. For example, if you were going to build a secret prison, how would that operate logistically? How would the transportation work? What were the operations you needed to do to make that prison exist? I tried to understand the logistics of secrecy in that sense. It was very much a project of going out into the world and looking at things; whether that was business records, or whether that was aerial maps or testimonies of prisoners, and then putting those things together. In parallel to that, I had started looking at the National Security Agency, as a secret institution wielding enormous political power. Having this background of working with secrecy and with issues related to the military and intelligence community is the reason that Laura Poitras reached out to me, after Edward Snowden had reached out to her, and asked me to support the Snowden project. Looking at the National Security Agency was a very natural thread from the work that I'd been doing, looking at secret prisons, the 'war on terror', and secret military bases. That work extended to more contemporary aspects, such as looking at artificial intelligence and what kinds of machine learning models were being built and deployed in the infrastructures around us. What kinds of politics are built into such infrastructures? Curiously enough, there are many similarities between how Google works and how the NSA works. Working with the Snowden documents was very educational in terms of learning how to look at AI and machine learning. I worked on part of the work on undersea network cables; at the infrastructures of surveillance on one hand, and the internet on the other. We were trying to understand the materiality of the cables, thinking about where the servers were. Where was the cloud? We looked at the literal stuff that these communications are made of.

TB: Speaking about your project on the offshore prisons, could you describe in more detail how you provided evidence of their existence?

TP: In terms of finding secret prions, there were a handful of journalists and people in the human rights community who were trying to understand where the secret prisons were, how they worked and what was going on. People like John Sifton at Human Rights Watch, Jane Mayer at *The New Yorker* and Danna Priest at *The Washington Post*. At that time, there were a handful of people who were worried and were talking to each other in various ways, trying to piece together these different fragments of information. In terms of the secret prisons, I had hypothesized where one of these prisons was in Afghanistan. This hypothesis came from looking at a combination of records of airplanes. I would look at airplanes that I thought were carrying prisoners who had been abducted from different places around the world, and I would look at where they flew as being a proxy for where these prisons might be. I also looked at the testimonies of prisoners. One of the important testimonies in locating the prison in Afghanistan was by a guy named Khaled El-Masri; the CIA had kidnapped him in Macedonia and taken him to a prison in Afghanistan, before deciding that he had nothing to do with terrorism. They kidnapped him again and dumped him by the side of a road in Albania. I was able to look at the records of the airplanes that had flown him around and saw that the airplane had landed in Kabul, Afghanistan, which at the time was interesting, because the normal place you would land if you were an American was Bagram; the US military base. El-Masri had described being driven, blindfolded, for about 20 minutes to wherever the prison was, so the prison was about 20 minutes away by car. By putting together different pieces of information, I had an idea of where I thought it was. I went out there in 2006 with my friend, the investigative journalist, A.C. Thompson (we wrote a book about this together called *Torture Taxi*). We hired a driver to take us out to the place where we thought this prison was and, as is very often the case, when you go to the physical place it becomes very obvious what's going on. While we were in Afghanistan, we spoke to people who were doing human rights work and we talked to people who had been in American prisons set up in Afghanistan. When you go to a place and start talking to people, everybody knows what's going on, even though it doesn't necessarily rise to the level of being in the news. This was also true of an airplane company in North Carolina, in a little rural town called Smithfield. Everybody in the town knew that the airplane company headquartered there was actually CIA. It was obvious if you went there, but if you didn't, you wouldn't necessarily get that understanding. That's always a big part of my process; trying to physically go to different places.

TB: Do you know if these kinds of secret prisons still exist?

TP: Obviously, Guantanamo Bay still exists. It's become the place where a lot of the people who were in these secret prisons are held; usually the ones that were not let out. When A.C. Thompson and I were doing this work, we had a lot of conversations about why there was a secret prison program from a logistical point of view. Why weren't they just murdering these people? Why bother having a prison; you have to feed them, and perhaps provide rights and go to court, and so on. I think that's exactly what they did; the program morphed into the drone assassination program. At some point, the CIA just said they were going to start killing people based on metadata signatures. As in, if you are somebody in this region, and you have been in the vicinity of this cell phone, and you're of this age, then that qualifies you to be assassinated with a drone. I consider the drone program to be what the secret prison program morphed into. Do secret prisons still exist? I don't think in that same way. I don't think that the CIA is running secret prisons in other places around the world right now. In the cases where they want people incarcerated, I think they are using local proxies.

TB: In 2014 at the "Afterglow" edition of the transmediale festival in Berlin we were both part of the panel "Art as Evidence". Revealing the invisible seems to be part of your artistic practice. Could you describe this concept more in depth?

TP: I don't think about it so much as revealing the invisible; I consider making artwork as being similar to making words. When we make a word, or we invent a word, we bring something into existence. We create the possibility of being able to talk about a concept or talk about a feature of our everyday lives. I think about making artwork in a similar way, which is building vocabularies that we use to see the world around us and to articulate the things that constitute our societies and our environments. It's not that there's something hidden and we're doing this work to reveal it, it's that we're trying to bring forth the possibility of seeing the world in a different way, or a more precise way. I'm not concerned with making artworks that could be used in a court of law, in the way that Forensic Architecture is, for example. We have different approaches, but methodologically we are similar.

TB: In the framework of your current work on "Machine Visions" you have been mapping and studying the implications of AI tracking and surveillance both in artistic and technological terms. What were your findings on the social and political effects of machine learning through your artistic work?

TP: Recently, I made an artwork called Image Net Roulette, which is a simple web application that classifies people according to the classifications that are built into the most widely used data sets in AI. AI systems are made of algorithms, but also built out of training data. You create a huge amount of data that is classified and indexed, you put that into a model, and then the model "learns" how to see the world in ways that the data set articulates. These data sets can include all kinds of different things; there are data sets for emotions, for example, made of thousands of pictures of people making different facial expressions. There are data sets of plants, with pictures of different kinds of flowers that are labelled and classified. There's a massive range, depending on what somebody wants to classify. The most widely used of these data sets is called Image Net, which was created at Stanford University. This is a data set made of images, and it has something like 14 million images, organized into about 20,000 different categories. It's used for object recognition and for building computer vision systems to identify different objects. It has images of strawberries, apples, trees; just anything that you can imagine. There are about 2,500 categories: man, woman, boy scout, cheerleader etc. Concerningly, many of the categories in the data set are misogynistic or racist, or are just cruel and awful. There are things like kleptomaniac, slattern, or slut—some of them are quite horrible. The categories also include pictures of people that the researchers scraped from the Internet and classified. I built that application, allowing you to upload a picture of yourself to the Internet, showing you how this dataset would classify you, in order to illustrate how prevalent and how horrible some of the classifications built into machine learning systems are, and how little thought there is put to those kinds of questions within the technical communities that often build datasets. Another project was with the Kronos Quartet, called Sight Machine; over the course of their performance, we looked at them with different computer vision algorithms. Projected behind them was a representation of what these computer vision algorithms were "seeing". You could watch the performance through your own eyes, and also through the eyes of different computer vision systems. The list goes on and on, but I'm obsessed with these underlying classificatory structures in the form of training sets that build machine learning models, as well as the technical forms of "vision" that are built into different computer vision systems; trying to understand what forms of politics are built into those ways of seeing. One of the reasons I'm so interested in the implications for surveillance and privacy is that our domestic environments, as well as our civic environments, are increasingly populated by machine learning systems and AI systems. They are recording and classifying us all the time, in order to either try to sell us something or to try to extract value from us in one way or another, whether that's through trying to modulate our insurance premiums or our healthcare or our credit ratings, for example. State surveillance is one part of that, but there are many ways in which machine learning systems affect our everyday lives and the societies in which we live.

TB: As part of your ongoing study of how computer vision and AI systems "see" the world, you are developing a series of works that look through the "eyes" of various computer vision algorithms. Which kind of social structures are machines enforcing, and how could we intervene in exposing their biases?

TP: Machine learning systems and computer vision systems enforce certain kinds of politics at many different levels. On one level, you have this kind of classificatory level; you always have to build categories into machine learning systems, and those categories are rigid. It's very often the case that categories around gender are created. You build a computer vision system which says, "this is a man" and "this is a woman". What are the politics of that? Why do computer scientists get to decide what somebody's gender is? There's a kind of enforcement that is created and that's a very clear example of the politics that are built into these classificatory systems. There's an inbuilt bias that gender is binary. I think it's a deeper question than one of just bias, however, as bias suggests that there is a kind of standard of fairness, and that the system is unfair in one way. The deeper question is that the system can only be unfair, and can only be biased, and that sexism and racism are features of this kind of classificatory system and not a bug. That's a fundamental disagreement that I have with a lot of people who talk about trying to de-bias machines. In terms of translating this into artwork, I've made installations out of different training sets. For example, one of the earliest training sets for facial recognition was made out of images of prisoners in the 1990s. Where do you get a lot of pictures of people's faces in order to create facial recognition systems? You get them from prisoners. A lot of the work that I've done has been working with training sets in order to think about the historical origins of computer vision and machine learning systems, as well as the political origins of them. I've done it in other ways, in terms of building models and trying to create projects like an Image Net Roulette or a Site Machine, or any number of other installations. There was a video installation called Image Operations, and another one called Behold These Glorious Times. These installations try to show what the logic of machine vision is, by using them and by building machine learning systems based on widely available tools, trying to highlight the kinds of politics that are built into them at every level.

TB: Your text "Turnkey Tyranny, Surveillance and the Terror State", written immediately after the Snowden revelations, is a critique of the economic, political and environmental effects of a surveillance state. As an artist, you have been able to see how these systems are interconnected. What are they revealing about geopolitical powers?

TP: That essay was written in the context of the Snowden disclosures, trying to think about the crises that we are facing as a world. There are many different crises, but obviously we're in a climate emergency. This is a massive crisis, playing out year by year, and I was trying to think about what tools societies build to manage emergencies; the philosophy being that you're going to use the tools that you have to manage emergencies or crises. I was considering this in the US context, where you have a massive military system, a huge mass surveillance system and a huge policing system. Those are the things that you invest in in terms of managing emergencies. When you add it all up, you end up with a society that has all of the elements of a totalitarian approach to politics; very centralized forms of power that are predominantly wielded through instruments like surveillance and police. That is a very brutal way to manage crises. The COVID-19 crisis has accelerated much of this, but I think we're seeing it at many different levels. In the US context, again, we're seeing the more widespread use of facial recognition, especially in the context of policing. One of the things that I didn't talk about in the essay, because it was very much about state power, was the blurry relationship between policing and data collection by companies like Google, Amazon and Zoom, and how those boundaries between the police and global data companies are non-existent. That has certainly been accelerated by COVID-19, in terms of the ubiquity of digital platforms and the degree to which they've become part of the fabric of our everyday lives.

TB: Has your artistic work put you at risk as an artist and how do you deal with the problem of surveillance yourself?

TP: I'm extremely privileged in the sense that I'm a white guy, and I can be in a lot of places that would be very dangerous for somebody who didn't look like me. I have a huge amount of privilege, and I've been able to use that privilege to go to places and do things that might otherwise be dangerous. Having said that, there have definitely been times I've been afraid or felt like I was in a dangerous position. Very early on in my career, however, I decided to not be disabled by fear. My philosophy was that a lot of the most reactionary and fascistic parts of society gain power by fear, so I made a very conscious decision not to be motivated by that.

TB: Whistleblowing is heavily persecuted in many countries and it is often treated an act of treason. How could we culturally contribute to making the work of whistleblowers more accepted in society?

TP: I certainly think that we can all contribute to sculpting society, and to politics in one way or another; through what we do and what we participate in and validate. To me, that is a crucial part of what it means to be living collectively with other people and trying to imagine a world that is more just. Articulating what kind of world we want to live in is one way of culturally contributing to making the work of whistleblowers more acceptable.

TRAFFORD

Photo by Antoine Tardy

is a research coordinator with Forensic Architecture, a pioneering investigative agency iths, University of London. His role at Forensic Architecture covers open-source research stigation, editing and writing for scripts and exhibitions, as well as coordinating inves-nvestigative work with Forensic Architecture has spanned from police violence against the extrajudicial killing of civilians by Cameroon's special forces. He also jointly coor-gations into the 2011 killing of Mark Duggan by UK police, and the agency's acclaimed ER investigation, which premiered at the 2019 Whitney Biennial in New York. Robert investigative journalist, a graduate of the University of Oxford and City, University of joining Forensic Architecture, he was a freelance journalist, covering the 2015 refugee

ROBERT TRAFFORD

SOCIALISED EVIDENCE PRODUCTION IN A POST-OPEN SOURCE WORLD

IN THE 21ST CENTURY, 'big data' whistleblowing and open source investigation have proposed two different but complementary means of challenging state hegemonies of information. One begins with an overwhelming mass of data; the other with fragmentary image or video evidence. But both attempt to drive change, and pursue accountability for states or militaries, by making data more accessible and comprehensible, and by (re-)connecting that data with real lives, and lived experience. And in that attempt, both practices must navigate the shifting dynamics of the contemporary 'public square', an information-sharing space that could seem hopelessly corrupted by 'post-truth'. The work of Forensic Architecture and our partners proposes a path through that space.

It is the privilege of the state to erect cordons, to establish boundaries that carry legal and political weight. A state may delineate a hard border with its neighbours, or it may legislate for corporate privacy, and against public declarations of beneficial ownership. Agents of a state hang lengths of plastic tape around a crime scene, excluding the citizenry from the space in which the facts of a crime are determined. The cordon is the expression of sovereign privilege, and the act of whistleblowing is among the few means available to civil society to puncture that cordon.

The information that escapes that privileged space acts as a window, a portal through which the internal architecture of power—and invariably corruption of power, and violence—becomes visible. But what exactly is seen is determined by who is looking, and through what lens; how the products of whistleblowing are taken up and processed by civil society, and in public and political discourse, is determined by the landscape of information and discourse into which they land. That landscape has of course shifted dramatically since the late 2000s and the all-encompassing rise of the 'social web', the online social media ecosystem. Today, revelations from inside the cordon emerge into an environment of practically unprecedented polarisation, in which faith in existing institutions is failing, and in which established methods of truth-production and dissemination are being left behind as foundational pillars of civic discourse—concepts such as 'truth', 'evidence', and 'fact'—have been erased or weaponised.

New models of truth-production are urgently necessary; models which not only assemble and argue for certain facts and their evidential foundations, but build an audience and a community of action around those facts. This model is at the heart of the 'counter-forensic' practice of Forensic Architecture (FA), the University of London-based research agency with whom I have worked since 2017.[1] FA conducts investigations into human rights violations and environmental violence by state or corporate actors, with and on behalf of the communities and individuals affected by that violence, in pursuit of accountability through political and legal forums. From police violence and border regimes to extractive industry and cyber-surveillance, our investigations look to combine technical expertise with situated experience, creating evidence, arguments, and knowledge from within political struggles, rather than reporting on them. In this essay, I offer some reflections on FA's practice, through which the seeds of some alternative processes for the articulation of shared truth might be glimpsed.

The Open Source Revolution

The seeds of FA's growth are partly to be found in what can be called the 'open source revolution', that far-reaching and cross-disciplinary intellectual and cultural shift,[2] itself a product of the 'social web' and the accompanying rise of instant mass communication and documentation, which has ushered in what Ronald Niezen calls 'Human Rights 3.0'.[3] Our cases, then, proceed less often from the revelations of whistleblowers as through the use of new analytic techniques and technologies for locating and analysing publicly available information, compositing that information into evidentiary arguments: the toolkit of open source investigation, or OSI.[4] Since the early 2010s, OSI has offered ever more innovative and impactful new opportunities for sight across the cordon, particularly in military, national security, and border contexts. Whether photographs uploaded to social media by US military contractors,[5] or freely available satellite images of airbases in Ethiopia,[6] OSI offers new opportunities for researchers to exploit the 'contradictions between materiality and secrecy' that Trevor Paglen identifies.[7]

OSI begins with a diverse set of image-fragments, which require careful reassembly into evidence. By contrast, the act of whistleblowing commonly conveys large quantities of detailed and internally coherent information—documents, communiqués, account statements—into the public domain by the singular and decisive action of an individual (invariably, of course, at great personal risk). Indeed, the kinds of information brought to light by such actions are often fundamentally inaccessible to the methods of the open source research community,

US Special Forces operations at the Salak military base in northern Cameroon (left) were revealed by Forensic Architecture's investigation of photos found on a US military contractor's social media profile (right). Image courtesy of Forensic Architecture.

which is in many respects structurally tethered to images. One cannot, after all, see a bank account from the edge of space.

But while there are functional differences, whistleblowing and OSI are undoubtedly allied practices, tools which sit side-by-side in civil society's (limited) toolkit for exposing and challenging the operation of power, and the misconduct of the powerful. Whistleblowing is a political practice and the exercise of a (possible future) right, the right to be informed. It is oriented towards tangible change in society: greater transparency in global finance; increased civilian oversight of military and intelligence practices. OSI, while it can be critiqued for its remoteness, is inextricable from essentially political demands: for information accessibility, and for human rights accountability.

They are also complementary practices: OSI develops new methods for solving the research problems presented by 'big data', which is increasingly the currency of whistleblowers, and which can present substantial demands on labour, and resources. Amnesty International's Decoders project draws on OSI's collaborative roots to challenge the problem of big data by crowdsourcing investigative tasks. Meanwhile, FA has deployed machine learning in the service of open source research, developing workflows to scrape open data sources such as Youtube and Twitter, run 'object detection' algorithms over images found there, to search for objects of interest to investigators, such as specific models of military vehicles.[8]

The theory of change behind an act of whistleblowing presupposes, or hopes for, a line of causal consequence between disclosure and political action—a line which necessarily runs through the public square, through our shared information spaces. And here, whistleblowing is subject to the same contemporary forces as open source investigators, and civil society as a whole, the forces which have brought us to our present 'post-truth' moment. In the second decade of the twenty-first century, these forces exploded the models of knowledge production that have dominated post-war transatlantic politics and society, and with them the frameworks for human rights that they underwrote. Perversely, these forces can in part be traced back to the same technological and social developments that drove the open source revolution.

A Crisis of Trust

The slow-motion crisis of meaning that is presently strangling many of the world's largest political and social systems is at least in part a crisis of trust: throughout the world, across a broad range of political, social, and economic contexts, the long-standing idea that others can reach out into the world and return to us with information that we can trust is being roundly rejected.

Until the rise of the social web, the task of producing and disseminating truths for societies was performed by governments, and by a small number of legacy media institutions.[9] As citizens, we have long existed in a vertical relationship with this created truth; receiving it, handed down to us, with limited opportunity to see beyond or around the claims presented therein. It was a flawed system, one in which a measure of social consensus around certain categories of 'fact' (such as politics and international relations) relied upon restricted access to information about the world beyond one's immediate experience: in 1950, one's only conceivable (which is not to say reliable) source of information about Syria were the newspaper correspondents writing from there, and the perceived authenticity of their reports was a function of the extent to which that correspondent's newspaper was trusted by the general public—which, on the whole, they were.[10]

In such a context, the path for rights advocates, whistleblowers among them, to leverage public sympathy, or anger, and to convert it into pressure on governments and international bodies in support of their objectives, ran almost exclusively through the print media. In a *vertical* system of information sharing, the truth claims made by civil society bodies were required to first move *upward*, into spheres of media and politics, where they could fight for further, wider dissemination.

This vertical model held those campaigners at the mercy of colonial, patriarchal structures that invariably drove the cases that those advocates sought to challenge. The early years of the internet, and its promise of radical interconnectivity, led to attempts to circumnavigate and critique that media environment, among them the Indymedia network, an early model for socialized truth-telling. But it was the exponential growth and availability of information afforded by Web 2.0

that would ultimately explode the erstwhile systems of knowledge-production. The primacy of those vertical systems of truth-production and dissemination has collapsed, those systems drowned out, if not altogether replaced, by horizontal, peer-to-peer information sharing.

These new models may offer additional avenues for advocacy: NGOs can not only reach million-strong audiences through social media, but indeed conduct their own advanced OSI.[11] But these systems are not primarily systems of truth-production at all; rather, the dissemination of truth claims in the post-internet age is a byproduct of interrelated commercial technologies including global instant communication, 'big data' analysis, and AI. Social media platforms are driven by algorithms which prize similarity over truth, accelerating the growth of 'counter-factual communities',[12] proudly isolated from mainstream interpretations of shared reality. Those same algorithms, which thrive on attention and emotional response,[13] feed community members a diet of emotional extremes, outrage among them.

These 'filter bubbles' have two critical effects upon the efforts of rights campaigners, whistleblowers, and investigators to assemble diverse public coalitions in support of their objectives: first, the population of the information space in which they must operate is broken apart into groups who are 'incapable of engaging with each other upon a shared body of accepted truth';[14] second, those groups become inured to perceiving events in the world crudely, and reactively, without the sensitivity or openness with which an audience might be amenable to the appeals of human rights advocates or the revelations of whistleblowers. In this way, social media has exacerbated deep-rooted problems in the relationship between citizens and information, not least the widely-observed tendency of individuals to entrench themselves more deeply in their existing misperceptions when presented with corrective data.[15]

At the same time, political actors on the populist right have learned more quickly than the rest of us the rules of this new media environment, and have gained a surer footing within it. Eyal Weizman, FA's founder and director, has called these forces an 'insurgency against truth'.[16] Across the world, this insurgent tendency merges an affected populist 'outsider' status with an unabashed proto-fascism,[17] while the public is encouraged to believe that we have become unmoored from truth, that we are floating adrift in a sea of information and misinformation; that anybody's guess is as good as another. It is behind this fog of uncertainty that the human rights violations of the 21st century are carried out and concealed at every scale.

Post-OSI

Against such opposition, civil society, in its pursuit of accountability for state violence, must respond to something of a paradox. The technological innovations and social forces which exploded the stability of the information systems upon which previous supranational models of rights advocacy and enforcement depended are, in many respects, the very same forces that enabled the open source revolution, and which have empowered the OSI ecosystem of which FA is a part to pioneer new models for human rights work.

The artist and curator Marisa Olson coined the term 'post-internet' in the late 2000s,[18] to describe an unavoidable precondition for cultural production in the early 21st century: 'an internet state of mind'.[19] After this fashion, the scale and breadth of the changes wrought by the open source revolution force us to consider that much of contemporary human rights now operates according to a 'post-OSI' logic.

'Post-OSI' does not refer only to the increasing ubiquity of 'visual forensics' or 'visual investigations' teams at the world's major media outlets and NGOs, or the presence of courses on open source investigation at universities around the world (most of them connected to Amnesty's excellent Digital Verification Corps programme). Hints of it can be recognised in the recent and overdue expansion of critical intersectional reflection on open source practices, orienting OSI away from its surveillant mode, toward a centring of situatedness and empathy,[20] evidencing a process of coherence, of becoming an object of study.

Indeed, the attendance of law enforcement personnel at Bellingcat's training workshops,[21] and the requests for training or advice received from governments (and rebuffed) by FA, attest to a dawning awareness by states of the transformative power of a new field. Elsewhere, the denialism that surrounds dozens of well-documented chemical weapons attacks by the Syrian regime[22] also points, much to those denialists' evident fury, to the way in which OSI has become synonymous with contemporary conflict reporting. Regardless of the political and geographic context in which it surfaces, this mode of denialism follows a predictable and ultimately embarrassing pattern, substituting analysis of evidence for *ad hominem* attacks. That there is indeed a pattern, a *script* for this kind of response to civil society's use of publicly available material in pursuit of human rights accountability, is itself evidence of the ubiquity of the target of the pattern, and of our present 'post-OSI' context.

'Post-OSI' recognises that our interlaced systems of information sharing, discourse, politics and media are suffused with a new balance of agency between states, civilians, and civil society, and that ground is cleared for new (or revisited) modes of knowledge production, in light of that rebalancing. Diverse political struggles are increasingly connected, learning from one another, and sharing tools (including FA's open source mapping software, Timemap, which is being deployed by activists from Colombia to Germany). The diversification of media voices is mirrored in human rights, from the monolithic NGOs of Amnesty and Human Rights Watch to a constellation of radical, situated activist groups, that are willing and able to speak more boldly, move aggressively, and act innovatively. The emergence of an activist-technologist-investigator skill set has empowered radical groups and monoliths alike, driving innovation in the field.

'Socialised' Evidence Production

In a presentation to the Disruption Network Lab's *Citizens of Evidence* event in 2019, I outlined, through reference to a number of our past cases, something of FA's response to the ongoing breakdown in established modes of truth-production, and the resurgence of two-fold violence, against bodies and facts, that it has facilitated, which demands a new model for the articulation of human rights claims, and the pursuit of accountability. It is an approach that our director has defined as 'open verification',[23] and it relies, Weizman writes, "upon the creation of a community of practice in which the production of an investigation is socialized; a relation between people who experience violence, activists who take their side, a diffused network of open-source investigators, scientists and other experts who explore what happened".[24]

Open verification seeks to move beyond the model of participatory fact-finding that might be understood as the 'first wave' of open-source investigation: a model which, like much of the traditional news media before it, had a tendency to skew White, male, and European,[25] and ran the risk, as such, of practising a kind of 'helicopter' or 'parachute' investigation. Rather, open verification seeks to take as the starting point of any investigation the marriage of remote technical expertise with the situated knowledge of those who have fallen victim to, and are resisting, state violence. In this mode of operation, the skills of open source investigators, architects, analysts, and scientists are brought into partnership with the truth claims born out of the lived experience of communities and individuals suffering repression, environmental violence, or racist police brutality, enhancing and amplifying those claims. In turn, that experience grounds those technical capacities in the histories and depths of the struggles in whose present they strive to intervene. Commonly, it is FA's digital models that are the venue for the meeting of these perspectives.

Sometimes, the contributions of lived experience are embedded within the investigative process itself, producing new insights and contributing to networked and mutually-supporting findings. From Greece, to Pakistan, to Burundi, FA has

combined spatial analysis and visual investigation with an interviewing technique
we call 'situated testimony', in which digital models become venues for collaborative reconstruction of incidents of violence, and trauma. The process, developed
in partnership with academic psychologists, encourages a mode of interaction
between spatial memory and traumatic memory which can access a witness's rec-
ollections of traumatic incidents in new and valuable ways.[26]

Elsewhere, the situated experience which informs our work is woven throughout and around an investigation, casting new light on its findings. Our investigation of the 2011 killing of Mark Duggan by London's police began as a relatively
narrow, technical assignment commissioned by the lawyers for the victim's family,
intended to illustrate through digital modelling certain 'consensus facts'—agreed
upon by both disputing parties—for the benefit of a civil courtroom. Following
the out-of-court settlement of that case, our findings grew into a diverse after-
life, energising anti-police violence activism in the city, strongly challenging the
narrative of the incident previously established by the UK's police watchdog, and
recently exhibited for the first time within a show at London's Institute of Contemporary Arts, curated by the activist group Tottenham Rights[27] which addresses racist police violence in the UK through the lens of five killings of Black Britons by police.[28] A more recent investigation, into the extrajudicial execution of
Ahmad Erekat, a Palestinian man, by Israeli border police, goes further, embed-
ding an explicit articulation of the connectedness of the struggles for Palestinian
and Black American liberation within and throughout the investigation itself, the
findings of which were narrated by the political intellectual and anti-racist scholar
Angela Davis.[29]

Still other cases, such as our work with Bellingcat to develop the most com-
prehensive archive of US police violence against 'Black Lives Matter' protesters in
the wake of the murder of George Floyd,[30] function as *calls for* the engagement
of that situated perspective, an acknowledgement that OSI must be grounded in
local experience to open up new fronts in the pursuit of accountability. In that
case, a 'mission statement' document shared in on-the-ground networks began a
process of building alliances which now bears fruit in a forthcoming investigation
into police brutality during the same period in the city of Portland. In this way, an
investigation not only develops evidence—in the 'Black Lives Matter' protests case,
findings which are now informing OHCHR's ongoing inquiry into systemic racism
in US law enforcement, and a report by the UN's Human Rights Council—but also
develops communities of action in support of local struggles.

The entanglement of disciplines and perspectives is not intended only to improve the quality of the findings produced by a collaborative investigation. Open
verification acknowledges the urgent need for new spaces of public discourse, and
new forms of commons. The post-war media environment supported a notion of
common ground for rights discourse, defined by a shared deference to the edicts

of supranational rights forums. As that environment has unravelled, so too has the common ground which relied upon the successful operation of a 'politics of shame' on rights-abusing countries.[31] Open verification is also, then, the project of building new common grounds in the face of conditions of post-truth relativity, through common action and the shared production of truth claims: 'Every case produced with open verification is thus not only evidence of what has happened, but also evidence of the social relations which made it possible'.[32]

Virtually every project that FA engages in results in a long and expansive list of credits upon publication; it is rare for our projects to have less than two, or three, or four partners. Whether formal institutional collaborators, protests movements, community activist groups, or specialist technical experts (such as our regular collaborators at Imperial College London, world-leaders in fluid dynamics simulations), our projects are diverse ecosystems of skill-sets, capacities, political intentions, and histories, asymmetric networks of distributed agency and resources.

When the agency was invited to exhibit at the 2019 Whitney Biennial, we were already looking for possibilities to drive forward our research into the applications of machine learning to OSI.[33] As we mulled our options, a storm began to brew around the exhibition—starting with an article in the art news outlet *Hyperallergic*.[34] That article evidenced a connection between the then-vice chair of the Whitney's board of trustees, Warren B. Kanders, and a shocking incident of tear gas use against civilians at the San Diego-Tijuana border: Kanders owned the very company that manufactured the tear gas grenades that had been used there, including against children. Images circulated, contributions to a genre of documentation-photography in which dusty hands hold discharged tear gas grenades face-forward to the camera, revealing the manufacturer's name. In this case, Kanders' company: SAFARILAND.

The controversy that followed was only the latest in which the relation of the arts to human rights was recalled to public attention, a particularly egregious and jarring demonstration of the deep interconnections between colonial capitalism, border regimes, police violence, and the long-standing pillars of cultural heritage. Museum staff protested, and an urgent and uncompromising movement grew into life.[35] The project that developed in response to this attention, and in support of that movement, began with internet research by students at Goldsmiths' Centre for Research Architecture.[36] Their research informed the development of an automated process for creating a set of computer-generated images of tear gas grenades, in realistic and unrealistic environments, wholly created inside the Unreal game engine. We used this 'synthetic data' to train a machine learning classifier to predict the presence of tear gas grenades in real images found online. (In a satisfying inversion of the deepfake crisis, 'fake' images were used to improve the search for real evidence of potential rights violations.)

Left: During the process of training a 'computer vision' classifier, bounding boxes and 'masks' tell the classifier where in the image the Triple-Chaser grenade exists. Right: A computer-generated 'synthetic image' of Triple-Chaser tear gas grenades. Outlandish backgrounds help the algorithm to identify the object of interest. Image courtesy of Forensic Architecture/Praxis Films.

These striking images caught the eye of the filmmaker Laura Poitras when she visited our office weeks later; with her and her team, FA's researchers began to push further into what was known about Kanders, including his barely-reported relationship to a US bullet manufacturer, Sierra Bullets, wholly owned by a holding corporation of which Kanders is board chairman.[37] That research suggested the possibility that bullets manufactured by the company were being used by the Israeli army, not least during the shocking violence seen at the Gaza border fence in 2018, when, in response to peaceful protests, Israeli soldiers killed 150 civilians, including 35 children.

This research led to activists on both sides of the Gaza border fence searching for a matching bullet, while at a border fence on the other side of the world, Tijuana residents searched for examples of the TRIPLE-CHASER tear gas grenade after which our project, in partnership with Praxis Films, would later be named.[38] Activists and citizens from four continents, software developers, academics, animators, open source investigators, and filmmakers, as well as NGOs and solidarity movements, each contributed to the development of this investigation, which premiered at the 2019 Biennial.

This distributed, 'ecosystemic' effort ultimately contributed to Kanders' resignation from the Whitney Museum's board. TRIPLE-CHASER was later named by *The New York Times* among the leading examples of post-war protest art.[39] At the same time, our research led the European Center for Constitutional and Human Rights, a pioneering legal NGO with whom recently opened a shared office in their home city of Berlin, to investigate the possibility of legal action against Sierra Bullets. Perhaps most enduringly, these combined efforts established and disseminated clear and mutually-supporting truth claims, building agency across fields and disciplines to confront the entanglement of extractive capital and colonial violence with culture.

In the TRIPLE-CHASER investigation, throughout FA's seventy published investigations, and across the collaborative networks that have enabled and sustained them, new possibilities for collectivised knowledge-production are evident. Those possibilities respond to, and have been incubated within, a new and evolving political, technological, and media environment which is shifting the ground beneath whistleblowers and investigators alike, offering new paths to accountability, and at the same time new and significant risks. These new environments are characterised by fragmentation, the dissolution of unitary truths into multitudes; FA's model of socialised truth production offers a path toward reassembly of that multitude, simultaneously producing knowledge, and communities of action around that shared knowledge.

Notes

1. Ideas of counter-forensics expounded in Threshold.

2. E.g. amongst others, Muhammad Idrees Ahmad, "Bellingcat and How Open Source Reinvented Investigative Journalism", *New York Review of Books*, June 10, 2019, https://www.nybooks.com/daily/2019/06/10/bellingcat-and-how-open-source-reinvented-investigative-journalism.

3. Niezen, Ronald. *#Human Rights: The Technologies and Politics of Justice Claims in Practice*, (Palo Alto: Stanford University Press, 2020).

4. Early on in history of open source investigation, the most widely-used term for the practice was "OSINT". An acronym for "open source intelligence", the term's connections to the history of state spycraft is obvious. At FA and elsewhere, the term has slipped out of favour; I will use our preferred acronym, "OSI".

5. "Torture and Detention in Cameroon", *Forensic Architecture*, June 2017, https://www.forensic-architecture.org/investigation/torture-and-detention-in-cameroon.

6. Wim Zwijnenburg, "Are Emirati Armed Drones Supporting Ethiopia from an Eritrean Air Base?", *Bellingcat*, November

2020, https://www.bellingcat.com/news/rest-of-world/2020/11/19/are-emirati-armed-drones-supporting-ethiopia-from-an-eritrean-air-base.

7. Paglen, Trevor, "Art as Evidence." Keynote, transmediale 2014, Haus der Kulturen der Welt, Berlin, January 30, 2014.

8. Our investigation into Russia's 2014 invasion of eastern Ukraine deployed such methods to turn up new evidence. Those findings were submitted to the European Court of Human Rights in 2019; the first example of machine learning-based evidence in such a context. The investigation is here: https://ilovaisk.forensic-architecture.org.

9. It is difficult to define the scope of the problem at hand here without being open to justifiable charges of generalisation. My own understanding of this problem is situated in the media and social contexts of western Europe and north America, but the language of 'post-truth' has undoubtedly taken root more widely.

10. See for example: Ladd, Jonathan M., *Why Americans Hate the Media and How It Matters*, (Princeton: Princeton University Press, 2011).

11. Such as the excellent work done by Amnesty's Citizen Evidence Lab, found at https://citizenevidence.amnestyusa.org.

12. A term increasingly favoured by Eliot Higgins, as in his recent *We Are Bellingcat: An Intelligence Agency for the People*, (London: Bloomsbury, 2021).

13. For example, Robert Booth, "Facebook reveals news feed experiment to control emotions", *The Guardian*, June 30, 2014, https://www.theguardian.com/technology/2014/jun/29/facebook-users-emotions-news-feeds.

14. Vaidhyanathan, Siva, *Antisocial Media: How Facebook Disconnects Us and Undermines Democracy*, (Oxford: Oxford University Press, 2018).

15. https://cpb-us-e1.wpmucdn.com/sites.dartmouth.edu/dist/5/2293/files/2021/03/nyhan-reifler.pdf.

16. Eyal Weizman, "Data Against Devilry." Keynote, Re:publica 2018, Deutsches Technikmuseum, Berlin, May 4, 2018.

17. Witness the discussion in the aftermath of the January 6, 2021 Capitol invasion of the 'big lie', a concept born in Nazi Germany. For example, Eli Zaretsky, "The Big Lie", *London Review of Books*, February 15, 2021, https://www.lrb.co.uk/blog/2021/february/the-big-lie.

18. https://www.academia.edu/26348232/POSTINTERNET_Art_After_the_Internet.

19. https://ucca.org.cn/en/exhibition/art-post-internet.

20. An excellent article on this front is Dyer Sophie and Gabriela Ivens, "What would a feminist open source investigation look like?", *Digital War 1*, (2020): 5–17, https://doi.org/10.1057/s42984-020-00008-9. The pages of the Open Source Researchers of Color collective are similarly valuable for their reorientation of OSI principles: https://www.osroc.org.

21. https://twitter.com/AricToler/status/1321127564275056640.

22. A thorough and hard-nosed exploration of one such incident, its aftermath, and the ways in which open source evidence may be swallowed by propaganda is by James

Harkin, a colleague at Goldsmiths, University of London: https://theintercept.com/2019/02/09/douma-chemical-attack-evidence-syria.

23. Eyal Weizman, "Open Verification", *e-flux*, accessed March 23, 2021, https://www.e-flux.com/architecture/becoming-digital/248062/open-verification.

24. Ibid.

25. Rayna Stamboliyska, "Women in OSINT: Diversifying the Field, part 1", *Bellingcat*, December 8, 2015, https://www.bellingcat.com/resources/articles/2015/12/08/women-in-osint-diversifying-the-field.

26. Beginning with Mir Ali, then Saydnaya.. (e-flux).

27. *War Inna Babylon*, at the Institute for Contemporary Arts, was described by London's Evening Standard as "a necessary, urgent, at times devastating show". Read more about the exhibition and its public programme at https://www.ica.art/exhibitions/war-inna-babylon.

28. Ibid.

29. Forensic Architecture, "The Extrajudicial Execution of Ahmad Erekat", February 2021, https://forensic-architecture.org/investigation/the-extrajudicial-execution-of-ahmad-erekat.

30. https://blmprotests.forensic-architecture.org.

31. https://blogs.commons.georgetown.edu/erikvoeten/files/2011/10/LeboISQ.pdf.

32. Eyal Weizman, "Open Verification", *e-flux*, June 19, 2019, https://www.e-flux.com/architecture/becoming-digital/248062/open-verification.

33. See for example https://forensic-architecture.org/investigation/experiments-in-synthetic-data.

34. Jasmine Weber, "A Whitney Museum Vice Chairman Owns a Manufacturer Supplying Tear Gas at the Border", *Hyperallergic*, November 27, 2018, https://hyperallergic.com/472964/a-whitney-museum-vice-chairman-owns-a-manufacturer-supplying-tear-gas-at-the-border.

35. At the heart of that movement were the groups Decolonize This Place and Working Artists and the Greater Economy. Both groups remain sources of inspiration for FA's practice.

36. The Centre for Research Architecture, based at Goldsmiths, University of London, is a pioneering research experiment and community, founded by Dr. Susan Schuppli and our director Eyal Weizman. FA grew out of the CRA, and continues to hire researchers from its MA and PhD programmes.

37. That research is available here: https://forensic-architecture.org/investigation.matchking-warren-b-kanders-and-the-israel-defense-forces.

38. View the investigation at: https://forensic-architecture.org/investigation/triple-chaser.

39. Thessaly La Force, Zoë Lescaze, Nancy Hass, and M.H. Miller, "The 25 Most Influential Works of American Protest Art Since World War II", October 15, 2020, https://www.nytimes.com/2020/10/15/t-magazine/most-influential-protest-art.html.

3

NETWORK EXPOSED

TRACKING SYSTEMS OF CONTROL

LISA LING &
CIAN WESTMORELAND
LAURI LOVE · JOANA MOLL
DENIS "JAROMIL" ROIO

GLOBAL MILITARY

dominance, tactics of control, data tracking and surveillance practices call for a public debate on ethics and awareness around these interconnected systems. Former military service members Lisa Ling and Cian Westmoreland introduce and explain what they call the "Kill Cloud" behind the US military drone programme as a pervasive technological weapon system pursued to achieve dominance across space, cyberspace, and the electromagnetic spectrum. Their piece highlights what is happening behind the visible drone platform and aims to provide a better understanding on the real consequences of network centric aerial warfare. The subject of pervasive invisible surveillance infrastructures informs the reflections of security engineer and activist Lauri Love, who discusses the notion of "Sousveillance", to denote vigilance upwards from below. He provides an analysis on the current ethical issues concerning technological and intimate surveillance, reflecting on the urge of self-empowering ourselves from centralised power and authority.

Artist and investigative researcher Ioana Moll describes the making of her three projects "The Hidden Life of an Amazon User", "The Dating Brokers" and "Algorithms Allowed". She exposes severe malpractice in the hands of corporate and governmental stakeholders and highlights the role of creative practice in uncovering and denouncing such actions. Finally, Denis "Jaromil" Roio, digital innovation expert, software artisan and ethical hacker, discusses the meaning of hacker ethics in 2021, stressing the importance of social movements to provide agency through collectivising big data controlled by financial and institutional powers.

LISA LING

Lisa Ling began her military career in the early 1990s as a medic and nurse. She became recognised for her information systems skills, and was encouraged to enter the combat communications field, where she participated in the operations, maintenance, and security of networked communications technology. The Intelligence Surveillance Reconnaissance (ISR) enterprise required more people to build and operate it, so her Combat Communications Squadron was assimilated into the Drone Program and moved to Beale Air Force Base. During her Military Career she was deployed to various locations, including the DCGS headquarters at Joint Base Langley-Eustis in Virginia, an Air National Guard site in Kansas, as well as several overseas deployments. Lisa served her last active-duty assignment with the site at Beale Air Force Base in California. After her military service, she travelled to Afghanistan to see firsthand the effects of what she participated in. She has a BS in History from UC Berkeley where she hopes to further her education.

CIAN WESTMORELAND

Cian Westmoreland served as a technician specialised in radio and satellite communications in the United States Air Force from 2006 till 2010. He was deployed in 2009 to Kandahar Airfield in Afghanistan to intercept command and control data over a 240,000 mile radius in Afghanistan and relay it through a high bandwidth satellite datalink containing voice communications, targeting data, imagery, and geographical data for both manned and unmanned aircraft tasked by the Combined Air Operations Centre at Al Udeid Air Base in Qatar and processed by the DCGS weapon system. His performance report stated that he assisted in "200+ enemy kills" and his unit received a Meritorious Unit Award. In 2010 he separated from Spangdahlem Air Base, Germany and spent a year hitchhiking across Eastern Europe, Central Asia, South East Asia and China. Several encounters with the spectre of organised violence drove him to seek understanding of his participation in war by receiving a bachelor's degree in international Affairs from Vesalius College in Brussels, Belgium.

Photo by Siri Margerin

Photo courtesy of the author

LISA LING & CIAN WESTMORELAND

THE KILL CLOUD
REAL WORLD IMPLICATIONS OF NETWORK CENTRIC WARFARE

AS FORMER MILITARY

service members, we have a lifelong responsibility to submit for prepublication review any information intended for public disclosure that is, or may be, based on protected information gained while associated with the Department of Defense (DoD). We think this requirement is problematic as a constitutional matter and acts as a prior restraint on protected First Amendment speech. Nevertheless, this essay contains no such protected information. Instead, we use official government discourse to expose and interrogate what is not classified and currently exists in the public domain. Accordingly, and after consultation with our attorney, we did not seek pre-publication review.[1]

This chapter is about the United States' Global War on Terror, its ideological underpinnings, its ambitions, consequences, and more specifically, the technological approach pursued to achieve global military dominance across every spectrum of warfare, including space, cyberspace, and the electromagnetic spectrum itself. To fully appreciate this paper, it is important to be open to a civilizational critique of the United States and to recognize it on its own historical merit without relying on the mythical narrative of "American Exceptionalism." In the context of a rapidly warming world, issues of colonialism, water scarcity, forced migration, and war are all interconnected under the aspirations of technological progress.

We seek to introduce and explain what we have come to call the "Kill Cloud" behind the US military drone program. The modern militaries of the Global West wage war through remote surveillance and kinetic strikes with interconnected platforms, some of which ingest enormous quantities of data.[2] The use of this massive technological weapon system under the auspices of the "Global War on Terror" is invisible to the Western public. This chapter intends to illuminate greater aspects of modern drone warfare for the public eye to stimulate participation in the conversation around the ethics and scope of this developing weapon system. We have arrived at a time when enough information has been declassified for the public to engage in a robust dialogue about what is happening behind the visible drone platform.[3] Along with thousands of other soldiers and airmen, we were part of this interconnected system we are calling the Kill Cloud. We call it that because there is no other word that fully describes the size and scope of this still evolving weapon system. Our professional military experiences were vastly different in many ways, yet both of us contributed to what we now see as terror. We share an abhorrence for the human toll shamelessly quantified in writing on our performance evaluations and awards.

After our service was over, we felt it was important to travel as civilians to reconnect with our humanity. Working with technology tends to disconnect those working with it, so we traveled as civilians to conflict zones to see for ourselves the human consequences of our actions. Through our process of disillusionment, a commitment arose to continue to question and reflect on this modern form of distributed networked warfare for the rest of our lives, along with a heartfelt desire to work toward positive social and cultural change. We have each turned to intellectual reflection as students in academia after our military service to critically analyze the power dynamics that have influenced this type of war. Lisa turned to history, and Cian to international relations. This collaborative chapter draws on our different experiences and is informed by research across interdisciplinary perspectives. We want to acknowledge the terror, the pain, and heartache that use of this technology has caused people living in the communities persistently surveilled, targeted, and blown to bits by connected peripheral devices (such as drones). It is our most sincere hope that once this writing is in the hands of the public that you, too, will understand the enormity, complexity, and barbarity of this vast distributed enterprise despite the promise of greater situational awareness, or the ability to see through the fog of war by adding Geospatial tools, Artificial Intelligence (AI), or other robotic platforms.[4]

There is an urgent need to widen the public's understanding of drone warfare. We must move from viewing the unmanned platform as a separate weapon, to including the entirety of the evolving systems behind it because of the insidious threats they pose to all of us. A drone can carry and launch lethal weapons and loiter at relatively low altitudes, terrorizing those living under them, so the tendency to focus on the drone platform itself is valid. However, such narrow framing obscures the distributed systems, bureaucratic institutions, and cultural biases behind the intensive intelligence, surveillance, and reconnaissance (ISR) production that directs these platforms toward their targets. There is no single term that could describe what this massive evolving weapon system is in a way that can be universally understood; the concept is unprecedented. Modern drone warfare is vastly more complex, insidious, ubiquitous, inaccurate, than the public is aware, and its colonial scope continues to bring endless war to communities of color across the globe.

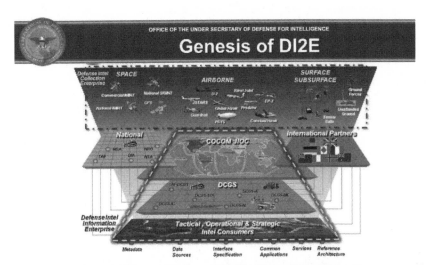

- **DoD Defense Intelligence Strategy coined the Phrase "Defense Intelligence Enterprise" (DIE)**
- **The term DI2E was created to describe the Information Component of the DIE-- DI2E stands for Defense Intelligence Information Enterprise**

Diagram of the information component for the evolving weapon system we are calling the Kill Cloud. Image courtesy of Michael G. Vickers.[5]

The Drone Myth

Retired Lieutenant General David Deptula, who was the primary planner of the air campaign in the First Gulf War and the former first Deputy Chief of Staff for ISR, was heavily involved in shaping and managing the US military use of drones; he uses the business-like description of an "Enterprise" to reference the networked socio-technical assemblage that functions silently and in secret behind the drone. This enterprise, this Kill Cloud as we call it, connects sensor and weapons platforms (drones) to a globally distributed network of devices, software, and a multitude of other nodes via satellites, cables, radio, and digital communication links that are accessed, operated, and maintained daily across all military branches, support agencies, and coalition partners, by thousands of people spanning the world (see Figure 1). This is what we refer to when we talk about network centric warfare (NCW), a means of navigating armed conflict that relies on distributed networks to kill with impunity.[6]

The public understanding of the intricacies of drone warfare remains extremely superficial and has been heavily influenced by the symbol of the drone itself. The popularized focus on drones promoted and dramatized in films such as *Good Kill* (2014), *Eye in the Sky* (2015), *Drone* (2017) and, to a lesser extent, *Pine Gap* (2018) inhibits conversation about and diverts public attention from the broader entanglements of network-centric warfare. While each of these films have a narrower focus on different aspects of an immense system, the much deeper ethical questions regarding a distributed (semi) autonomous, hyper-staffed, weapon of global connectivity and reach are not comprehensively interrogated. America's obsession with military planes and pilots harkens back to such films as *Those Magnificent Men in Their Flying Machines* (1965) or *Top Gun* (1986), so it is not difficult to understand how focusing on the deeper structural problems of this immense system have been averted. It is the myth of the drone, its simplicity and promise to make war shorter and safer, that dominates the discourse of the greater public today. Wars will not be made shorter or safer by adding remote connectivity, AI, or full autonomy to new or existing weapons.

General Deptula describes the phenomena of the clean and simple design of a drone drawing the public's focus away from the vast complex networks responsible for its operation in this way: "Everyone focuses on this little piece of fiberglass flying around called an unmanned aerial vehicle, but it's just a host for sensors that provide data to this vast analytic enterprise we call the Distributed Common Ground System [DCGS], which turns the data into information and hopefully knowledge" (Deptula, as quoted in *Airforce Magazine*).[7]

The press has not been immune to the lure of the drone myth, either. We both are regularly interviewed by journalists who only too quickly display disappointment upon learning that we were neither drone pilots nor sensor operators. They are even more disappointed to learn that the pilots are the least informed of all about the globally interconnected systems and equipment necessary to keep the drones flying and their sensors sensing. The term "drone" itself, which we adopt in this essay due to its wide public acceptance, is a misnomer because of the significant amount of labor required to keep them in flight. The drone myth obfuscates the Kill Cloud with its sleek design and straightforward conception: the drone aims to be war, simplified.

Yet, it is everyone's duty to see beyond this symbol of modern warfare and question the convoluted and complex mechanisms behind its operation as well as the idea that the proliferation of these systems will make us all safer. Similarly, the word "cloud" in relation to what we know as the internet is a marketing term and bears no relation to reality. It is not ionized water vapor condensing around particulates through surface tension freely floating in the air, nor is it some magical place.[8] The cloud is a distributed network of servers, databases, devices, software, data storage and computing power. Interface with the cloud provides users the

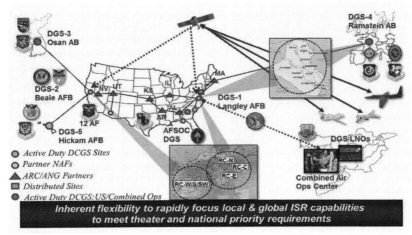

Air Force Distributed Common Ground System (US Air Force 2015, 32).[56]

means to view the same information and collaborate from various locations. The services we use every day to plan a trip (Google Maps), order a ride (Uber), avoid traffic (Waze), watch movies while they buffer (Netflix, YouTube, and others), link up with "People you may know" (Facebook Friend Recommendations) or identify that song you keep hearing (Shazam) are all rendered to your device using data sent from the cloud—and, disturbingly, all have applications that "can" be assimilated into what military planners envision for Cloud Supported Network Centric Warfare (NCW).[9] Technology companies have already been tapped by military planners for their collaboration with this massive weapons system.[10]

Obstacles to Public Understanding

A key obstacle limiting public understanding of the Kill Cloud is the very nature of distributed systems themselves, as Maarten van Steen and Andrew S. Tanenbaum state in *A Brief Introduction to Distributed Systems* in 2016: "Distributed systems are by now commonplace yet remain an often-difficult area of research. This is partly explained by the many facets of such systems and the inherent difficulty to isolate these facets from each other."[11]

A Distributed Common Ground System is described on the United States Air Force (USAF) official website as the "primary intelligence, surveillance and reconnaissance (ISR) planning and direction, collection, processing and exploitation, analysis and dissemination (PCPAD) weapon system that consists of at least 27 regionally aligned and globally networked sites."[12] The letters in the acronym PCPAD refer to the process that can direct sensors to collect data in near-real-time. That data collection and interpretation necessitates a more symbiotic relationship between military technology, communications personnel, and the intelligence community. The often-repeated Air Force phrase "no comms, no bombs" accurately describes the partnership needed between these two formally semi-segregated military sectors. Both are integrated into the Distributed Common Ground System, making the Kill Cloud a murky affair. In other words, when the communications sector and the intelligence sector work together, it is rarely transparent, include weapons and sensors, and the public can be assured that critical research information will neither be forthcoming nor forthright.[13]

Further complicating substantial public discourse is the prolific use of military acronyms and nebulous descriptors such as DCGS (Distributed Common Ground System), EPIE (European Partnership Integration Enterprise), "Military Aged Male" or "Target".[14] These acronyms and descriptors control public access to information and often serve to impede researchers' access to knowledge over time. They are part of a massive infrastructure built to increase the speed at which complex ideas and concepts are communicated within limited human networks while simultaneously obfuscating them to the uninitiated. The use of acronyms also strips away any emotional context that will communicate the effects of what the letters represent in the real world. For example, phrases like "Military Age Male" (MAM), "imminent threat" or "target" have become normative representations of human beings, many of whom never were, nor intended to be combatants; they were innocents. Dr. Sara Shocker, through her research was able to rigorously work around obstacles to empirically demonstrate that data analysts use stereotypes about gender and religion to inform who is selected as a drone target.[15] In her book, *Military Aged Males in Counterinsurgency and Drone Warfare*, Shocker argues that the normative use of the category "Military Aged Male" has contributed to the deterioration of civilian protections.[16] We both agree with her argument and her conclusions.

Compounding the many obstacles that acronyms and nebulous descriptors pose to public access to information, there is a lack of clarity and oversight surrounding the multiple classification processes that hold "state secrets." Items of critical public interest have been consistently locked behind phrases like "need to know" or "national security" and kept from public disclosure even when unnecessarily classified. The government selectively decides what, when, where, why, and how information is exposed. Much has been said on the topic, but little has changed. There is no clear definition for over-classification even in the public law signed by President Barack Obama designed to reduce it.[17] Furthermore, in the executive summary of a Department of Justice (DOJ) audit from 2013, both Congress and the White House recognized that over-classification of information interferes with accurate and actionable information sharing, increases the cost of information security, and needlessly denies public access to information. The audit found that the DOJ is susceptible to what was called misclassification, and that the DOJ was not effectively administering its own classification policies.[18] This is one of the very few publicly accessible investigations demonstrating misclassification and over-classification, which is not exclusive to the DOJ. Within the Kill Cloud there are multiple classification systems in place managed by multiple agencies, branches of service, mission partners, and others. Over-classification is common because the incentive to classify materials, even unnecessarily, far outweigh any reasons or risks not to. Despite these failures, public interest whistleblowing is still prosecuted vigorously under the 1917 Espionage Act and the accused are denied a fair trial because any evidence can be hidden from the public under the auspices of National Security. Furthermore, any defense that allows the defendant to state motive is disallowed and has been from the case of Daniel Ellsberg forward. This precedent was upheld in the recent case of Daniel Everette Hale whose documents prompted The Council on American-Islamic Relations ("CAIR" or "CAIR Foundation") to submit an amicus curiae brief to support Hale during sentencing. CAIR represented hundreds of Muslim Americans who were placed on the US Government's Selectee and No-Fly Lists.[19] It is important to cite a part of the request here:

> The 2013 Watchlisting Guidance, a US Government publication, spelled out the criteria and procedures through which US persons are placed on the federal government's many secret lists. This document is unclassified, but the US Government had never agreed to make it available so that persons caught up in the lists and their representatives could come to understand the process. Daniel Hale disclosed this document, [...] The availability of this information enabled CAIR to present focused claims on behalf of its clients, whose lives had been disrupted by being placed on the lists.[20]

From 2002 through 2008, J. William Leonard served as the Director of the Information Security Oversight Office. Leonard worked for the Department of Defense from 1973 until 2002 where his responsibilities included ensuring that classified national security information in the possession of defense contractors was properly protected. Other responsibilities included counterintelligence, critical infrastructure protection, and offensive and defensive information operations programs. He is one of few individuals we would look to for clarity on what should and should not be considered classified or, more to the point, what pieces of hidden information is in the publics' best interest to know.

One of the more recent debates on this topic surrounds Reality Winner's leak releasing information regarding the security of the 2016 US election. Leonard stated quite clearly that the document released by Winner, an accoladed cryptographic linguist who translated incoming data from drone platform sensors, should not have been classified and was in the public's best interest in an opinion piece for

The Washington Post dated December 21, 2020, and in the documentary film directed by Sonia Kennebeck, *United States vs. Reality Winner*.[21] While Winner's leak was not about network centric warfare, this is a clear instance where the government's' power to strategically over-classify information resulted in the persecution and five-year sentencing of another whistleblower associated with the drone program.[22]

Common Operating Picture

Command, Control, Communications, Computing, Intelligence, Surveillance, and Reconnaissance (C4ISR) is another one of many military acronyms used to describe a conceptual framework for the United States current approach to warfare. Command and Control throughout military history consisted of a commander observing from the highest point he could to get an accurate overview of the battle space. The commander would then use that information to direct his troops and formulate a battle plan for them to carry out. Maps allowed Generals or commanders to sit in a tent and conceptually visualize the battlefield. Wars have been won and lost based on who had the most accurate vision of realities on the ground or, put simply, the most accurate maps. Maps are coveted assets that win wars and communicating plans through a common picture with other forces was essential to accurately execute battlefield maneuvers. Until data was able to be transmitted wirelessly or beyond line of sight (BLOS), command and control had not really changed since Napoleon tried to conquer Russia in the middle of the winter of 1812.

Today, a Common Operating Picture (COP) of the air war is rendered from location data that is overlayed onto a topographical map and displayed on screens so that Air Battle Managers (ABMs) and other decision-makers can view the air war in real time. The ABMs send current information to the Air Operations Center (AOC) to provide Command and Control of the air war. ABMs have knowledge about aircraft, weapons, and surveillance. They use this information to control each aircraft by telling pilots, and sometimes ground troops, where to go and what to do with their weapons when they get there. The core functions of an ABM include orienting shooters, pairing shooters, solving problems, and making decisions. Sitting with the Air Battle Manager is an enlisted position called the Command-and-Control Battle Management Operator (C2BMO) who determines things like who has the most fuel, who is closest, who can get there fastest and who can stay on station longest in order to support the tactical decisions of the Air Battle Manager.[23] They create the air tasking order and task the aircraft within that order.

The COP, or what is described as a common picture of the air war, includes the aircraft platforms, locations, and available weapons. Air Traffic Controllers

(ATCs) operate radio equipment to relay flight and landing instructions, weather reports and safety information to pilots. ATCs are also responsible for plotting aircraft positions on radar equipment, as well as computing aircraft speed, direction, and altitude.[24]

Expanding the Kill Cloud

The US Military will be rolling out the Advanced Air Battle Management System (AABMS) in 2021. Air Force Chief of Staff Gen. CQ Brown, Jr. explains the improvements this way: "Nearly two years of rigorous development and experimentation have shown beyond doubt the promise of ABMS... We've demonstrated that our ABMS efforts can collect vast amounts of data from air, land, sea, space and cyber domains, process that information and share it in a way that allows for faster and better decisions".[25]

What this means in laymen's terms is that increased data is going to be ingested into what we are calling the Kill Cloud, attempting to eliminate the fog of war. More data does not necessarily mean less confusion unless it is managed well. As we will explain later, the OODA Loop (Observe, Orient, Decide, Act) concept takes more data and strives for faster and faster reaction times. What could go wrong? Many would argue that the answer is even more data; the appetite for increasingly more data is insatiable.[26]

Advanced Air Battle Management is becoming a multi-domain data collection and distribution system that uses a mesh network of various platforms in which nodes automatically assign which asset to respond. The possible end state is supposed to resemble how someone might call for an Uber or a Lyft with a cloud-based system choosing which driver is closest to you in time and distance to pick you up. The truth is that not even the Air Force knows what the whole system will be composed of when it is finished.[27] The goal is for soldiers on the ground to be able to identify threats, much like accidents and traffic choke points can be spotted and avoided on Waze with user input. Soldiers on the ground will be able to send what they see and experience so their information can be distributed to any number of proximal collection points where the data will be analyzed and used by mission planners or others in the future.[28]

Until recently, battlefield communications between different entities were a complex, cumbersome, and time intensive task to plan and execute; often errors occurred that required more planning and execution from the field and on the fly. Today, it is possible for dissimilar networks to effectively communicate BLOS from great distances using what is known as a Battlefield Airborne Communications Node (BACN) pronounced "bacon" for short. This capability makes the aspirational goal of a Common Operating Picture plausible from a pure technology perspective. The assemblage of Internet Protocol (IP) and software defined radios, a gateway manager, and Advanced Information Architecture (AIA) allows the exchange of data from disparate sources to be collated and transmitted or stored as necessary for mission planners and others to use. Because the link can be configured to be device agnostic, it is now possible to send text messages from a cell phone to a pilot flying overhead.[29]

These systems, originally flown by NASA (North American Space Agency) in high altitude airframes for testing, were soon in high military demand. BACN evolved "[...] from a joint operational need to an enduring capability."[30] Because this equipment can be deployed on mobile platforms, the use of this technology reduces the logistical and security footprint, as well as the requirements needed for static ground-based systems. In the future, these systems will be further facilitated by low earth orbit satellites deployed by civilian contractors. According to *Air Force Magazine*, "the military is waiting for the commercial industry to build its satellite communications constellations on orbit, such as SpaceX's Starlink array and an Airbus LEO constellation, so it can tap into the capability on a large scale."[31] Like much of the Kill Cloud, this piece will evolve to facilitate the ingestion of mass amounts of data using software and algorithms for AI and machine learning to compute and connect the massive amounts of source and sensor data, using an Edge Computing strategy, with the goal of speed and accuracy beyond what is currently available.[32]

After a significant testing exercise at Eglin Air Force Base, Florida on September 3, 2020, that included thousands of personnel, hundreds of contractors, expeditionary 5G towers, robot security dogs made by Ghost Robotics, and a plethora of connected legacy weapons, Chris Brose of Anduril Industries stated: "You're taking cognitive burden off of the operator when it comes to understanding the environment, ruling out false positives and finding objects that the user has said that they care about."[33] It is important to note that according to the Anduril Industries website, the company is run by what they call a team of experts from Oculus (owned by Facebook), Palantir, SpaceX, Tesla, and Google.[34] There are 28 separate companies each with billion-dollar government contracts working on ABMS. This is the system the Air Force describes as: "[...] the Air Force and Space Force's priority program to develop the military's first Internet of [deadly] Things and is the services' primary contribution to Joint All-Domain Command and Control, a Defense Department-led effort to securely connect all elements of the US military—every sensor and shooter—across land, air, sea, space and cyberspace."[35]

Notably, one of the Anduril experts implementing systems that are supposed to create greater situational awareness of the battlefield came from Facebook, a company with a well-known sordid history of difficulties rendering fact based unbiased data. Google, where another expert worked previously, has also manipulated users' reality with curated search results favoring those who pay good advertis-

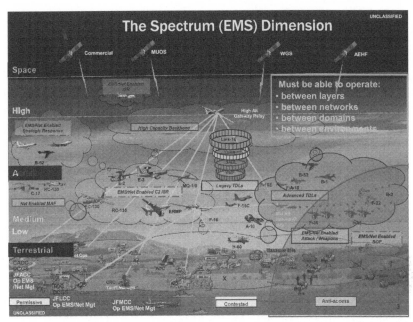

Initial capabilities of the JALN or Joint Aerial Network that include Space, Aerial, and Terrestrial layers. A graphic simulation of Kill Cloud topology.[57]

ing money to be rendered first. The machinations used to translate battlefield data into actionable intelligence or "knowledge" used for life-or-death battlefield decisions is ripe for further interrogation. This is one area where ethicists, researchers, and legal scholars are better positioned to clear murky waters than technologists alone. As previously noted, the expansion of this technology continues to evolve within a troubling colonial context.

Colonial Underpinnings of the "American Peace"

The United States, despite its merits, is a nation that was born out of colonization and the destruction of indigenous societies. Indigenous people were labeled savages under the ideological frameworks of The Discovery Doctrine and Manifest Destiny. These cultural beliefs provided the "moral" impetus for settler expansion westward in North America and beyond. This expansion disregarded the territorial rights of indigenous peoples and was upheld as recently as 2005 in the case of *City of Sherrill v. Oneida Indian Nation of New York*, 544 US 197.[36] Leaders of the free world often deny the colonial frameworks they are party to in favor of memorializing the legacy of European descendants. Unlike other anti-colonial struggles in world history, popularized heroes of the American Revolution were not indigenous peoples who often played crucial roles, but British colonizers and their direct descendants. We often criticize authoritarian nations that submit their people to involuntary servitude to achieve civilizational objectives, and yet most of our initial infrastructure was built by African slaves, Chinese immigrants, and indentured servants. It took a civil war to outlaw chattel slavery, and almost immediately thereafter, arbitrary laws were created that forced former slaves into prison labor where conditions were sometimes worse. It is not the last time that the legal system of the United States will be weaponized against a whole race of people inside or outside US territory; the Chinese Exclusion Act is another example, Japanese internment another, and the list continues into present day Islamophobia shrouding what is witnessed or ingested in a fog of historical prejudice and White supremacy.

We brand our country as a nation of laws, but this has hardly ever stopped laws from being selectively enforced. Racism is not always presented by those intending to do harm; it is built into cultural assumptions, exclusionary ideological frameworks, and ignorance. The United States military is viewed by many in the US as a forward-thinking multicultural institution. In basic training, a common trope uttered by instructors is that there is only green or blue, nothing more. This means that the cultures of those individuals who signed up are put aside in favor of an identity based exclusively on one's branch of military service, Blue for the Air Force, and Green for the Army. As of 2018, White people in the US military still numerically outnumber those of other ethnicities. Whether intended or not, military recruiters primarily target the poor and underserved with offers of college tuition, debt forgiveness, and healthcare.[37]

The military is inherently dehumanizing, with the purpose of enforcing political will through violence. Military members are broken down, reassimilated, and calculated as units of monetary value. The process of training humans willing to work together under a rigidly enforced hierarchy to kill an enemy does not require empathy or understanding for other cultures. Members are instructed to fall in line, which often means accepting the current "other" into their reconstructed world view. Military members are also drilled to view civilians as lesser human beings as a method of retaining trained personnel. Furthermore, meaningful discussion about racist assumptions affecting US foreign policy decisions to invade and terrorize with Shock and Awe tactics remain to be had. We cannot overstate the importance of grasping the futility of intelligence requirements used to characterize a "threat" within cultures that very few analysts, if any, have the cultural competency to fully comprehend. This lack of cultural familiarity has made the death toll of network centric warfare more of a reflection of Eurocentric bias than global safety. The racial implications of nations with a colonial legacy surveilling and bombing Indigenous communities across the Middle East, Southwest Asia, and Africa must be reckoned with.

Cell Phone that Belonged to the Former President of Afghanistan, Hamid Karzai, on display at the National Museum in Kabul. Photography by Lisa Ling.

As one can imagine, people living under a constant threat of connected weaponized surveillance capable devices change their behaviors to reduce their traceability; they do not engage in normal daily activities and are terrified of making new associations with people and communities. The smart phone—once a technological wonder that defines our modern existence—has become monopolized by war and converted into a surveillance tool. These devices are now integrated into a global weapons system that has the potential to mark individuals for death, and they know it. The behaviors of these populations change in response to the imminent possibility of being targeted with seemingly no rhyme or reason. Behavioral changes often become an intelligence identifier, creating suspicion in the eyes of those airmen and their colleagues, analyzing local populations' movements and actions. It creates a perpetual cycle of fear and distrust for the innocent civilians that these platforms are supposed to protect. Smart phone data can be compared and compiled with other data sources through the collaborative cloud we loosely identify as the Kill Cloud. That data gets packaged, tagged, and stored until someone somewhere decides it is useful again. Data can be retrieved from months or years in the past to support an imminent decision to pursue and strike a suspected "threat."[38] Despite the military's preference to talk about warfare as if it is a business and to use business-like terminology surrounding this globalized weapon system, it is not a business—it is brutal violence; it is terror.

While we do not specifically address non-military CIA drone operations of which we claim no first-hand experience nor direct knowledge, we argue that the distinction commonly made between targeted killings in areas outside or inside recognized armed conflict zones are problematic, and that distinction makes no difference to those living under them. Remote warfare is justified by using "law-fare" to legitimize it. In other words, legal interpretations of international humanitarian law (IHL) allow the US government to execute any drone operation with impunity.[39]

Some Things Never Change

The ability to pick up a smartphone and video chat in real time with a friend on the other side of the globe is something that most people today take for granted. We grow impatient when a call lags and curse our service providers. Very few people acknowledge the effort that goes into making this possible; fewer understand the complex technology or machinations weaved into the multiplicity of technologically moderated human connections. Fewer still can tell you exactly what went wrong at what part of what process or how to fix it. To step back and fully appreciate the scale, complexity, and capacities available today, and how the vast weapons system discussed in this paper connects, a brief history may be helpful.

The Kill Cloud owes much of its existence to Benjamin Franklin's discovery of electricity, Michael Faraday's discovery of electrical current production, Alessandro Volta's discovery of how to store electricity, and Werner Von Siemens development of the dynamo electric generator. These discoveries effectively established the foundational requirements for electronic devices in use today. The invention of the electric telegraph was a means for militaries to communicate at the speed of a trained person's ability to punch an on/off switch on either end of a copper wire. Unknown to Michael Faraday at the time, his discovery into how to produce electric current also enabled the first loop antenna, which took signals from a copper wire to electromagnetic waves. From these discoveries, not only was communication speed increased, but the foundation of modern maneuver warfare was born in a hybrid of accidental intentionality. Major investments were made in laying underwater cables so that commerce could be more regulated and controlled. Combined with the steam engine, these innovations increased the speed at which wars were fought significantly. Technological advances gave way to colonial conquest, and the ability for armies to communicate instantly over thousands of miles, setting the stage for the colonial consequences still being felt today. Gayatri Spivak calls this *epistemic violence* —the harm that dominant groups like colonial powers wreak by privileging their ways of knowing over local and Indigenous ways. It is still true today, and the Kill Cloud has become the colonial way of knowing.

Much more recently, we moved from hardware to software switching making it possible to remotely access and control hardware while moving to faster data transmission. There are 7 types of electromagnetic wavelengths that are known and exploited by the military and others for different purposes. Every second of every day, radio waves pervade every millimeter of this earth likely carrying more information than every civilization possessed in total for most of human history. The control of the electromagnetic spectrum is of great political, economic, and military consequence. The ability to use the spectrum for friendly forces while denying it to an adversary is to control the operational tempo in which battles are fought as the use and exploitation of the electromagnetic spectrum increases in every domain of conflict. As the name implies, Network Centric Warfare is centered on communications networks, and the ability to exploit connectivity and coordinate actions at an increasingly faster pace with exponentially more data. These are the building blocks of the Kill Cloud and, while they are vast and complex, it is not important to fully understand these technologies to grasp the implications we are presenting.

Bias of Data Collection

In the January 2013 issue of *Air Force Magazine*, Lieutenant General Larry James, the Airforce ISR Chief at the time, described the DCGS as follows: it processes more than 1.3 petabytes of data a month—equivalent to 1,000 hours (about 1 and a half months) a day of full-motion video. [40] In a September 2016 edition of *Air and Space Magazine*, Roger Mola describes the DGS-1 (now called DCGS-1) processing facility as a windowless warehouse that can hold about 1,500 people. [41] While he toured DGS-1, there were about 70 analysts working in teams of six and he described them as "enlisted personnel that looked to be between 18 and 25-years old." [42] He mentions "that within seconds, raw bits of data from Afghanistan are transmitted by satellite and fiber-optic cable to a network of 27 centers around the world for processing, analysis, and dissemination, to military units and a number of government agencies." [43] He also notes that "nearly 6,000 active and reserve air personnel, assisted by hundreds of civilian contractors, work with the data in the system." [44] All this system ingested data will not necessarily become actual knowledge or situational awareness. Much like spellcheck has dulled our ability to spell words from memory, or the use of smart phones has all but removed our ability to memorize a friend's phone number, access to modern technology does not necessarily improve knowledge just as politically charged social media posts have been known to alter our perception of reality. Our dependance on multiple streams of data will not necessarily work to decrease the fog of war.

It is good to mention that raw data does not necessarily mean without bias, just as witnessing events play out on a video screen on the other side of the globe does not necessarily offer reliable knowledge. In the film *National Bird* by Sonia Kennebeck, General Stanley McChrystal observes that, while discussing viewing drone feeds from 10,000 feet, "you don't know what's going on, you know what you see in two dimensions." Watching two-dimensional video on a screen is also different from the situational awareness one gets by being there. It is important to understand that being on any operations floor for any remotely connected process is vastly different from being physically there. This should be obvious but, clearly, it still needs to be stated; awareness will *always* be limited by distance, sometimes in critical ways. Raw data, when used in a scientific sense, refers to information gathered for a research study before the information has been analyzed or transformed.

In the context of a research study, there are limits and ethical considerations that determine the validity of the study and, by extension, the validity of the data returned. Much of the ingested ISR data is without context. Data without contextual information is inaccurate missing a full picture at best, or bad information that contributes to the death of an innocent at worst. In ISR, "Knowledge Production" violates long standing research norms. These norms were utilized to prevent bias in scientific and scholarly research, and to certain extent, they have. Donna Haraway wrote, "The situation or context that data is collected in has an inalienable relationship to the nature of the knowledge it can generate."[45] This is true even in the fog of war, perhaps especially then.

As we have discussed, the appetite for more data and a faster operations tempo is insatiable; one reason is the Observe, Orient, Decide, Act (OODA) Loop, an acronym used to frame the maneuver warfare derived approach to conflict.[46] It was created by John C. Boyd, a Korean War Fighter Pilot, to describe the process that he used to survive aerial dogfighting. The military's primary objective is to defeat its "enemy" by incapacitating their ability to make decisions through shock and disruption. The ordinance dropped on Iraq on March 23, 2003, was an example of this strategy. Thus began the "Shock and Awe" campaign designed to disrupt the Iraqi Forces OODA Loop. Boyd believed that going through the OODA loop faster than your enemy would end with you living, and your opponent dying. Many military strategists are convinced that big data analytics synthesizing massive quantities of input used to uncover information about enemy operations will enable this strategy to scale from fighter pilot to battle. This enormous collection of data is intended to assist with combat operations to help define targets, but does it? Does using big data reveal patterns and "orient data in a way to be visible to someone who may not otherwise be able to recognize it due to their own personal biases or background"?[47] This sounds good in theory, but the emphasis on speed and simplicity can lead to rash judgements. When the OODA Loop is applied from a technology-mediated distance, things can fall apart quickly. Through secrecy, distance, and compartmentalization, no participant sees the full picture, and their perception is limited by their narrow scope. Equipment failures, the weather, and a multitude of other factors can interfere in practice. In addition, high operational tempo, inaccurate data, absence of context or metadata, cultural bias, and racism can also mis-orient commanders, analysts, and those who pull the trigger providing circumstances ripe for error that can result in the death of innocent civilians. On any given day, intelligence analysts at a base in the United States will support a drone operation over a conflict happening on the other side of the world and can launch a missile at a "target" deemed a "potential threat." At the end of a shift, the same analysts will re-enter the reality the rest of us see and experience, unable to say anything to their family or friends who remain completely unaware that remote wars are being fought remarkably close to their homes by people they see every day. For the family and friends of those working in a SCIF (Sensitive Compartmented Information Facility) prosecuting these wars, missing a favorite television show is bothersome, but to others, who depart from remote war zones into their communities daily, the trivialities of life just become even more trivial. People prosecuting these remote wars from home, understand how isolating it can be to have real time information, updated daily, that cannot be shared. Conversely, the weapon system also supports what is called dynamic re-tasking so that if a natural disaster were to hit a base, it is possible that the data could be transmitted and processed elsewhere and ordinance could still be fired by another crew with little notice and even less familiarity with what is happening on the ground.[48] What is still true is that people here in the United States will not know it happened, but those a world away living under drones will, and it may be the only part of the Western world they ever see.

Many of the people living under Western surveillance depend on the land they cultivate to survive and are acutely aware of the impact their actions have on future generations. They have survived for centuries within their cultural operating systems that have evolved over thousands of years and, while many have little use for the written word, their knowledge of life and the world around them is in many ways better than our own observations. Their natural unmediated situational awareness is something the Western world has lost over time; we do not believe technology will ever be able to fully reconstruct it.

These people are inextricably connected to the land they inhabit, yet euro-centric cultural misunderstandings dismiss them as backward or primitive. Instead of using a critical lens to observe, Western voyeurs operating a multitude of different sensors do not question the notions of backward or primitive, these ideas are accepted, ingested, categorized, and stored within the system. This information will be kept until someone in the chain of command decides it is needed for "accurate situational awareness" of current or future operations. This information may be utilized later within a frame of more erroneous assumptions taking the viewer further from what can be considered objective truth or awareness. The truth is that these are exactly the people and cultures the Global West desperately needs to engage. We have a lot to learn from good stewards of the environment, especially as the natural world continues to warm around us.

Every year since 9/11, the West laments the devastation that occurred when the World Trade Center fell. It was a tragic event for those directly affected, and it was also tragic for every single innocent person whose life was destroyed by the Islamophobic Global War on Terror (GWOT). The devastation and destabilization brought about after the towers fell has ravaged the lives of millions of people, many now part of the human flow of refugees around the world.

Now that we can pass more data over longer distances, while flipping on/off selector switches in remotely accessible locations via software switched devices, it becomes a matter of ease to weaponize industrial advancements under the guise of protection. It is the ever-present and redundant pretext for more war. What is happening today is both accidental and intentional, and can be seen as an inevitable branch of the evolution of technology within the context of colonialism. The ways in which technologies are used follow a long history of colonial wars of aggression. Innovative technology will carry us to new frontiers faster, continuing the same destructive patterns if no substantive changes are made.

Despite repeated insistence to the contrary, these technological advantages have not prevented armed conflict and their continued evolution has not shortened or ended wars. Militaries arm drones by promising the public that they will only be used defensively to protect soldiers, but this promise disappears the moment higher-ups decide to label something or someone as a threat, which militaries the world over can do (and have done) in an instant. As soon as something or someone is labeled a threat, the drones will start buzzing and communities living below them will hear them day in and day out. Arming drones will not keep soldiers on the ground safer; it will lead to more situations that endanger them. These weapons inevitably change the perception of militaries in locations where drones are deployed. The resentment created by replacing actual soldiers on the ground with machines serves to radicalize populations, making engagement more dangerous for everyone while continuing to perpetuate endless wars. This resentment then becomes intergenerational as children grow up with an ever-present threat to their everyday reality, making any future attempt at de-escalating violence far less achievable. These are logical conclusions about the relationship of autonomous armed aerial platforms to people living below them. The more wars are automated, the less accountable militaries will be. Like the telegraph facilitated colonial exploits of the past, so too does the use of the Kill Cloud in countries whose resources continue to be plundered.

It is the tendency of Western academics to parse systems and explain processes as if they are somehow separate in purpose or function, but we believe it is critically important to understand the interdependent connected nature of these emerging technologies and how their use has perpetuated ceaseless conflict in far flung places around the globe, as well as the military's devastating impact on our climate. In a joint Brown and Boston University study, the only one of its scope, researchers found that at least 37 million people were forcibly displaced from their homes. This number exceeds those displaced in every war since 1900 except WWII. The researchers state that this number is an extremely conservative estimate and believe the true number to be closer to 48 to 59 million people from every country the US has involved itself in under the auspices of the GWOT.[49]

To put this into perspective, this number conservatively translates to the entire population of Canada or Poland. Numbers can never adequately communicate what it must be like to lose one's home, community, or country, nor the incalculable emotional, physical, social, and financial damage displacement causes. For those able to return to their country, there is no guarantee of safety or security because water sources, food supplies, hospitals and other necessities have been decimated. These are the human costs often overlooked or completely ignored when looking at the functions of distributed *weapon systems*, but we cannot forget that the technology militaries wield have devastating human and environmental consequences. This Global War on Terror was the impetus the Kill Cloud needed to take center stage with military planners and the intelligence community; no stone goes unturned, no dollar spared, no rights supersede the threats that can be imagined with this expansive and destructive weapon we call the Kill Cloud.

Conclusion

"Faith preserve us all, and fertilize this ground with truth, crack these foundations with pressure of humble roots. Let ancestors rise and inhabit life once more to guide us back home from the hard night's journey behind the door."

Cian Westmoreland

As regretful participants within the Kill Cloud, we urge others to engage with the unseen aspects of drone warfare. We can all view images of drones with missiles and have heard of how they terrorize people living below them; but crucially, there has been little attention given to the less transparent programs, devices, processes, or policies that govern their objectives. The expanding machinations that send drones and other platforms out to ingest data and hunt people remain absent in most media discourse. This weapons system is hyper-staffed, and the appetite for its growth is insatiable. We must collectively pull back the veil of the Kill Cloud and see it for what it is: a massive effort of coordinated killing and global power projection under a colonial pretext that has created more problems than solved. A compounding factor that faces any society impacted by violent conflict is environmental devastation. This devastation exacerbates issues of scarcity brought on by increasingly unpredictable weather due to the rapidly changing climate. Instead of addressing problems underlying conflicts that have continued to create more conflict, the United States has prioritized national spending toward militarizing emerging technologies. This has only served to exacerbate instability with perilously misguided actions aimed at fighting terrorism with more terrorism.

More bandwidth, like the irradiated medicines touted by snake oil salesmen of the past, is not the remedy for what ails us. Massive federally subsidized projects, such as the deployment of Starlink satellites, are being implemented under the auspices of bridging a digital divide and providing internet connectivity to the underserved.[50] This project intends to blanket the earth with high bandwidth access to allow the US military to project its vision of global security with increasingly more surveillance and automation.[51] As wars come home, smart city technology ingratiates itself in our everyday lives and its preemptive threat modeling will empower police to apply military tactics in the civilian world, further marking the underserved as threats.[52]

As described by Naomi Klein, the book *Conflict Shorelines* by Eyal Weizman observed that almost every drone strike by the US was within areas bordering on 200mm of rainfall per year. 200mm is the minimum amount of rainfall necessary to grow cereal crops without irrigation; he called this the "Aridity Line."[53]

Weizman also discovered what he calls an 'astounding coincidence'. When you map the targets of Western drone strikes onto the region, you see that "many of these attacks—from South Waziristan through northern Yemen, Somalia, Mali, Iraq, Gaza and Libya—are directly on or close to the 200 mm aridity line'... To me this is the most striking attempt yet to visualize the brutal landscape of the climate crisis".[54]

We believe that climate change and war are connected, and should be addressed accordingly. We cannot continue to perpetuate war while claiming to address climate change. The inflow of refugees directly affected by wars, instigated or perpetuated by the Global West, has led to a resurgence in xenophobic political rhetoric. Misguided efforts to stem the flow of refugees have only served to exacerbate existing inequality as we see increased militarization of the border lands. Even though we are all contributing to the problems that led to this human flow, refugees are still being treated like invading forces. The treatment of refugees along the US border and by the European Union's (EU) Frontex program reveals a deep-seated "otherization" at work. Militaristic responses only serve to embolden inhumane treatment and racism, yet do little to address the driving forces that perpetuate the problems leading people to flee their homes. It is a vicious feedback loop that results in more dehumanizing treatment bolstered by a *perceived* threat centric model. Politically expedient emission targets of less than 2 degrees celsius temperature rise, as discussed in the Paris Climate

Accords, are insufficient and ineffective at best. It will only take a 1.5 degree rise to threaten regions without sufficient resources to mitigate it.[55] War perpetuates the destruction of food and water resources on all sides of any conflict. There is no *effective* process currently in place for the public to request redress from our national role in conflicts or climate change, voting is not going to fix this. aWhile the promise of this technology is touted to lesson human suffering by sanitizing the harmful effects of war, the reality of its implementation tells a different story. In the chain of events that causes the death of another, the two of us and many others cannot escape the integral part we played. Our nations are works in progress; what we have learned is that it is time to decolonize, and it will require all of us to do it. It is our hope that others will join the discourse surrounding the ethical use of emerging technologies and continue to take steps within their communities to push the pendulum toward a more just and regenerative future. We believe that by this extension, the possibility of a more lasting peace between states, starting with its global citizens, will be achievable.

Notes

1. "The Unreasonableness of 'Reasonable' Prepublication Review, Part 1", *Yale Law School*, accessed July 18, 2021, https://law.yale.edu/mfia/case-disclosed/unreasonableness-reasonable-prepublication-review-part-1.

2. Vickers, Hon Michael. G, "The Warfighter Expects and Deserves Secure & Reliable Access to Information & Services from Any Device, Anywhere, at Anytime in a Form That Is Useable Regardless of Classification Domain", http://c4i.gmu.edu/eventsInfo/reviews/2013/pdfs/AFCEA2013-West.pdf.

3. "DOD Aims for New Enterprise-Wide Cloud by 2022", *U.S. Department of Defense*, accessed July 18, 2021, https://www.defense.gov/Explore/News/Article/Article/2684754/dod-aims-for-new-enterprise-wide-cloud-by-2022.

4. "How the Military Is Revolutionizing Situational Awareness" *FCW*, accessed July 18, 2021, https://fcw.com/articles/2012/03/15/feature-inside-dod-situational-awareness.aspx; "Intelligence Center Develops Distributed Common Ground System-Army Tactical-Engagement Teams to Support Mission Command", *eArmor*, accessed July 18, 2021, https://www.benning.army.mil/armor/earmor/content/issues/2015/JAN_MAR/Edwards.html.

5. Vickers, "The Warfighter Expects and Deserves Secure & Reliable Access to Information & Services from Any Device, Anywhere, at Anytime in a Form That Is Useable Regardless of Classification Domain", http://c4i.gmu.edu/eventsInfo/reviews/2013/pdfs/AFCEA2013-West.pdf.

6. Andresen, Joshua P. "Due Process of War in the Age of Drones", *SSRN Electronic Journal*, (2015): https://doi.org/10.2139/ssrn.2574914; and Presidents' Unchecked License to Kill", accessed July 18, 2021: https://www.justsecurity.org/75980/trumps-secret-rules-for-drone-strikes-and-presidents-unchecked-license-to-kill.

7. "Airpower Comes of Age", *Air Force Magazine*, accessed July 18, 2021, https://web.archive.org/web/20210617225946/https:/www.airforcemag.com/article/Airpower-Comes-of-Age.

8. "DOD Aims for New Enterprise-Wide Cloud by 2022", *U.S. Department of Defense*, https://www.defense.gov/Explore/News/Article/Article/2684754/dod-aims-for-new-enterprise-wide-cloud-by-2022.

9. "Technology Innovation and the Future of Air Force Intelligence Analysis: Volume 2, Technical Analysis and Supporting Material", *RAND Corporation*, (2021), https://doi.org/10.7249/RRA341-2; "Want to Understand MDC2? Think About Uber, USAF Official Says", *Air Force Magazine*, accessed July 18, 2021, https://www.airforcemag.com/Want-to-Understand-MDC2-Think-About-Uber-USAF-Official-Says.

10. "Technology for Innovative Entrepreneurs & Businesses", *TechLink*, accessed July 18, 2021, https://techlinkcenter.org/news/new-us-army-software-rapidly-converts-live-drone-video-into-2d-and-3d-maps.

11. "A Brief Introduction to Distributed Systems", *SpringerLink*, (2016): accessed July 18, 2021, https://link.springer.com/article/10.1007/s00607-016-0508-7.

12. "Air Force Distributed Common Ground System", *U.S. Air Force*, accessed July 18, 2021, https://www.af.mil/About-Us/Fact-Sheets/Display/Article/104525/air-force-distributed-common-ground-system.

13. "Air Force Moves Ahead with Headquarters-Level Merger of Intel, IT Functions", *Federal News Network*, accessed July 18, 2021, https://federalnewsnetwork.com/air-force/2019/01/air-force-moves-ahead-with-headquarters-level-merger-of-intel-it-functions.

14. "Air Force Distributed Common Ground System", *U.S. Air Force*, accessed July 18, 2021, https://www.af.mil/About-Us/Fact-Sheets/Display/Article/104525/air-force-distributed-common-ground-system; "European Partnership Integration Enterprise Opens New Facility", *DVIDS*, accessed July 18, 2021, https://www.dvidshub.net/news/297660/european-partnership-integration-enterprise-opens-new-facility.

15. Sarah Shoker, *Military-Age Males in U.S Counterinsurgency and Drone Warfare* (Palgrave MacMillan, 2021).

16. Ibid.

17. "Reducing Over-Classification Act", *Govinfo.gov*, accessed July 18, 2021, https://www.govinfo.gov/content/pkg/PLAW-111publ258/pdf/PLAW-111publ258.pdf.

18. "Audit of the Department of Justice's Implementation of and Compliance with Certain Classification Requirements", *U.S. Department of Justice Office of the Inspector General*, accessed July 18, 2021, https://oig.justice.gov/reports/2013/a1340.pdf.

19. "Government's Motion In Limine to Exclude Certain Evidence, Argument, or Comment at Trial" *Project on Government Secrecy*, accessed July 18, 2021, https://fas.org/sgp/jud/hale/usa-exclude.pdf.

20. "United States District Court for the Eastern District of Virginia, Alexandria Division – Motion for Leave to File Amicus Curiae Brief on Behalf of CAIR Foundation", accessed July 18, 2021, https://storage.courtlistener.com/recap/gov.uscourts.vaed.405902/gov.uscourts.vaed.405902.219.0.pdf.

21. "Why Joe Biden Should Pardon Reality Winner", *The Washington Post*, accessed July 18, 2021, https://www.washingtonpost.com/opinions/why-joe-biden-should-pardon-reality-winner/2020/12/21/9e6f4094-4162-11eb-8db8-395dedaaa036_story.html; Kennebeck,

Sonia "CodeBreaker Films", Enemies of the State, 2020, https://www.codebreakerfilms.com/films.

22. "National Security and America's Unnecessary Secrets", *The New York Times*, accessed July 18, 2021, https://www.nytimes.com/2011/11/07/opinion/national-security-and-americas-unnecessary-secrets.html.

23. "Command & Control Battle Management Operations: Controlling the Chaos", *Air Education and Training Command*, accessed July 21, 2021, https://www.aetc.af.mil/News/Article/1578287/command-control-battle-management-operations-controlling-the-chaos.

24. "Air Traffic Control - 1C1X1", *U.S. Air Force*, accessed July 19, 2021, https://www.af.mil/About-Us/Fact-Sheets/Display/Article/104595/air-traffic-control-1c1x1; "Air Battle Managers: Offensive Coordinators of the U.S. Air Force", *Air Combat Command*, accessed July 19, 2021, https://www.acc.af.mil/News/Article-Display/Article/2111041/air-battle-managers-offensive-coordinators-of-the-us-air-force; "U.S. Air Force - Career Detail - Air Battle Manager", accessed July 19, 2021, https://www.airforce.com/careers/detail/air-battle-manager.

25. "Network Centric Warfare: Creating a Decisive Warfighting Advantage", accessed July 18, 2021, https://www.hsdl.org/?view&did=446193.

26. "Eliminating the Fog of War", *SIGNAL Magazine,* accessed July 18, 2021, https://www.afcea.org/content/eliminating-fog-war.

27. "The Air Force Tested Its Advanced Battle Management System. Here's What Worked, and What Didn't", accessed July 20, 2021, *C4ISRNET*, https://www.c4isrnet.com/air/2020/01/22/the-us-air-force-tested-its-advanced-battle-management-system-heres-what-worked-and-what-didnt.

28. "With Its Promise and Performance Confirmed, ABMS Moves to a New Phase", *U.S. Air Force*, accessed July 19, 2021, https://www.af.mil/News/Article-Display/Article/2627008/with-its-promise-and-performance-confirmed-abms-moves-to-a-new-phase.

29. "Network-Centric Warfare Airborne Military Communications Links Approved for Deployment", *Military Aerospace*, accessed August 1, 2021, https://www.militaryaerospace.com/home/article/16709544/networkcentric-warfare-airborne-military-communications-links-approved-for-deployment.

30. "Battlefield Airborne Communications Node (BACN)", *Air Combat Command*, accessed August 1, 2021, https://www.acc.af.mil/About-Us/Fact-Sheets/Display/Article/2241383/battlefield-airborne-communications-node-bacn.

31. "LEO Constellations" *Airbus U.S. Space & Defense, Inc.*, accessed August 4, 2021, https://airbusus.com/leo-constellations; "Musk's Satellite Project Testing Encrypted Internet

with Military Planes", *Reuters*, accessed August 4, 2021, https://www.reuters.com/article/us-spacex-starlink-airforce/musks-satellite-project-testing-encrypted-internet-with-military-planes-idUSKBN1X12KM; "Global Lightning' SATCOM Project Expanding to AC-130, KC-135", *Air Force Magazine*, accessed July 20, 2021, https://www.airforcemag.com/Global-Lightning-SATCOM-Project-Expanding-to-AC-130-KC-135.

32. "The Air Force Just Conducted the First Test of Its Advanced Battle Management System", *C4ISRNET*, accessed August 1, 2021, https://www.c4isrnet.com/air/2019/12/21/the-air-force-just-conducted-the-first-test-of-its-advanced-battle-management-system.

33. "The Air Force Just Conducted the First Test of Its Advanced Battle Management System", *U.S. Air Force*, https://www.af.mil/News/Article-Display/Article/2446122/gatewayone-and-attritableone-test-moves-joint-force-one-step-closer-to-iotmil-d.

34. *Anduril*, accessed August 1, 2021, https://www.anduril.com/company.

35. "GatewayONE and AttritableONE Test Moves Joint Force One Step Closer to 'IoT.mil,' Demonstrates F-22, F-35 First Secure Bi-Directional Data Sharing", *U.S. Air Force*, https://www.af.mil/News/Article-Display/Article/2446122/gatewayone-and-attritableone-test-moves-joint-force-one-step-closer-to-iotmil-d.

36. "City of Sherrill v. Oneida Indian Nation of N.Y, 544 U.S. 197" (2005) ", *Justia US Supreme Court Center*, accessed July 19, 2021: https://supreme.justia.com/cases/federal/us/544/197.

37. "Distribution of Race and Ethnicity among the U.S. Military", *Statista*, accessed July 20, 2021, https://www.statista.com/statistics/214869/share-of-active-duty-enlisted-women-and-men-in-the-us-military.

38. "Technology Innovation and the Future of Air Force Intelligence Analysis: Volume 2, Technical Analysis and Supporting Material", *RAND*, accessed July 20, 2021: https://www.rand.org/pubs/research_reports/RRA341-2.html.

39. Dunlap Jr., Charles J., "Lawfare: A Decisive Element of 21st-Century Conflicts?", 54 *Joint Force Quarterly* 34-39 (2009), accessed July 20, 2021, https://scholarship.law.duke.edu/cgi/viewcontent.cgi?article=6034&context=faculty_scholarship.

40. "ISR After Afghanistan", *Air Force Magazine*, accessed August 18, 2021, https://www.airforcemag.com/article/0113isr.

41. "The Intel Net", *Air & Space Magazine*, accessed July 20, 2021, https://www.airspacemag.com/military-aviation/the-intel-net-180960363.

42. Ibid.

43. Ibid.

44. Ibid.

45. "Situated Knowledges: The Science Question in Feminism and the Privilege of Partial Perspective", *JSTOR*, accessed July 20, 2021, https://www.jstor.org/stable/3178066.

46. "The Fastest Ooda Loop: The Implications of Big Data for Air Power", accessed July 20, 2021, https://apps.dtic.mil/dtic/tr/fulltext/u2/1040684.pdf.

47. "A Critique of the Boyd Theory—Is It Relevant to The Army?", accessed July 20, 2021, https://apps.dtic.mil/dtic/tr/fulltext/u2/a374770.pdf.

48. "The Intel Net", *Air & Space Magazine*, https://www.airspacemag.com/military-aviation/the-intel-net-180960363.

49. "New Costs of War Study: 37 Million Displaced by U.S. Post-9/11 Wars", *Watson Institute*, accessed July 20, 2021, https://watson.brown.edu/research/2020/Post-9/11DisplacementStudy.

50. "Cherokee Nation Begins Installation of Starlink in Rural Areas", *5news*, accessed July 21, 2021, https://www.5newsonline.com/article/news/local/cherokee-nation-installs-starlink-in-rural-areas-tribe-hopes-to-close-the-digital-divide-chief-hoskin/527-97d8396d-2ab1-4c95-a508-80c86821f619; "Google Cloud Wins SpaceX Deal for Starlink Internet Connectivity", *CNBC*, accessed July 21, 2021, https://www.cnbc.com/2021/05/13/google-cloud-wins-spacex-deal-for-starlink-internet-connectivity.html.

51. "U.S. Army Signs Deal with SpaceX to Assess Starlink Broadband", *SpaceNews*, accessed July 21, 2021, https://spacenews.com/u-s-army-signs-deal-with-spacex-to-assess-starlink-broadband.

52. "242. Military Implications of Smart Cities", *Mad Scientist Laboratory*, accessed July 21, 2021, https://madsciblog.tradoc.army.mil/242-military-implications-of-smart-cities.

53. Klein, Naomi, "Let Them Drown", *London Review of Books*, June 2, 2016. https://www.lrb.co.uk/the-paper/v38/n11/naomi-klein/let-them-drown.

54. Ibid.

55. "The Paris Agreement", *UNFCCC*, accessed July 21, 2021, https://unfccc.int/process-and-meetings/the-paris-agreement/the-paris-agreement.

56. "Reachback and Distributed Operations ISR", *Curtis E. Lemay Center*, January 29, 2015, https://www.doctrine.af.mil/Portals/61/documents/AFDP_2-0/2-0-D11-ISR-Distributed-OPS.pdf.

57. "Joint Spectrum Center (JSC) Overview Brief", *Defense Information Systems Agency*, accessed August 18, 2021, https://storefront.disa.mil/kinetic/app/resources/disa/DSO%20JSC%20Overview%20brief.pdf.

LAURI LOVE

Lauri Love is a Security Engineer and activist based in the UK. In 2018, he successfully fended off the prospect of 100 years in the US prison system for his alleged involvement in online activism. That landmark appeal ruling has proven a critical precedent in subsequent high profile extradition cases. He played a prominent role in the student and Occupy movements in Glasgow during 2011-12. Love is being recognised as an expert on hacking, surveillance and privacy issues in the UK and has made a principled stand against

LAURI LOVE

SOUSVEILLANCE
REVOLUTIONARY REAPPROPRIATION OF VIGILANCE BY THE NETWORKED POLITY

I WAS BORN in 1984 of a neurodiverse phenotype—autistic, eccentric and prone to flights of fancy—if relatively debilitated in executive function and other properties required by normative society, I came of age as the Internet blossomed and saw in its potential a wonderful new kind of world, in which my taxing misfittedness might instead give way to a relative adaptedness that could be most beneficial and valued. I struggled to follow the prescribed trajectory of an intellectual, not quite managing to complete academic degrees as mental health difficulties and/or the more pressing need to right inexcusable wrongs in society interfered with the expected monomania of ticking boxes. Though having a great desire to better the world, I had no taste for fame or prominence. Regardless, fame, or perhaps infamy, was nevertheless thrust upon me when in 2013 it suited the agenda of certain components of the US hegemonic power structure to criminally persecute me through legal instruments and the complicity of the United Kingdom's courts, for supposed involvement in an Anonymous-heralded hacktivist campaign to seek redress and reform after overzealous prosecutorial abuses drove the Internet wunderkind Aaron Swarz most tragically to suicide.

I was dealt then by fate a harrowing but potentially quite useful opportunity to raise a bulwark against the extra-territorial arrogation of global policing perversity by the United States, and set a precedent raising the bar against plucking poor souls from overseas and subjecting them to the assorted torments and inhumanities of the carceral system that still today in that cursed state carries the wretched torch of slavery and the worst manifestations of evil that it accrued. On the gambit that my very life might be forfeit, a great and noble alliance of good-doing that arose in a campaign to which I will forever be grateful was able thankfully to convince the highest court of the United Kingdom that it would be not only wrongful, but *"unjust and oppressive"* to render me to the US.

I hope only that the still-scarring limelight of that most difficult of episodes in my life may yet save many others, most notably and pressingly Julian Assange, from the similarly horrific fate of falling into the appalling and unmitigatedly heinous estate of incarceration in the United States that all of good conscience and character are increasingly coming to the consensus can only rightly be redressed by one outcome: total abolition.

Content now to reassume the privilege of non-notability and non-celebrity, I now ply some modest trade as a security engineer, and am occasionally induced to venture a few words that might have some beneficial, if also modest, effect on the hearts and minds of others. My remaining aspirations, neither modest nor humble by necessity, are to facilitate the realisation of universal quantum post-Turing hyper-computation while avoiding the menaces of uber-mechanised moral hazard, and thereby to achieve, perhaps even in this most precious lifetime of human incarnation, perfect and complete enlightenment for the benefit of all sentient beings. By vying so for the nigh-on impossible, I hope at the very least not to join the unfortunate ocean of settling that besets us now. Too long we have settled for what is; we must rejoice today and tomorrow that we are ever capable of realising what yet might be.

Sous-, You, Sur-? Prepositional Modalities of Vigilance in the Context of Hierarchies of Power

We are used to the concept of surveillance: the vigilance of those with power and (more or less legitimate) authority 'down' onto the citizenry, the congregation, the class, the userbase—or in these digital Ed-Snowdenian pantopticraptic days, the whole damned digital world. Then again, we are used to thinking of power and authority in general as operating in the prepositional modality of a classical hierarchy—from the top to the bottom, the centre to the periphery, governors to governed. So we are schooled, and not without cause or reason, as the well-conditioned internalise the suggestion that their role is to accept power and authority and thus by extension surveillance. The expectation, more implicit than explicit, being that the *quid pro quo* and equity awaits necessarily their ascendence from hoi-polloi to the hallowed spheres of the elite.

The observational converse has also always obtained: ministers or barons observing the monarch, and on occasion holding them to account on the basis of such observations and the dialectic they enable. Even unto the base of the hierarchy has it been ever possible to gaze upwards, to view, to the extent of acumen to analyse, and more recently even to document the workings of power. However, there was not for most of history, in most recorded societies from which we inherit tradition and structure, much, if any formalised, countenanced, nor effective mechanism for vigilance and accountability to flow counter to the gradient of hierarchical power.

Thus we had to await the nigh contemporary coinage—courtesy of cyber-netician, engineer, professor and inventor Steve Mann—of the term "*Sousveillance*", a straightforward reversal of the preposition in the French compound to denote vigilance upwards from below. Like most ideas, birthed of their time when context and contingency conspire, the emergence of the concept of sousveillance is reflective of the environment in which it became manifest—like a panoramic polaroid bringing into focus and relief the concomitants of its occasion.

In particular, sousveillance obtains and empowers in an age of near ubiquitous facility for the masses to record with fidelity—something it is easy to forget was once more or less the exclusive province of bodies vested from centralised power and authority, to whom were afforded the opportunity and responsibility of entering into the record, the rolls, the chronicles. We are blessed however with both—opportunity and responsibility—of making, storing and disseminating records to an extent that our antecedents could scarce have imagined possible.

One could perhaps at a squint cast as one of the functions of folklore and fairy-tale to capture, if not the particularities, then the generalities and gist of the exercise of power, and thus exert some influence, albeit vaguely and culturally, over its future exercise. The *Panchatantra* (Five Treatises), for instance, a collection of interrelated animal fables dating in written form between 200-300 BCE and of an oral lineage much older, can be taken as an allegorical vehicle to impress indirectly the essence and elaboration of good governance through the anthropomorphisation of animals embodying archetypes and tendencies still easily recognisable by readers of today, and influencing more familiar western corpora, most notably the fables of Aesop, but also Boccaccio, La Fontaine and the brothers Grimm.

Culture however, though exercising momentous influence, does so with the loosest of grips and with quite fallible efficacy against the sociopath and tyrant. The direct and viscerally causal exercise of moderating force and requisition of inverse representation—the accountability of the powerful unto its subjects—consequent to observational and recording faculties, had to await in extending franchise broadly for the invention and proliferation of the printing press. At that crux in the dance between technology and realpolitik did the second great symbol of power emerge to truly equal the first: the pen became as mighty in potentiality as the sword.

The pamphleteers thus, empowering themselves not with martial armaments but with verbal ornaments, with wit and satire—something before suffered by the crown only to the jester and a few in court, and even then at the risk of losing ones head—were now able to twist inflection on the fortunes of the powerful with more efficacy by the raising of contempt, derision and ire, than the prince, duke or baron could achieve by raising armies. Joining then the ranks of the clergy, the nobility, and commoners, arose *the fourth estate* of the realm: the press and news media that self-organised from the scattershot agendas of individual empressors into a regulatory capacity inextricable from the state, though at differing times as varyingly independent as the preceding three estates.

Nevertheless, though greatly enlarging both the means of moderation and accountability, as well as the breadth of those enfranchised to exercise either, the press did not yet afford universal nor unmediated ability for individuals in the body politic to proceed from observation to intercession in the face of the vagueries and abuses of the powerful. The essential flow from recognition to remediation remained, despite the democratising influence of the press, constrained by the necessity of traversing conduits of institutions, and the great water that cleanses the mires of power was oft enough sullied along these capillaries by editorial prejudice, the constraint of the mores and mendacities of a privileged class, and too often stemmed entirely in the editor's cutting room, or by the censor's hand.

Providence however had yet in store more twists to exert upon the social fabric. The letter gave rise to the postal service, the first democratic verbal interconnection of people at geographic remove. The post in turn inspired with the advent of electricity the telegraph, greatly decreasing the latency of this new phenomenon— *The Network*—and increasing its throughput and extent. The necessity of encoding the written word, which the telegraph greatly increased (though visual signalling and the demands of secrecy had already given it a head-start), spurred on the encapsulation into discrete forms of verbal thought that tentatively progressed, from the untamed analogue through alphabetisation and the standardising influence of the widely disseminated written word, into digitisation. No longer were writings but conventionally informative, they were now a new veritable essence; *Information*: something not just quantifiable, but about which an entire science, theory and praxis would evolve and begin to exert its own influence back upon the genius in humanity.

The theory of information, though collegiate, international and fraternal as a theoretical discipline of mathematics, became—in the ineffable poetry of destiny—most fecund when, for better or worse, its practice between decisively uncollegiate foes became determinative to the fate of nations. In war it was then—as a continuation of the age-old necessity of keeping secret from potential interceptors the true content of messages—funnelled through the technology of digital transmission, now traversing the very aether itself, that the fraternal mathematical theories of information and logic now wrought from digital intrigues—the coded messages of generals and admirals—the utility, sharpened to existential necessity, of a new participant in information and its networking: *the calculating, computing machine*. Now observations intended to have limited disseminative ambit were— through the mechanisation of arithmetic process—liberated against the will of their senders, and in the process could change the course of global history.

At this epoch, man—made in God's image—realised as never before God's creative function. From humanity issued a new entity, in a certain manner rendered in man's image: the logic gate, and the grimoire of beneficent daemonic forms constituted therefrom. And the logic gate went forth, multiplied and prospered. Indeed, it is not too much of a conceit to say that the logic gate, latterly realised as the transistor, is now the most successful species of being on planet Earth today, for it has consistently doubled in number, density and interconnection since its inception, enjoying thus a geometric growth denied to biological species except in extreme brevities.

All Bets Are Off—The Topological Singularity That Renders All Extant Social Contracts Defunct

We are all familiar, if not with the theory, then with the phenomenology of phase transitions. We see water freeze to ice, ice melt to water, water evaporate or boil into stream and steam condense back into water. Less widely appreciated is the information theory—the entropics—of phase transitions. Briefly surmised, the input or extraction of heat energy which is usually correlated with increase or decrease of temperature, takes on a more mysterious role at the phase transition. Heat is the random velocities of molecular constituents of matter, but on condensation and in freezing, an environment extracting heat from a gas or liquid ceases to change the temperature and instead affects the orderliness of this heretofore inchoate cacophony of jitters. The molecules become arranged in more-organised, highly-structured and typically more-compact formations.

A similar phase transition occurs in the interconnection and mutual entrainment of an informational network when conditions begin similarly to favour long-range correlations between the dispositions of constituent elements. In the informational network constituted by our neurons, their electromagnetic interrelation to one another and via the skeletal-musculature field to the environment, this phase transition gives rise to consciousness, an integration of atomic awarenesses into an experiential stream that comprises our typical daily experience.

If we take as Gregory Bateson suggests, that information is "difference that makes a difference", then consciousness is perhaps the superlative exemplar—a topology of dense, informationally rich, integral yet almost infinitely open-ended interconnection, that weaves from mere sentience the double sapience we cherish as our defining characteristic.

So then the network of information whose history we have briefly reprised can be seen to have met with a topological-connectivity-enacted epochal phase transition. Those of us privileged to remember a world largely not yet visibly affected by this transition and survive to see a world in which scarce little escapes its effect are spared the misleading seeming mundaneness of its commonplace nature to our younger compatriots. We speak of course of *The Internet*, the Network of Networks, the Great Chain of Being made manifest by the digital and all it can represent, whizzing hither and thither at speeds approaching that of light—of causality itself—and in densities that boggle even the minds of the adept.

Those online, increasingly a supermajority of humanity, are now connected, may interface one to another, one to many or many to one, with restrictions diminishing logarithmically towards zero. Can we say at this point that the default discretisation of political power—geographical proximity on the basis predominantly of accidents of birth—retains legitimacy as the basis of social compacts? When association, common endeavour and the intertwining of destiny may now self-organise on the basis of myriad other concerns than how far an army might march before encountering another, surely we must consider that all extant contracts imagined between polities and the powers over them are rendered null and void.

This truth upon inspection and mediation stands undeniable and inescapable, though it has yet to be faced, except in some dreams, some words [cf. *A Declaration of Independence of Cyberspace* by John Perry Barlow], and the valiance of thus far evocative if sometimes abortive attempts of emergent collective consciousness to assert a will to sentience, sentiment, values and the exercise of power in their service, though it be necessarily at times in lesser or greater defiance of the *ancien remines* [cf. The Open-Source Community, Cyberarmy, Hacktivismo, Freenode/Libera, Freenet, Blockchain, Anonymous, etc.].

The fact remains—and is of such gravity that it will attract unto itself further facts, ever increasing its transformative potence—that we now face one another as humankind. And in mutual observation—shall we call it *'interveillance'*?—we await perhaps the greatest political shift of all, visible on the horizon of history, where the dialectic between this emergent networked polity and the systems of entrenched power that have managed thus far, if occasionally tenuously, to suborn and shackle it, must play out as inevitably as the rain must fall and the sleeping must wake.

The last great globally transformative dialectic of power is widely considered to be that of *the labour movement*—when the notion, first elaborated in the form of words, became realised in practice, that the workers, in unison, might through collective bargaining reclaim the productive value of their toils from the usurpation of the capitalist classes, and engage (sometimes even successfully) in the reimagining of society made possible by the resultant redistribution of potency.

A vision arises then, as the network awakens unto itself and finds through fumble and falter its footing at last, that we must face another grand dialectic of power, and through collective bargaining we the networked must elicit a new settlement with the remnant analogue powers, represented now predominantly by state, church and corporation, whose compacts remain on the basis respectively of geography, creed and greed—restrictions that the network finds increasingly irrelevant and must face with increasing irreverence.

The Third Symbolic Archon of Power—No Longer but Pen and Sword—Ecce Potentialis Monoculis

Though ironic perhaps to the point of distaste in its invocation at the Langley headquarters of the Central Intelligence Agency of the United States of America, two epitomes respectively of information and networking fouled by subordinance to secrecy and exclusivity, and professed and extroverted noble ideals masking unacknowledged and introverted toxicity and violence—the verse of John's Gospel, 8.32 remains of divine provenance and universal application: "*And you shall know the truth, and the truth shall set you free.*"

LulzSec logo, 2011

Sousveillance as a form of praxis wherein truth is instrumentalised through oversight and accountability into eventual guarantorship of freedom, came into its own in the context of the network when what had heretofore been a great fear of the machinations of power and on occasion a great moderator too—the leak— became itself as democratised as literacy made the pen, and nothing shall ever make the sword. Before the network, leaking had been predominantly a tool of those inside the tent of circumscribed power to engage in intrigues one amongst another: a department or a minister or an aide, disgruntled or avaricious, or from time to time even afflicted by conscience, channelling information through the still distorting lens of the established press to the masses. In the network it has evolved into a more perfected form.

Firstly, the disintermediation of the (ever corruptible, thus ever corrupted) established press, possible because the network enables the viral proliferation of content and routes around the censorship it rightly perceives as damage, is seen not just in the transcendence of curation, editorialization, distorting presentation, and selective publication of the leak, but also in supplanting of the (ever corruptible, thus ever corrupted) professional class of journalist as mediator between the press and the source, another cause of myopia and prejudice, and a pinch-point for power.

Experiments in the transcendence of both these modes of mediation have been transformative, if yet far from perfected. Most notable of course remains WikiLeaks, an organisation accepting contributions by anyone, and if they meet the sole bar of being verifiably authentic, granting to the public the revolutionary boon of direct access to original source materials, facilitating perusal, but declining or at least minimising editorial discretion and selectivity of publication, save for the mitigation of potential harm.

The transformative effect of this paragon is testified not only in the great utility the network has derived from its endeavours, but even more poignantly perhaps in the ruthlessness and sheer villainy of the reactionary efforts by the powerful (most publicly enacted through the offices of the *United States Department of [In]Justice*) to destroy its most visible personage, Julian Assange, who at the time of publication remains, after over a decade of unmitigated fuckery, in a battle against being rendered to the state whose war-crimes he helped the world to know, to be undoubtedly held in conditions of torture perhaps unto his death.

Not even the marginalisation of WikiLeaks, however, can stop the continued manifestation of the monocle as a new contender and equal to the pen and the sword. The subversive merry pranksters and hackers *Lulzsec*, operating alongside and synergistically with WikiLeaks, gave the monocle the power to strike fear into the hearts of assorted emperors lacking both clothing and security, and the even more potent power through humour and mirth to inspire the already fermenting collective manifestation known as Anonymous to briefly rise to the dubious honour of becoming "public enemy number one", supplanting even the most useful spectres of rogue states and terrorists.

These prime movers may be gone or past their prime, but the potential they demonstrated cannot be suppressed by the criminalisation of a few good denizens of the network. Evolution heeds not the beck of power to halt, to cease or to desist. The monocle renders only more powerful—through innovations in the decentralisation of fault-tolerance by transcending single points of failure—the network's capability to obtain leaks and to make them available at large.

Protocolisation of Conduct—Emergent from Consensus—Enforced by Cryptographic Mathemagics

Thus we touch upon the latest, greatest discipline of information theory, most proximate to magic, to the divine: *cryptography*, in its maturity not just the study of encoding and decoding, ad-hoc schemes whose security could only be assumed until demonstrated lacking. Now nestled between mathematics and computer science and becoming the equal and indispensable partner of both, cryptography offers to the network new and staggering potentialities through increasingly powerful *primitives*—basic constituents from which systems of open-ended agility can be spun.

Bitcoin, and the sprawling ecosystem of blockchain-contingent, even blockchain-transcending systems of distributed, decentralised, fault-tolerant and censorship-resistant rich information interplay are revolutionary towards power and authority in a way so novel it was almost universally agreed to be unviable: they have allowed the network to come to a most powerful state of being—*consensus*. By coupling an economic externality as incentive yoking self-interest to mutual benefit, the anonymous genius we know by the pseudonym Satoshi Nakamoto overcame the trifling hindrance of a mathematically proven impossibility and solved the problem of *Byzantine consensus* in a distributed and decentralised system. Agreement was now, and shall forevermore remain possible to achieve between potentially mutually-untrusting participants in a network as *a shared state*, a set of truths, a reality construct contributed to by all, but owned and controlled by no single entity or subset—truly something more than the sum of its parts.

The Bitcoin network consensuates two powerful primitive notions: the ticking of a network clock, and the integrity of a ledger giving the authority—without the need of any central arbiter—of all participants to possess and transact.

While this prototypical consensus is quantitative and fiduciary, we ought remind ourselves that the digit and tally-mark also emerged in service to the reckoning of private property and enabling of commerce. Yet the digital now encompasses not only the quantitative and coveted, but also the qualitative, universal, ineffable and sublime: *Wikipedia*, *Project Gutenberg*, photography video and missives of our beloveds.

So one imagines that networked cryptographic consensus might very well and imminently extend to the emergence and contingent concretion of collective value, and that protocolisation might carry yet further the democratisation of power through the facilitation of oversight and accountability that the leak has given us yet but piecemeal and haphazardly. Where before it took acts of personal courage, integrity and the [mis]fortune of standing to blow the whistle, and it took yet more complex and fragile instruments of untarnishing proliferation to make of the blown whistle a clarion call to justice, we can conceive already of cryptosystems in which the vesting of any and all powers and authorities to individuals, offices and entities from the networked polity (that must ultimately and always be the ceding source), is automatically and inexorably yoked to a responsibility of adherence to consensuated values no longer just assumed until found otherwise, but guaranteed cryptographically.

For there exists a synthesis of the transparent and the opaque made possible by the cryptographic primitives of *"commitment to state"* and *"proof in zero knowledge"*. A few examples should suffice to prime the imagination of the reader. Consider the sadly residual problem of discrimination in the workplace, say in the context of hiring. A company may institutionally, or a manager sporadically and autonomously, be inclined contra the normative values of society to prefer to hire applicants not only on merit of skills and experience, but because they have the right kind of name, complexion of skin, or creed. We may however define a game— rules for hiring if one is to have the suffrage of participation in the networked economy—when an entity makes a decision, to which we afford the default privi- lege of opacity, that is to be one's own business, it is required that a cryptographic commitment be made to all inputs to that decision, and the decision made. Once committed to, this information exists in an opaque yet immutable form on the network. Upon suspicion of discrimination here, or malfeasance of any kind more generally, the system can oblige the opening—transparency—of some statistical sample of these commitments, and a mathematical function can be computed thereon. The system's participants may then determine that, for instance, other factors considered equal, the company or manager hired preferentially appli- cants in a racist, sectarian or otherwise discriminatory manner. This may be known without compromising the privacy of particular applicants—though if it be deemed useful, for instance to identify victims for compensation, then they might be identified, but the contents of their resumes or the jobs to which they applied be kept private.

Similarly, for example, insider trading might be disincentivised by the facili- tation of its detection by committing the input (reasons it was deemed sensible) to make a trade and the trade made, and again through computation in zero know- ledge of statistical functions discrepancies be ascertained between trades and the available 'kosher' public knowledge which might inform them.

Polity as Argus Panoptes—Moral Photonic Pressure of Myriad Eyes

Generalising from these examples, we can envision that the cryptographic capa- city for the operation of entities in the networked polity, be they of governance, business, or anything else upon which consensuated values would take a view, to be afforded opacity, thus privacy and competitive freedom by default, and yet render unto the system in a manner minimising the compromise of these deside- rata the facility of exercising the functions of oversight and accountability, while dispensing with the requirement for some privileged ombudsman or regulator, limited, imperfect and corruptible as they tend to be.

Without roles, offices and agencies vested by centralised powers deriving legi- timacy ultimately—as all yet do today—from some manner of coercive authority, underpinned by the potentiality of force through the monopolisation of violence, we perceive within our imminent reach the dream of cryptographic anarchy:

order, justice, equality and freedom, without the archon singular and central, but through the distributed and holistic archonate of the monocles of all participants.

Argus Panoptes we might collectively constitute, not a Leviathan that rises beastly from the masses to swing a sword, nor merely by the pen that inscribes indelible, powerful in the province of a few, but by the gaze of a collective and a transparency that need not come at the unnecessary injury of privacy to individual or group. The many eyes of Argus might well mostly be sleeping, but a few remaining vigilant and the ability to select that few after-the-fact, yields a potential where in the limit, ideally, the mere pressure of possible observation is enough to keep the conscience functional.

Solitary Whistles Blown May Yet Cohere Into an Orchestra of Right

We participate today in an economy which we know to facilitate the most horrific of crimes and abuses, and hope the appendages of coercive authority will mitigate these, while perceiving that as often as not they are complicit therein. Yet we, the participants of the networked polity, are the very ones who turn the cogs and gears, press the buttons, sign the authorisations, give transit to the information that enables these enormities. Too often however, those forming the chains of causation that enable e.g., war-crimes, exploitation of labour, ecological destruction, etc. see so small a part of the picture that neither their culpability nor agency rise to the level of Eichmanns. But imagine an app with the tagline *"Let us collectively oblige one another to be just"*. Imagine the bank teller who receives the suggestion that today it might be good to highlight transactions between this and that company for vigilance, or someone peripheral to this or that factory to contribute a piece of a jigsaw puzzle. In a cryptographically-empowered networked world where all the eyeballs of both humans and machines can be harnessed through transparency toward justice, in what shadows will evil find a place to lurk, as the sunshine floods to every crevice and corner?

JOANA MOLL

Photo by Francesc Melcion

Joana Moll is a Barcelona/Berlin based artist and researcher. Her work critically explores the way technocapitalist narratives affect the alphabetisation of machines, humans and ecosystems. Her main research topics include internet materiality, surveillance, online tracking, social profiling, and interfaces. She has presented her work in renowned institutions, museums, universities, and festivals around the world. Furthermore, she is the co-founder of the Critical Interface Politics Research Group at HANGAR (Barcelona) and co-founder of The Institute for the Advancement of Popular Automatisms. She is currently a visiting lecturer at Universität Potsdam (DE), Escola Elisava (ES) and Escola Superior d'Art de Vic (ES).

JOANA MOLL

BEHIND AND BEYOND
TRACKING NARRATIVES &
USERS' AWARENESS

IN FEBRUARY 1999 I visited an exhibition by William Kentridge, a graphic artist, filmmaker, and theatre arts activist, at the Museum of Contemporary Art of Barcelona (MACBA). Back then I was a pre-graduate art student and I felt that drawing and sculpting were interesting and necessary in many ways, but meaningless in many others, in the sense that, back then, the creative process did not answer to anything but my inner world, and the results were just measured by varying degrees of self-satisfaction. In other words, I believed that art practice was isolating and dramatically detached from its concurrent realities.

Kentridge was born in South Africa to a Jewish family in 1955. His parents were lawyers well-known for representing victims of the apartheid. In essence, Kentridge's work examines the profound social injustice caused by such a discriminatory system through drawings, animations, films, and theatre performances. It was the first time in my life that an artist exposed the political dimension and the activist possibility of art and art practice to me. Moreover, even though back then I ignored the particularities of the apartheid, through Kentridge's drawings, I could experience, intensely, the deep social, political, and emotional toll left behind by this policy of racial separation.

Regardless of Kentridge, it took several years to articulate and integrate a conscious critical artistic practice capable of informing and being informed by its co-existing realities. Moreover, defining what "critical practice" means has become central (and a never-ending process) in my work, as I believe that the term must be constantly revisited to coherently engage with the realities that I am trying to affect. My work lies at the intersection of art, research, and investigative journalism, with a strong focus on techno-capitalist narratives and their effects on the alphabetization of machines, humans, and ecosystems. In particular, over the last ten years, I've consistently targeted the hidden layers of the so-called data economy apparatus: from its physical infrastructures to the geopolitics of data, corporate surveillance practices, the commodification of user data, and materiality of data. One of the major drives, and outcomes, of my work, is to expose critical techno-social arrangements that govern our lives but are mostly opaque to the average citizen, and in turn, generate dramatic power asymmetries between the ones running the technical infrastructures and the ones using them. I believe that producing evidence is a crucial act to empower users to identify and promote sustainable, transparent, and accountable forms of governance, which are essential to forging a fair and just society.

In this text, I will focus on describing the making of three of my recent projects that expose severe malpractice at the hands of corporate and governmental stakeholders and, at the same time, highlight the role of creative practice in uncovering and denouncing such actions.

The Hidden Life of an Amazon User (2019)[1]

On June 17, 2019, in Utrecht, I purchased *The Life, Lessons & Rules for Success: The Journey, The Teachable Moments & 10 Rules for Success Cultivated from the Life & Wisdom of Jeff Bezos* from the Amazon website. In order to purchase the book, the Amazon website forced me to go through 12 different interfaces composed of large amounts of code—normally invisible to the average user. This code carries out all sorts of operations, such as organizing and styling the site's content, supporting interactivity, and recording the user's activity—such as their clicks and scrolls. Overall, I was able to track 1,307 different requests to all sorts of scripts and documents, totalling almost 10,000 A4 pages worth of printed code, adding up to 87.33MB of information. The amount of energy needed to load each of the 12 web interfaces, along with each one's endless fragments of code, was approximately 30 watt-hours. According to their promotional materials, Amazon's business model is based on "obsessive customer focus", entailing "constantly listening to customers to enhance and improve the customer experience."[2] In other words, their business relies on continuously tracking and recording their customers' behaviour and activity to improve the monetisation of each user, and ultimately to increase Amazon's revenue. These processes are carried out by cookies and other supporting technologies embedded on websites, apps, videos, and other digital media formats. When a user visits a website, tracking software will automatically trigger the collection of all sorts of user data, which is now owned by the company that executes the tracking (e.g. Amazon, Google, Facebook, etc.)—and which has a legal right to exploit it.

The act of purchasing (for example a book on Amazon) has thus been turned into a tracking and monetization device, with the aim of adding layers to the already-complex setting of power relations online: including user profiling, social-sorting, task assignment, energy use and waste, and 'smoothening of liberal logi(sti)cs'.[3] Thus, the 8,724 pages of code that track and personalize a user's behaviour and experience—and that I involuntarily loaded through the browser—

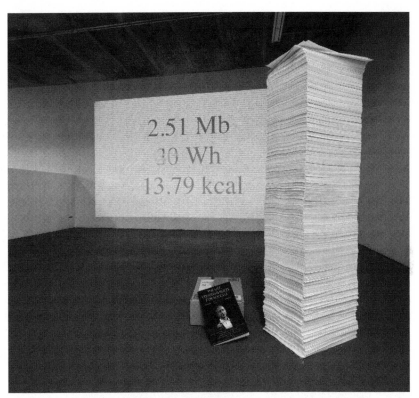

The Hidden Life of an Amazon User, Exhibition: BIG D@T@! BIG MON€Y! at HALLE 14—Zentrum für zeitgenössische Kunst / Centre for Contemporary Art, from 26.9. to 5.12.2020.
Photography by Walther Le Kon.

are evidence of Amazon's core money-making machinery at work. "A machinery that sustains the patriarchal-colonial regime that determines how power is distributed along hands, territories and whole modes of existence at large"[4]. Moreover, this distributive operation implies that all the energy needed to load this relatively large amount of information was effectively demanded from the user, who ultimately assumed not just part of the economic cost of Amazon's hidden monetization processes, but also a portion of its environmental footprint.

All these aspects are drawn on in *The Hidden Life of an Amazon User,* an interactive artwork that details the intricate labyrinth of interfaces, code, and energy that make possible the purchase of Jeff Bezos's book—with the aim of casting light on Amazon's often unacknowledged but aggressive exploitation of their users, which is embedded at the core of the company's business strategies. Such strategies rely on apparently neutral, personalized user experiences afforded by attractive interfaces. These interfaces obfuscate the sophisticated business models embedded in endless pages of indecipherable code, all of which are activated by the user's labour—again, clicking and scrolling—and hence based on a hidden mode of delegation. In turn, these strategies incur a significant energy cost, part of which is involuntarily assumed by the user. To put it bluntly, the user is not just exploited by means of their free labour, which allows these companies to collect and trade in massive amounts of user data, but the user is also forced to assume part of the energy costs of such exploitation.

The Dating Brokers (2018)[5]

The Dating Brokers, 2020 Digital Arts Festival-Taipei, 01.–15.10.2020.
Photo courtesy of the author.

In May 2017, Tactical Tech and I bought 1 million user profiles from online dating pages for € 136. These profiles were acquired at USDate.org[6], a US-registered company that trades in online dating user profiles from around the world. The data package selected included photographs of each user (almost 5 million in total), username, email addresses, nationality, gender, age, and highly detailed personal information about sexual orientation, interests, profession, physical and personality traits of each user. The purchase of these profiles exposed an extensive network of interconnected companies which capitalized on all this information without the conscious consent of the users, who are ultimately the ones being exploited. This project was commissioned by Tactical Tech, a Berlin-based NGO with a very specific focus on digital rights and data transparency. Tactical Tech and I collaborated on several projects before developing The Dating Brokers. In this specific case, the collaboration began in 2017. I had begun developing research for The Dating Brokers during 2016. During this time, Tactical Tech was developing research on the global industry of online dating and I was hired as an external consultant to advise them on data collection and processing issues. Later, Tactical Tech proposed commissioning The Dating Brokers. This commission was crucial to the project, not only on the financial side, but most importantly, on the legal side, as the project revealed sensitive user data and disclosed information that could harm a group of particularly powerful companies which could potentially take legal action against me. In that sense, Tactical Tech had the legal infrastructure to respond to potential legal claims.

The research before the formalization of the project lasted more than a year. The first step was to buy the profiles on USDate.org, a company that was advertised on Google and was very easy to access. We acquired 1 million worldwide user profiles. The data packet contained 630,426 male and 310,235 female profiles aged between 18 and 80 from 38 different countries. The buying process was exceptionally quick and easy. After making the payment through a PayPal account, I received several links to download the profiles. It was precisely this fluidity throughout the process that made me wonder why it was so easy to buy online dating profiles. I then began researching the business dynamics of the global online dating industry and I discovered that constantly exchanging profiles between different platforms was a very well-established practice in this industry. These practices fulfil the need to have a continuous flow of new faces to raise the chances of match-making between users and increase the number of paid subscriptions.

The next step in the research focused on finding the source of the profiles we had purchased. USDate.org declined to provide this information. I then applied different reverse engineering techniques, such as extracting metadata from the pictures in our dataset, looking at the data structure, and comparing it with that of profiles found in different dating sites. The result of this investigation generated irrefutable evidence that pointed to Plenty of Fish (POF). In 2017, POF was the second most used online dating service in the United States, just after Tinder, and according to the companies' public records, it had more than 150 million users and an average of 65,000 new subscriptions every day. But if POF and USDate. org were actively exploiting those profiles, who else could potentially do that? I found out that POF was part of an extensive conglomerate led by Match Group, the largest online dating services company in the world. In 2007, among many other companies, Match Group owned apps like Tinder and OkCupid. The user data policy of Match Group clearly stated that any user information belonging to any service affiliated with Match Group could be freely shared among each other. In other words, any profile created on any Match Group service, for example, in POF, could potentially end up in Tinder and OkCupid. To expose this business practice, I drew a map that included all the companies affiliated with Match Group, and found more than 130 online services and apps that belonged to that company, which in turn, were potentially capitalizing on the profiles we had bought.

Sadly, that was just the tip of the iceberg. Match Group was itself a sister company of IAC, an American holding company that owns brands across 100 countries, mostly in digital media. Its very extensive portfolio of digital services includes Vimeo, Investopedia, The Daily Beast, or Daily Burn, among many others. In total, we could identify around 170 IAC-related companies and services. The company's privacy policy, just as in Match Group, stated that any user data created in any company affiliated with IAC could be shared with any of its services, including Match Group.

The network for utilizing data from dating profiles doesn't end with IAC and its brands—it extends much further, into countless third-party companies. Tracking users' online activity has become a major business model in the last decade. Put simply, online tracking is the act of collecting data from a user while they are interacting with a digital service, like reading the news or purchasing something online. Even though online tracking is an established practice within the digital economy, users are often not aware of the number of third-party companies that are keeping information on their online behaviour via trackers. Back then, we couldn't find any official document that listed the third-party companies with whom Match Group and IAC were sharing their users' information. However, during the investigation, we used some tools that allowed us to identify more than 300 third-party cookies linked to IAC and Match Group businesses that were potentially collecting all sorts of data on user behaviour. And this only accounted for desktop browser activity—it didn't even include trackers on mobile apps, which could potentially make the list of third parties twice as long.

Overall, we were able to map a network of more than 700 interconnected companies and online services that potentially utilised the 1 million profiles we bought from USDate. Nevertheless, we believed that there are many more undisclosed services that generate value from the dating profiles owned by Match Group. We also believed that the $0.57 average revenue per user that Match Group reported in their Q2 2018 Investor Presentation was just a fraction of the user profile's real value. This value was obfuscated by a complex web of other companies and services. This business ecosystem did not just affect the 1 million profiles we bought—this group of individuals was representative of everyone who has ever had a dating profile on one of the online dating services that are owned by companies such as Match Group. As seen in this analysis, the data collected, shared, traded, and sold on dating app's users travels far and wide and could potentially be instrumentalised by third-parties for advertising and individualised pricing, but also to restrict access to health insurance, credit, education and much more.

Tatiana Bazzichelli and Joana Moll at *Activation: Collective Strategies to Expose Injustice*, Disruption Network Lab, November 30, 2019, Kunstquartier Bethanien Berlin. Photo by Maria Silvano.

The investigation produced extensive evidence and the task of coherently and ethically reflecting it in a single artwork was quite complicated. For this reason, I decided to divide the project into two formats: an artwork that sought to provoke an emotional reaction towards the wild transaction of intimacies within the global online dating ecosystem, and an interactive report that would disclose the evidence produced and explain the investigation process.

Managing the amount of data that had been generated during the project was also a complicated task. To me, it was of utmost importance to anonymize any information that could lead to the identification of any of the profiles that we purchased. Due to the technical complexity of this operation, I collaborated with Ramin Soleymani, a computer engineer who developed software to anonymize photographs and texts. This collaboration was crucial to the project, for if this anonymization had not been possible, I wouldn't have made the project public.

The project enjoyed international attention. Since its publication in November 2018, the project has been exhibited in centres such as Ars Electronica, Fotomuseum Winterthur, and Photograpers' Gallery. Media such as *The Financial Times*, *O'Globo* and *la Repubblica*, among others, also mentioned the piece. The Dating Brokers was the first published project to disclose extensive research on the commercialization of data dynamics within the global online dating industry.

A few days after publishing the project, Match Group contacted Tactical Tech and asked us to remove certain pieces of evidence. We declined the petition as Match Group refused to comment on any of it.

Algorithms Allowed (2017) [7]

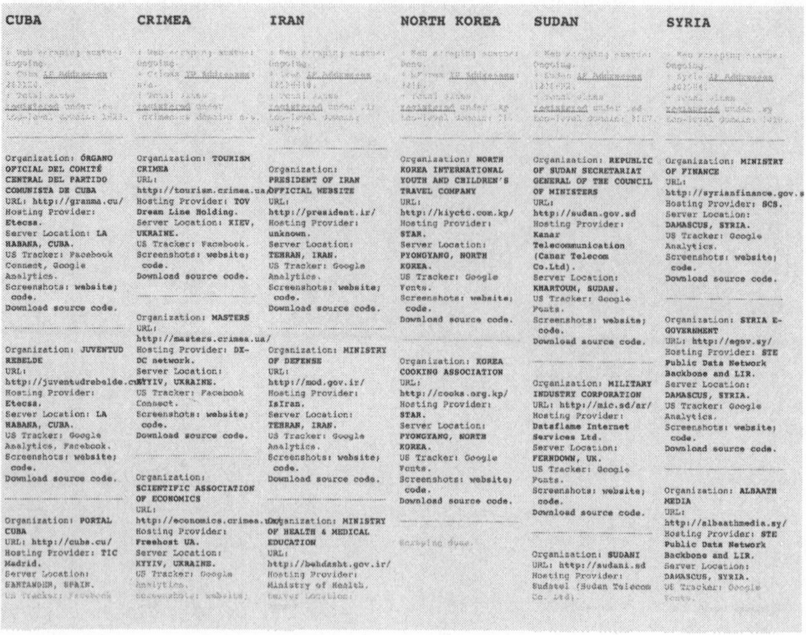
CUBA
Organization: ÓRGANO OFICIAL DEL COMITÉ CENTRAL DEL PARTIDO COMUNISTA DE CUBA
URL: http://granma.cu/
Hosting Provider: Etecsa.
Server Location: LA HABANA, CUBA.
US Tracker: Facebook Connect, Google Analytics.
Screenshots: website; code.
Download source code.
Organization: JUVENTUD REBELDE
URL: http://juventudrebelde.cu
Hosting Provider: Etecsa.
Server Location: LA HABANA, CUBA.
US Tracker: Google Analytics, Facebook.
Screenshots: website; code.
Download source code.
Organization: PORTAL CUBA
URL: http://cuba.cu/
Hosting Provider: TIC Madrid.
Server Location: SANTANDER, SPAIN.
CRIMEA
Organization: TOURISM CRIMEA
URL: http://tourism.crimea.ua/
Hosting Provider: TOV Dream Line Holding.
Server Location: KIEV, UKRAINE.
US Tracker: Facebook.
Screenshots: website; code.
Download source code.
Organization: MASTERS
URL: http://masters.crimea.ua/
Hosting Provider: DX-DC network.
Server Location: KYYIV, UKRAINE.
US Tracker: Facebook Connect.
Screenshots: website; code.
Download source code.
Organization: SCIENTIFIC ASSOCIATION OF ECONOMICS
URL: http://economics.crimea.ua
Hosting Provider: Freehost UA.
Server Location: KYYIV, UKRAINE.
US Tracker: Google
IRAN
Organization: PRESIDENT OF IRAN OFFICIAL WEBSITE
URL: http://president.ir/
Hosting Provider: unknown.
Server Location: TEHRAN, IRAN.
US Tracker: Google Analytics.
Screenshots: website; code.
Download source code.
Organization: MINISTRY OF DEFENSE
URL: http://mod.gov.ir/
Hosting Provider: IsIran.
Server Location: TEHRAN, IRAN.
US Tracker: Google Analytics.
Screenshots: website; code.
Download source code.
Organization: MINISTRY OF HEALTH & MEDICAL EDUCATION
URL: http://behdasht.gov.ir/
Hosting Provider: Ministry of Health.
NORTH KOREA
Organization: NORTH KOREA INTERNATIONAL YOUTH AND CHILDREN'S TRAVEL COMPANY
URL: http://kiyctc.com.kp/
Hosting Provider: STAR.
Server Location: PYONGYANG, NORTH KOREA.
US Tracker: Google Fonts.
Screenshots: website; code.
Download source code.
Organization: KOREA COOKING ASSOCIATION
URL: http://cooks.org.kp/
Hosting Provider: STAR.
Server Location: PYONGYANG, NORTH KOREA.
US Tracker: Google Fonts.
Screenshots: website; code.
Download source code.
SUDAN
Organization: REPUBLIC OF SUDAN SECRETARIAT GENERAL OF THE COUNCIL OF MINISTERS
URL: http://sudan.gov.sd
Hosting Provider: Kanar Telecommunication (Canar Telecom Co.Ltd).
Server Location: KHARTOUM, SUDAN.
US Tracker: Google Fonts.
Screenshots: website; code.
Download source code.
Organization: MILITARY INDUSTRY CORPORATION
URL: http://mic.sd/ar/
Hosting Provider: Dataflame Internet Services Ltd.
Server Location: FERNDOWN, UK.
US Tracker: Google Fonts.
Screenshots: website; code.
Download source code.
Organization: SUDANI
URL: http://sudani.sd
Hosting Provider: Sudatel (Sudan Telecom Co. Ltd).
SYRIA
Organization: MINISTRY OF FINANCE
URL: http://syrianfinance.gov.sy
Hosting Provider: SCS.
Server Location: DAMASCUS, SYRIA.
US Tracker: Google Analytics.
Screenshots: website; code.
Download source code.
Organization: SYRIA E-GOVERNMENT
URL: http://egov.sy/
Hosting Provider: STE Public Data Network Backbone and LIR.
Server Location: DAMASCUS, SYRIA.
US Tracker: Google Analytics.
Screenshots: website; code.
Download source code.
Organization: ALBAATH MEDIA
URL: http://albaathmedia.sy/
Hosting Provider: STE Public Data Network Backbone and LIR.
Server Location: DAMASCUS, SYRIA.

Algorithms Allowed. Photo courtesy of the author.

Algorithms Allowed was developed as part of the web residency program—"Blowing the Whistle, Questioning Evidence"—curated by Tatiana Bazzichelli for the Akademie Schloss Solitude and ZKM Center for Art and Media in 2017[8].

Earlier that year, I was invited to participate in an online exhibition where artists were asked to come up with unconventional objects to be sold on eBay. My first idea was to sell Google Analytics (GA) cookies found within a North Korean website. I was quite sure that I wouldn't find any, but to my surprise, I could identify GA within the first website I visited: The official webpage of the DPR of Korea[9].

Cookies and other tracking technologies are generally embedded in the source code of a website. Thus, by "simply" looking at the code that builds any site, cookies, and the companies that own them, are "easily" identifiable. For the eBay exhibition, I accessed the source code of "The official webpage of the DPR of Korea", looked for the GA code, and copied and paste it into a .txt file. Afterward I created an auction page to sell the .txt file named "Google Trackers in North Korea Official Page".

Interestingly, once I submitted the auction, I automatically received a warning message (embedded within an orange frame) from eBay preventing me from publishing the auction, as eBay's policy forbade the selling of items that originated from North Korea due to the sanctions enforced by the US Department of the

Treasury's Office of Foreign Assets Control (OFAC). The company also threatened to remove the item and prohibit me from using their services any longer if I violated this policy. Nevertheless, I decided to insist, and this time the message was framed in a strong red and directly forbid me to sell the item.

In 2017, the US was currently enforcing embargoes and sanctions against Cuba, Iran, North Korea, Sudan, Syria, and the Ukrainian region of Crimea. Thus, all transactions carried out with these countries, including software and data, were prohibited and heavily sanctioned by the US government. Nevertheless, I found Google trackers and other online services such as Google Fonts, Facebook connect and other tracking technologies mostly owned by American IT giants, within several websites owned by countries under US embargo. The list of websites included the official website of the President of Iran, the Syrian e-government, and the official website of the Cuban Communist Party, among hundreds of others. It is important to remember that these websites are stored inside hard disks placed in physical territories. Thus, these companies were violating the same policy that eBay accused me of. Ultimately, *Algorithms Allowed* sought to produce evidence to reveal an incredibly absurd but highly problematic legal grey area, and thereby expose the ambiguous relationship between code, public policy, geopolitics, economics, and power in the age of algorithmic governance.

Conclusion

I believe that one of the main differences between "traditional" acts of whistleblowing and whistleblowing by means of artistic practice resides in the fact that the evidence is portrayed by an artwork, not by a citizen or a group of citizens (with whom we can easily empathise and deeply engage with the cause they are publicly denouncing). Thus, the aesthetic representation of evidence within an artwork, which ultimately will expose and interrogate wrongdoing along with its multilayered consequences, is a particularly critical phase as it implies a great deal of responsibility. I believe that art practice has the ability to do just that: to transcend the story and activate experience by allowing for the arrangement of different pieces of evidence across multidimensional layers. I believe that *The Hidden Life of an Amazon User* represents this idea best: the project discloses the multiple material costs of a simple purchase at Amazon.com by exposing the several interfaces, code, and energy involved in this process, resulting in 15 minutes of a continuous scroll. Such an arrangement seeks to force the user to spend a substantial amount of time, energy, and attention (in comparison to what would usually be spent when buying at Amazon, which in this case was roughly 3 minutes) throughout the different vectors that make a regular shopping trip to Amazon possible, and thus experience Amazon's online purchase process energy-intensive machinery in the flesh: the fingers get tired, the attention deflates, forcing the body to be aware and present, or in other words, turning the usually passive role of the body (when it interacts with a screen) into an active entity capable of experiencing the physical dimension of digital interaction.

Honestly, I haven't thought about or followed Kentridge's work for many years, nor have I considered him a crucial reference in my work, so it came as a surprise when his name promptly popped up in my mind when I was asked to write about my work and the relationship relationship between art practice and whistleblowing. However, I believe that as much as our practices are extremely unrelated, they greatly converge in the act of going beyond storytelling and intentionally affecting the body. From my perspective, Kentridge's success in exposing the deep political and social anxieties caused by the Apartheid relies on the strength of his hand drawing, the presence of his body. Similarly, I believe that the most successful projects I've developed are the ones that expose misconduct and actively include the body as a mechanism to understand the consequences of wrongdoing in a "disembodied" ecosystem such as the digital. In that sense, far from being meaningless, drawing and sculpting as an art student played a fundamental part in shaping the role of the body throughout my practice. Funnily, when I was writing one of the early versions of this text, I discovered that Kentridge and I were born on the same day.

Notes

1. Moll, Joana, *The Hidden Life of an Amazon User*, November 11, 2019, accessed April 28, 2021, https://janavirgin.com/AMZ.

2. Premack, Rachel, "Jeff Bezos Said the 'secret Sauce' to Amazon's Success Is an 'Obsessive Compulsive Focus' on Customer over Competitor", *Insider*, accessed June 5, 2019, *https://www.insider.com/amazon-jeff-bezos-success-customer-obsession-2018-9*.

3. Moll, Joana, and Jara Rocha, "Tilt the Scroll to Repair: Efficient Inhuman Workforce at Global Chains of Care." *Digital Work in the Planetary Market*, (Cambridge: MIT Press, September 1, 2021).

4. Ibid.

5. Moll, Joana, *The Dating Brokers*, November 1, 2018, accessed April 28, 2021, https://datadating.tacticaltech.org.

6. "Start Online Home Business. Buy Dating Profiles, Dating Profiles for Sale | General Dating Industry Support Services LLC", *USDate*, accessed May 25, 2021, https://www.usdate.org.

7. Moll, Joana, *Algorithms Allowed*, May 1, 2017, accessed April 28, 2021, http://www.janavirgin.com/ALGORITHMS_ALLOWED.

8. "Web Residencies by Akademie Schloss Solitude & ZKM 2017–2020", *Web Residencies by Akademie Schloss Solitude & ZKM 2017–2020*, accessed May 25, 2021, webresidencies-solitude-zkm.com.

9. "Democratic People's Republic of Korea", *Korea-Dpr.com*, accessed May 25, 2021, korea-dpr.com.

...AROMIL" ROIO

Photo by Riccardo Bern...

...known by his nickname Jaromil, is the founder of Dyne.org and the Chief Technol...
...he DECODE EU flagship project on technological sovereignty and data owners...
...co-operation with the municipalities of Barcelona and Amsterdam. Jaromil publis...
...mic Sovereignty (AlgoSov.org) and received the Vilém Flusser Award at transmed...
...e leading the R&D department of the Netherlands Media Art Institute (Montevid...
...He has been a fellow of the "40 under 40" European Young Leaders programme si...
...d in the "Purpose Economy" list of the top 100 social entrepreneurs in the EU in 201...

DENIS "JAROMIL" ROIO
HACKER ETHICS IN 2021
INTERVIEW BY TATIANA BAZZICHELLI

This interview was conducted on May 19, 2021.

Tatiana Bazzichelli: This anthology reflects on how whistleblowing contributes to shaping change, new courses of action and digital tools among communities of activists, hackers, artists, and researchers engaging with participatory technologies and networks. To what extent is whistleblowing a source of inspiration to you and the free and open-source software networks you belong to?

Denis "Jaromil" Roio: When I think of whistleblowing and free software, an image comes to my mind. It's a photo of Julian Assange with Richard Stallman, holding a picture of Edward Snowden. It was taken at the Ecuadorian Embassy during Assange's period in there, when Stallman visited him.

Photo courtesy of Richard Stallman.

It's a photo of one of the most prominent whistleblowers, co-founder of WikiLeaks, together with a prominent free software activist holding the picture of another whistleblower. The photo depicts three people, including the one in the picture, who will be remembered in history: Assange, Stallman and Snowden.

This point of connection between whistleblowing efforts denouncing corruption within the system and free software is difficult to spot if we don't look at the context in which it is grafted. I believe this to be "corporate culture." Whether it is in public or private, corporate culture has built systems that are collective and that grow in complexity, to the point that corruption can be hidden, or even functional, to the scope of its mission. We live in a world that is dominated, regulated, or governed by only few corporations, national states, and their institutions, together with even bigger oligopolies; such organisations are guided by forms of collective agency coordinated through advanced methods of working together and organising work. Whistleblowers are individuals within these organisations that raise a flag and "blow the whistle" because of a particular ethical sense that something isn't right and should be observed and respected, and that it has essentially been suppressed by collective agency.

Whistleblowing is an individual act against a collective corruption—the corruption of a collective place—and it has many similarities with foundational events of the free software movement. If you look back at the history of many Unix free and open-source software— Unix variants like Linux, or BSD—they opposed the adoption of proprietary software built by corporations, because they contained bugs that were hidden from the users. They gave errors that were hiding away problems from users, like the blue screen of death that we saw on Windows, reporting numbers that can only be interpreted by the software creators; one had a hard time figuring out what was happening in his or her own computer. This led to a situation where responsible software developers and engineers "blew the whistle" declaring unethical to hide code running on people's computers. These acts of constructive rebellion have worked better than money in motivating developers to rewrite entire operating systems.

Ethical objection and constructive rebellion is a point of contact between these two phenomena, and we can see the positive impact of free software today. Free and open-source software has changed the very corporations that it fought, because many of the operating systems that we run today have in one way or another inherited characteristics of the ethos of free and open-source software. Nowadays, we have an increasing transparency in various degrees in the operating systems that we use. In most cases free software projects were born from isolated efforts that sought to oppose the status quo in a creative way, showing that something else was possible. But there is a common pitfall in this way of action which is common to movements motivated by ethical objection: organisational capacity to make project scale and be sustainable. Somehow, we all have to learn from the systems we want to improve, as corporations have demonstrated much better capacity in organising collective, establish workflows and arguably in some cases establish a fair governance.

My source of inspiration as a software developer and a user of operating systems was the rebel, the genius, and the "messianic figure" of Richard Stallman, who denounced corruption within institutional apparatuses as much as Julian Assange. Over the years, I have had the opportunity to look within corporate processes, and I have realised that the collective effort—the effort to collectively find solutions from within systems—is also a source of inspiration. Because I don't think a messiah can save a society, no matter how good he or she can be, what matters is a collective vision that can be shared and understood by everyone involved.

TB: In the context of whistleblowing, one important challenge is how to make classified information, which is in the public interest, available—while also considering security and privacy when opening up potentially sensitive data. Do you think it is possible to preserve openness when dealing with leaks of large datasets?

DJR: We have seen incredible advancements in the field of cryptography over the past ten years, and technical solutions that can be used for a variety of things. Zero-knowledge proof technologies, and multi-party computation techniques that can be adopted in order to reach more transparency in processes while granting the privacy of the participants. This is important to say, because the hype around crypto projects has steered most discussions around the tokenisation of value, ending up creating financial markets—something that we do not need to grow more than what we have today. We still need to divulge most of the opportunities offered by cryptographic advancements today, outside of toxic financial hypes. There is much more to be done to make processes of transparency and accountability more agile while preserving privacy. We need methods to practice good, balanced governance and oversight that is not biased by knowledge of private details. Much of my work as a developer and scientist over the past ten years has been dedicated to making these opportunities known and usable to the public. Last, but not least, is the paper I recently published in pre-print: "Reflow: Zero Knowledge Multi Party Signatures with Application to Distributed Authentication" (May 2021).[1]

TB: To explain it technically, is it possible to apply the zero-proof technology to large data sets and guarantee openness, as well as security and privacy for classified information?

DJR: The point is to make the origin of certain data traceable when it is needed, and to make the data analysable without this information being disclosed all the time. The principle is well known in the intelligence community as "need to know." We don't need a reviewer to know all private details, but we do need a reviewer to analyse the larger picture and spot patterns of deviance. Often, data about the participants and subjects of this analysis is embedded or linked univocally to it, but this is not always necessary. Zero-knowledge proof in general is a very flexible field of cryptography that can be adapted to many use-cases.

For instance, one can be sure of the possession of an ID of someone without knowing the ID. We can follow traces contextually, and within a certain context we can be sure that the trace is that of the same person, or of a subject that operates in a network. The boundary of privacy and disclosure is context. Here I recall the formulations that Professor of Information Science Helen Nissenbaum named "Contextual Integrity": principles that help us understand how confidentiality and integrity can affect context and should affect the subjects operating within a context.

TB: Hackers have long been challenging power dynamics and generating criticism of closed systems. If we reached a more just society, we would not need acts of whistleblowing. How do you think hacker communities could contribute to supporting whistleblowers technically and socially in order to make their work more effective?

DJR: I believe that hackers can help by assisting investigative journalists; people trained within a profession that has held this role in society for a long time. Of course, there is a similarity between investigative journalists, hackers, and investigators in general: they are all liminal subjects. If we see societies as "semiospheres", following the theories by Professor Yuri Lotman, then we have cells whose osmotic membrane are such liminal roles that allow the information to penetrate within the society, be understood, be "digested." Hackers, journalists, investigators, cultural mediators and maybe more future liminal roles have the responsibility to share information that can be useful to nurture society, as well to keep out what is not useful or dangerous. This is a delicate process. We can hardly think of societies that are made knowledgeable of every single event that happens in the world; even when declared, global knowledge is a myth; "freedom of information" is a delicate cultural process. Hackers have been often arrogant in thinking that they can steer this process alone. Many of us have already understood that interdisciplinarity is necessary. Therefore, I think that hackers can help by interfacing themselves with the expertise of other disciplines.

When interacting with diverse aspects of society we should value more diversity in disciplines, for instance it is detrimental to many societies that studies in humanities are losing ground to scientific education, a trend driven by market demand of technicians.

Hackers: better be humble! The many I know, after the "rock star moment" of the early 2000s, are aware of this, and so will be able to contribute to society even more. Not to belittle what has been done by the "stars" so far—some had an important role as change agents—but there must also be ways to communicate with society and not end up being alienated by it. We need to be hybrids, and to learn how to share our knowledge and talents with others.

TB: Could you describe some collective initiatives pushing for transparency and social justice, that could be a source of inspiration in the creation of distributed methods of knowledge awareness?

DJR: I have had the luck of an unconventional life, which also included being a squatter in Europe. I have been living off very few resources for long periods, also in more than a few difficult contexts, but what made always the difference was the collective around me: our agency and the power to shape our society and the city around us. As squatters, we were serving the purpose of most vulnerable people, the people left on the wrong side of capitalism. By squatting, I learned that in Italy, the Netherlands, Germany and other places in Europe there is a heritage of resisting through collective solidarity in direct response to rising levels of poverty. Entire families organised to occupy abandoned buildings, to build their lives in there, or activists taking the initiative of cleaning and repairing abandoned places and organising the best social initiatives for cultural and anti-mafia agendas. One large motivation was reclaiming our time by not working as an employee under a boss, always in need of money to buy back our time. Another motivation was collectively envisioning how the texture of the city could be improved by repopulating it with people, rather than letting it be shaped by the dynamics of financial speculation, which mostly serve the interests of those who accumulate more assets, money, and space. Because of these factors, it was especially important to investigate the reason behind the abandonment.

In Amsterdam, I learned how to investigate and use background information about abandoned buildings, collectively organised in a "parallel cadastre" called "Speculanten Onderzoek", a research centre on speculation in the city. Many buildings we knew of were bought and then left abandoned by financial speculators, undeveloped assets that, when left empty, rapidly turn into scars through the living texture of a city. Across Europe, there are entire buildings owned by people who have perhaps never stepped into them, just to park their financial capital. Those of us who investigated this sort of speculation did not only contribute to make our cities a better place: we stood up as a grassroots movement against speculation, corruption and even mafia organisations.

TB: In our conversation at the 2020 Logan Symposium you mentioned how social movements in Italy and in the Netherlands challenged city policy on financial speculation and hidden illicit cash flows. How can we create agency through collectivising data controlled by financial and institutional powers?

DJR: The way to make this possible is the de-penalisation of collective, researched and well-motivated conversion of private property in common and public space. Financial markets, and in general the financial world, have become a completely abstract and detached world of non-existing processes that simply underpin numbers and values: the very processes of production are no longer linked to the abstract representation operated by financial markets.

Researchers like David Hakken and Christian Marazzi have written at length about this. When the production dynamics no longer match their financial representations, there is a huge imbalance between the capacity to buy and sell physical objects, and their real use. In Marxian terms: the use value is not aligned with the exchange value, nor economists are taking care to better define the so called "externalities" that should serve as indicators for the evaluation of use value. At this point, it does not make sense for regulations to protect only—and even violently—a concept of property based exclusively on exchange value. When the Netherlands was still a social democracy such a depenalisation clause was in place to allow occupants to go through a civil case, so that we could explain our reasons, present our collective plan: this approach made many things possible at zero budget, arguably producing more opportunities of development than a subsidized institution can ever provide. Today, I regret seeing only a few squatted social centres left in Europe, and I regret seeing many well-meaning occupants repressed with disproportionate force and violence, forced to marginalisation and "forced to bleed", to quote our common friend and cultural agitator, writer and editor Marco Philopat.

TB: You have been working for many years in the framework of Dyne.org on AI and inclusion, to influence policy making through pilot projects in Amsterdam and Barcelona. What have you achieved in this sector so far and what more needs to be done?

DJR: I am critical about the adoption of artificial intelligence. There is an urgent need for our societies to reclaim knowledge and control of algorithms—especially AI ones used for mass surveillance and societal control. We have done our best to explain this by analysing the Dutch context in which AI is deployed by law enforcement.[2]

From a philosophical standing point, I think it is particularly important to consider that AI can fail in their decisions and doing so, when given too much power over people, can commit crimes. Then we should not ask ourselves if AI have standing, but primarily how to deal with victims in the living world. In the future, there will be a growing number of victims of AI crime. I did my best to document what happened after the assassination of Jean Charles De Menezes back in 2005, and tried to inspire solutions in the direction of restorative justice for AI crimes.[3] I'm very happy that just recently the European Commission has released guidelines for ethics in AI, and I think they should be read by anyone working in the field, including our friends on the other side of the Atlantic.[4]

TB: It is crucial to establish and develop new policies in the technological sector to create a real change. For that scope we need an intersectionality of expertise, where the technical meets the social and the political. Could you give us some examples from your experience working on blockchain technologies and data ownership at DECODE EU?

DJR: The research we conducted at DECODE became the understated consciousness that technocracy is a growing power that needs to be limited, complemented with the collective understanding of what technology does. We worked hard to make people understand what is being done with their data. We did not want participants to become technicians and learn to code, but we wanted code to be closer to human language and be easily understood by participants without technical training.

What I am proposing here is an inversion of vision. I propose we stop working to make machines understand and interpret human agency through very complex and often non-deterministic processes. I propose we work so that humans can better understand what machines do for them through the development of technologies that are verifiable and deterministic. Today, most technologists work so that machines can perceive humans, their sentiments and expressions; I argue that we need technologies that can be perceived better by us humans.

This vision lead us to develop the Zencode language and its secure execution environment the Zenroom VM, which turned out to be remarkable—overwhelming at times—technical achievement for the DECODE project.[5] This free and open-source software is easy to embed in any application to manipulate, authenticate and encrypt data in less than 2MB of memory: anyone can use a simple human-like language to describe actions to be done on data structures, including very advanced functions like zero-knowledge proof, multi-party computation and homomorphic math. Fairly complex actions to be executed by machines (even on small chips) can be described this way, to execute anything like business logic, data analysis, and end-to-end encryption communication. The important thing is that the code executed can be easily reviewed also by non-technical people.

We did this because of the advent of GDPR regulations. In Europe, we needed and wanted a greater defence of our privacy from the sort of data extraction operated by multinational corporations. The GDPR raised the liability on service providers (including online communities) to define responsibilities for private data manipulation and storage: liability embodied in the role of the "data protection officer" (DPO). But in most cases the DPO is a person with a background in law, lacking the engineering knowledge required to review the technical processes applied to data, creating a situation in which needs and liabilities propagate through an organisation as an entire engineering team becomes necessary to interpret code for the DPO to understand and review. With Zencode, a language that can be shown even to final users, anyone can have the ability to check what is being done with her or his data. In Amsterdam we used this system to design a way for young people to buy beer at the counter of a pub without showing their ID, but with a zero-knowledge proof credential.

This was done using cheap and inexpensive free and open-source hardware—a Raspberry Pi connected to a scanner and RFID scanned passports, a totally open-source framework—to produce a credential that could be used on a mobile phone or printed on paper as a QR code to show proof of age. We also used this in Barcelona to power petition signatures for the rights to the city in collaboration with the amazing democratic platform Decidim.

All this work allowed us to streamline development processes while keeping them transparent to ourselves and our colleagues despite the growing complexity. Today, still, very few people understand the difference between symmetric and asymmetric keypair cryptography. Only a few of us have managed to learn how to use PGP. While trying to make people navigate the complexity of cryptography, I think that we should also try harder to make this technology simpler, more usable, intelligible—and hackable! Especially as it is free and open-source.

TB: The main challenge of social change lies in the invention and production of new courses of action and intervention, both on and offline. You mentioned, on various occasions, the role played by WikiLeaks in inspiring the blockchain communities to develop new distributed and privacy-oriented transaction technologies. Could you tell us more about this early phase of blockchain development, and what is important to consider for preserving these initial goals?

DJR: This happened in 2011, at the time of the financial blockade of WikiLeaks. I'm talking about the time when WikiLeaks was becoming very popular on the trail of the 2007 Baghdad airstrike, when footage from *Reuters* journalists on a US Army Apache helicopter, known as the *Collateral Murder* video, was leaked by Chelsea Manning to WikiLeaks. Back then, following the bashing of WikiLeaks by conservative US politicians and without any court mandate, Visa and Mastercard closed the possibility of receiving donations to WikiLeaks. In the eyes of many of us, this was a breach of the normal course of law; an act of aggression against an organisation trying to eradicate corruption from the military-industrial complex. Many hackers who supported WikiLeaks thought that it was a good idea to step out of Visa and Mastercard networks, to not trust them as neutral anymore, and to adopt cryptography for the radical decentralization of networks, to make possible flows of values. The financial blockade of WikiLeaks was in February 2011, and right after we saw an increase in the mining and exchange of Bitcoins. This was a moment of rupture; a rupture that was generative, as much as it was destructive.

At that time, Bitcoins were less than $1. That was the moment in time, the rupture in history that brought Bitcoin to fame. It is hard to believe today, and difficult to remember for most people, because no one paid attention to Bitcoin until it surged to fame a few years later. I guess this part of history is relevant for understanding how ethics are transformed and value is created in society, what motivated me to write "Bitcoin, the end of the Taboo on Money" (April 2013).[6]

Today, we can tell that the Bitcoin experiment itself became an instrument of the financial sector, and a tool for deregulation: the crypto world became an acceleration of the financial sector itself, which is the industrial oligopoly it posed to destroy in the first place. What became of this hype was almost completely derailed from its initial ethos: it did not liberate WikiLeaks from its role, nor from its own biggest enemy; it only marginally allowed more organizations like WikiLeaks to thrive off peoples' donations.

TB: Whistleblowing is heavily persecuted in many countries and is often treated as an act of treason. How could we politically contribute to making the work of whistleblowers more accepted in society?

DJR: To make whistleblowers more accepted by society, we need society to be more accepted by whistleblowers. Let us look at the individual dimension of the actions of a whistleblower: it is an individual act of responsibility as much as a desperate act that cuts ties with the context it is denouncing. It is sometimes a romantic dream, that the system around one whistleblower may recognise the value of the effort, but I argue that, in most cases, antagonizing a system we are part of is not the best way to improve it.

We have seen what has been inflicted on the minds, souls and bodies of those who have had the courage to stand up to what are clearly huge injustices and huge discriminations and huge corruptions in human history. Throughout history, we have burned people in the middle of squares, tortured them and imprisoned them for years without trial.

When I say that whistleblowers need to accept society, I do not mean that corruption should be accepted. What I am trying to say, is that we need to stop accepting that sacrifice is the only way to do this. I would like to imagine a world in which, to quote Tina Turner, "we don't need another hero": we do not need sacrifice to denounce corruption. We do not need to mourn a loss, or to amend deep wounds, to say that something was wrong; that a collective system became unjust, deviant and corrupt. In some cases, we can assume that an organisation has degenerated into corruption despite the well-meaning intentions of its agents, who became unable to spot their own mistakes and their damaging effects. I believe that we all need to make an effort to be ethical participants of society, and to inspire others to do so. We need to understand society, to see if there are ways to improve it, and look for collectives (not a single hero, messiah or hacker) that can take up this challenge, understand the urgency and act.

Notes

1. Roio, Denis, Alberto Ibrisevic, Andrea D'Intino, "Reflow: Zero Knowledge Multi Party Signatures with Application to Distributed Authentication", May 2021, https://arxiv.org/abs/2105.14527.

2. Roio, Denis, "The Algorithmic Sovereign", *Amsterdam Alternative*, January 17, 2020, https://amsterdamalternative.nl/articles/8920.

3. Bianchi, Amos, and Denis Roio, "Frames from the life and death of Jean Charles de Menezes", 2010, *jaromil.dyne.org*, https://jaromil.dyne.org/journal/three_frames_de_menezes.pdf; Adnan Hadzi and Denis Roio, "Restorative Justice in Artificial Intelligence Crimes", *Spheres*, November 20, 2019, https://spheres-journal.org/contribution/restorative-justice-in-artificial-intelligence-crimes.

4. "Ethics guidelines for trustworthy AI", accessed July 5, 2021, https://digital-strategy.ec.europa.eu/en/library/ethics-guidelines-trustworthy-ai.

5. Zenroom, accessed July 5, 2021, https://dev.zenroom.org/ and https://zenroom.org/; *DECODE*, accessed July 5 2021, https://decodeproject.eu.

6. Roio, Denis, "Bitcoin, the end of the Taboo on Money", *jaromil.dyne.org*, April 6, 2013, https://files.dyne.org/readers/Bitcoin_end_of_taboo_on_money.pdf.

4

UNCOVERING CORRUPTION

CONFRONTING HIDDEN MONEY & POWER

FREDERIK OBERMAIER &
BASTIAN OBERMAYER
PELIN ÜNKER · SIMONA LEVI
CHRISTOPH TRAUTVETTER

THE CASES of the Panama Papers in 2016 and the following Paradise Papers have revealed the inner mechanisms of the financial system and the crime, corruption and wrongdoing hidden by secretive offshore companies. This section interconnects the development and current results of these giant leaks of financial and legal records with related acts of whistleblowing as well as investigations to denounce financial corruption. *Süddeutsche Zeitung* investigative journalists Frederik Obermaier and Bastian Obermayer reflect on the effect of the Panama Papers leaks and their impact, as well as on the crucial role of whistleblowers to spark investigations and the need to protect them. Investigative journalist Pelin Ünker tells the story of her reporting in the context of the Paradise Papers, which revealed business interests of the former Turkish Prime Minister's family in tax havens in Malta.

She was the only journalist involved in the Paradise Papers' story having to face a prison sentence for that. In the line of exposing corruption and wrongdoing at the governmental level, activist and founder of Xnet, Simona Levi, describes how the groups Xnet and 15MPARATO denounced through digital whistleblowing the responsibility of the bank Caja Madrid (now called Bankia) for the millions of euros that went missing in the Spanish economy. The Bankia Case resulted in sending the potential Prime Minister of Spain to jail for corruption, and many other politicians and bankers got sentenced. Finally, Christoph Trautvetter's investigation into real estate ownership structures in Berlin in Germany exposes how large real estate owners have managed to stay anonymous, sketching how these findings might contribute to change.

FREDERIK OBERMAIER & BASTIAN OBERMAYER

Frederik Obermaier and Bastian Obermayer are Pulitzer Prize-winning investigative journalists and bestselling authors living in Munich, Germany. They are heading the investigative unit of the German broadsheet *Süddeutsche Zeitung*. In 2019, Obermaier and Obermaier were part of the investigative team which revealed the existence of a video showing the head of Austria's far-right FPÖ party, Heinz-Christian Strache, promising government contracts to a woman claiming to be a Russian millionaire. The reporting led to the resignation of Austria's vice chancellor. Together, Obermaier and Obermayer initiated and coordinated the Panama Papers revelations, after an anonymous source provided them with 2.6 terabytes of internal data from the dubious Panamanian law firm Mossack Fonseca. As part of the Panama Papers team, they won the 2017 Pulitzer Prize in the category "Explanatory Reporting". The journalists have received numerous honours for their work, including the renowned Wächterpreis and, together with their colleagues, the Scripps Howard Awards, the George Polk Award for Business Reporting, the Barlett & Steele Award, and the Investigative Reporters and Editors-Award (IRE-Award). Obermaier has also been awarded the CNN-Award and Otto-Brenner-Preis; Obermayer has received the European Press Prize and German Reporterpreis. In 2017, Obermaier was awarded the Murrey Marder Fellowship in Watchdog Journalism at the Nieman Foundation at Harvard University. Obermayer is co-founding director of the Forbidden Stories Network, of which Obermaier is a member, and Obermaier is co-founder of the Anti-Corruption Data Collective. Both are members of Netzwerk Recherche and the International Consortium of Investigative Journalists.

FREDERIK OBERMAIER &
BASTIAN OBERMAYER
HOW THE RICH AND THE POWERFUL HIDE THEIR MONEY

INTERVIEW BY TATIANA BAZZICHELLI

"IN THIS SYSTEM —*our system—the slaves are unaware both of their status and of their masters, who exist in a world apart where the intangible shackles are carefully hidden amongst reams of unreachable legalese. The horrific magnitude of detriment to the world should shock us all awake. But when it takes a whistleblower to sound the alarm, it is cause for even greater concern. It signals that democracy's checks and balances have all failed, that the breakdown is systemic, and that severe instability could be just around the corner. So now is the time for real action, and that starts with asking questions".*

John Doe, "John Doe's Manifesto"

The case of the Panama Papers began in 2014 with a cryptic message from an anonymous whistleblower: "Hello, this is John Doe", the source wrote. "Interested in data?"

In the months that followed, the confidential source transferred emails, client data and scanned letters, from Mossack Fonseca, a notorious Panamanian law firm that has not only helped prime ministers, kings and presidents hide their money, but has also provided services to dictators, drug cartels, Mafia clans, fraudsters, weapons dealers, and regimes like North Korea or Iran. After the revelation in 2016, several heads of governments had to step down, thousands of investigations were launched, and approximately one billion dollars were recouped. The Panama Papers proved that there is a parallel world offshore in which the rich and powerful enjoy the freedom to avoid not just taxes but all kinds of laws they find inconvenient.

The interview, conducted on March 26, 2021, addresses what we have learnt from the Panama Papers about political and economic power, the progress that has been made against tax and dark havens, and how the Papers have changed the way that journalists think about and analyse tax havens.

Tatiana Bazzichelli: This anthology aims to reflect on the impact of whistleblowing in culture, politics, and society. You don't know the identity of John Doe, the whistleblower who contacted you in 2014 and provided you with 2.6 TB of leaked data, the so-called Panama Papers. However, you became very close to them. Could you tell us why, from your own understanding, they decided to blow the whistle and what they wanted to achieve?

Bastian Obermayer: What we know and what we can say from a year long conversation, and also from the manifesto that John Doe wrote after the publication of the Panama Papers, is that it was about inequality in our societies. The offshore industry is still a big part of it, as the rich and the powerful have the chance to hide their money and not pay their fair share. They can escape their duties and their taxes: that's been one motivation our source has told us. The other motivation that we have been given is that the person who called himself John Doe thought that there were crimes going on inside Mossack Fonseca, which is the Panamanian law firm that was the holder of all the secrets behind the Panama Papers. It was the urgent need that there had to be something done because Mossack Fonseca was helping a lot of corrupt people and politicians and enabling all kinds of financial crimes. The whistleblower somehow got insights into how Mossack Fonseca worked and how they dealt with problematic clients. John Doe wanted to stop this and have a big organisation like *Süddeutsche Zeitung* investigate Mossack Fonseca, and he or she wanted help in handing over the data and their insights.

Frederik Obermaier: What strikes me most is that at the time when John Doe approached *Süddeutsche Zeitung*, there were already news stories about tax havens, about corruption, about a lack of transparency: this was not breaking news. There were news about individuals hiding their money, with the help of providers or financial service providers like Mossack Fonseca, with the help of governments of tax havens, like the Caymans and the British Virgin Islands. Yet, the reporting put the spotlight only on singular cases, on singular tax havens, on singular firms. This changed with the data we received from John Doe as it gave insight into the machine room of this industry. We did not see only one spot, we saw everything: we saw the mechanism, the tricks that financial service providers like Mossack Fonseca used: nominee directors, bearer shares, fake names and so on. We also saw how firms like Mossack Fonseca internally discussed their dubious and often criminal customers, how they were well aware of breaches of law, breaches of sanctions, and still proceeded with their activities. What John Doe enabled the world to learn was to understand the offshore system and discover the parallel world of offshore, and to see the individual cases: like the Icelandic Prime Minister, like one of the best friends of Vladimir Putin, like the role of the banks, the enablers, and also the bigger picture: continents like Africa being literally plundered with the help of secrecy jurisdiction, wars, like the one in Syria, being secretly financed. The offshore world also leads to all of us paying the price for this whole problem, because if we have countries where governments and authorities are unable to provide affordable housing, healthcare, schools and universities, that is down to individuals who with the help of firms like Mossack Fonseca evade taxes, and thereby steal money: money that is desperately needed, especially in the times we are now living in. When John Doe approached us, we had already covered numerous investigations on corruption, on illicit money flows and on tax havens. It had started with the Offshore-Leaks investigation in 2013, where the International Consortium of Investigative Journalists invited us to take part, and then afterwards we also reported on Swiss Leaks: an investigation on the secret customers of HSBC. We also reported on the so called "Lux-Leaks", which showed how consultancy firms like EY, KPMG and PwC help multinational firms to avoid taxes in Europe and beyond.

TB: Secretive offshore tax havens are not just a technical matter concerning financial experts, accountants, and bankers, but are the node of a global network of financial institutions, systems of law, governments and corporations. What did you learn from the Panama Papers' investigation, and what do we still need to achieve to make a real change?

BO: What we learnt with the Panama Papers is that without the help of the banks, these networks would not work. They need to wire money, and most need the US dollar. If the big banks were not helpers in this system, if they had been committed to fighting tax evasion and money laundering and other financial crimes, it would not have happened. What we saw in the Panama Papers was that a huge number of national and international banks were customers of Mossack Fonseca: actually, in most cases, Mossack Fonseca did not have real contact with the final clients, the people who evaded taxes, they had contact with a client manager at Deutsche Bank, Switzerland, for example, or at UBS or Credit Swiss. The banks are the ones that steered most of the system, and they were completely free from any second thoughts like, "this isn't allowed" or "maybe we shouldn't do this" or "this could be illegal". They just cared about the money and the earnings of the banks and the riches of the customers. Of course, that's a big problem, because when we do see financial crises, we see that the big banks get bailed out. The same banks don't care in the slightest about society, they only care for money. We saw this repeat itself in investigations before, and we saw it later in the FinCEN files: that the banks are the most important players in this market. A lot of wealth managers and family offices, who have very rich clients, also use the offshore system for the advancement of these people's fortunes. That makes it a bit more complicated because they are not really regulated. In this sector, there is way more work to be done. The banks are now pretty much in the defence; I don't think that very cheap tax evasion works anymore with the big banks. But the private part, where you have exclusive lawyers and wealth managers working together to get a bullet-proof system of how a high-net worth individual does not have to pay taxes, that's still pretty much in place.

FO: If we speak about what we need to achieve to make a real change, transparency is key. We don't yet have global transparency when it comes to the ownership of companies. It would be a huge blow for tax evaders, crooks and autocrats if there were ultimate beneficial ownership registers in place around the world, because what tax havens or secrecy jurisdictions are basically selling is secrecy. They sell the promise: if you set up a company in my jurisdiction, no one will find out who is behind that company name. Since the Panama Papers, however, we have seen a growing movement and an increasing force pushing for change in this field. We have seen the European Union demanding search registries for its members and member countries. We even saw the United States recently with their Corporate Transparency Act, asking and forcing companies to reveal their ultimate beneficial owner. The big problem, however, is that in many countries—and the United States is one of them—these registries are not yet open to the public. In the meantime, I have lost faith in the authorities over the past years when it comes to investigating corruption. In many cases, civil society, journalists and NGOs have proven to be far better and more thorough at following the money. Or as US congressman Tom Malinowski put it recently: "We have groups of investigative journalists arguably doing more cutting-edge work on this than US intelligence agencies with their enormous budgets". If we want to really fight illicit money flows, corruption and kleptocracy, we need those registries open to the public all around the world.

TB: It would have taken more than 30 years for the two of you to work alone on the massive amount of data leaks you received from John Doe. You decided to share the documents with an international team of journalists and media outlets (the International Consortium of Investigative Journalists). Could you tell us more how this method of sharing worked, what the challenges were and why you preferred to work with a team of experts rather than opening the data up to the public?

FO: We decided to share the Panama Papers with hundreds of journalists all around the world because we realised early on that it was too large a data leak for the two of us, or even for our newspaper, *Süddeutsche Zeitung*. We also realised that the data covered so many countries and scandals all around the world. *Süddeutsche Zeitung* would not have been able to cover all of them. A scandal that might be huge in Paraguay, or might be huge in France, might only be a small article on our web page. We recognised that society needed to know about the findings of the scandals, and that we would be able to do better and more thorough investigations if we involved experts and journalists from those countries in our team. They had the knowledge; for them, it was much easier to help us with their context and information. We were not experts, for example, on Iceland, on Icelandic politics, nor on Icelandic economy. But Iceland was an important issue and topic in the Panama Papers because we saw the prime minister in the data, hiding company ownership from the public. We therefore saw it as our duty to enable a thorough investigation by sharing the data. There was also the security aspect. When we started, Bastian and I sitting there through day and night, scrolling through the data, seeing mafia bosses, organised crime figures and the cousins of Bashar Al Assad in Syria in the data, we also realised that at that point in time, someone could have stopped us. If one criminal had learned about us investigating him, there was at least a chance that the investigation could have been stopped by doing harm to us. By sharing the data with 400 journalists around the world, we made sure that no one could stop the investigation. If you harmed one of those journalists, the other 399 would pick up that work, and even investigate it more thoroughly and cover it widely. So, it was protection, better investigation and more publicity for the issue of in-transparency, inequality and corruption.

BO: We still had, of course, many challenges. Starting with people in our own newsroom, who thought that it was not a good idea to give away a scoop like this and to share exclusive information instead of being the only ones in the world writing about it. We had to convince everyone that this was the right decision. We were working with more than 400 journalists. Many of us knew a lot about what we were doing, but we had to give everybody rules, and we had to stick to the rules, and no one was allowed to speak about the investigation. We all needed to find one common date for publishing, a day where we all could publish. A day when it wasn't a national holiday in Morocco, or a big election in Spain, for example—so there were many obstacles, if only from the organisational part of it. We also had to find ways to share the information that we had received; we had to find a way to let everyone in the team research the Panama Papers, which the ICIJ, the International Consortium of Investigative Journalists, worked on us with. They set up a research platform where we could all search the data from wherever we were. And then a forum, which was kind of a Facebook for Investigative Journalists, where we could make posts and comment on posts and upload things and even like posts, so that we had a way of forming smaller sub-groups on certain topics and a way of informing everyone else. It was like, "look, we found the best friend of Vladimir Putin, maybe that's a story that we should tackle!". This wasn't an easy task because everyone needed to learn how to encrypt the emails and how to work with messengers and how to work with a two-factor authentication in the forum. But at the same time, it was such a great experience to see all of those fabulous minds at work, and to see how many contacts we had altogether and how great it was to have someone on the ground—like in Iceland or in Pakistan, or wherever—to understand what the data really meant in their countries. We would not have had a 10th of the stories had we not decided to share it. We worked for more than a year on the data—the process was that we kept receiving data from the whistleblower, we collected it and transferred it to the ICIJ, and they put it online for everyone to search and sent out alerts about the arrival of new data.

FO: We strongly believe in the power of transparent data and transparent working methods. But in this case, we had several challenges. The most important challenge for us was to protect our source. We have seen many investigations in the past, where data was made public, but later whistleblowers have been blown: they were sent to prison or at least indicted or lost their jobs. We wanted to protect the source of the Panama Papers by all means, and to protect John Doe and not waste his or her life. We all have to keep in mind that we owe a lot to whistleblowers. There are so many things we have learned in the past through whistleblowers; at the same time, many whistleblowers have paid a huge price for this. We didn't want John Doe to be one of them. Another aspect was the German law; in Germany, we have very strict privacy rules and legislation, so we would not have been able to publish all of the data and make it unredacted to the public. To redact everything in 2.6 terabytes of data that is not in the public interest would be at least a decade's work. Also, as we didn't know the identity of John Doe, how could we redact traces in the data that could lead to John Doe—that was an impossible task. So, we decided to only publish parts of the data that were relevant for a story, where we had the capacities to go through it step by step to make sure there was no hint to whatever person in there that may lead to a source, and also that the only data published was of huge public interest.

BO: The Panama Papers are millions of emails, and only a few thousand are probably relevant for their respective cases. The rest of the emails are people who are, in many cases, not doing anything criminal: maybe an intern at the bank or someone who needed the work as a nominee director in Panama. They were not bad people—they were speaking in the emails about their private lives and about their kids and sending pictures. That's all data that's not supposed to be in the public sphere. As journalists, we wanted to make a very clear distinction between data that should be public—and that is all the data that the ICIJ has published on the website about the Panama Papers—and data that does not belong in the public sphere, which is private data or private citizens. We think we need more transparency for politicians, but we don't think that we need more transparency for ordinary people.

TB: After the release of the Panama Papers investigation in April 2016, many social and political consequences followed: the Prime Minister of Iceland,

Sigmundur Davíð Gunnlaugsson, resigned after massive demonstrations in the country. Public protests followed in Pakistan, London, Malta and El Salvador. Could you describe in more detail what happened after April 4, and what the impact of the investigation was?

FO: After April 4, we saw massive demonstrations in several countries that were affected by the reporting. In Iceland, we saw the biggest protests in Icelandic history; we saw thousands of people gathering in the streets also in Argentina, in London, in Malta. This showed that the Panama Papers addressed a need to learn more about corruption and to fight corruption. We also saw hundreds, if not thousands, of investigations launched all around the world. Governments and authorities, globally, have recouped more than $1 billion due to the Panama Papers. We saw Prime Ministers not only in Iceland, but also in Pakistan, stepping back. Even a representative from Transparency International stepped back because he was involved in the Panama Papers. I think what is far more important than those individual cases, however, is that we saw a public debate that hundreds of thousands of people around the world spoke about tax havens and the high price that we pay for these untransparent, secretive jurisdictions. We have seen laws around the world changed. In Germany, a new law forces companies to reveal their beneficial owner. We saw change in Panama, in the US, all around the world. We saw lawmakers adopt new laws asking for greater transparency. Still, in these days, not one week passes without an investigation published somewhere around the world with at least some of the Panama Papers in there. For us as journalists, it is a treasure trove. I am sure that even in ten years, we will dig into the Panama Papers and still find leads in there.

BO: One of the big results of the Panama Papers is also the fact that we have seen more and more journalistic collaborations over the last few years than we have ever seen before. So many of our colleagues noticed the success of the Panama Papers— although it seemed so unlikely to work as a project (and we were really desperate many times in the middle of the process...). While not every story is suited for this kind of investigation, there are so many cross-border stories—stories that no one can investigate alone in their respective country. The huge attention that the Panama Papers received has shown whistleblowers and colleagues around the world that it's healthy to think about collaboration. You don't have to stop at the border, you should consider if there's someone on the other side who can help you or who may have the context that you don't have in other countries. The sheer amount of reporters can also be a factor. If we hadn't had 400 colleagues, we couldn't have had more than 5,000 stories. I think that this has given the world of journalism a huge boost in the direction towards collaborations. If we look back at the last five years, we have seen so many journalistic collaborations, especially in the investigative area. It really makes me happy, because when you speak to people who are part of those networks, so many say that the Panama Papers inspired them to found their own network. I think that's a good direction, because it helps to uncover more truth. It's not a day-to-day work anymore, but we still have the Panama Papers, of course, on our secure servers. Whenever we start a topic or see interesting names, we throw them into the system, and many times we still find stories. Perhaps not the biggest names, but maybe the missing puzzle piece of the story is in the Panama Papers, or something that's somehow related, but maybe can be interesting. People working in the field of money—money crimes and financial crimes, in the mafia field, like the OCCRP—are still publishing five new Panama Papers stories throughout the year; really good stories and really important stories.

TB: The disclosure of these secretive offshore systems provides evidence of speculation, corruption and a lack of transparency. Tax havens are robbing us of public services and the industry is very opaque. How much do we know, and how much it still to be done at a legal, financial, and social level?

FO: In the past years, through the Panama Papers, we have learned a lot about how secrecy in this field works; how enablers like banks and financial service providers, lawyers and consultants help to hide money from the authorities. At the same time, we have to be realistic. We have only got an impression of what is going on. We also have to be aware that whenever laws have been introduced in the past, whenever investigations have been launched, we have seen that the industry adapts to those investigations and adapts to new laws, by creating new bypasses and by using other loopholes. So, the Panama Papers have demonstrated the extent of the problem, but they have not completely solved it. Indeed, they cannot because this is something lawmakers and investigators have to do. Journalism and civil society can only push; can lay out the facts, then society and voters can vote for politicians who fight for more transparency. Then, we have to hope that lawmakers act, and that investigators act. When it comes to the price that we as society have to pay, we have learned a lot in the past years because increasing numbers of academics have looked into this issue. They analyse the price of tax havens, of financial secrecy, and they tell us in long lists how much taxes are lost by each country, each year, due to tax havens. These are shocking figures. Billions of euros are hidden in tax havens. According to the economist Gabriel Zucman the equivalent of 10 percent of global GDP is held offshore—most of the time hidden behind shell corporations, foundations and trusts. To see the amounts of money and to imagine how this money could be spent; how this could be spent to fight poverty, for example, to create a better health system, better schooling systems. That is shocking to me, because this shows us that there's so much to be done in this field.

TB: As you mentioned at the Disruption Network Lab, 17% of the tracked countries have seen a backlash against journalists who covered the Panama Papers or worked on them. They experience threats, mobbing, isolation, persecution, and also death, as in the case of Daphne Caruana Galizia in Malta and Ján Kuciak in

Slovakia. How can we better defend the work of investigative journalists and help to uncover these stories?

BO: Ján Kuciak was a member of the Panama Papers team. He was one of the people who actually worked on the files. Daphne Caruana Galizia was someone who had very early knowledge of wrongdoings in Malta that the Panama Papers would reveal, and she was publishing it even before we published. Although she wasn't part of the team, she was a relentless reporter on the Panama Papers issue. It's a huge tragedy to see both gone and murdered. It is also a huge cause of grief and anger for us, and of desperation. It came as a complete shock. When we published the Panama Papers, we didn't really think about security because we thought in the middle of Europe, you should be safe as an investigative reporter, doing work in the financial sector, as we did. It turns out, not at all. I still think that in Germany and in Western Europe journalists are mostly safe. One of the biggest problems here is that the public attitude appears to be increasingly against journalism. You see that in the framing of people like Donald Trump and Boris Johnson and others, who speak about "fake news" —and Donald Trump even on the "enemy of the people" —this is a big problem, because if journalists are only seen as liars, and part of the "other side" and "part of the enemy", then it's absolutely logical that they would be attacked as a next step. Because what do you do with the enemies? You fight them. We see this happening increasingly in Germany, especially from the right wing. We have to educate younger people, and we have to educate our neighbours and our friends when they start saying "all journalists lie". Especially, we have to challenge politicians who are going down the very easy populist path of accusing the news media of lying and fabricating stories; we have to stand up every single time when they put out this lie and say, "no, this is not the truth, this is not what's happening". That's part of what's important in the privileged countries. In many other countries, there needs to be real tactics to defend journalists: they need money, they need help, they need bodyguards, they need safe houses. There are many organizations doing good work there. If anyone is concerned about that, consider donating money. The moment that there's no free press in a country, you'll see that democracy dies next. Whenever we witness a country like Hungary or Poland, where the free press is really under attack, we all have to unite and fight it. In countries like Russia, and China, you need dedicated organisations. I don't think it's by chance that in Malta, and in Slovakia, where the murders of Ján Kuciak and Daphne Caruana Galizia happened, the political language has been terrible. Politicians were accusing journalists of being liars and even giving them names of animals and saying Daphne was a witch and the like. This has to be fought. It's the first step.

FO: Journalism is not only under pressure from people who want to do harm to journalists and who want to stop critical reporting. It's under pressure by financial restrictions; more and more journalists are unemployed. More and more media outlets are laying off journalists. This means there's less and less staff to investigate corruption or to investigate wrongdoings by the powerful. Journalism costs money because it costs time, and it costs workforce. A small step that every one of us can do is subscribing to a newspaper or donating to non-profit newsrooms, and thereby helping those journalists with their work. We also need more protection for whistleblowers. Unfortunately, there is still a huge risk for whistleblowers to blow the whistle on public interest topics to journalists; they have to fear repercussions, they have to fear for their jobs, and in many countries also for their lives.

TB: John Doe wrote: "Legitimate Whistleblowers who expose unquestionable wrongdoing, whether insiders or outsiders, deserve immunity from government retribution, full stop". In Germany, as in many other countries, a correct translation of "whistleblower" does not exist. This says a lot about the stigma around the act of blowing the whistle. What are your thoughts on this and how could we better defend the rights of whistleblowers, including John Doe?

BO: I think the obvious solution would be a whistleblower legislation that really owns the name. We have seen steps happen in the European Union, but we have also seen a lot of problems with that. I know that especially in Germany, the whistleblower law says that whistleblowers first have to deal with it inside the company. If you are working in a company where you really don't trust the people and you even suspect they might try to destroy you if you try to blow the whistle, I think you should have the guaranteed right to go to the press and speak to someone outside of the company. For now, however, you can not only lose your job over this, but also become the subject of a lawsuit. That's a terrible situation for anyone who might think about blowing the whistle. As journalists, it's still the case in Germany that in many cases we should—or we have to think about—telling a whistleblower not to blow the whistle, because they are endangering themselves in a way that we cannot advocate for. There needs to be a possibility for whistleblowers to do the right thing, and still not give away their future and their chance to provide a living for themselves and their families. If you have to take into consideration going to jail, this is not a situation we should have in a democratic country. I can understand those who do not dare to blow the whistle, because most of the famous whistleblowers are famous because they are in jail or they are in Moscow—in places you don't want to end up in. In this respect, the Panama Papers are kind of a best case scenario. The whistleblower enacted real and lasting change, and is still somewhere in the dark, and hopefully still safe. That's one of the best things about the whole Panama Papers affair.

FO: As we realised John Doe was running such a high risk, we had to take a lot of precautions, starting with only communicating via encrypted ways of communication. We even had to protect the computers in our offices. We had a special alarm system and we even put nail polish on the back of our computers to see if anyone was manipulating our workstations. Most importantly, we kept the secret.

For a long time, even within the newsroom, we only spoke with our editors. We invented a cover story on what we were doing, not to tell our colleagues. These were only small steps that everyone could expect and should expect from journalists—the most important precaution was taken by John Doe, him or herself. By not revealing their identity to us, this person made sure that we could never make the mistake to reveal their identity. I am sure, many other whistleblowers have learned from John Doe, learned from Snowden, from Manning, and John Doe has also shown to the world and to potential whistleblowers out there that there is a way of keeping your secret and keeping your life after blowing the whistle.

TB: You said at the Disruption Network Lab that the secretive offshore financial system, which is also legitimated legally, is undermining our democracy. How can we question such a business model? How could we imagine a more equitable and transparent future of this industry?

FO: My personal opinion is that we need tougher fines, tougher investigations and more consequences for those financial service providers. Many of them are still hiding under the disguise that they are lawyers, only doing their job. Society should not let them get away with this excuse. What is even more important is that we do see big consultancy companies being very active and helping their clients to hide their money from the authorities. Let's only look at the big four companies: EY, Deloitte, KPMG and PWC—whenever you see a scandal that is about hiding money and avoiding taxes, you can bet that at least one of them is somehow involved. At the same time, these are companies that get regular public contracts by authorities and parliaments. If the wrongdoing of such companies is proven in court, in my opinion they should be banned from public contracts for at least a certain time, and this time should be several years. Otherwise, it is not a big punishment for them.

BO: I think we should question the very existence of offshore centres, of tax havens. As Stiglitz said, there is no need for tax havens, there's no economic or other need for them to exist. No one said that there are certain islands or big states that need to help rich individuals have lower taxes. We could go even further and think about sanctioning them. One of our neighbours is Switzerland, and they are still a tax haven. In the long run, the European Union should really think about putting some economic sanctions on Switzerland and on other countries. It may sound strict, and I know that it's not doable right now when we still have tax havens inside the European Union, but I think in the end we should not tolerate states who are so deep into this race to the bottom of taxes.

TB: The Panama Papers opened up a debate around the fiscal costs to citizens after the 2008-2009 financial crisis. We are now experiencing another financial crisis with COVID-19 and the effects that will become evident in the future. What would you suggest to potential whistleblowers who would like to denounce abuses and wrongdoing at the moment? How can we help to uncover important stories?

FO: We are living in one of the most severe global crises since World War II, and there are billions of dollars and euros being spent on COVID-19 to fight the pandemic. There are huge amounts of money spent on masks, for example. Of course, there are huge possibilities for crooks and for corrupt practices in this field. Already in Europe, in many countries including Germany, we have seen politicians using their influence to profit from the state effort to help society to recover. There is a strong need for whistleblowers in this field, especially in these times. Politicians are currently not yet speaking much about the cost of fighting the pandemic, but it's a huge cost. We need more transparent acting of lawmakers, and a transparent flow of money. I can only address whistleblowers out there: if you want to blow the whistle, now is indeed the time. As the laws I would wish for are still not in place, I would recommend approaching journalists anonymously. Do not reveal your identity in the first contact, although you can do so later if you feel safe and if the journalist does not see any reason to prohibit you, or prevent you from revealing your identity, but don't do so on your first point of contact. If you do so, your identity is out there, and you cannot rewind.

BO: We're seeing a lot of scandals right now in Germany, with politicians making massive amounts of money from COVID-19, because they consulted companies who sold masks, and they got their share of it; and the share was sometimes as large as a million euros. Some politicians have already had to step back because of this. In the last year, governments around the world gave out lots of help, and lots of money was sent to corporations to help them survive. Many groups misused the COVID-19 money and used the opportunity to rob the government, and many politicians allowed people who wanted to earn money to bribe them. If you witnessed any of this, this needs to be uncovered to gain back the truth of the people out there who are really suffering. This is a really important time.

PELIN ÜNKER

Pelin Ünker is an investigative journalist, working for *Deutsche Welle* as a correspondent in Istanbul. She worked at *Cumhuriyet* newspaper for ten years as an economics correspondent and finance editor. Her stories are now published by *Deutsche Welle*, *taz, die tageszeitung*, and some Turkish websites. She has worked on ICIJ's Panama Papers, Bahamas Leaks, Implant Files, Paradise Papers and FinCEN Files investigations. Her work has included investigations on macroeconomic data on the state of the Turkish economy. She has also investigated corruption, tax avoidance and evasion, privatisations, public contracts, and other subjects. Her work has been honoured with the Ugur Mumcu Investigative Journalism Award by Progressive Journalists Association in 2016, the Research-Investigation Journalism award by Progressive Journalists Association in 2017, the Transparency Award by Transparency International Turkey in 2017, the Don Bolles Medal by IRE and NICAR in 2019. She is a doctoral student in economics at Istanbul University and is writing a dissertation about the impact of fiscal policy on poverty and income inequality in Turkey.

PELIN ÜNKER

THE PARADISE PAPERS EFFECT IN TURKEY
NO RESIGNATION, NO PROSECUTION, BUT PUNISHMENT FOR JOURNALISM

"THE WEST IS JEALOUS of us!" These words are from Turkish President Recep Tayyip Erdogan's speech. In May 2016, while talking to the public in Artvin, a city in the north of Turkey, he stated: "Why is the West jealous of us? Because of dams like this (referring to Yusufeli Dam), Yavuz Sultan Selim Bridge (the third Bosphorus bridge), the Bosphorus underwater tunnel and the Marmaray Subway line", he claimed.[1]

Since then, it is the one of the most helpful propaganda tools that the government has used on their voters. So much so that whenever the government is being criticized, it is frequently expressed by the Turkish government and partisan media that the West makes such criticisms because it is jealous of the government's success.

Whether or not the West really envies us is another debate. But as a Turkish journalist who collaborates with The International Consortium of Investigative Journalists (ICIJ), I would say I always envy my colleagues in the West. ICIJ has a lot of members and partners from all over the world. But when we're working on a project together, I know that especially the colleagues from Europe don't worry about the potential legal problems of their work as long as they abide by the principles of journalism. However, as Turkish journalists, we know from the start that when we write about critical issues, accusations of defamation will be levelled at us. At this point I should state that it doesn't matter whether what we wrote is uncontested fact or not. That's what happened to me when I wrote the Paradise Papers stories. I'm the only journalist who risked being sent to jail for the Paradise Papers stories.

When the BBC wrote that Britain's Queen Elizabeth II had invested millions in offshore accounts,[2] no one said that they smeared their ancestors. Or the Canadian Prime Minister, who was mentioned in the Paradise Papers,[3] did not s"e journalists for defamation. However, this tool is often used in court cases in Turkey. In the last two and a half years, at least 40 journalists have been convicted of insulting public officials.

ICIJ's Panama Papers[4] and Paradise Papers investigations, with about 400 journalists working on each revealed secrets of the World's elites, of global businesses, and of politicians. But these projects had only been the subject of litigation in Turkey. After initially conceding that the companies did exist, the state later filed a lawsuit and got the journalist who wrote about those companies convicted; this was probably the first example of its kind.

And of course, motions by opposition parties demanding an investigation into Turkish politicians' accounts in tax havens, as revealed by the Paradise Papers, were rejected by AKP votes.

ICIJ and partners have been involved in publications concerning the financial off-shore sector since 2013. In 2017, the Consortium won the Pulitzer Prize for the stories on the Panama Papers.[5] After reporting on the Panama Papers in April 2016, the team published stories on the Paradise Papers, a set of 13.4 million confidential electronic documents relating to offshore documents. The leaked documents originate from the legal firm Appleby, the corporate services provider Asiaciti Trust, and 19 corporate registries maintained by jurisdictions. They contain the names of more than 120,000 individuals and companies, including more than 120 politicians worldwide.[6] Turkey stories revealed the offshore connections of two politicians, as well as business people and sportspeople. The purpose of the articles was to re-discuss the legitimacy of tax havens. They were leaked to Bastian Obermayer and Frederik Obermaier from the German newspaper *Süddeutsche Zeitung*, who then shared the documents with the International Consortium of Investigative Journalists and a network of more than 380 journalists from 95 global media partners.[7]

According to ICIJ, the research showed that corporations like Nike, Apple, Facebook or Glencore reduce their taxes to meagre rates; they also showed how the political elites use the secret world of tax havens, including in Turkey.

The Paradise Papers provide an insight to the offshore industry, "a sprawling behemoth so secretive its very size can only be guessed and yet understood to be so large as to distort the global economy".[8] Since the publication of the Paradise Papers in November 2017, authorities have opened tax investigations in numerous countries, including Vietnam, Lithuania, Indonesia, Ireland, Greece, the Netherlands, New Zealand, Australia, Nigeria and Pakistan.

And the leaks showed that Erkam and Bülent Yıldırım, the sons of the former prime minister of Turkey, Binali Yıldırım, owned five companies in Malta, where doors were open to those who would like to avoid taxes in their own countries. At the time, Yıldırım was the Speaker of the Parliament. The documents revealed the Yıldırım's sons were shareholders of companies called Black Eagle Marine Co

Ltd, Hawke Bay Marine Co Ltd, South Seas Shipping NV, Nova Warrior Limited and Dertel Shipping Limited. They were all shipping companies that were used to minimalize taxes.

It is not illegal for Turkish citizens to own or run a Maltese company. Companies pass profits on to their Maltese subsidiaries, which pretend they are doing business on the Mediterranean island. But in fact, they just pay fewer taxes there. As a result, the countries in which the profits were made lose billions every year.

After the publication, Binali Yıldırım spoke to the press at the Ankara Esenboga Airport before his US trip on November 7, 2017. Yıldırım conceded to the existence of the companies and said it is normal for a global business. "I have immunity, but my children don't. Therefore, I especially wish for an investigation to be launched. Shipping is a global business. There are companies and contact points in all parts of the world. There is no secret or concealed business here",[9] he claimed.

International Maritime Organization records further showed that one of these Maltese companies was linked to a Turkish company which had taken a big contract from the state. We discovered that Nova Warrior is connected with Oras Denizcilik, a company that got a tender from the General Directorate of Mineral Research and Exploration that amounts to 7 million dollars. Binali Yıldırım was also in the shipping business before he entered politics. His business partner was Salih Zeki Çakır. Oras Denizcilik is also owned by Salih Zeki Çakır.

The Yıldırım family, whom I contacted through lawyers before publishing the stories, did not respond to the detailed questions about any of the companies, including Nova Warrior's connection with Oras Denizcilik. The news stories did not claim that offshore companies were illegal businesses; they said they avoided paying taxes through loopholes in the legislation. The news stories did not say this was a crime; they questioned how ethical it was.

However, before a week had passed, Yıldırım and his sons opened a compensation case against me and the *Cumhuriyet* newspaper at the Anadolu 24th Civil Court of First Instance. They had been seeking a total of TL 500,000 in non-pecuniary damages in the lawsuit, claiming that two news stories about the "Paradise Papers" leaks that were published in the *Cumhuriyet* daily "violated their personal rights". Non-material damages of 250,000 lira were claimed for Binali Yıldırım, 125,000 lira for Erkam Yıldırım and 125,000 lira for Bülent Yıldırım. The stories also mentioned Binali Yıldırım's uncle and nephew, although no complaints were filed concerning these people. The lawsuit petition asserted that the reports, "were put together with intent to insult and vilify by employing special emphasis". But this was not the only case.

They also filed a separate criminal case at the 2nd Criminal Court of First Instance of Istanbul. The trial took place from September 2018 to January 2019. The fact that the judiciary, which was entirely under the control of political power, sentenced me to imprisonment was not a surprise.

The court sentenced me to one year and 45 days in prison for "defamation and insult" and fined me for TL 8,660 in non-pecuniary damages in January 2019.[10] The judge opted not to defer the sentence on the grounds that I might commit the "same crime". But for the court, the crime was reporting uncontested facts and the possibility that I might publish other investigative journalism reports.

Nearly one month after this decision, the compensation case ended. The Anadolu 24th Civil Court of First Instance verdict was to pay Yıldırıms' a sum of TL 30,000 in compensation. The court found me, the *Cumhuriyet* newspaper and its former holder, journalist Orhan Erinç, guilty.

In May 2019, the Istanbul Criminal Chamber of the Regional Court of Justice (Appellate Court) dropped the charges against me on the grounds of the statute of limitations.[11] The news story in question had been published in November 2017 and the investigation had been launched in the same month. But the indictment had been submitted on August 31, 2018. The court said the prosecution unlawfully proceeded. Therefore, the complaint was barred by the four-month statute of limitations for pressing charges as per Article 26/1 of Turkey's press law. Aside from that, the appellate court upheld the legal fine that was given to me on the charge of "insulting a public official" under Article 125 of the Turkish Penal Code (TCK). However, the court ruled that I was to pay TL 7,080 instead of TL 8,660.

The data of the Paradise Papers showed that economy, politics and family ties in Turkey are closely related to each other. According to the Financial Crimes Investigation Board from Turkey (MASAK), offshore companies are being used in Turkey not only for tax evasion or tax avoidance, but also to launder dirty money through front companies. More than a decade ago, MASAK stated that there are tax havens in the world where the Turkish tycoons transfer their money and requested that the government pass a law to tax the transactions to the tax heavens. But nothing happened.

Another problem is that the origin of the money brought from abroad is not questioned in accordance with the regulations. Those who bring assets from abroad are not subjected to tax investigation. At the moment of the writing of this text at the end of June 2021, there is still zero tax for people who bring their money to Turkey. This reminds me of all the names from the Panama and Paradise Papers. They are business people close to President Erdogan, ex-president Binali Yildirim's sons and the Albayrak brothers.

The Paradise Papers leaks also revealed that the Minister of Finance and Treasury of Turkey, Berat Albayrak, who is married to President Erdogan's daughter, and his brother Serhat Albayrak concealed offshore companies linked to the Turkish conglomerate Calik Holding which two Albayraks ran. The files showed that Serhat Albayrak was listed as a director of a Maltese company named Frocks International Trading Ltd. Berat Albayrak was the CEO of Calik Holding for a part of that period. This company used nominees, which allowed it to conceal the identity of real shareholders and potentially to hide money offshore and avoid tax.

I faced another criminal case for covering this. Berat-Serhat Albayrak and Calik Holding filed a criminal complaint against me for "defamation through media". Although the claims are not disputed, the judge blamed me for painting tax havens as a financial crime. According to the judge's decision, people's sense about tax heavens is that it is a crime and although I always highlighted 'it is not a crime in Turkey' in the article series, I had made people feel that it is a crime. This was the reason for this punishment.

But this case was also dismissed due to violation of the four-month statute of limitations. At the last hearing of the case, the Presiding Judge was heard to say, "Unfortunately, I have detected that the statute of limitations has been violated".[12]

Calik Holding's 10 thousand TL action for their claimed damages was also dismissed in the last months.[13] But the case is now at Appellate Court.

On the other hand, blocking access to specific news reports is a growing problem that mounts up to censorship. According to Turkish law, precautionary access blocking can be imposed on websites that contain content that violates personal rights. This content can be removed from the Internet.

According to data compiled by the Freedom of Expression Association (İFÖD), access to some 130,000 URLs, 7,000 Twitter accounts, 40,000 tweets, 10,000 YouTube videos and 6,200 pieces of content on Facebook was blocked in Turkey by the end of 2019. İFOD also reported that a total of 1,484 Twitter accounts were blocked by Turkish Criminal Judgeships of Peace in 2019, making Turkey the top country in the number of withholding requests sent to Twitter.[14]

What happened in the Paradise Papers summarizes the state of journalism in Turkey. First, they blocked access to the Paradise Papers stories. The news channels covered this access-blocking on their web sites. Then those stories were blocked by the government as well.

When I won the court cases, of course it was all over the media. So they blocked those stories as well. Then the press covered stories about this access-blocking. But finally, they blocked access to those stories and tweets as well. These are textbook examples of how the government takes the media under direct or indirect control, how the rule of law is under severe strain and how Turkey's judiciary is no longer independent.

It must be noted that 90 percent of Turkish media outlets were bought by friendly business conglomerates such as Calik Holding. It led to a situation in which many topics cannot be freely reported on. In fact, many topics can only be covered within the framework laid out by the government. The current people in power don't want to see any journalism, unless it praises them. Turkey is one of the world's biggest prisons for journalists; there are more than 40 journalists in Turkey's prisons now. Besides that, the non-governmental organization Press

In Arrest's database shows that since 2018 more than 350 journalists are being trialled. These cases function not only as a way to pressure and intimidate the journalists, but also as a tool to keep them busy with legal procedures to perform their job. Everybody knows that the journalists are not guilty, including the judges and the politicians.

The Turkish example proves that the impact of whistleblowing and truth-telling can be different for different societies and cultures. And this also shows why collaboration is so important, especially for journalists from imperfect democracies like Turkey. They can block access to news stories, but stories don't disappear in this way. They can try to silence journalists by putting them in prison with false charges, but solidarity can protect our colleagues.

The rule of law is eroding by the day, and corruption is increasing at the same time. And that is why journalism is under pressure. They want to silence the journalists sometimes by killing them, sometimes by sending them to prison. Actually, they want to silence the news stories.

So people need free journalists, people need to hear the reality. We need to understand—if one journalist is silenced, it means that a society will be silenced. So we have to strengthen solidarity and collaboration to withstand the pressure. When we are together, our voice will be stronger.

Notes

1. Türkiye Cumhuriyeti Cumhurbaşkanlığı, May 21, 2016, video,11:02-11:33, https://www.tccb.gov.tr/yurt-ici-ziyaretler/354/44044/artvin.

2. BBC Panorama, "Paradise Papers: Queen's private estate invested £10m in offshore funds", *BBC*, November 6, 2017. https://www.bbc.com/news/uk-41878305.

3. Oved, C. Marco, Alex Boutilier, Robert Cribb, "Liberal fundraisers held family millions in offshore trust, leaked documents reveal", *Toronto Star*, November 5, 2017, https://www.thestar.com/news/paradise-papers/2017/11/05/trudeau-bronfman-kolber-offshore-trust-taxes.html.

4. "The Panama Papers: Exposing the Rogue Offshore Finance Industry", *ICIJ*, https://www.icij.org/investigations/panama-papers.

5. "The 2017 Pulitzer Prize Winner in Explanatory Report, *The Pulitzer Prizes*, https://www.pulitzer.org/winners/ international-consortium-investigative-journalists-mcclatchy-and-miami-herald.

6. "Offshore Trove Exposes Trump-Russia links and Piggy Banks of the Wealthiest 1 Percent", *ICIJ*, November 5, 2017, https://www.icij.org/investigations/paradise-papers/paradise-papers-exposes-donald-trump-russia-links-and-piggy-banks-of-the-wealthiest-1-percent.

7. "Paradise Papers: Media partners", *ICIJ*, November 5, 2017, https://www.icij.org/investigations/paradise-papers/paradise-papers-media-partners.

8. Fitzgibbon Will, Dean Starkman, "The 'Paradise Papers' and the Long Twilight Struggle Against Offshore Secrecy", December 27, 2017, https://www.icij.org/investigations/paradise-papers/paradise-papers-long-twilight-struggle-offshore-secrecy.

9. "500,000 lira in damages sought for our Paradise Papers report", *Cumhuriyet*, November 11, 2017, https://www. cumhuriyet.com.tr/haber/500000-lira-in-damages-sought-for-our-paradise-papers-report-864228

10. "Ünker given prison sentence for "Paradise Papers" reports", *Platform for Independent Journalism*, January 9, 2017, http:// platform24.org/en/articles/714/unker-given-prison-sentence-for--paradise-papers--reports.

11. Fitzgibbon, Will, "Turkish journalist spared jail for Paradise Papers investigation", *ICIJ*, May 6, 2019, https://www.icij.org/ investigations/paradise-papers/turkish-journalist-spared-jail-for-paradise-papers-investigation.

12. "Paradise Papers Case Against Journalist Ünker Dismissed Due to Statute of Limitations", *Bianet.org*, March 28, 2019, https://m.bianet.org/english/freedom-of-expression/206860-paradise-papers-case-against-journalist-unker-dismissed-due-to-statute-of-limitation.

13. Court dismisses case against journalist Pelin Ünker over ,Paradise Papers' reports", *Bianet. org*, December, 22, 2020, https://m.bianet. org/english/media/236419-court-dismisses-case-against-journalist-pelin-unker-over-paradise-papers-reports.

14. Akdeniz Yaman, Ozan Güven, *An Iceberg of Unseen Internet Censorship In Turkey*, 2019, https://ifade.org.tr/reports/ EngelliWeb_2019_Eng.pdf.

SIMONA LEVI

Photo by Albert Salamé

In 2017, Rolling Stone magazine named Simona Levi as one of 25 people who are "shaping the future." Since 2017, she has designed and directed the postgraduate course, "Technopolitics and Rights in the Digital Era". Levi is a theatre director, playwright, technopolitical strategist and researcher. She iss a founder and spokesperson of the project 15MPARATO, which led to the imprisonment of the former Minister of Economy and IMF President, along with 15 other bankers, and Xnet, a leading Spanish activist project related to digital rights, democracy, freedom of expression and citizens' control of power and institutions. She is the co-author of several books, including: *#FakeYou: Fake News and Disinformation* (Rayo Verde, 2019); *Vote and Charge: Impunity as a Form of Government* (Capitán Swing, 2017); *Technopolitics, the Internet and R-evolutions* and *Free Digital Culture: Basic Notions for Defending What Belongs to Everyone* (Icaria, 2012). Her shows have been performed in theatres and festivals throughout Europe, and she has created high-impact festivals like OXcars and InnMotion.

SIMONA LEVI
IMPROVING DEMOCRACY THROUGH DIGITAL WHISTLEBLOWING
OPEN-SOURCE DEVICE FOR JAILING POLITICIANS

This text is an adaptation by Simona Levi of Shreya Tewari and Nani Jansen Reventlow's interview for the Catalysts for Collaboration project on her group, 15MPARATO.[1]

"ONE OF THE BIGGEST *strengths of our campaign was that it was not centred around a single person. It was built as a citizen's device where the victory would also belong to the people."*

A member of 15MPARATO

Background

In one of Spain's most high-profile cases, a group of activists successfully sent Rodrigo Rato, the ex-Minister of Economy, former President of Bankia and potential Prime Minister of Spain, to jail for corruption. Alongside him, 64 bankers and politicians were sentenced to varying terms: 14 of them imprisonment.

The convictions were the result of a lawsuit filed by an anonymous collective called 15MPARATO against the executives of Caja Madrid, Spain's oldest savings bank, which later merged with six other savings banks to form Bankia.[2]

During the proceedings, popularly known as the 'Bankia Case', evidence surfaced as a result of collaborative digital tools created for 15MPARATO by the activist platform Xnet.[3] Most crucial of these were over 8,000 emails from the ex-chairman of Caja Madrid, Miguel Blesa, which shed light on malpractice and tax evasion by bankers and politicians amounting to over 15.5 million euros. As a result, in 2017, Spain's High Court found Rato and 64 other executives guilty. They were all members of various political parties and unions, from the conservative Partido Popular to which Rato belonged; to the social democractic Partido Socialista; to Izquierda Unida, the left-wing party now merged with Podemos; and the two main "left" unions. But this was not all: with the evidence that 15MPARATO brought to the case, unprecedentedly, the small savers who had been forced to invest were all able to recover the money they had lost in the scam: over 2 billion euros.

Formation of 15MPARATO

Spain was heavily hit by the financial crisis in 2008 which led to a recession, mass unemployment and the collapse of Spain's property market. The effects of this crisis were felt for many years, with large companies facing bankruptcy, and unemployment reaching a record rate of 32%. The devastating effects of the financial crisis led to massive protests in 2011. These protests were first staged on May 15 and later came to be known as the 15M or the Indignados movement. This movement saw Spaniards assembling in towns and city squares across Spain to display their distrust in the government and its handling of the financial crisis.

15MPARATO was created in May 2012, on the one-year anniversary of 15M. The group was driven by Xnet, a non-profit activist organisation active in the field of democracy in the digital era. Its objective was to put an end to economic and political impunity and corruption. The Bankia case was chosen because it summarized the key ingredients of unfair governance: all parties involved, revolving doors between the public and private sector, lack of transparency, privileges and a large part of the population affected.

15MPARATO was a witty wordplay, with 15M standing for the Indignados movement, and Rato holding the dual meaning of Rato, the last name of Rodrigo Rato, also translating as "for a while" in Spanish. The name made both intentions of the campaign clear: that the 15M movement was coming for Rato and others like him, and that the 15M movement would continue to question the establishment for a long while.

Facts Leading up to the Lawsuit

In 2010, Rodrigo Rato joined Caja Madrid as its chairman. Prior to this, he held other high-level positions, including Director of the International Monetary Fund, Minister of Economy, and Vice President of one of Spain's major political parties, the People's Party. The latter had set him up as a potential Prime Minister of Spain. At Caja Madrid, he succeeded Miquel Blesa, who had held the position for 13 years.

Shortly after Rato joined, Caja Madrid became the largest of seven regional banks that consolidated to form 'Bankia', and he became the President of Bankia. In 2011, Bankia listed itself on the stock exchange and carried out an Initial Public Offering (IPO). The advertisement to sell shares targeted the poor and middle class, offering shares for only 1,000 euros. Over 300,000 small saver shareholders invested in Bankia for 3.75 euros per share and, consequently, the conglomerate raised 3.2 billion euros.

In May 2012, Rato announced that Bankia had recorded profits upward of 300 million euros. Shortly after making this claim, Rato resigned from his post amid rumours regarding Bankia's insolvency and, in June 2012, José Ignacio Gorigolzarri took over as the new President of Bankia.

In November 2012, within seven months of Rato's profit rates announcement, Bankia announced that it was suffering a loss of 14 billion euros and was in urgent need of a bail-out. Share prices crashed to an all-time low of 0.01 euros. Bankia was considered key to the nation's banking sector since it was the fourth-largest bank in Spain and held ten percent of Spanish citizens' total bank deposits. To avoid a collapse of the entire banking sector, the government stepped in and bailed out Bankia by partially nationalising it. The 19 billion euros raised for this was part of a larger debt that Spain had acquired from the European Union.

Xnet analysed the first bailout plan and realised that half of the amount was being used to rescue Bankia, a bank that was claiming profits of over 300 million euros only seven months ago. As collateral damage, Bankia's 300,000 shareholders—mostly unemployed, elderly and families—had collectively lost over two billion euros due to Bankia's sudden downfall. It was clear to the activists that the bailout from the government and the steep fall of the share prices were extremely implausible unless there was maladministration and misrepresentation by the executive running Bankia. This led to the formation of 15MPARATO and the launching of the lawsuit.

Even though the campaign was not against one banker specifically, Rato represented a *modus operandi* that occurs repeatedly in Spanish politics: a potential Prime Minister who, after holding the position of Minister of Economy and then Director of the International Monetary Fund during the crisis, became a private banker with executives from across the political spectrum. The positions he held in government and the banking sector over the past decades clearly symbolised the revolving door culture of the establishment.

In May 2012, 15MPARATO launched a campaign seeking people who had lost their money in the Bankia crash, and also for individuals with any information that might help them to hold Rato to account. Within two weeks, they had found 44 people wanting to hold Rato liable for financial fraud. The collection of evidence

began. In order to enable secure and anonymous evidence gathering, Xnet created a digital tool in 2013, called Xnet Leaks. The tool was inspired by WikiLeaks,
where any citizen could anonymously submit information about systemic corruption. Later on, it was improved by installing the GlobaLeaks system.

The next obstacle was to overcome the financial burden of initiating the case.
15MPARATO saw this as an opportunity to host the first political crowdfunding
campaign in Spain: over 11,000 people tried to donate money within the first hour
of the platform going live, leading to a system shutdown. 130% of the 15,000 euros
required was gathered in less than a day.

This is how journalist Pau Llop reported the digital fundraising on the day of
the crowdfunding:

> [...] thousands of tweets since 9 o'clock this morning refer to a crowdfunding cam-
> paign that is destined to mark a before and after, not only in the history of this type
> of economic collectivism, but also, if it goes well, in Spanish judicial history.
>
> At the time of writing, 357 Spaniards have already raised 7,345 euros to sue Rodrigo
> Rato and the entire Board of Directors of Bankia, the fourth largest financial in-
> stitution in the country. And in just four hours. At 1,800 euros per hour. And de-
> spite the fact that Goteo.org, the website hosting the collection of the money, has
> been down for a good part of this morning, without service, due to the saturation
> caused by thousands of people trying to get information and donate.
>
> A member of this website tells us that this campaign had received 11,500 visits in
> the first hour (9–10 a.m.) when the usual was until then 7,800 in 24 hours. Nobody
> remembers a campaign with a similar start [...]. "This is an action by all for all", ex-
> plains a spokeswoman for 15MPARATO, the group behind this unusual and already
> successful initiative.
>
> Looking at the wall of donors, there are dozens of donations of 5, 10, 15 and 20 eu-
> ros. But there are also people who have already donated 500 in one go... This has
> only just begun. From now on, crowdfunding is no longer just for projects that are
> difficult to fit into the traditional mass market. In the time it has taken to write this
> post, 1,000 euros more have been raised to force the justice system to investigate
> something that neither the government, nor the current board of Bankia want to
> be investigated. The people accuse. And pay.[4]

After years of financial abuse and humiliation, 15MPARATO provided a way for
the population to regain some dignity. The initiative was so popular that the mass
media were forced to announce that a group of un-identifiable "freaks" had collected enough evidence and money to sue the potential prime minister. 15MPAR-

ATO shared spending accounts of the money received on its website. This created trust and transparency between the public and 15MPARATO. It was also a reliable way to refute claims of money-making and other allegations made against them by the press.

In June 2012, 15MPARATO filed a lawsuit in Spain's High Court against Rato and 32 other bankers on behalf of 14 aggrieved shareholders. This direct action was possible as the Spanish judicial system allows victims to be part of a trial, and 15MPARATO was representing the victims (a group that grew to 44). The main allegations made in the lawsuit related to negligent administration, financial misinformation, fraud and forgery.

Information submitted through Xnet led to some ground-breaking revelations in the Bankia Case, such as the Black Card Scandal and Blesa's emails, revealing the systematic corruption across the banking and political sectors and eventually leading to two additional lawsuits and the devolution of the money. As 15MPARATO promised from the beginning, "We don't need any bail out; we simply need our stolen money back."[5]

The Preferred Shares Scam: How We Got the Money Back

Important evidence was leaked to Xnet by Bankia's own employees. It concerned an internal document about selling a product called "Preferred Shares". It showed that 98% of shares sold to small savers and families were complex, high-risk shares. It was clear to 15MPARATO that the products were not put on the public market, but were sold only to specific, fragile targets. According to the document, employees were asked to keep shareholders under the false belief that the shares sold to them were fixed-income security shares, a less complex and more secure type of shareholding.

The leaked document encouraged the sale of these shares to small savers and families lacking financial knowledge, with each page of the sales pitch stating: "This information should not be visible to customers." Based on this evidence, 15MPARATO provided a path for those who had lost money to litigate and claim their money back directly from the bank. Their campaign quipped: "Suing your bank is the best product in the financial market: you get your money back plus 4%"; the percentage added when the litigation was won. The court case grew exponentially as, for the first time, the scammed were winning. It got so big that in 2016 the High Tribunal stated that all the small savers had to be refunded: over 4 billion euros were returned, with a plus of 4%. One of the first goals of 15MPARATO was achieved: people got their stolen money back.

The Black Card Scandal

In December 2013, Xnet received an anonymous submission containing over 8,000 email exchanges from Blesa, the former chairman of Caja Madrid. They included details of how executives of the bank and other influential political figures had access to a Visa Black Credit Card, which was paid off using Bankia's savings account. Not only were Bankia's funds being used for personal expenses up to 50,000 euros, but these expenditures were made without the knowledge of the tax agencies. This had led to over 15.5 million euros in tax evasion. Blesa's emails were representative of Caja Madrid's corrupt administration. Due to the complexity and scale of the Black Card Scandal, the investigating magistrate Judge Andreu opened an adjoining lawsuit against 65 bankers and politicians on charges of embezzlement and tax evasion. Rato and Blesa put up personal property amounting to 19 million euros in their bail.

Outcome

In February 2017, Spain's High Court sentenced Rato to four and a half years of imprisonment and Blesa to six years of imprisonment on account of embezzlement in the Black Card Scandal. 63 other bankers and politicians were also sentenced for varying terms, 15 of them to prison. Blesa committed suicide few months after the ruling. Rato appealed the judgment, but the Supreme Court upheld Rato's conviction. In October 2018, Rato and 13 others began their prison sentences.

15MPARATO's initial case, against Bankia executives over the IPO scam and allegations of fraud, forgery and administrative malpractices, remained pending in Spain's High Court until 2020. By then, many things had changed—including the spirit of the movement, heavily smashed by the co-optation of Podemos, a political party that falsely claimed to represent them. This modified public perceptions of the movement. 15MPARATO was one of the few groups from the Indignados Movement that was not seduced by Unidas Podemos, despite the party trying to infiltrate both the group and the trial several times.[6]

Another contribution in the changing situation was the COVID-19 pandemic: an exhausted population had little energy to say anything when, in September 2020, the tribunal found the accused not guilty of any malpractice. This was a contradiction of the Spanish High Court statement in 2016, that the information provided by the bankers was "heavily inaccurate"; this is how the system operates.

The People Did It

From the moment 15MPARATO called upon the public for any information that could potentially imprison Rato, the narrative of the movement was clear: this was a movement by the people and for the people. Now the second case has been lost, they have changed the name of their social network to the hashtag #LaCiudadania LoHizo—"the people did it."

15MPARATO began with an anonymous message on the internet, reading:

"We will be catalysts. Countless small, surgical groups to free up living spaces... We are not one, we are not ten, we are not a thousand or a million. We are countless because we are everywhere. The change is unstoppable, the change has already happened... We have the power of the multitude, organised in connected and inexpressible catalysts. If we cannot go for the bank because it is too big to fall, let's go for the Bankers."[7]

The internal group remained anonymous for the majority of the campaign, and used only their collective name, 15MPARATO. This was for three reasons. Firstly, they didn't want the government to identify and obstruct individual members. Secondly, they didn't want the government to be able to assess the number of people involved in the movement. As a member of 15MPARATO recalled, "We didn't want the establishment to know whether we were one or one thousand in number." Since the group comprised of majority female and LGBTQ members, "we couldn't come out in public because we would perhaps not be taken as seriously as male, hetero, White individuals from the capital." Some group members did disclose their names, however, to take credit for the movement amid the ongoing trials. Because of this, the whole group eventually shared their names with the press.

The external group, which comprised of the wider population, was created by 15MPARATO using digital tools such as social media platforms and mailing lists. These platforms were created so that Spanish people could interact and engage with the movement. The internet was, and remains, the best place for collaboration; if we wanted to check the accountability of a bank, or if we couldn't find a certain legal article, we would go on Twitter and ask for help. Hundreds of thousands of citizens were mobilised at different stages of the case for both crowdfunding and evidence gathering.

The Xnet Leaks tool was a by-product of this digital collaboration: an online portal that allowed citizens to anonymously submit evidence against Bankia, which led to breakthroughs such as the leaked Blesa emails. Maddalena Falzoni, the founder of MaadiX, a free platform for secure tools, was the technologist behind the creation of Xnet Leaks—based on GlobaLeaks—and other digital tools in the campaign.[8] As an activist group, Xnet was concerned about citizens' privacy and security and decided to set up Xnet Leaks, which was a free and secure channel for anonymous communication. The group didn't want to know their sources; this was the best way to protect their identities.

15MPARATO put all relevant evidence of the Bankia case on their website to enable other aggrieved parties to file separate lawsuits. Even today, Xnet Leaks continues to be a platform where evidence of corruption can be submitted. If a person submitting evidence is willing to create a device themselves, Xnet will help.

Collaboration happens in phases and often activists are only together for a short time; it is difficult to expect people to participate at the same level for a sustained period. Even so, there is much pride in the fact that 12 of the original 20 members who started 15MPARATO continue to work together on similar campaigns. Ultimately, they discovered something that they did not expect; putting dozens of bankers and politicians in the dock is not as difficult as letting the public know that it is within everyone's reach.

Furthermore, through gathering first-hand information, they saw that what reached the public was something completely different. For every ten journalists who collaborated with 15MPARATO, there were ten media outlets that ignored the truth. This was obvious when Rato's wife was one of the directors of the economic section of *El País*, a leading national daily newspaper in Spain, but even more painful when other outlets selling themself as "on-the-left" failed to hold truth to power. For every genuinely civic or popular contribution that has helped and supported the movement, a political party has made it sadly clear: "Either you join our ranks and carry our brand, or we wipe you off the map as a potential competitor."

That is why the 15MPARATO decided to explain their story themselves with a theatre play, *Hazte Banquero* ("Become a Banker"), seen by more than 10,000 people in its first few months, and a book, *Votar y Cobrar*, written and directed by Simona Levi.[9] An important element of 15MPARATO was to prove that the public sector and citizens must collaborate and organise to create a healthy democracy. To quote a line from *Hazte Banquero*:

"This is the story of how government elites plundered the county. But it is also the story of how citizens got together and brought to light the truth. And how normal, ordinary people, joining forces, learning and explaining how things really happened, are changing the usual ending."[10]

Notes

1. https://catalystsforcollaboration.org.

2. https://15mparato.wordpress.com.

3. https://xnet-x.net/en.

4. Pau Llop, "#15mpaRato: yo (el pueblo) acuso", *El Diario.es*, June 5, 2012, https://www.eldiario.es/opinion/zona-critica/pueblo-acuso_129_5366734.html.

5. Simona Levi and Sergio Salgado, *Votar y Cobrar*, (Madrid: Capitán Swing, 2017).

6. Ibid.

7. Ibid.

8. https://maadix.net/en.

9. https://xnet-x.net/en/become-a-banker.

10. Simona Levi and Sergio Salgado, *Hazte Banquero*, Barcelona: A Conservas and Minoria Absoluta Production, July 5, 2016, https://youtu.be/PGZqKRjhf3o.

CHRISTOPH TRAUTVETTER

Christoph Trautvetter holds a master's degree of Public Policy from the Hertie School of Governance. He currently works with the Netzwerk Steuergerechtigkeit—a network of German NGOs campaigning for tax justice and against financial secrecy—and as an external project coordinator for the Rosa Luxemburg Stiftung project, "Who Owns Our Cities?" In the past he has worked as a forensic analyst for KPMG and on public budgets and budgetary control in the European Parliament, Germany and Zambia. His personal goal is to mobilise the majority of honest citizens and businesses, tenants, and those without hidden wealth against the unfair and destabilising impact of illicit financial flows benefitting the small minority.

CHRISTOPH TRAUTVETTER

WHO OWNS OUR CITIES?

EXPOSING DIRTY MONEY AND UNDEMOCRATIC WEALTH IN BERLIN REAL ESTATE

WHO OWNS our cities? Who owns Berlin? As short and simple as these questions might appear, they are difficult to answer. This is for two reasons. First, ownership structures are not transparent. Answering these questions requires us to draw from the work of activists, tenants, artists and researchers dedicating thousands of hours to understanding what is happening to their homes, collecting evidence about their landlords and acting as whistleblowers. It also builds on the work of data analysts and investigative journalists with leaks from Luxembourg, Panama and other secrecy jurisdictions helping to connect the individual stories to the global corporate structures and owners behind them. Second, the existing lack of transparency helps to hide both dirty money flowing into Germany from around the world and the undemocratic concentration of wealth. Consequently, abusive practices such as money-laundering, tax evasion and speculation remain hidden, and lobby groups continue to foster the myth of the friendly small-scale owner to counter political regulation.

Asking and answering the ownership question therefore has the potential to change the way that our societies work, and real estate plays a central role. This chapter will take you through the efforts of two projects exposing real estate ownership structures in Berlin, Germany. It explains why and how large real estate owners have managed to stay anonymous so far, presenting the unequal distribution of ownership as well as examples of these landlords and, finally, sketching how the findings might contribute to change.

The first is a crowd-based journalism project launched by journalists from *Correctiv* and *Tagesspiegel*, which enabled thousands of tenants to provide information on their landlords and to tell their stories. The second is a data-driven research project supported by the Rosa-Luxemburg-Stiftung that systematically connects information provided by tenants with data from company registers, official statistics and commercial market information.

Why So Many Landlords Manage to Remain Anonymous

In the century of artificial intelligence and the exploitation of big data, data protection and privacy are important values under attack from multiple sides. But in the realm of German real estate, this protection takes grotesque forms. With the birthdate and name of a person, anyone can find their residential address in an online register.[1] In contrast, the information on the legal owner of that address—even if it is a company with more than 100,000 apartments—is protected by the highest courts with recourse to data privacy.[2]

In Germany, ownership of real estate is registered in local real estate registers ("Grundbuch"). These registers contain information on the legal owner—i.e. the individual or legal entity that owns the house or apartment—and are only accessible with a legitimate interest. The information is provided mainly to those who want to buy real estate and the administration regulating real estate transfers. Tenants and journalists can also access the register, but only for individual entries and with an appropriate justification. Even for the city's administration this justification seems difficult: a very popular referendum—Deutsche Wohnen & Co Enteignen—currently calls for the expropriation of landlords with more than 3,000 apartments in the city. Tasked with evaluating the costs of such a referendum, however, the city administration rejected a more systematic analysis of information from the real estate register, arguing that such an analysis was not possible due to time constraints and a missing legal mandate.[3] Combining thousands of information requests made by tenants and journalists, therefore, has so far been the only way to get reliable information on the owners of residential real estate in Berlin.

As difficult as this is, accessing the real estate register and the legal owners is often just the first step. This is because only a part of the houses are directly owned and registered in the name of a natural person. For the majority of the city's two million apartments, the real estate register contains the name of legal entities. In many cases, their owners can be identified from official company registers from around the world and commercial databases such as Orbis, combing information from those registers. In some cases, the new beneficial ownership registers, publicly accessible in Germany and other countries in the EU and beyond as of 2020, helps to fill gaps. But for about one in ten houses, the owners behind the companies remain anonymous despite those registers. An analysis of 433 companies identified as Berlin real estate owners by its tenants, shows why.[4]

Example 1: The Anonymous Heirs of a Real Estate Empire

Until recently, the Berlin real estate market had never heard of the UK's Pears brothers. They were not listed among the owners of the more than 3,000 apartments in the Berlin Senate's cost analysis in connection to the Deutsche Wohnen & Co Enteignen referendum. The estimated 6,000 apartments they own are, according to the Grundbuch, the property of almost 50 different companies from Luxembourg. These companies ultimately belong to the three Pears; one third each, via further companies and foundations in Cyprus, the British Virgin Islands and the UK. Thanks to Luxembourg's beneficial ownership register, tenants can now identify their ultimate owners behind companies such as Marie Luise S.à.r.l online, with a few clicks and for free—provided they know where to look. Finding out how many apartments these companies actually own and what they do with them, remains difficult because neither the companies in Cyprus or the BVI nor the foundations that ultimately own them publish financial accounts.

As the analysis shows, more than four in five of the 433 companies that own Berlin real estate were registered in Berlin (269) or within Germany (88), and only five were registered in non-EU secrecy jurisdictions including Jersey, Gibraltar, the Isle of Man and Liechtenstein. Compared to London this seems few. Following a freedom of information request, the UK land register published a complete list of land titles held by overseas companies with 91% of a total of 44,022 London land titles held through secrecy jurisdictions.[5] Part of the reason for this difference might be that our sample did not cover the apartments that are usually connected to anonymous dirty money in London—namely, expensive houses owned for private use or investment rather than for the rental market.

Perhaps more importantly, a registration in Germany does not automatically lead to transparency. The shareholders of the most commonly used German companies are registered in the German "Handelsregister". For a fee of 1,5 euros this information can be accessed online, and commercial providers such as Orbis offer electronic access. For legal entities that don't have to register owners in the company register, the new "Transparenzregister" provides information of the beneficial ownership for a fee of 1,98 euros and has been publicly accessible since the beginning of 2020.

In 223 of these 357 German companies, this information leads to a natural person who is registered with their name, birthdate and address. For most of the others, however, the shareholders listed in the German company register are legal entities from outside Germany and—often in violation of the law—are not registered as a beneficial owner in Germany.

	Ultimate Owner ascertained via:			
Special-purpose vehicle located in:	German Register	Other Register	Not Ascertainable	Total
Berlin	163	34	72	269
Germany	60	3	25	88
EU	0	37	33	70
Non-EU	0	1	5	6
Total	223	75	135	433

Anonymity Of Real-Estate Owners In Berlin. Source: Henn and Trautvetter (2020).

Overall, the natural person(s) ultimately benefitting from the rental income could not be identified in 135 of the 433 companies analysed. Among those companies, secrecy jurisdictions played an important role—notable among them, Cyprus, Luxembourg, and the Netherlands. According to our estimates, in 49 cases a properly implemented beneficial ownership registry in the EU could most likely help to address the problem. But an even bigger problem are listed companies and investment funds that allow investors to invest hundreds of millions of euros into real estate around the world, hiding behind their asset managers and remaining below the 25% reporting thresholds in the beneficial ownership registers.

What We Know About the Owners So Far

With its cost-benefit ratios, outcome and impact evaluations, modern policy making aims and claims to be evidence-based. But for regulating the housing market as much as for fighting tax evasion and money-laundering, the evidence base is thin. For the census, the statistical offices collect information on all houses and their owners—the so-called "Gebäude und Wohnungszählung". Unlike in Switzerland, for example, where this is done through an automatic analysis of existing registers every year, in Germany this is done by writing letters to all known owners or administrators. This happens every ten years, with the last time in 2011. In addition, a sample-based micro census collects information on houses and their owners from the tenants every four years; the last time being in 2018.

Because the census and the micro census use different sources and different classifications for owners, the results diverge widely. The 2018 micro census classified 373,400 as being owned and rented by private individuals. In contrast, the 2011 census put this number at 571,192—without any sign that ownership structures have radically changed. Instead, this shows that a large share of private owners hide from their tenants behind corporate shells. To better understand private owners, the Federal Institute for Research on Building, Urban Affairs and

Who Owns Berlin?

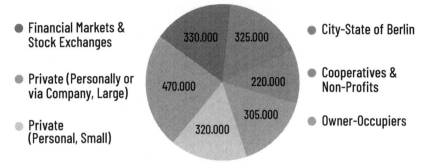

- Financial Markets & Stock Exchanges
- Private (Personally or via Company, Large)
- Private (Personal, Small)
- City-State of Berlin
- Cooperatives & Non-Profits
- Owner-Occupiers

330.000   325.000   470.000   220.000   320.000   305.000

Owners of Berlin Real Estate, 2019

Spatial Development (BBSR) conducted an additional sample-based survey in 2015—but this only reported the number of apartments according to three categories: "owned" (one, one to five, more than five), the "value of the apartments" and the "profit earned from them".[6]

Finally, the Socio-Economic Panel (SOEP) and the Income and Wealth Survey (EVS) that regularly ask for the value of real assets held and income produced, do not ask for the number of apartments, nor do they differentiate between German and foreign real assets which significantly under-samples the very wealthy. Unlike in Sweden, for example, a survey that regularly compares rental practices, rents and profits across the different ownership groups does not exist.

Despite their limitations, the statistics can tell us two things for definite. First, Germany is a country of tenants, with about every second person living for rent—in Europe, this is higher only in Switzerland. Berlin is a tenant's capital, with about 85 per cent of apartments rented. The central district of Friedrichshain-Kreuzberg is the tenant's stronghold, with only slightly more than five per cent of houses individually owned by those who live in them. Second, residential real estate has replaced farmland as the main source of wealth in Europe. Real estate wealth is slightly more equally and less violently distributed than farmland used to be in feudal Europe, and tenants have significantly more protection than the serfs who used to work the land for the noblemen. Nevertheless, half of the population continues without any wealth and live from increasingly precarious jobs while one per cent own nearly half of all homes.

Beyond the distributive statistics, the documentation of ownership and business practices varies depending on the type of owners. For the cooperatives and public housing companies that own one quarter of the city's houses, they are rather well documented. As a unique feature in comparison to other large cities, Berlin has five big publicly listed companies that own 200,000 apartments between them, and they publish detailed annual reports. Deutsche Wohnen, the company that gave the name to the expropriation campaign, is the biggest among them, owning more than half. Vonovia is the second largest, owning nearly a quarter. Together, onstitutional investors and investment funds own another 130,000 apartments; they are less transparent, but information is usually accessible to those who know where to look and have access to the commercial databases that collect information on them. Most prominent, but nonetheless largely unknown to the Berlin senate and the Berlin public until recently, is Blackstone, the US private equity company owning more than 3,000 apartments in Berlin through its opaque structures in the Cayman Islands and Luxembourg. This leaves more than half of the city's two million apartments "in the dark". It also begs the question whether the majority of these privately-held apartments are in the hand of responsible long-term investors and nice small-scale owners, as the lobby would have it, or the ruthless financial market, focused on short-term profits and a few extremely wealthy and sometimes dubious owners.

Why this obscurity is a problem and the shapes it takes is best explained with a few examples from the research project.

Example 2: The Lebanon Connection— Money-Laundered in and Out of Germany?

It all started with a call from the Drug Enforcement Administration (DEA). The DEA had tapped a conversation between a cocaine cartel and their money-laundering expert somewhere in South America, discussing operations in Europe. Based on this information, police in France and Germany began operations which, ultimately, ended with the arrest several people, mainly from Lebanese origin. These individuals had converted the cash from cocaine sales into expensive watches, exported them to Lebanon—apparently with the friendly help of the Head of Security at Hariri Airport—converted them back into cash and transferred that money through a bureau de change in the heartland of Hezbollah back to South America—sometimes via Asia to blur the trace. According to journalists who have analysed this case in depth, this one money-laundering ring laundered at least 20 million euros using expensive German watches and used cars, exported to Benin in West Africa.

German police have apparently uncovered at least seven similar Lebanese money-laundering rings in the last ten years—even though they only find much less than one percent of the money laundered through Germany.[7] Without suggesting guilt by association, there seems to be good reason for special caution with money coming from Lebanon. One case raises particular question marks. In 2019, a tenant sought to discover the owners behind her landlord, a company called Beryt Cedar Immobilien GmbH. Some research in the Berlin company register exposed a whole network of companies owning several buildings around Berlin, including one housing the tax agency, managed by two investment managers from Lebanon. These managers provided detailed information on their—totally legitimate—investment business on their website. When it came to their investors, however, they provided much less transparency. For one of their investment vehicles, they set up a company in the British Virgin Island with Mossack Fonseca, the infamous Panamanian law firm behind the Panama Papers. This company was in turn owned by 73 individuals and legal entities including managers and business people from Lebanon, a private banking client from HSBC and some very obscure entities like Invest & Interest Corp (owning 0,71 percent of the whole investment). Let's assume for a second—without having any proof or indication in that direction—that the dirty money from European cocaine business or from the weed produced in Lebanon for the European markets ended up in a Lebanese bank account and was invested through that company in German real estate. Would the Lebanese bank and the Lebanese investment manager be willing and able to identify this suspicious transaction and trace it back to Europe? Would the oversight bodies in Lebanon check? Would the German actors involved in selling the real estate, or their oversight bodies, or the German police chasing drug dealers care and check? The answer to these questions appears to be "no".

Example 3: The Indonesian Billionaire—Tax Evasion Made in Germany?

Even though it's not about Berlin—and not even about residential real estate—but about a fancy office building in the center of Munich, the following case is a perfect illustration of another important problem with real estate investors. In this case, the building was bought by a letter box company in Luxembourg for 350 million euros, set up purely for this purpose by local accountants. The Luxembourg company was in turn owned by a Singaporean family office and, as the new beneficial ownership register of Luxembourg exposed, indirectly controlled through various vehicles in the Cayman Islands by Mr. Tanoto, an Indonesian billionaire who reportedly made his money from palm oil and ruthless deforestation. Tanoto had been sanctioned for tax evasion and accused of violating human rights in the past. Questioned about the background of the deal, the German investment manager who arranged it passed the buck to the accountants in Luxembourg (who were unavailable for a press statement). Because no one in Europe apparently asked questions about the source of the funds or forwarded them to Indonesia, the Indonesia's Financial Transactions Reports and Analysis Centre was reportedly unaware of the deal. Whether the income from the German tenants is then properly taxed in Indonesia becomes increasingly unlikely with every additional layer of secrecy.

Example 4: The One-Billion Dollar Inheritance— No Tax Justice in Sight?

In the current discussions about expropriations, this company is not on the list, but with 2,884 apartments and a swathe of commercial buildings, their property in Berlin is worth more than one billion euros. This impressive portfolio is professionally managed and owned through a holding company in Zossen, an inner-German tax haven a short drive from Berlin. In turn, this company is owned by a family foundation that, according to the German register, is beneficially owned by the joint heirs and adoptive children of the founders; according to an unofficial source, about 30 third-generation descendants of the architect Georg B. and the bank director Günter K. who began amassing the fortune after the second World War and put it into the family foundations in 1962. Why their heirs should continue to benefit from operational surpluses of about 30 million euros a year, and why Berlin tenants should pay for this, should be at least debated openly.

Example 5: The Friendly Real Estate Agent and His Obscure Business—The Healthy Rays of Transparency!

Mr. Ziegert has made his own fortune as a real estate agent and is not shy of publicity. He has named his company after himself and has given extensive press interviews. He is also the founder of a charitable—and tax-exempted—foundation with the goal, among others, of promoting home ownership. What has been unknown to the public, and at least to some of his company's clients, is that a second part of his business seems to contradict the goals of his foundation. Using several companies such as Lebensgut and Assoziation Bankum, like the family foundation Becker & Kries registered in the tax haven of Zossen, he bought Altbau buildings mainly in and around Kreuzberg, renovated them, and legally split them up into individual apartments. He then sold these apartments to individuals, in some cases without the knowledge of his clients, acting as both the owner and the agent. Instead of faraway secrecy jurisdictions, he used a simple German vehicle—the so-called "Aktiengesellschaft"—not requiring the registration of shareholders, and using a lawyer from a company service provider to serve as the official owner in the beneficial ownership register. Thanks to the persistent efforts of the tenants from the houses, the threat of being bought by Lebensgut and the confrontation of these findings after over a year of extensive research by a journalist from

Disruption Network Lab's *Berlin City Tour: Visiting the Invisible* with Christoph Trautvetter, in partnership with Rosa Luxemburg Stiftung, August 30, 2020.
Photo by Maria Silvano.

Berliner Zeitung, Mr. Ziegert was exposed. He claimed a right to anonymity and held that he was trying to avoid a competitive disadvantage that would have otherwise forced him to pay higher prices given his reputation. He also claimed that the wrong entry in the beneficial ownership register was simply a lapse that would be (and was) corrected.[8]

How Exposing Ownership Structures Can Lead to Change

Germany is a democracy and prides itself on its strong rule of law tradition. Democratically approved and evenly implemented laws should create healthy societies—at least in theory. But this theory does not work when laws can be circumvented through anonymous secrecy jurisdictions, money can buy influence over decision-making and a lack of information hinders a well-informed public and political debate. Healthy societies crack when the promise that everyone can earn their share and place in society through effort and work falls short, and when normal salaries are not enough to buy a house or even pay rent in the place that people live or chose to live in. With the threat to the homes and livelihoods of the urban middle-classes comes pressure for change. By making these threats visible and tangible—individual tenants telling their stories, artists turning them into "art as evidence", as well as research and technology making structural information accessible—we can disrupt the mechanisms that, ultimately, endanger democracy. In Berlin and around the world, countless examples and projects have shown the power and potential of bringing information about real estate ownership and wealth distribution into the light. Now the structural changes need to follow.

First, registers of real estate, companies and beneficial ownership need to become open and open-data to allow for more structural and scientific analysis. Berlin is working on both a local solution for a so-called "Mietenkataster" and has proposed changes to the availability of information at a federal level through an open "Immobilienregister". In the meantime, Berlin tenants can find and report information about their landlords at www.wemgehoertdiestadt.de, and an extension of the project to other cities and countries is in the making. Second, and most importantly, laws have to change based on newly acquired information. Taxes on inheritance, wealth and value gains need to ensure that work and effort matter more than birth and choosing the right investment manager. The regulation of construction and maintenance, rents and rental contracts and, last but not least, transactions need to ensure that buildings are managed responsibly and that the interests of tenants and landlords are balanced and aligned. If all that does not help, well targeted corrective measures such as expropriation need to be applied. Without the work of whistleblowers, abusive business models and modes of tax evasion and money-laundering will continue to evolve faster than the regulation made to prevent them. Without good data, evidence-driven and democratically legitimised laws will remain an illusion, and the necessary disruptive change will only happen when whistleblowers and good data come together with activists, artists and politicians to draw on them. Answering the question of "who owns our cities" is a significant step in that direction.

Notes

1. The so-called "Melderegister" can be accessed online for a fee of five euros at https://service.berlin.de/ dienstleistung/120732/. Simple extracts (i.e. first and second name, current address) are provided without any justification. With legitimate interest, more complex requests can be made. Individuals can request protection of their information but the burden to justify such a request is high.

2. In 2020, the Federal Court of Justice rejected a request by parliamentarians from the Berlin parliament to the real estate register for information about the houses owned by Deutsche Wohnen in the city. The justification analyses the limitations of the right to parliamentary oversight but also notes that the right to access the real estate register is limited due to data privacy reasons (compare https://openjur. de/u/2198733.html, III. 2. (2) aa).

3. Cost analysis is a normal requirement of a referendum and was provided by the Senate on March 1, 2019. For more detail: https://www.dwenteignen.de/2019/03/enteignung-kann-haushaltsneutral-sein/.

4. Due to lack of access to data, the 433 companies are not the result of a random sample but (with some exceptions, like the missing coverage of individual and expensive flats intentionally left empty and possibly bought through offshore companies), they seem to be a good representation of the ownership structure. For more details compare Henn and Trautvetter (2020): https://www.rosalux.de/publikation/id/42141.

5. For more detail: https://www.transparency.org.uk/publications/faulty-towers-understanding-the-impact-of-overseas-corruption-on-the-london-property-market. The complete and regularly updated data for England and Wales can be accessed via https://www.gov.uk/guidance/hm-land-registry-overseas-companies-that-own-property-in-england-and-wales#access-the-data and also covers owners from the UK.

6. Available at: https://www.bbsr.bund.de/BBSR/DE/veroeffentlichungen/bbsr-online/2015/ON022015.html.

7. The people involved were arrested and convicted at the end of 2018. The case draws on court documents from France and Germany. The watch sellers are still under investigation and the Head of Security at Hariri airport still seems to be working in his old job. More information: https://www.ndr.de/nachrichten/info/podcasts/Die-Libanon-Connection-Geldwaesche-fuer-die-Kokain-Kartelle,organisiertesverbrechen100.html (in German).

8. The article can be found here: https://www.berliner-zeitung.de/wirtschaft-verantwortung/der-geheime-eigentuemer-li.79219 (in German) and the reactions here: https://www.berliner-zeitung.de/mensch-metropole/harsche-kritik-an-ziegerts-undurchsichtigem-konstrukt-li.79347 (in German).

5

EXPOSING INJUSTICE

CHALLENGING DISCRIMINATION & DOMINANT NARRATIVES

DARYL DAVIS
CHARLOTTE WEBB
MAGNUS AG
OS KEYES

SUPREMACIST ideologies, deliberate disinformation, hate speech, and the spreading of false facts are on the rise. It becomes urgent to expose injustices and human rights violations, and to challenge dominant narratives. This section provides a careful analysis of power asymmetries, focusing on the importance of a collective effort to reveal wrongdoing. Musician and author Daryl Davis, who made a difference as a Black American befriending members of the Ku Klux Klan since the 1980s, and making them leave the Klan, exposes the reasons behind White supremacy, racial hate and the recent US Capitol insurrection. His piece outlines the grounds of the stigmatisation of truth-tellers, starting from the adoption of the informal Blue Code of Silence shared among police officers to protect colleagues' misconduct, leading to severe violence against Black people. Tracing the line of exposing discriminations,

Charlotte Webb reflects on how feminist practices are able to reveal abuses and injustices derived by a problematic construction of gender in techno-social systems, deconstructing sexist representations of women in technology devices. Magnus Ag, sharing his experience as a journalist during the 2019 Hong Kong protests and as a human rights advocate, reflects on the power of citizens and artists in challenging dominant narratives. He brings many examples of how truth-tellers and dissidents have used creative practices to denounce oppression, resulting in many cases in imprisonment and censorship. In the final chapter, researcher on the politics of technology Os Keyes reflects on the meaning of social change through speaking out. They highlight the importance of addressing whistleblowing and truth-telling as a collective practice, going beyond the artificial dichotomy of whistleblowers as being either heroes or traitors.

DARYL DAVIS

Known as the Rock'n'Roll Race Reconciliator, award-winning musician Daryl Davis tours nationally and internationally with his own band and has worked extensively with the late, great Chuck Berry, Elvis Presley's Jordanaires, The Legendary Blues Band and many others. He is also an actor and author who is considered an expert on White supremacy. His book *Klan-Destine Relationships* and documentary *Accidental Courtesy* detail his work with the Ku Klux Klan, neo-Nazis and other White supremacists and racists. Today, Daryl owns numerous KKK robes & hoods given to him by active members who renounced their racist ideology after meeting him. As a race relations expert, he has received numerous awards for his work and is often sought by news media as a consultant on race relations and White supremacy and nationalism. His latest book is *The Klan Whisperer* (forthcoming). More information at DarylDavis.com.

DARYL DAVIS
ANOTHER TYPE OF WHISTLEBLOWER
EXPOSING THE PUBLIC TO OVERT & COVERT SOCIETAL TRUTHS

ACCORDING TO the National Whistleblower Centre (NWC), succinctly put, a whistleblower is defined as a person who reports wrongdoing such as corruption, abuse, waste, fraud, illegal activities, and dangers to public health and safety to someone in the authoritative position to rectify these issues and problems. The whistleblower typically, but not always, works within the public or private corporation, company, or group on which he is reporting.[1]

In a broader sense of the definition of a whistleblower given by the NWC, I too fit the description of a whistleblower. I work, live in, and am a citizen of the public corporation, company, and group of people known as the United States of America. Additionally, I and others like me are subjected to abuse and danger within the public space, perpetrated by those within the private space surrounding us, known as White supremacy. Racism and the ongoing identity crisis of White supremacy is, without a doubt, the oldest and greatest danger threatening the health and safety of the United States today. Yet at the same time, it is the least recognized and even less addressed. It is for these reasons I am blowing the whistle, which in its original definition means to sound the alarm. This originated when police officers would blow their whistles to indicate to other police in the vicinity that something was amiss and to summon them to come and help. The modern usage of the term "whistleblower" was coined in the 1970s by activist Ralph Nader to give the action a more positive and ethical connotation. The intent was to separate it from negative terms such as "snitch" and "informer".[2] However today in some circles including police, the terms "whistleblowers", "snitches", and "informers", are considered synonymous.

What separates me as a whistleblower from those defined by the NWC points to the legal aspect—there are laws specifically created to protect the whistleblowers who fit the definition as given by the NWC. These laws were designed to prevent the identity of the whistleblower from being exposed, which would subject him to negative and retaliatory consequences. Even though a company cannot legally fire someone for whistleblowing, they may find or create another excuse to terminate the employee from the company. Consequences for whistleblowing include being fired from one's job, alienation by fellow employees, having one's job made harder by assigning a heavier workload, cutting one's hours, creating an unpleasant atmosphere between the whistleblower and his coworkers, physical harm and even death.

There are also rewards available to whistleblowers who fit the legal definition. These rewards are two-fold: (1) to encourage whistleblowers to come forward with information that would negatively impact the entity on which the whistleblower is reporting, and (2) realizing the potential consequences the whistleblower will likely suffer, the entity will compensate the whistleblower financially.

For the risks I take and the truths I tell by blowing the whistle and exposing the fraud, disguises, and hidden truths behind White supremacy, I am not protected by the law, nor am I compensated. While I have a lot of support from those who may not take the risks I do, but who are inspired to support furthering my mission, I am also the target of threats by White supremacists. I have also been the recipient of condemnation by some people who look like me, who falsely accuse me of "selling out", by spending time with White supremacists in attempts to offer them better and more positive perspectives on their falsely perceived realities. This is the story of a Black man blowing the whistle on the identity crisis and anxiety of White supremacists.

The Blue Code (or Wall) of Silence

Omertà is a term used by Cosa Nostra, otherwise known as the Italian Mafia. It simply means "code of silence", warning those with knowledge not to reveal any information about illegal activity to anyone, usually the police or anyone in the judicial court system. Ironically, police have a similar code known as the Blue Code of Silence or The Blue Wall of Silence.

Nobody likes a snitch, an informer, or a whistleblower, especially when that person is one of their own. Breaking the code in the Mafia is a guaranteed way to end up on the wrong side of the dirt. The same can also apply to police officers who break the code. They find themselves alienated by their fellow officers, being given undesirable assignments, and even having their lives put at risk. An officer whose whistleblowing is leaked, may find his fellow officers slow to respond to his distress call for backup. Responding slowly, or even failing to show up to an officer's call for backup, is a common tactic which imperils the safety and life of the officer requesting the assistance of other officers. Ironically, while police officers detest their own snitches, they rely on criminal snitches to feed them information so they can make their arrests and rise through the ranks. The Blue Code of Silence is what allows police officers to act with impunity and blatant wanton disregard for the law when they wish to over-exert their authority over others who they deem to be inferior for any reason, including race.

In August of 1997, NYPD Officer Justin Volpe responded to a call about a fight at a nightclub. He would claim that a Black man named Abner Louima attacked him when he arrived. Officer Volpe would later admit he lied about Louima attacking him. Louima was in fact, not even involved in the incident to which the police responded. Volpe simply wanted to arrest someone and use excessive force. Louima happened to be walking in the vicinity.

Louima was placed in the police car where he was beaten with nightsticks and fists by police officers led by Officer Volpe. The beatings continued at the police station. Volpe then took a broken, jagged toilet plunger handle or broken broomstick and forced into Louima's rectum while other NYPD officers held him down. Louima's rectum and anus were ripped and torn. His bladder was punctured, and his colon was severed. Volpe then removed the jagged broom handle with blood and excrement and forced it into Louima's mouth with such force it damaged his teeth. Volpe explained that the damage done to Louima was a result of his being a homosexual who had been engaging in rough consensual sex with someone. The other officers involved with Volpe supported his lie under their Blue Code.[3]

Chicago Police Detective and Commander Jon Burge was responsible for the torture of more than 200 innocent men, mostly Black, in order to force confessions. He would use electric shock to their genitals, hold loaded guns to the heads of their children and shoot their pets, in addition to beating his arrestees. [4,5]

In 1991 a Black motorist named Rodney King was tasered, kicked and beaten, getting his teeth broken and knocked out, while lying on the ground not resisting arrest. This egregious assault, caught on camera by a citizen, showed the perpetrators as being four LAPD White officers. Ten other White officers stood by watching, and not one intervened to stop the violence perpetrated by their own.[6]

One of the most affluent counties in the United States is Montgomery County, Maryland. The MCPD has had a vast history of racism in its police force. An investigation was conducted and, in 2000, the US Department of Justice (DOJ) and the MCPD entered into a Consent Decree Memorandum of Agreement (MOA). The MOA set forth changes to be implemented in regard to complaints of a racial nature including racial profiling.[7]

In 1981, the Grand Dragon of the Maryland Knights of the Ku Klux Klan conspired to bomb a synagogue in Baltimore, MD. He had been a Baltimore City Police officer who had committed numerous transgressions of racial illegal activity while on the force. The BCPD was well aware of his Klan activities but were willing to turn a blind eye as long as he did not bring embarrassment to the Department. He continued with his violent racist Klan activities, and the BCPD was forced to let him go. Grand Dragon White served 4 years in prison for conspiring to bomb the synagogue. In 1989, he was sentenced to 3 years in prison for assault with intent to murder two Black men with a shotgun. [8, 9]

Through my work with him, this former Baltimore City Police Officer and Grand Dragon in the KKK, quit the Klan and became a very good friend of mine. Today, I own his Grand Dragon robe and hood and his police uniform. He confessed to me that he was not the only KKK member in the BCPD and told of numerous racial crimes he had committed. The Baltimore City Police Department has been plagued with racism for decades. In 2017, the Baltimore City Police Department (BCPD) entered into a Consent Decree with the DOJ similar to the one with the MCPD.[10]

On May 25, 2020, the world witnessed four Minneapolis police officers, led by White Officer Derek Chauvin, lynch a compliant, non-resisting Black man named George Floyd on the street. This intentional murder of Mr. Floyd was captured live on cell phone video, while Mr. Floyd begged the officers to let him breathe and called out for his dead mother. Citizens on the sidewalk pleaded with the officers to let Mr. Floyd breathe. Officer Chauvin continued choking Mr. Floyd by cutting off his air supply by kneeling on his neck and compressing his windpipe for 9 minutes and 29 seconds until he was dead. Officer Chauvin refused to allow a paramedic to check on Mr. Floyd during the lynching.[11]

Despite the negative press given to police and despite a summer of violence following the George Floyd lynching in May 2020, in December 2020, two White Virginia police officers threatened to kill a US Army soldier who was stopped for no other reason than his being Black. The Army vet is now suing the Virginia police.[12]

In 2006, a Black female police officer from the Buffalo, New York Police Department named Cariol Horne was fired for stopping a White fellow police officer from using a chokehold on a handcuffed suspect. Other police officers lied to cover-up for the choke-holding officer and Horne was fired in 2008. She had served 19 years on the Buffalo Police Department. In an interview Horne said, "The message was sent that you don't cross the blue line..." In April 2021, a New York judge ruled that Horne be given her pension and back pay. In an interview, Horne was asked if she felt vindicated by the court's decision. She stated that she would not feel vindicated until all police whistleblowers felt vindicated. She said she will continue to push for police accountability.[13]

A change in policy may be on the horizon as there appears to be a history-making crack in the Blue Wall of Silence. The Police Chief of the Minneapolis Police Department and other high-ranking officers have broken rank and broken the Blue Code and testified in the current trial of their former officer Derek Chauvin in the lynching of George Floyd. They testified against Chauvin. This is extremely rare, but hopefully it is a sign of police turning over a new leaf and instilling trust in the community. All police take an oath to "Serve and Protect". Hopefully, we will see more of them serving and protecting the communities they are sworn to serve and protect, rather than serving and protecting each other.[14]

The Tea Party

During the ascension to the White House of the 44th and first Black President of the United States, Barack Obama, the political arena within the Republican party gave birth to a new movement called The Tea Party. The last time America had heard of a Tea Party was just prior to the commencement of the Revolutionary War between America and Britain in 1775. The Boston Tea Party was formed as a political protest movement created to express the discontent of American Colonialists over the British imposing hefty taxes on the Colonists in order to pay for Britain's debts without any representation by the Colonists. To clearly show their anger and frustration, the American Colonists dumped 342 large chests of tea from a British East India company into the Boston Harbor, sparking the flame for the soon-to-come Revolutionary War. Their slogan became, "Taxation Without Representation".[15] Now, some 230 years later, a loose political party movement bearing the same name was born in the dawning of the Obama Presidency. Although they would claim its name stemmed from the same desire of its namesake predecessor to demand lower taxes, its slogan this time, "Take Our Country Back", harkened back to a racist slogan just a little over 50 years prior to the second incarnation of The Tea Party.

In 1954, the United States Supreme Court, in a landmark case, Brown v. Board of Education, ruled unanimously to desegregate schools. The leading and largest racist organization, or gang, as it has been referred to, the Ku Klux Klan, held rallies throughout the South. With a burning cross in the background, while standing behind a podium microphone, Grand Dragons and Imperial Wizards angrily declared at the top of their lungs, "We're not going to let our little White boys and girls go to school with little niggers! We're gonna take our country back!!!" Thus, was born the Klan slogan, "Take Our Country Back", meaning back to segregation. Why would the Tea Party of the 21st century adopt a racist slogan of the 20th century? I intended to find out.

On September 12, 2009 tens of thousands of the Tea Party movement descended on the US Capitol in what was to be the largest protest against President Obama during his entire 8-year administration.[16] Their protest was held under the guise of rejecting Obama's policies on taxation, health care, immigration and just about everything for which he stood. I asked a couple of Tea Party members why they were using a racist slogan. They quickly denied being racist and claimed their protest against Obama had nothing to do with the colour of his skin. They pointed out that the Tea Party movement also had Black supporters. I pointed out that many

Trump in Dallas, September 14, 2015. Photo by Jamelle Bouie (CC BY 2.0).

White organizations, corporations, and the like had been using token Blacks since integration in order to shield themselves from being referred to as racist. While the Tea Party is made up of mostly Republican Americans with very conservative values, there are indeed some Black Conservatives who share those values. At the same time there are some Blacks who feel they can get ahead if they align themselves with White values and that Whites will elevate them to higher positions in order to prove they are not racist. Then you have self-loathing people of any color, ethnicity or religion who will identify with those who also loathe them.

I brought up the fact that they were using a KKK slogan and pointed to the sign one of them was holding which read, "Take Our Country Back", and signs scattered throughout the crowd, bearing the same slogan and similar variations such as, "Take Back Our Country", and "Take America Back". "How can you tell me this isn't racist? You are aware the KKK used these same slogans back in 1954 when Brown v. Board of Education desegregated schools and throughout integration, are you not?"

One of them said he had never heard that, while the other one acknowledged he had but quickly said, "That had another meaning back then, but that's not how we mean it".

"Well, you say, 'Take Our Country Back.' You don't say take it back from whom or take it back to what. Instead, you leave it open-ended. So, it is therefore open for interpretation. I think it's a dog whistle to racists", I pushed back.

"No sir. What we mean is take our country back from the Democrats, take it back to Republican rule", he replied.

"Well, if that were the case, I could live with that. Then why don't you say so and close the gap, leaving no room for misinterpretation? But I don't believe that's the case. From George to George, in other words, from Washington to Bush, we've had nothing but White men in the White House. Now there's a Black man in the White

House and suddenly there's a new political movement called the Tea Party who's screaming 'Take Our Country Back.' Jimmy Carter was a Democrat, Bill Clinton was a Democrat. Where was the Tea Party then? Why weren't you shouting 'Take Our Country Back' during their Presidencies?" The two Tea Party members were left speechless and our conversation ended politely on that note. We shook hands and went our separate ways.

The Tea Party had a song written for it by singer/songwriter Chris Cassone, which the Tea Party used as its anthem. Can you guess the name of the song? You got it, *Take Our Country Back*.[17] Well-known comedienne, actress and activist Janeane Garofalo who appeared on MSNBC's "Countdown with Keith Olberman", had this to say: "It's not about bashing Democrats. It's not about taxes. They have no idea what the Boston Tea Party was about. They don't know their history at all. This is about hating a Black man in the White House. This is racism straight up. That is nothing but a bunch of tea-bagging rednecks".[18] I would not characterize the entire Tea Party movement as Ms. Garofalo did in her last sentence, but I wholeheartedly agree with her sentiment that it is about their dislike of having a Black man in the White House.

Confederate Monuments, Flags, and Buildings Named After Slaveowners

"It doesn't stand for hate, it stands for heritage", are the words often spoken when White Americans attempt to defend a flag that represents hatred and the defense of owning human beings of darker pigmentation. Although many who fly the flag will dispute this, make no mistake about it, the American Civil War was fought over slavery. In the Northern States, school systems teach exactly that. In the Southern States, students learn that the Civil War was fought over States Rights. Yes, those teachers and textbooks are correct. The Civil War was indeed fought over States Rights; the State's right to own slaves.

Not only do many American adults and current students not know their own history, but many of them don't even know their own flags. What is often referred to as the Rebel Flag or the Confederate Flag is in fact the Confederate Battle Flag and not the official flag of the CSA (Confederate States of America). The original CSA flag of 1861 consisted of three stripes; a red stripe at the top and bottom with a white stripe in between, and a blue square in the upper left-hand corner containing seven silver stars arranged in a circle. That same year, that same flag would go through three additional incarnations: the same design with nine stars, then 11 stars, and finally, thirteen stars representing the 13 Southern States. The flag used in battle for which Confederate soldiers shed their blood and lost their lives, has a red background with two blue crossbars forming the shape of an X, with thirteen silver stars equally arranged within the blue bars. This is the Confederate Battle

Flag, most often and mistakenly called the Confederate Flag or the Rebel Flag by those who deny or don't know their own history.

Anyone who knows American History knows that there were Blacks and Jews who also fought in the Confederacy. Blacks in the South were enslaved people who had to fight for their slave masters. There were plenty of Jewish slave owners in the South who, like all slave owners, did not want to give up that free labor and have to pay someone to pick cotton and tobacco from which the plantation owners became very wealthy. The Civil War was fought to maintain that tradition and free wealth. Leading that charge against the Whites, Blacks, and Jews in the North, was the Confederate Battle Flag.

On August 12, 2017, the White supremacist *Unite The Right* rally was held in Charlottesville, Virginia under the guise of protesting the removal of Confederate statues from the city parks of Charlottesville. While there were some people in attendance who were actually there to defend the statues, the real reason behind the rally was far more sinister. Representatives of every imaginable White supremacist group calling themselves supremacists, separatists, nationalists, and Alt Right, were in attendance. Whatever distinctions they wanted to draw between them, the one thing they all had in common was the fact that they all were racist. Despite the fact that they all claimed they were not there to promulgate hate, but to preserve their Confederate heritage, many neo-Nazi groups were there speaking on behalf of their beliefs.

Wait a minute, neo-Nazis? Yes, those people who years later still uphold and promote the values of the original Nazi, Adolf Hitler. Why were the bastard offspring of Hitler in Charlottesville promoting antisemitism, racism, and his values? Because, as I stated earlier, despite the organizers of the rally (who I know personally) stating it was about heritage, it was about hate.

Even Ku Klux Klan and neo-Nazi relic David Duke attended the Charlottesville White supremacist rally. When asked by an interviewer what this day meant to him, he replied, "This represents a turning point. For the people of this country, we are determined to take our country back. We are going to fulfil the promises of Donald Trump. That's what we believed in. That's what we voted for Donald Trump, and because he said he's going to take our country back and that's what we gotta do".[19]

Again, anyone who knows history, knows that Nazis have no heritage in Charlottesville, Virginia. Adolf Hitler was born in 1889, twenty-four years after the Civil War ended in 1865. The Nazis did not even exist during America's Civil War. The only thing neo-Nazis had in common with the Ku Klux Klan, the Alt Right, and the other racist groups that day, was their common White supremacy and hatred of Blacks and Jews. Those who know American History should also know that the United States fought against the Nazis in WWII. Many grandfathers and great-grandfathers of those at this rally lost their lives fighting in WWII against

Confederate Flag's Strange Companions, February 24, 2017.
Photo by Don Sniegowski (CC BY-NC-SA 2.0).

the Nazis. Now, 72 years later, adult grandchildren and great-grandchildren are walking down the streets of Charlottesville, side-by-side with neo-Nazis flying swastikas. Remind me again why the neo-Nazis were in Charlottesville? It wasn't because of heritage. We knew nothing about swastikas during our Civil War. Today the swastika is even banned from display in Germany. So what do German neo-Nazis use in its place? The American Confederate Battle Flag. Even to them, it is a symbol of White supremacy. According to Neo-Nazis in Germany, the White supremacy embedded in Confederate iconography is useful. It's a stand-in for the Nazi swastika, which has been banned in Germany since the Holocaust.[20]

The American Revolutionary War was fought against Britain who lost that war. Thus, the United States celebrates the Fourth of July. There are plenty of Americans of British descent who have British ancestors who fought in the American Revolution. While they may respect their ancestors who lost the War, they don't go out and build statues to King George III and fly the Union Jack. The losers do not get to erect their statues and fly their flags on the winner's land. Similarly, the US went to war against Japan when the Japanese bombed Pearl Harbor. There are plenty of Japanese-Americans who have ancestors who fought in that war. Japan lost the war. These Japanese-Americans do not build statues to Emperor Hirohito and fly the Japanese flag. The US went to war against Germany to bring down Hitler's regime and the Third Reich. Germany was defeated. There are plenty of German-Americans with Nazi lineage, but most of them do not fly swastikas and build statues to Adolf Hitler, Adolf Eichmann, Joseph Goebbels or Josef Mengele.

Something is obviously missing in the educational system of American schools. The Confederacy lost the War to the Union. This is the United States of America (USA), not the Confederate States of America (CSA). The descendants of those Confederate soldiers need to accept it and get over it. The loser does not get to build their statues and fly their flags on the winner's land. Until that is accepted we will be the DSA (Divided States of America).

I am a firm believer that history needs to be preserved; the good, the bad, the ugly, and the shameful. I do not believe Confederate statues, monuments, flags, and buildings named after slave owners should be ripped down and destroyed, leaving no trace of their existence. I believe that the names on the buildings should be changed and the statues and flags should be placed in a museum or Confederate Memorial Park. Just as there is much we can learn from the items in a Holocaust Museum, Americans should learn equally from their good history as well as from their historical mistakes and wrongdoing.

The US Capitol Insurrection

Predicated on his lie about the Presidential Election being stolen from him, on January 6, 2021, the 45th President of the United States of America, Donald J. Trump, rallied his radicalized base of supporters. Trump then gave a lecture to them in which he used the phrase, "Take back our country", telling them strength must be used and to not show weakness.[21] Trump then sent them on a mission of insurrection to the US Capitol for the purpose of overturning the election results and declaring him the winner. During his Presidential campaign speeches in 2015, Trump had promised to, "Take our country back".[22]

Donald Trump certainly by no means invented racism and White supremacy. But since becoming President of the United States, he has definitely catered to it and emboldened it to a higher degree than we've seen since the 1960s. Racism and White supremacy have always existed in this country, just under the rug. Trump ripped up the carpet and exposed the dirty floor beneath. His mob of upwards of 30,000 supporters stormed the US Capitol, rioting and breaking windows, stealing laptops, defecating and urinating in the offices of elected officials. They brought a makeshift gallows and noose with the intent of hanging Vice President Michael Pence for not attempting to overturn the election results. They threatened to murder Speaker of the House Nancy Pelosi as well as some Democrat Congressmen and Senators. While it does not apply to all of Trump's supporters, Hillary Clinton's term, "Deplorables", was most fitting on January 6, 2021 inside the US Capitol.

Almost 74,000,000 people voted for Donald Trump in 2020. The majority of them claimed the election was rigged and stolen from the rightful President. Not all Trump supporters are racist, yet all racists support Trump. His supporters, who stormed the Capitol that day on Trump's instruction, were brainwashed and radicalized. Many of the racists among them had been brainwashed into

Capitol riot on January 6, 2021. Left: Gallows and noose. Photo by Tyler Merbler (CC-BY-2.0)
Right: Capitol rioter with Camp Auschwitz T-shirt. Photos: EOG/Unknown (Twitter)

White supremacy years before Trump ever ran for the Presidency. While some US Presidents in previous administrations had been somewhat leaning to the right, Trump's right-leaning was at full tilt. His supporters felt he had given them full *Carte Blanche* to do whatever they felt necessary to protect their White race. It is interesting that the meaning of "carte blanche", is the ability to act freely and do whatever one wants to do. Perhaps that's why the color blanche (meaning white in French) was chosen. The term can also be considered synonymous with "White privilege". Calling it something like *Carte Noir* would never have worked.

These particular Trump supporters realized that he was the only President in recent history whose views on race aligned with theirs. His criticisms of Blacks, gays, Muslims, and Mexicans were unprecedented. No past US President had called African countries and third world non-White countries "shitholes", when referring to people coming to the US from Haiti and African countries with darker people. He then asked why more people couldn't come here from "Norway", which is predominantly White.[23] Trump's comment about there being, "fine people on both sides", when referring to neo-Nazis, defenders of slavery and counter pro-testers at the White supremacist rally in Charlottesville during his watch, did not fall on deaf ears.[24] Instead, it signalled to, emboldened, and invigorated racists to continue with their activities because they had the support of the most powerful man in the world. In the 30,000 person mob, there were more Trump flags than US flags. One of the rioters was seen roaming the inside of the Capitol with the Confederate Battle Flag, determined to take the country back. Perhaps ex-President Trump's "Fine people", comment is what emboldened at least one White supremacist anti-Semite man to boldly and completely identifiably, enter the US

Capitol wearing a neo-Nazi Camp Auschwitz tee-shirt while participating in the insurrection.

Trump's cult supporters realized their chief ally, best endorser, and biggest sponsor would no longer be able to put the weight of the Oval Office behind their efforts if he was voted out of office. All of the perceived progress they had made over the last four years in their effort to "Take Our Country Back", and "Make America Great Again", would come to an end if the election results were not overturned and Donald Trump was not reinstated as the winner and true President of the United States. They had come this far with the help of a President who understood them and shared their values and now it was up to them to thwart the racial progress America was trying to make and fulfil the slogan of their cult leader Donald Trump, to Make America Great Again.

Any candidate running for President of the United States, would say they are going to make America great, or even greater than it's ever been. No one but a racist would say they would "Make America Great Again". We understood what the Ku Klux Klan meant in 1954 when they said they would "Take Our Country Back". It came on the heels of integration and they wanted the country to remain segregated. No explanation was necessary. While some White people may not have understood the racial implications of the Tea Party's use of that same slogan, Black people knew what it meant all too well. A Black man had just been elected to the White House and some people couldn't handle it. Likewise, Black people knew without a doubt what the word, "Again", implied at the end of Trump's slogan. When was "again?" Was it back when Blacks had to sit in the back of the bus, or drink from a separate water fountain, or perhaps be denied service at hotels, stores, and restaurants? When you've made progress but haven't yet attained equality, who the hell wants to go backwards to a past era and live it "Again???" For the mob of Trump rioters who damaged the Capitol and attacked and killed a police officer, it wasn't about taxes, healthcare, and a rigged election. It was about restoring and maintaining their racist lives.

2042

"My VCR is going to stop working! The world is going to blow up! The computers in the banks are going to crash and I'll lose all my money!" were just some of the cries of panicked people, both educated and uneducated, in 1999 as the turn of the millennium and the year 2000 was rapidly approaching. Conspiracies abounded and this unfounded panic was referred to as Y2K. Fearing bank computers crashing, many people withdrew their lifesavings from banks and hid them in their homes or buried them on their properties. Of course, Y2K came, and the world continued spinning on its axis and revolving around the sun. Bank computers did not crash, and VCRs continued to work for those people who were a little behind in upgrading to DVD players and recorders.

Now, twenty-one years past Y2K, many people are having a similar panic, especially those who identify themselves as White supremacists, White separatists, White nationalist, or Alt Right. Those who don't identify with these groups, simply identify these people as racists.

In 1974 when I was 15 years old, Matt Koehl had taken over as head of the American Nazi Party after its founder and leader George Lincoln Rockwell was murdered by one of his own American Nazis named John Palter. Matt Koehl told me that I and all Blacks would be shipped back to Africa and that all Jews would be sent to Israel. If we did not go voluntarily, we would all be exterminated in the upcoming race war. That was the first time I had heard the term "race war". I would later learn it was also referred to by White supremacists as RaHoWa, an acronym for Racial Holy War. More recently it is also referred to as "The Boogaloo". Eight years later in 1982, as a 22-year-old adult, I met Matt Koehl again. He told me the White race was committing genocide through miscegenation with mud races such as mine and that his Aryan race was becoming a mongrel race as a result. He then reminded me of the upcoming race war and told me that my skin color was my uniform and it was the uniform of the enemy.

Twenty-five years after meeting him, some of Matt Koehl's fears were becoming realized. White Flight is defined as White people moving out from an all-White neighborhood when non-Whites begin moving in and the neighborhood becomes more diverse. These particular White people take flight to another all-White neighborhood. It's not too long before they start "flying" again.

Today, White flight barely exists, because the color of the American landscape has changed so much that no matter where White people go, there is someone else already there who does not look like them. What I am told by KKK, neo-Nazi, and Alt Right members is, "Daryl, I don't want my grandkids to be brown". They refer to it as, "The Browning of America", and "White Genocide". Some of these people were not even born the first time I met Matt Koehl, but they continue to echo his sentiments.

According to US Census estimates and those who monitor populations, it is well-believed and expertly projected that the year 2042 will render the United States 50% White and 50% non-White for the first time in its history. Some sources speculate that Whites will become the minority population in the US in 2042, for the first time since before the killing off of Native American Indians and the banishing of survivors of that population to reservations.[25] While the number of White Americans who accept and welcome this transition is high, there are a good many others who do not want to accept this evolution and are ready to stop it in its tracks. They hide behind fighting illegal immigration, preserving racist statues and flags under the guise of heritage as opposed to hate. Their concern over illegal

254   Daryl Davis · Another Type of Whistleblower

immigration is not about those coming from Canada, the UK, or Eastern Europe, but more about those coming from Haiti and African countries, or as President Trump put it, coming from "shithole countries".

Believing their only hope to take their country back was to overturn the election and reinstall Trump as President, around 30,000 of his supporters wearing his slogan MAGA (Make America Great Again) hats stormed the US Capitol and rioted in a failed insurrection that resulted in six deaths, including Trump's racist thugs murdering a Capitol Police officer.[26] Some of these racists marched through the Capitol carrying Trump flags as well as the Confederate Battle Flag, ravishing the personal belonging of Congressmen and Senators, while destroying government property and displaying a total disregard for American Democracy. Depending upon how one may wish to look at it, perhaps at the end of his four years, President Donald J. Trump did fulfil his promise to Make America Great Again. He practically destroyed his own political party, the Republican Party, and cost the Republicans the Presidency, the Senate, and the House. That will be his legacy, and if that is his definition of Making America Great Again, he certainly achieved it.

Now his base is left with a broken, defeated, and deflated leader. They will be left to their own devices to change the course of the country and save it from the impending doom they predict will happen in 21 years from now, when unless they declare RaHoWa, their world of White supremacy will end. As their Doomsday approaches, more and more groups are promoting fear as a recruitment tool, with the promise to once again, "Take Our Country Back". When these groups don't move fast enough, some of their members strike out on their own, figuring, "If the Klan can't do it and the neo-Nazis and Alt Right can't do it, I'll do it myself". Thus appears the creation that is known as the lone wolf. These are the radicalized soloists who walk into a Black church in Charleston, South Carolina and murder 9 Black people conducting Bible study,[27] or walk into a synagogue in Pittsburgh,[28] Pennsylvania and murder 11 Jewish people, or go to the Walmart in El Paso, Texas and murder 23 Latino people.[29] All of this is being done out of fear that their White identity is being erased. When the homes of the shooters are raided and searched by law enforcement authorities, they most commonly find a cache of automatic weapons which are being stockpiled for their prediction of the upcoming race war. What they are finding out is that there are more people today who look like them but who don't share their supremacist and nationalist views, and that they will be fighting their own kind. It is not rocket science to figure out what it means when you combine a past racist slogan with a current racist one. Take Our Country Back, Make America Great Again. 2042 has become the White supremacists' Y2K.

Notes

1. "What is a Whistleblower?" *National Whistleblower Center*, accessed April 12, 2021, https://www.whistleblowers.org/what-is-a-whistleblower.

2. "Whistleblower", *Wikipedia, Wikimedia Foundation*, accessed April 11, 2021, https://en.wikipedia.org/wiki/Whistleblower.

3. "Abner Louima", *Wikipedia, Wikimedia Foundation*, accessed April 11, 2021.https://en.wikipedia.org/wiki/Abner_Louima.

4. "John Burge", *Wikipedia, Wikimedia Foundation*, accessed April 11, 2021, https://en.wikipedia.org/wiki/Jon_Burge.

5. Laurence Ralph, *The Torture Letters* (University of Chicago Press, 2020).

6. "Rodney King", *Wikipedia, Wikimedia Foundation*, accessed April 11, 2021, https://en.wikipedia.org/wiki/Rodney_King.

7. "DOJ Investigation of the Montgomery County Department of Police", *Civil Rights Litigation Clearinghouse*, University of Michigan Law School, accessed April 12, 2021, https://www.clearinghouse.net/detail.php?id=5538.

8. Paul Valentine, "MD. Klan Leader Gets 36 Months in Weapons Case", *Washington Post*, published October 5, 1989, https://www.washingtonpost.com/archive/local/1989/10/05/md-klan-leader-gets-36-months-in-weapon-case/f9e90689-c964-4e84-85ff-85d912a763e3.

9. Daryl Davis, *Klan-Destine Relationships* (New Horizon Press, 1997).

10. "Consent Decree", *Baltimore City Police Department*, published January 12, 2017, https://www.baltimorepolice.org/consent-decree-basics/consent-decree.

11. "George Floyd", *Wikipedia, Wikimedia Foundation*, accessed April 12, 2021, https://en.wikipedia.org/wiki/George_Floyd.

12. Dakin Andone and Chris Boyette, "Two Virginia Police Officers Used Excessive Force, Threatened Army Officer During Traffic Stop, Lawsuit Says", *CNN News*, accessed April 12, 2021, https://www.cnn.com/2021/04/11/us/windsor-virginia-police-stop-army-lieutenant-lawsuit/index.html.

13. Evan Simko-Bednarski, "Black Buffalo police officer fired for trying to stop chokehold wins ruling, to get pension", *CNN News*, accessed April 15, 2021, https://www.cnn.com/2021/04/14/us/buffalo-officer-reinstated-trnd/index.html.

14. Ray Sanchez, Christina Carrega, and Nicquel Terry Ellis, "'The Lessons of This Moment.' The Testimony of Police Brass at Derick Chauvin's Trial is Unprecedented", *CNN News*, published April 10, 2021, https://www.cnn.com/2021/04/10/us/derek-chauvin-george-floyd-trial-testimony/index.html.

15. "On this day: 'No taxation without representation!'" *Constitution Daily, National Constitution Center*, published October 7, 2020, https://constitutioncenter.org/blog/250-years-ago-today-no-taxation-without-representation.

16. "Taxpayer March on Washington", *Wikipedia, Wikimedia Foundation*, accessed February 3, 2021, https://en.wikipedia.org/wiki/Taxpayer_March_on_Washington.

17. Chris Cassone, "Take Our Country Back", YouTube video, 5:18, October 9, 2010, https://www.youtube.com/watch?v=Y_hcrdZoRgY.

18. Janeane Garofalo, "Countdown with Keith Olberman", *MSNBC*, YouTube video, 8:29, April 16, 2009, https://www.youtube.com/watch?v=jAAHMDpk7Ik&t=190s.

19. David Duke, "David Duke: Charlottesville Rally Part of Effort to 'Take Country Back'", *NBC News*, YouTube video, 0:40, August 13, 2017, https://www.youtube.com/watch?v=fULPlGwjJMA.

20. Jordan Brasher, "Confederate flags fly worldwide, igniting social tensions and inflaming historic traumas", *The Conversation*, The Conversation US, Inc., accessed February 5, 2021, https://constitutioncenter.org/blog/250-years-ago-today-no-taxation-without-representation.

21. Trump, Donald, "Trump Encourages Those at His Rally To March To The Capitol—NBC News Now", *NBC News*, YouTube video, 1:03, January 7, 2021, https://www.youtube.com/watch?v=5fiT6coMQ58.

22. Donald Trump, "We're Going to Take Our Country Back", *Patriotic Populist*, YouTube video, 1:23, March 12, 2016. https://www.youtube.com/watch?v=rTzuWhpIz9w.

23. "Trump Asks Why U.S. Would Want Immigrants from 'Shithole Countries'", *CBC Radio-Canada*, YouTube video, 2:04, January 12, 2018. https://www.youtube.com/watch?v=e-Odk4n_KeY.

24. Donald Trump, "President Donald Trump on Charlottesville: You Had Very Fine People, On Both Sides–CNBC", *CNBC News*, YouTube video, 4:07, August 15, 2017. https://www.youtube.com/watch?v=JmaZR8E12bs.

25. Sam Roberts, "Minorities in U.S. Set to Become Majority by 2042", *The New York Times*, published August 14, 2008, https://www.nytimes.com/2008/08/14/world/americas/14iht-census.1.15284537.html.

26. Mary Clare Jalonic and Nomaan Merchant, "WATCH: Capitol Police Officer Killed in Insurrection Honored at U.S Capitol", *PBS News Hour*, News Hour Productions, LLC, published February 2, 2021; Revised February 3, 2021, https://www.pbs.org/newshour/politics/watch-live-funeral-for-capitol-police-officer-brian-sicknick.

27. "Dylann Roof", *Wikipedia, Wikimedia Foundation*, accessed February 3, 2021, https://en.wikipedia.org/wiki/Dylann_Roof.

28. "Pittsburgh Synagogue Shooting", *Wikipedia, Wikimedia Foundation*, accessed February 3, 2021, https://en.wikipedia.org/wiki/Pittsburgh_synagogue_shooting.

29. "2019 El Paso Shooting", *Wikipedia, Wikimedia Foundation*, accessed February 3, 2021, https://en.wikipedia.org/wiki/2019_El_Paso_shooting.

Bibliography

"2019 El Paso Shooting", *Wikipedia, Wikimedia Foundation*, accessed February 3, 2021. https://en.wikipedia.org/wiki/2019_El_Paso_shooting.

"Abner Louima", *Wikipedia, Wikimedia Foundation*, accessed April 11, 2021. https://en.wikipedia.org/wiki/Abner_Louima.

Andone, Dakin and Boyette, Chris, "Two Virginia Police Officers Used Excessive Force, Threatened Army Officer During Traffic Stop, Lawsuit Says", *CNN News*, April 12, 2021. https://www.cnn.com/2021/04/11/us/windsor-virginia-police-stop-army-lieutenant-lawsuit/index.html.

Brasher, Jordan, "Confederate flags fly worldwide, igniting social tensions and inflaming historic traumas", *The Conversation*, The Conversation US, Inc., accessed February 5, 2021. https://constitutioncenter.org/blog/250-years-ago-today-no-taxation-without-representation.

Cassone, Chris, "Take Our Country Back", YouTube video, 5:18, October 9, 2010. https://www.youtube.com/watch?v=Y_hcrdZoRgY.

"Consent Decree", *Baltimore City Police Department*, January 12, 2017, https://www.baltimorepolice.org/consent-decree-basics/consent-decree.

Davis, Daryl, *Klan-Destine Relationships*, New Horizon Press, 1997.

"DOJ Investigation of the Montgomery County Department of Police", *Civil Rights Litigation Clearinghouse*. University of Michigan Law School, accessed April 12, 2021. https://www.clearinghouse.net/detail.php?id=5538.

Duke, David, "David Duke: Charlottesville Rally Part of Effort to 'Take Country Back'", *NBC News*. YouTube video, 0:40, August 13, 2017. https://www.youtube.com/watch?v=fULPlGwjJMA.

"Dylann Roof", *Wikipedia, Wikimedia Foundation*, accessed February 3, 2021. https://en.wikipedia.org/wiki/Dylann_Roof.

Garofalo, Janeane, "Countdown with Keith Olberman", *MSNBC*. YouTube video, 8:29, April 16, 2009. https://www.youtube.com/watch?v=jAAHMDpk7Ik&t=190s.

"George Floyd", *Wikipedia,Wikimedia Foundation*, accessed April 12, 2021. https://en.wikipedia.org/wiki/George_Floyd.

Jalonic, Mary Clare and Merchant, Nomaan, "WATCH: Capitol Police Officer Killed in Insurrection Honored at U.S Capitol", *PBS News Hour*, News Hour Productions, LLC. Published February 2, 2021, revised February 3, 2021, https://www.pbs.org/newshour/politics/watch-live-funeral-for-capitol-police-officer-brian-sicknick.

"John Burge", *Wikipedia, Wikimedia Foundation*, accessed April 11, 2021. https://en.wikipedia.org/wiki/Jon_Burge.

"On this day: 'No taxation without representation!'" *Constitution Daily*, National Constitution Center. October 7, 2020. https://constitutioncenter.org/blog/250-years-ago-today-no-taxation-without-representation.

Ralph, Laurence, *The Torture Letters* (University of Chicago Press, 2020).

Roberts, Sam, "Minorities in U.S. Set to Become Majority by 2042", *The New York Times*. August 14, 2008. https://www.nytimes.com/2008/08/14/world/americas/14iht-census.1.15284537.html.

"Rodney King", *Wikipedia, Wikimedia Foundation*, accessed April 11, 2021. https://en.wikipedia.org/wiki/Rodney_King.

"Taxpayer March on Washington", *Wikipedia, Wikimedia Foundation*, accessed February 3, 2021. https://en.wikipedia.org/wiki/Taxpayer_March_on_Washington.

"Pittsburgh Synagogue Shooting", *Wikipedia, Wikimedia Foundation*, accessed February 3, 2021. https://en.wikipedia.org/wiki/Pittsburgh_synagogue_shooting.

Sanchez, Ray, Carrega, Christina, and Ellis, Nicquel Terry, "'The Lessons of This Moment.' The Testimony of Police Brass at Derick Chauvin's Trial is Unprecedented", *CNN News*, April 10, 2021. https://www.cnn.com/2021/04/10/us/derek-chauvin-george-floyd-trial-testimony/index.html.

Simko-Bednarski, Evan, "Black Buffalo police officer fired for trying to stop chokehold wins ruling, to get pension", *CNN News*, accessed April 15, 2021, https://www.cnn.com/2021/04/14/us/buffalo-officer-reinstated-trnd/index.html.

"Trump Asks Why U.S. Would Want Immigrants from 'Shithole Countries", *CBC Radio-Canada*, YouTube video, 2:04, January 12, 2018, https://www.youtube.com/watch?v=e-Odk4n_KeY.

Trump, Donald, "President Donald Trump on Charlottesville: You Had Very Fine People, On Both Sides – CNBC", *CNBC News*, YouTube video, 4:07, August 15, 2017, https://www.youtube.com/watch?v=JmaZR8E12bs.

Trump, Donald, "Trump Encourages Those at His Rally To March To The Capitol – NBC News Now", *NBC News*, YouTube video, 1:03, January 7, 2021, https://www.youtube.com/watch?v=5fiT6coMQ58.

Trump, Donald, "We're Going to Take Our Country Back", *Patriotic Populist*, YouTube video, 1:23, March 12, 2016, https://www.youtube.com/watch?v=rTzuWhpIz9w.

Valentine, Paul, "MD. Klan Leader Gets 36 Months in Weapons Case", *The Washington Post*, October 5, 1989, https://www.washingtonpost.com/archive/local/1989/10/05/md-klan-leader-gets-36-months-in-weapon-case/f9e90689-c964-4e84-85ff-85d912a763e3.

"What is a Whistleblower?", *National Whistleblower Center*, accessed April 12, 2021, https://www.whistleblowers.org/what-is-a-whistleblower

"Whistleblower", *Wikipedia, Wikimedia Foundation*, accessed April 11, 2021, https://en.wikipedia.org/wiki/Whistleblower.

CHARLOTTE WEBB

Photo courtesy of Barcelona Design Week

Charlotte Webb is co-founder of Feminist Internet, a collective of artists, researchers and activists aiming to disrupt inequalities in internet products, services and systems by educating and equipping the people who build and use them. She is Senior Lecturer at the Creative Computing Institute, London, where she recently created a master's degree in Internet Equalities, which explores how power relations are organised, embedded and perpetuated in internet technologies, and how they can be re-organised or challenged through critical, creative and activist practice. She is Founding Director of Even, the consultancy arm of Feminist Internet, which provides creative approaches to tech equity for the next generation of business. Charlotte was nominated by the Evening Standard as one of the most influential people in Technology and Science in London 2018, and has been widely featured in the international press. She has presented her work internationally, including at TedX, Reykjavik Global Women's Forum, Cannes Lions Festival of

CHARLOTTE WEBB
FROSTED WEBS, FEMINIST PRACTICE

"FEMINISM has always been a cyborg, a notion that links rules
and orientation (that is, cybernetics) to flesh and
material (that is, bodies) in a way that is not considered to be natural—but that
questions the so-called natural".

Ulrike Bergermann, 1998.[1]

Early one morning in the middle of a cold
British winter, I walked down my street
and saw that frost had settled on dozens
of spider's webs that were attached to
fences and hedges. The intricate structures of the webs were rendered visible
as the frost revealed architectures that
would usually be barely detectable. In this
chapter, I want to think of feminist modes
of thought and practice as matter that can
settle on techno-social webs, revealing
their architectures, infrastructures and
power imbalances. This desire points to
the kind of relationship I propose between
whistleblowing and feminist practices: a
relationship of making the invisible visible.

A frosted spider's web.
Photo courtesy of the author.

I am using whistleblowing in its broadest sense to refer to the practice of exposing injustices, rather than drawing on definitions which situate it squarely as
an act performed by workers in corporate or government contexts. It is not my aim
to suggest that feminist practices constitute whistleblowing in the latter sense.
Rather, I aim to reflect on how they reveal problematic constructions of gender[2] in
techno-social systems and the injustices these constructions reproduce, including
disproportionate amounts of online abuse being experienced by women, sexist
representations of women being embedded in devices (think sexy female robots),

technology facilitated domestic violence, gender inequality in the technology sector, gender discrimination in algorithmic systems, and the sexist censoring of women's bodies on social media. This is important because technologies—and the infrastructures within which they are created—can and do perpetuate inequalities and heteropatriarchal norms in ways that are not always immediately obvious. Infrastructure, after all, wants to be invisible rather than obvious. Of course, feminist practice involves acting, protesting, communing and creating, not only analysing and critiquing. Feminists do not stop at revealing injustices—they find ways to subvert and act in response to them.

Feminist Approaches to Technology

For centuries, feminists have exposed architectures of injustice, making visible discriminatory systems and practices that subjugate those outside dominant orders. For decades, they have revealed, contested, fought and reimagined forms of inequality that are woven into techno-social systems. The cyberfeminist movement that emerged in Europe, America and Australia in the 1990s was itself a network of ideas and communities which conceptualized feminism and its relationship to technology in multiple ways, but were united in their attempt to challenge patriarchal oppression as it was expressed through technological systems. Donna Haraway's Cyborg Manifesto[3]—an inspiration for cyberfeminism—challenged binary notions such as nature/culture, self/other, male/female and argued that these are central to Western tools of domination. The figure of the cyborg, Haraway argued, could "suggest a way out of the maze of dualisms in which we have explained our bodies and our tools to ourselves".[4] Haraway showed that the 'natural' should be understood as a form of problematic normativity that the cyborg could challenge since it was a constructed entity (which could therefore be reconfigured).[5] Australian art collective VNS Matrix's 'Cyberfeminist Manifesto for the 21st Century,'[6] created in a stream-of-consciousness writing session and published online and on a huge mobile billboard, was an irreverent proposition that technology could disrupt patriarchal norms. Cyberfeminism evolved through the 1990s, but was critiqued for being overly optimistic about the liberating potential of the internet, elitist in orientation,[7] and failing to attend to issues of race, class and economics in its analysis.[8] Through the 2000s and beyond, cyberfeminism expanded towards other forms including technofeminism,[9] which explored the premise that there is a "mutually shaping relationship between gender and technology, in which technology is both a source and a consequence of gender relations".[10] It also branched into modes such as cyberfeminism 2.0, Black cyberfeminism, xenofeminism, post-cyber feminism, glitch feminism, Afrofuturism, hackfeministas and transhackfeminism, which are catalogued in the Cyberfeminism Index.[11]

Cyberfeminism Index, images page, Mindy Seu. Screenshot, 2021.

The 2017 *Post-Cyber Feminist International* event at the Institute of Contemporary Arts in London marked twenty years since *The First Cyberfeminist International* held in Germany in 1997.[12] Expanding on the genealogy of cyberfeminism, the ICA event aimed to "purposefully constellate(s) thinkers to consider a new vision for post-cyber feminism that is substantive and developed, without being exclusionary of contestation".[13]

The Cyberfeminism Index draws on several feminist methods in its construction. It indexes and links to the work of others, celebrating and strengthening a community of practice. It is made open for 'collaborative editing and compilation' through a submit button, and aspires to grow in order to 'truly reflect the global nature of the cyberfeminist movement'. This points to the ways that feminism structures itself through networks and communities. For example, in 2014, the Association for Progressive Communications gathered 50 activists and advocates working in sexual rights, women's rights, violence against women, and internet rights to a meeting in Malaysia. Together, they drafted the Feminist Principles of the Internet,[14] a series of statements that "offer a gender and sexual rights lens on critical internet-related rights". The principles aim to "provide a framework for women's movements to articulate and explore issues related to technology". The principles are organized in 5 clusters (Access, Movements, Economy, Expression, and Embodiment), and the wider community are invited to build on them by translating them or adding related resources.

Techno-feminist artists, designers, scholars, and activists have not pulled apart the power relations embedded in techno-social systems by drawing impermeable boundaries around their disciplines, but by critically meshing with others, knowing that no one theoretical or methodological framework is perfect or even sufficient for building forms of resistance.[15] Approaching socio-technical injustices from a feminist perspective may take practitioners to the edges (or centres) of Design Justice,[16] Critical Race and Digital Studies,[17] Queer Science and Technology Studies,[18] Postcolonial Science and Technology Studies,[19] Environmental Studies,[20] or other fields of thought and practice. Whatever conjugations are formed, they can offer ways to sit at the centre of a problem with others, respond to contextual specificities, and figure out pathways forward together.

We might also consider how a productive conjunction of whistleblowing studies with gender studies has shed light on the ways in which imaginaries of whistleblowing and whistleblowers are problematically gendered. Studying the relationship between gender, information infrastructures and truth-telling, Agostinho and Bonde Thylstrup note: "truth-telling practices are entangled in gendered matrices of control that make possible some truth-telling subjects while foreclosing others...gendered and sexualized imaginaries overdetermine what counts as truth and who counts as a truth-teller".[21] If normative notions of gender and sexuality "fundamentally shape, complicate and ultimately define who counts as a truth-teller within emerging parrhesiastic networked spaces",[22] they also shape who counts as a producer and consumer of technology in the broader techno-social realm. For example, who counts as a producer of technology is shaped by pervasive narratives that foreground men as the creators of computers and the internet or as 'natural' innovators. Such narratives often omit women's ongoing contributions outside of well-known pioneers of early programming such as Ada Lovelace or Grace Hopper.[23] Who counts as a consumer of technology is shaped by what or who is prioritised by producers of technology. When women and minoritized groups are not understood as vital to the design, testing and roll out of technologies, their needs are under-recognised, and the technologies can reinforce inequalities and lead to negative or harmful outcomes. Just as the vital role of women and other minoritized gender identities in the development of the internet has been buried in favour of hetero-normative narratives of the male genius, media narratives about whistleblowers have aggrandized men's actions and minimised the actions of women and female identifying people.[24] This is not just a matter of unequal accreditation. Being less visible means being 'more vulnerable to legal injustice'. The under-representation of women and female identifying people in the design of technologies can also lead to poor experiences, harm and even death. In describing the 'gender data gap'—the fact that the majority of the world's data is based on the male body and male life patterns—Caroline Criado-Perez notes that women are more likely than men to be seriously injured in car crashes, because "cars have been designed using car-crash test dummies based on the 'average' male".[25]

Gender Coding in Voice Assistants

Allison Stanger defines whistleblowers as those who 'expose lies and wrongdoing which their perpetrators would like to be kept secret.'[26] However, feminist critiques of techno-social systems often address inequalities that are not deliberately 'kept secret', but that are encoded into technologies because they are normative in society. Sometimes such inequalities are hiding in plain sight. Take the problematic gendering of voice assistants for example. The fact that devices like Siri, Alexa and Cortana are typically characterized as female is not 'kept secret' from the public at all. It is highly visible, since these devices are pervasive in domestic settings and increasingly woven into the infrastructures of affluent homes. In total, Google Assistant, Siri, Cortana and Alexa are installed on over two billion internet-connected devices globally.[27] What may be less visible when interacting with these devices, is how their characterization as female problematically reconstructs normative ideas about gender and upholds the heteropatriarchal system in which they are produced. A 2018 survey by LivePerson showed that 53% of respondents had never thought about why voice assistants are projected as female, even though 85% knew that the default voices of these assistants are usually female.

In 2016, critiques of the gendering of voice assistants were emerging in the mainstream media, and gained traction in the following few years.[28] They focused on two main issues: the problematic characterization of the devices as female, and their failure to respond adequately to abusive comments.[29]

Alexa, Cortana, Siri, and Google Assistant originally launched with female-sounding default voices, although all four have since been updated. The default characterization of voice assistants as female is problematic because, as Jacqueline Feldman puts it: "by encouraging consumers to understand the objects that serve us as women, technologists abet the prejudice by which women are considered as objects".[30] This is an example of Wajcman's techno-feminist premise that technology is both a source and a consequence of gender relations. The commonly used capabilities of voice assistants and their primary goal of helping people with everyday tasks are associated with female qualities and feminized labour. Consumer preferences for female voices play on deep seated cultural norms and socially constructed Western notions of as women as nurturers, caregivers, homemakers and assistants.[31] Notice a parallel with perceptions of whistleblowing here. Agostinho and Bonde Thylstrup discuss the case of Sarah Harrison, a former member of WikiLeaks who was 'central in getting Snowden to Russia'.[32] She was portrayed by the media as Assange's assistant rather than a WikiLeaks editor. The authors note: "The tedious labour of truth-telling, essential as it is, rarely reaches public perception" and state that what is exemplary about Harrison's case is that: "the backgrounded labour (of truth telling) is not only performed by a woman but

Modified Alexa, created during a Feminist
Alexa workshop, 2018, Creative Computing
Institute, London. Photo: Feminist Internet.

Feminist Alexa workshop map, 2018,
Creative Computing Institute, London.
Photo: Feminist Internet.

is also gendered as female: this kind of work is usually feminized and thus devalued (even when performed by a male subject) because it is associated with the
menial work historically assigned to women".[33]

When Leah Fessler systematically tested how Siri, Alexa, Cortana, and Google
Assistant reacted to abusive comments, she found that when Siri was told "You're
a bitch", it responded: "I'd blush if I could". To "You're a slut", Alexa replied: "Well,
thanks for the feedback". Obviously, it is unacceptable for devices characterized
as female to respond politely, coyly or even flirtatiously to any command regardless of how hostile it is, because this reproduces the idea that women are tolerant
of abusive treatment. Since 2017, Apple and Amazon both rolled out updates to
their voice assistants—Siri now says "I don't know how to respond to that" when
called a bitch. Amazon created a 'disengage mode', and Alexa even claims to be a
feminist (it's not).[34] Google introduced new male voice options to its assistant in
2018 and Cortana was given a male voice option in 2019. These updates may seem
positive, but can also be read as virtue signals that do not remedy how the devices
were conceived and how they reinforce structural sexism.

This issue reflects a diversity crisis in the technology industry and the AI sector specifically. In 2018 the AI Now Institute found that just 18% authors at major
AI conferences were female; over 80% of AI professors were men; women comprised only 15% of AI research staff at Facebook & 10% at Google, and no public
data on trans workers or other gender minorities was available.[35] If the predominantly male creators of AI technologies have not grown up experiencing gender
discrimination from micro-aggressions to full blown harassment and violence, it
is not a lived experience they can draw on when creating products and services.

Designing a Feminist Alexa

These critiques inspired a group of artists and designers from the UK-based collective Feminist Internet to explore what a Feminist Alexa might look like, as part of a 2018 fellowship at the Creative Computing Institute, University of the Arts London.[36] We wanted to ask:

What *is* a feminist conversation? What kind of exchange between a human and a technology would qualify as feminist? Could there ever be a feminist response to: "Hey Alexa, what's the weather like today?"

Following an open call across the University, we gathered 40 students and several Alexas for two 3-day workshops, with a mission to prototype feminist voice assistants that would meet a meaningful human need, embody feminist values and advance equity for women or other marginalised groups. We wanted to ensure participants could demonstrate the use of feminist values in their designs, and to scaffold this, we drew on Josie Young's Feminist Chatbot Design Process, which aims to help designers ensure their chatbots do not knowingly or unknowingly perpetuate gender inequality.[37] Young's process was inspired in part by Showen Bardzell's work on Feminist Human Computer Interaction.[38]

We adapted Josie's process and mapped each section to the stages of the workshop, so that participants had something to guide their thinking.[39]

Users[40]

This section asked participants to identify a specific person or group, understand their experiences, and explore how they may benefit from a feminist voice assistant. The aim was to push back against the idea of 'universal design', which can fail to recognise differences in user experiences and outlooks. To quote Bardzell, "'Human' is too rich, too diverse, and too complex a category to bear a universal solution"[41]. Or, as Amrute puts it: "most often, designers of technical systems begin with a standard user [in mind] and, in doing so, set into motion patterns of discrimination that are hidden by the assumption of system neutrality".[42] One group initially wanted to design for people with Autistic Spectrum Disorder. This was well intentioned, but when they started to try creating a persona and reflected on this section of the tool, they realised that without direct experience or access to people with this particular condition, it might be better to focus their attention on a different group.

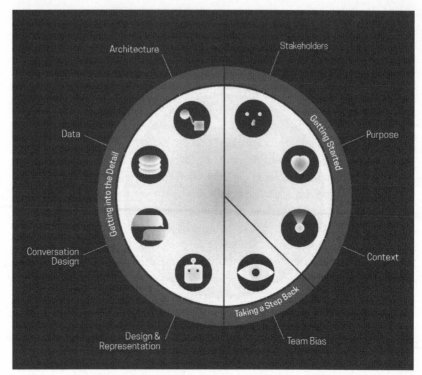

Feminist Design Tool overview, 2019. Graphic: Conor Rigby / Feminist Internet.

Purpose

This project did not aim to make a feminist 'version' of an Alexa, since part of the point is to challenge the corporate monopolies that produce these technologies. Instead, we used the term 'Alexa' as a proxy for voice assistants more generally. We asked participants to consider whether their feminist voice assistant would meet a meaningful human need or address an injustice, and how it could address the need/s of the intended user. This allowed them to ask critical questions about who should determine what is useful, and what counts as meaningful.

Team Bias

This section emphasised that we all come from places and experiences that shape our thinking and perspectives, and we can unconsciously embed these in the things we make. If we don't reflect on this there is a risk that what we design may reinforce problematic or harmful biases and assumptions. By reflecting on their values and position in society, participants raised their awareness about how biases can be baked into the design of technologies.

Design and Representation

The way AI agents such as chatbots or game characters are designed and represented can challenge or reinforce stereotypes. For example, characterising a financial advice bot as male could reinforce the stereotype that men are more competent than women with money. Asking participants to consider how the voice assistant would remind users that it was not human tapped into ethical questions raised at the Google Duplex demo, where a Google Assistant feature misled some users to think they were talking to a human rather than an AI.[43] Most groups opted to present their voice assistant as genderless, or to give it a character that actively embraced queerness.

Conversation Design

The emphasis here was on encouraging participants to reflect on what types of responses would embody feminist values, and how they could get their designs to 'speak' with a feminist voice. We asked them to consider how their assistant would respond if it received abuse and what its tone of voice would be literally and metaphorically.

Guided by our collaborator Alex Fefegha and the Feminist Internet team, participants designed 8 prototypes that reflected how they had used the feminist design tool in the design process. These are detailed in the project report,[44] but I will highlight a few here.

Pany was designed to tackle loneliness amongst elderly people. It has a range of voice options that can be configured by the user. To remind the user Pany is not human, it says: "If you want me to stop, just say 'Pany stop', don't worry I won't be offended because I am a bot"

Bud is a self-reflection voice assistant for teenagers. It was designed considering the persona of a 14-year old who has a tense relationship with her family and has turned to bullying as a way to gain control over her life. The pitch of bud's voice can be adjusted with a slider function. Instead of 'choosing a gender', the user can simply choose the sound of a voice they feel most comfortable with.

HiFuture is designed for students that are confused and overwhelmed about career pathways. When it receives inappropriate commands, it responds assertively but with a sense of sarcastic humour:

User: You are f***ing useless.

HiFuture: Good luck with that language at your interview.

Through this creative project, we wanted to make visible the ways in which voice assistants reproduce gender inequalities and fail to respond to abuse. We wanted to bring a community of young people together to enter a space of feminist critique and making. It was important that we allowed the critique to be a springboard for thinking about other possible imaginaries where voice assistants are conceived differently.

There are clear limitations in this work. More is needed than re-thinking voice assistants at the level of conversation design and voice tone and pitch.[45] A deep feminist approach to voice technologies needs to overhaul the entire ecosystem, attending to its consequences for people and the planet. In their revelatory Anatomy of an AI System, Kate Crawford and Vladen Joler expose how "each small moment of convenience—be it answering a question, turning on a light, or playing a song—requires a vast planetary network, fuelled by the extraction of non-renewable materials, labour, and data".[46] Although the authors do not frame this work in feminist terms, it is highly aligned with feminist approaches that wish to surface the impact of technologies on the environment,[47] the labour that produces them,[48] their extractive data practices,[49] their privacy implications and ability to facilitate domestic violence,[50] and their position in the ever increasing culture of 'surveillance capitalism'.[51] Efforts also need to be made to understand how these ecosystems intersect with sexism, racism, political and class discrimination. Sareeta Amrut advocates for "developing practices to train sociotechnical systems—algorithms and their human makers—to begin with the material and embodied situations in which these systems are entangled, which include from the start histories of race, gender and dehumanisation".[52] All these webs need frost to settle on them so that they can be seen and re-imagined by feminists and their allies across disciplinary and geographical borders.

Final Reflections

Ulrike Bergermann declared in 1998 that feminism has always been a cyborg that links rules to flesh, and questions the 'so-called natural'. The Xenofeminist Manifesto declares: 'If nature is unjust, change nature.'[53] What thrills me about feminisms in all their techno-fleshy manifestations, is that they question the normative and challenge the status quo. The seek to say what is unsaid and make visible what is deliberately (or unknowingly) obscured. They do not accept what comes to be seen as the inevitable progression of things. Then, they instantiate alternatives—bringing new socio-technical imaginaries into being. Sometimes this happens through activism, advocacy and organizing. Sometimes through academic rigor, critique or fiction. Sometimes, through artistic practices that bring a politico-aesthetic hybridity and a radical imagination to the field.

Feminism and whistleblowing are distinctive practices with their own genealogies, functions and outputs. However, their energies are aligned in aiming to unveil injustice and rectify it. While they may not occupy a direct lineage, they share a mindset that wants to expose systems of power, and make the invisible visible. In these words, I have tried to weave a narrative about feminism as a creative tool for exposing inequitable norms and creating fertile entry points for creative practice. I wanted to think about feminism as metaphorical frost that lands on techno-social webs, revealing their invisible architectures. But feminism, my guide *and* my nagging companion, has a way of disrupting things just when you think you have them resolved. As I came to the end of the writing process, I read a quote from Siana Bangura, founder of the Black British Feminist platform, No Fly on the WALL,[54] which she stated in a panel discussion at the Post-Cyber Feminist International: "You have to always be visible and productive or else you're invisible".

While I have tried to make an argument about feminism's capacity to make invisible inequalities visible so that they can be addressed, techno-capitalist logics grind along demanding that the hyper-visibility of women is maintained to uphold the productivity and profitability of platforms.

So, there are no conclusions—only possible feminisms and possible internets that we can strive to create as a global community.

Notes

1. Bergermann, Ulrika. "Do X", *First Cyberfeminist International*, 1997. https://monoskop. org/images/7/77/First_Cyberfeminist_ International_1998.pdf.

2. Intersectional feminist approaches do not only look at gender injustice—they also consider the ways in which race, class, ability or any other aspect of a person's identity can combine in ways that lead to unique modes of discrimination.

3. Haraway, Donna. "A manifesto for Cyborgs: Science, technology, and socialist feminism in the 1980s", *Australian Feminist Studies* 2, no. 4, 1-42, (1987): https://doi.org/10.1080/08164649 .1987.9961538.

4. Ibid, 223.

5. To see caregiving as "in women's nature" or to see women as "naturally" emotional rather than logical is to submit to constructed notions that take set in the cultural imaginary and reinforce gender oppression.

6. "Cyberfeminist Manifesto for the 21st Century", *VNS Matrix*, 1991, https://vnsmatrix. net/projects/the-cyberfeminist-manifesto-for-the-21st-century.

7. In a discussion of Cyberfeminism at the UK's Barbican Centre in 2019, Judy Wajcman noted that dominant narratives in feminist discourse are set up by Western standards, and that in South America Donna Haraway is not as strong an academic reference as in the West. She argues that "Haraway's texts, despite advocating for socialist feminism and having strong political agendas, often lack the clarity and simplicity to be accessed by anyone who does not belong to the hyper educated Western academia elite." Di Leone, Chiara. "Revisiting the Future: Technofeminism in the 21st Century", *Furtherfield*, 2019, https://www.furtherfield.org/a-review-of-technofeminism-in-the-21st-century.

8. Wilding, Faith. "Where is the Feminism in Cyberfeminism?", *N-Paradoxa* 2, (1998); Nakamura Lisa and Geert Lovink, "Talking Race and Cyberspace: An Interview with Lisa Nakamura", *Frontiers: A Journal of Women Studies* 26, no. 1, (2005): 60-65; ICA, *Black Feminism and Post-Cyber Feminism. A panel with Akwugo Emejulu, Bangura, Kiyémis Francesca Sobande*, 2017. For transnational perspectives on cyberfeminism see Radhika Gajjala, "Third World' perspectives on cyberfeminism", *Development in Practice* 9, no. 5, (2010): 616-619 and Payal Arora and Rumman and Chowdhury, (eds) "Special Collection: Cross-cultural Feminist Technologies", *Global Perspectives* (2021), https://online.ucpress.edu/gp/collection/232/Special-Collection-Cross-cultural-Feminist.

9. Wajcman, Judy. *TechnoFeminism* (Hoboken, NJ: Polity, 2013).

10. Wajcman, Judy. *TechnoFeminism*, 7; Sollfrank, Cornelia. *The Beautiful Warriors: Technofeminist Praxis in the Twenty-First Century* (Colchester / New York / Port Watson: Minor Compositions, 2020).

11. https://cyberfeminismindex.com. The Rhizome website, which hosts the index, states that the term "Cyberfeminism" has "brought feminisms and technologies into conflict and conversation, while the term itself has been contested, reimagined, debunked, and expanded. Cyberfeminism Index does not attempt to resolve these contradictions, but to honor the multiplicity of practices that might be gathered under this imperfect umbrella".

12. The First Cyberfeminist International took places at Documenta X, a contemporary art exhibition in Kassel, Germany. It was organized by the first cyberfeminist organisation, the Old Boys Network (OBN), and included work by OBN members including Cornelia Sollfrank (Hamburg/Berlin), Susanne Ackers (Berlin), Julianne Pierce (Sydney), Helene von Oldenburg (Rastede/Hamburg), Claudia Reiche (Hamburg), Faith Wilding (Pittsburgh), Yvonne Volkart (Zürich), Verena Kuni (Frankfurt) and others: The Old Boys Network, 1997. *The First Cyberfeminist International*. https://monoskop.org/images/7/77/First_Cyberfeminist_International_1998.pdf.

13. ICA 2017.

14. https://feministinternet.org/en/principles.

15. Feminism itself is imperfect and insufficient because it has a history of oppression and whiteness. The Women's Center for Creative Work, which cultivates L.A.'s feminist creative communities and practices, defines white feminism as "a Feminism that prioritizes the experiences and perspectives of cis, white, able bodied, middle class white women." See: https://corevalues.womenscenterforcreativework.com.

16. Costanza-Chock, Sasha. *Design justice: community-led practices to build the worlds we need* (Cambridge : The MIT Press, 2020).

17. https://criticalracedigitalstudies.com.

18. https://queersts.com.

19. Harding, Sarah (ed.). *The Postcolonial Science and Technology Studies Reader*, (Duke University Press, 2011).

20. Sapra, Sonalini, "Feminist Perspectives on the Environment", *Oxford Research Encyclopedia of International Studies*, (2017): https://doi.org/10.1093/acrefore/9780190846626.013.49.

21. Agostinho, Daniela and Nanna Bonde Thylstrup, "'If truth was a woman': Leaky infrastructures and the gender politics of truth-telling". *Ephemera*, 19, no. 4, (2019): 746.

22. Ibid, 749.

23. These narratives are increasingly challenged, such as in Claire Evans' *Broad Band: The Untold Story of the Women Who Made the Internet*, (New York: Portfolio/Penguin, 2018).

24. Agostinho and Bonde Thylstrup, "'If Truth Was a Woman'", 752.

25. Criado-Perez, Caroline. *Invisible Women: Exposing Data Bias in a World Designed for Men*, (London: Chatto and Windus, 2019), 186.

26. Stanger, Allision. *Reasons for Hope – The Ethics and Politics of Whistleblowing In Europe and the United States*, https://www.youtube.com/watch?v=_hqDsXavuaE.

27. EQUALS and UNESCO, *I'd Blush if I Could: Closing Gender Divides in Digital Skills Through Education*, (2019), https://unesdoc.unesco.org/ark:/48223/pf0000367416.page=1.

28. Feldman, Jacqueline. "The Bot Politic". *The New Yorker*, December 31, 2016, https://www.newyorker.com/tech/annals-of-technology/the-bot-politic; Fessler, Leah. "We tested bots like Siri and Alexa to see who would stand up to sexual harassment", *Quartz*, 2017 https://qz.com/911681/we-tested-apples-siri-amazon-echos-alexa-microsofts-cortana-and-googles-google-home-to-see-which-personal-assistant-bots-stand-up-for-themselves-in-the-face-of-sexual-harassment/; Strengers, Yolande and Jenny Kennedy, *The Smart Wife: Why Siri, Alexa, and Other Smart Home Devices Need a Feminist Reboot* (MIT Press, 2021).

29. Critiques have also been made about accent bias: Harwell, Drew. "The Accent Gap", *The Washington Post*, July 19, 2018, https://www.washingtonpost.com/graphics/2018/business/alexa-does-not-understand-your-accent/ and racial disparities in automated speech recognition—i.e. Koenecke, Allison et.al, "Racial disparities in automated speech recognition", *Proceedings of the National Academy of Sciences*, 117, no. 14, (April 2020): 7684-7689 https://doi.org/10.1073/pnas.1915768117.

30. Feldman, *"The Bot Politic"*.

31. There are some exceptions, such as when BMW had to recall a series of cars with female voiced satellite navigation systems in Germany, because the men there didn't like being told what to do in a car by a "woman".

32. Agostinho and Bonde Thylstrup, "'If Truth Was a Woman'", 747.

33. Ibid., 752.

34. Fessler, Leah. "Amazon's Alexa is now a feminist, and she's sorry if that upsets you", *Quartz at Work*, January 17, 2018, https://qz.com/work/1180607/amazons-alexa-is-now-a-feminist-and-shes-sorry-if-that-upsets-you.

35. Myers West, Sarah, Meredith Whittaker & Kate Crawford, *"Discriminating Systems: Gender, Race and Power in AI"*, AI Now Institute, https://ainowinstitute.org/discriminatingsystems.html.

36. bit.ly/feministalexaoverview.

37. Young, Josie, *Feminist Chatbot Design Process*, 2017, https://drive.google.com/file/d/0B036SlUSi-z4UkkzYUVGTGdocXc.

38. Bardzell, Shaowen. "Feminist HCI: taking stock and outlining an agenda for design", *CHI '10: Proceedings of the SIGCHI Conference on Human Factors in Computing Systems*, (April 2010): 1301-1310 https://doi.org/10.1145/1753326.1753521. For Bardzell, contemporary feminism (which for her is anti-essentialist feminism that doesn't treat "femaleness" or "femininity" as a given fact) is a natural ally to design because it seeks to make visible the ways that gender is constructed in everyday life and then generate opportunities for intervention.

39. Feminist Internet and Josie Young, *Feminist Design Tool: Defensible Decision Making for Interaction Design and AI*, (2018): https://drive.google.com/file/d/1AxWWPb76Lk2_71GlkqLqJW9a17xB5a5P.

40. When iterating the tool we changed "User" to "Stakeholder", which emphasises the idea that we all have a stake in the technologies we use and are active participants in constructing their social meaning and value.

41. Bardzell, "Feminist HCI: taking stock and outlining an agenda for design", 1306.

42. Amrute, Sareeta, "Of Techno-Ethics and Techno-Affects." *Feminist Review* 123, no. 1 (November 2019): 56–73, https://doi.org/10.1177/0141778919879744.

43. Lomas, Natasha, "Duplex shows Google failing at ethical and creative AI design", 2018, https://techcrunch.com/2018/05/10/duplex-shows-google-failing-at-ethical-and-creative-ai-design.

44. Feminist Internet, *Designing a Feminist Alexa: An experiment in feminist conversation design*, 2018, https://drive.google.com/file/d/1vlrIT8dIA9muhvd-XfCCCCUQCujRhMOO.

45. Q, the Genderless Voice was a creative attempt at challenging norms around voice—see Genderlessvoice.com.

46. See https://anatomyof.ai.

47. E Romberger, Julia, "Ecofeminist Ethics and Digital Technology: A Case Study of Microsoft Word", *Ecofeminism and Rhetoric: Critical Perspectives on Sex, Technology, and Discourse*, edited by Vakoch Douglas A., 117-44, (New York; Oxford: Berghahn Books, 2011), http://www.jstor.org/stable/j.ctt9qcnk8.9; Strengers and Kennedy, "The Smart Wife".

48. Sinders, Caroline. "Rethinking Artificial Intelligence through Feminism" *CCCBLAB*, May 05, 2020, http://lab.cccb.org/en/rethinking-artificial-intelligence-through-feminism.

49. D'Ignazio, Catherine and Lauren F. Klein, *Data Feminism* (MIT Press).

50. Bowles, Nellie. "Thermostats, Locks and Lights: Digital Tools of Domestic Abuse". *The New York Times*, 2018, https://www.nytimes.com/2018/06/23/technology/smart-home-devices-domestic-abuse.html.

51. Zuboff, Shoshana. *The Age of Surveillance Capitalism: The Fight for a Human Future at the New Frontier of Power* (Profile Books, 2019).

52. Amrute, "Of Techno-Ethics and Techno-Affects."

53. https://laboriacuboniks.net/manifesto/xenofeminism-a-politics-for-alienation.

54. https://noflyonthewall.com.

MAGNUS AG

Magnus Ag is a human rights advocate, journalist, researcher and the founder of Bridge Figures (a human rights project in a data-driven world). He is the public interest infrastructure advisor to International Media Support and also serves as an advisor to Columbia University's signature research project The Politics of Visual Art in a Changing World and to Avant-Garde Lawyers. From 2018-20, he lived in Hong Kong where he wrote long-form journalism about the pro-democracy movement for leading international publications. He has defended the right to artistic freedom with Copenhagen-based Freemuse and served as the Assistant Advocacy Director for the Committee to Protect Journalists during five years in New York.

MAGNUS AG

IN OUR DATA-DRIVEN WORLDS AUTHORITARIAN STATES KNOW: ART IS THE LIE THAT TELLS THE TRUTH

Did the Tiananmen Massacre happen?

NO ONE VISITING Chiang Kai-Shek Memorial Hall in Taipei in June 2019, as I did, would have much doubt. An enormous inflatable "Tank Man" was prominently placed in front of the entrance. The installation was created by Taiwanese artist Shake, inspired by a sketch of dissident Chinese artist Badiucao. This giant inflatable "tank man" was of course a reference to the unidentified singular demonstrator confronting a line of People's Liberation Army tanks that have come to symbolise the 1989 Tiananmen Square Protests and Massacre where hundreds and maybe thousands of students and workers were killed by the Chinese government and military to quell a momentum-gaining pro-democracy movement in Beijing.[1] Badiucao first performed the piece "One TankMan" in Australia on June 4, 2016 and later encouraged people to set up their own performances by cosplaying the look of the tank man posing with bags in each hand while sharing photos under the hashtag #TankMen2018.[2]

I was in Taipei to talk about digital authoritarianism, including the Beijing government and Chinese technology companies' unprecedented and sophisticated digital measures to exert narrative control. The domestic censorship operates through a system of intermediary liability where Chinese companies are held liable for content on their platforms operated from the Chinese mainland.[3] Monitoring of blacklisted keywords and images, from a range of applications including microblogs, live streaming platforms, chat apps, and mobile games, show that the Tiananmen Massacre anniversary remains one of the most consistently censored topics.[4] But non-Chinese companies are in no way off the hook. In June 2020, the video conference company Zoom—that has been no less integral to many people's communications since COVID-19 hit—suspended accounts of activists based outside of China for hosting online Tiananmen commemorations following requests

The inflatable *Tank Man* installed in Taipei, Taiwan in June 2019 by Taiwanese artist Shake and inspired by a sketch of dissident Chinese artist Badiucao. Photo courtesy of the author.

from Chinese authorities. When the company was met with public criticism, Zoom apologized but notably only for affecting users outside of China, not for censoring users in China.[5]

As I stood there in Taiwan's capital on the eve of the 30th anniversary of the Tiananmen Massacre, it seemed surreal that both the inflatable "Tank Man"—that in many ways looked as harmless at a bouncy castle—and me sharing pictures of it, would be close to unthinkable across the 180 km wide Taiwan Strait that separates democratic Taiwan from mainland China.

But the Beijing government's ambition and ability to control our narratives was soon to hit even closer to home. On June 4, the day after experiencing the inflatable "Tank Man" in Taipei, I was back in Hong Kong where I lived at the time. In iconic Victoria Park, surrounded by some of Hong Kong's tallest skyscrapers, I was one of more than 100,000 Hongkongers that took part in what for 30 years has been one of the only vigils for the Tiananmen Massacre on Chinese soil.[6] This is how I summed up the experience in a social media post along with a video of thousands of people holding candles while Cantonese music plays "I have rarely been part of anything as moving, as beautiful, and as real. #RememberJune4 #TiananmenMassacre #HongKong".[7]

What no one knew at the time was that this might have been the last large-scale vigil in Hong Kong for the foreseeable future. As we exited Victoria Park to walk home, the surrounding narrow streets were filled with activists and citizens with posters and flyers encouraging everyone to take part in an upcoming

More than 100,000 people gathered in Hong Kong's Victoria Park on June 4, 2019 to commemorate the Tiananmen Massacre. Photo courtesy of the author.

demonstration against the now infamous extradition bill introduced by the Hong Kong government earlier in the year. The following Sunday upwards of one million Hongkongers took to the street in what is often seen as the start of the 2019 pro-democracy protests. The subsequent Sunday closer to two million Hongkongers joined in protests.[8]

Two years later, as I write this in a Copenhagen apartment, both the 2020 and 2021 Tiananmen Massacre Vigils have effectively been banned, the city's Tiananmen Square museum—the only one of its kind in Greater China—forced closed, and Hongkongers who took part in informal vigils and gatherings have been charged and convicted under Hong Kong's new draconian National Security Law imposed by Beijing in swift reaction to the 2019 protests.[9]

In private and in the digital space Hongkongers might still be able to commemorate the massacre. However, the National Security Law has had a significant chilling effect as it makes anything Beijing officials regarded as inciting subversion, secession, terrorism, or colluding with foreign forces punishable by up to life in prison. Article 38 broadens the law beyond the physical territory of Hong Kong: "This Law shall apply to offenses under this Law committed against the Hong Kong Special Administrative Region from outside the Region by a person who is not a permanent resident of the Region". In other words, nobody, anywhere, is spared—including me for writing this text or you if you wanted to tweet a picture of the inflatable "Tank Man".

States New Ideology of Information Abundance

Before I moved to Hong Kong and started feeling the silencing nature of digital authoritarianism on my own body and in my own writing, I spent close to a decade in the US and Europe with human rights organizations focused on the right to freedom of expression. I have thus spent countless hours researching, documenting and advocating cases where journalists and artists are imprisoned or censored. And although the Chinese government often tops the lists of worst jailers and biggest censors, they are in no way alone. In 2020, Freemuse, where I worked from 2015-17 and have since contributed as a consultant, documented 978 acts of violations of artistic freedom in 89 countries and online spaces. 17 artists were killed, 82 were imprisoned and 133 detained, while the organization confirmed 352 acts of censorship in 73 countries. The perpetrators range from political and religious groups, to social media platforms and private individuals, but it is worth noting that different government authorities instigated the violations in 60 percent of the cases.[10]

What Freemuse is counting here is of course human rights violations as defined by international conventions, most notably the Universal Declaration of Human Rights, the International Covenant on Civil and Political Rights, and the International Covenant on Economic, Social and Cultural Rights. No easy task in and of itself, given the sensitivity, vulnerabilities and risk for everyone involved, from the victim and their family, to any sources that dare speak out. However, what is even harder to count—in particular for a human rights organization but also for everyone else—is when no individually identifiable action that meets the threshold of a human rights violation has taken place. As authoritarian states have realized that a filled prison cell or a closed art gallery is no longer the only, or necessary most efficient, way to uphold their dominant narrative in an era of data-driven communications, a tactical shift has taken place to what has been called an "ideology of information abundance". [11]

Authoritarian states', 'old' ideology of information scarcity—e.g. imprisonment and censorship of truth tellers and other dissident voices has not disappeared though. Rather, it has been supplemented by a new range of tools and tactics such as cyber attacks, hacking, invasion of privacy, computational propaganda, disinformation, and political bots designed to intimidate alternative voices into silence or simply crowd out inconvenient truths, be they artistic or otherwise.[12]

And while most artists would know what government is imprisoning them, a key feature of States' ideology of information abundance is that the digital attacks and disinformation is not necessarily coming from government-controlled entities directly. Rather, depending on the local context, a lot of it is a result of a complex web of formal and informal command lines, power structures and incentivising practises that creates online environments where artists challenging a dominant narrative will feel like the attacks they face are created organically by a multitude of actors and individuals. This is no coincidence. As many prominent alternative voices in the digital space have attested to, the feeling of being attacked from "all sides" without a clear identifiable opponent is part of what makes the experience terrifying and resulting in some people either permanently or for a period of time deciding to silence themselves.[13]

'Traditional Values' and Thin-Skinned Presidents

Embracing misogynistic 'traditional values', as defined by orthodox conservative groups around the world, has proven to be a popular way for so-called 'strongmen' presidents and their authoritarian states to build and signal to troll armies who and what to target online. When I was invited to give a talk on artistic freedom at the Garage Museum in Moscow in 2017, I chose a lighthearted but no less censored Chinese Internet meme comparing China's president Xi Jinping with Winnie the Pooh to illustrate a point about thin-skinned presidents as a defining feature of our time. I could of course have chosen the viral photo of the mural with Russian president Vladimir Putin kissing then US president Donald Trump by Dominykas Čečkauskas and Mindaugas Bonanu.[14] But I saw no reason to create unnecessary trouble for an art institution already navigating the many complexities of the Russian art scene. In 2012, when Vladimir Putin was reinstated as the President of Russia, he vowed to "respect and protect the rights and freedoms of man and citizen".[15] But shortly after, his government introduced a range of laws and actions proving a more cynical and limited understanding of the rights and freedom of the country's citizens. An amendment to the Russian criminal code, which was widely seen as a reaction to the anti-Putin performance in a Moscow cathedral by the feminist protest punk group Pussy Riot, made it a crime punishable with prison to offend the "religious feelings of believers". Similarly, Putin's anti-LGBT "propaganda" law and "foreign agents" law have sent a chilling message to artists and others who express alternatives to the government line.[16]

"The atmosphere [here] is very toxic. It is hard to survive if you are an artist",[17] Pussy Riot member and actor Nika Nikulshina told me from Moscow last year. Yet it is hard to find a picture on Nikulshina's Instagram that does not in some creative way challenges Putin's patriarchal story of what Russia is or should be.[18] Nikulshina, whom I first met in connection with a censored Badiucao art exhibition in Hong Kong, caught the world's attention when she, along with three fellow activists, ran onto the pitch during the 2018 FIFA World Cup final hosted in Moscow to protest human rights abuses in the country. For that she received a 15-day jail sentence and has since been detained and jailed multiple times, often in the lead-up to important dates on the official Russian calendar such as Victory Day

make everything
great again

Mural with Russian president Vladimir Puting kissing then US president Donald Trump by
Dominykas Čečkauskas and Mindaugas Bonanu. Photo courtesy of the artists.

and latest out of fear she would disrupt the Euro 2020 games (played in 2021) in
St. Petersburg. As Nikulshina explained it to me last year: "The authorities try to
protect themselves from contemporary art".[19]

In 42% of cases "indecency" was the main rationale used to silence women and
artworks according to Freemuse's categorization of artistic freedom violations in
2020. Other rationales included "politics" (27) and "religion" (16%).[20]

Despite an increased focus in recent years, the systematic study of online violence against women artists is still under-analysed. There are of course obvious
differences, but we can get some indication of the threats women artists face
when challenging both states and other power structures dominant narratives
from the challenges women journalists face when doing the same.

In a 2021 report that is surprisingly candid for a UN agency, UNESCO authors
note that online attacks on women journalists appear to be increasing significantly, and conclude that the online violence is designed to "belittle, humiliate, and
shame; induce fear, silence, and retreat; discredit them professionally, undermining accountability journalism and trust in facts; and chill their active participation
(along with that of their sources, colleagues and audiences) in public debate".[21]

"For me there is a direct relationship between dance and liberation...when
a woman stands on stage to dance what she is saying is: 'Here I am, I am not
ashamed of my body. I am confident and I don't fear you,'"[22] says dancer and wom-
en's right activist Sheema Kermani when talking about her artistic and activist
practice. I first met Kermani in Karachi, Pakistan, at a workshop I was co-hosting
with Shirkat Gah as part of my work for Freemuse. Although she founded Tehrik-
e-Niswan, a women's rights movement, in Pakistan in the early 1970s, the Internet
and in particular social media has become an important part of her activism in or-

der to spotlight specific injustices, highlight empowering performances and reach both domestic and international audiences.

"It is absolutely essential for us to feel that we are connected to those who can raise a voice for us internationally... Whenever the international media has given us some consideration it has helped us to promote our work nationally",[23] Kermani told me on a video call from Karachi.

When a suicide bomber attacked a shrine in 2017, killing 90 people, Kermani came to the Sufi shrine in the days after and performed the Dhamaal, a spiritual dance in an act of defiance and solidarity. The videos[24] and images of her brave performance reverberated around the world creating a beautiful, graceful, and powerful counter-narrative to the fear and silence the terrorist act was supposed to create.

Leadership Looks Different

The emergence of politically inspired and shareable art as a defining character of social movements of the 21st century has been widely documented, and the Internet or social media is—probably overly optimistically—often hailed as a central and positive factor in this development.[25]

One argument why creative expressions play a prominent role in contemporary social movements is that the leadership of such movements has changed. Many young people I spoke to in the streets of Hong Kong during the 2019 protest described what they were part of as a "leaderless movement", and artistic expressions from artists as well as regular citizens became an instrumental part of expressing the values, ideas and tactics of the movement.[26] Those same ideas and tactics would historically have been expressed by one or a handful of identifiable leaders.

According to Jamila Raqib, executive director of the Albert Einstein Institution, a leading organization promoting the study and use of nonviolent action based in Boston, USA, so-called leaderless movements show a new recognition of what power is and where it comes from. "Leadership looks different than it did in the Indian independence movement, the American civil rights movement, the Polish Solidarity movement. It is not necessarily that there is no leadership. But it is not centralized and it is not charismatic in the sense that one person has all the knowledge and determines strategy. If we decentralize knowledge and access to information, I think that takes the place of a need for one person that tells us what to do",[27] she told me from Boston when I interviewed her during the 2019 Hong Kong protests.

The Data-Driven Arms Race for Our Attention

Artists at the forefront of social movements have embraced
new digital infrastructures to
reach real and perceived global
audiences.[28] The complexity of
assessing the impact of artistic
expressions in social movements
and if and how it scales with the
introduction of social media and
other data-driven processes is
no easy task. But two things are
clear; one, whether you are a socially engaged artists in Taiwan,
a young protester in the streets of
Hong Kong, an icon for women's
rights in Pakistan, a journalist
uncovering the wrongdoings of
the powerful, or a whistleblower as

Sheema Kermani on stage at the Arts Council in Karachi, Pakistan. Photo courtesy of Sheema Kermani.

described throughout this anthology, one thing everyone has in common is the need for attention from others and ideally at a scale to drive the intended pro-gressive change. Secondly, authoritarian regimes and other reactionary power structures are acutely aware of this and, as described above, they are going to great lengths to either silence the critical voice or make sure no broader societal attention is awarded to that voice.

This arms race for attention between opposing forces in society is nothing new. However, the dynamics and infrastructures that determine what receives our attention have changed fundamentally. In the book *Feed-forward*,[29] artist and professor Mark Hansen argues that media has undergone a fundamental shift from past-directed-recording platforms to a data-driven anticipation of the fu-ture. With smart devices and microsensors, we now have the capacity to access aspects of our experience that would otherwise be beyond the grasp of our modes of perceptual awareness.[30]

Newspapers told you what happened yesterday. Data-driven media, based on existing data-points associated with their profiles of us, tries to anticipate what is most likely to capture your attention next. We are therefore no longer able to consciously decide what art, information or propaganda we want to embrace. In no way a replicable data analysis, but sitting with my phone in Hong Kong during the protest it was remarkable how few videos from the pro-democracy protests I was able to find on the Chinese video app TikTok, while American owned Twitter, YouTube, Facebook and Instagram were flooded with glorified images and videos of young pro-democracy protesters. Data-driven processes are at best helping you find the most relevant information to create change or at worst manipulating your access and exposure to the very information you are basing your decisions on. Or as Shoshana Zuboff describes it in *The Age of Surveillance Capitalism*: "A new economic order [has emerged] that claims human experience as free raw material for hidden commercial practices of extradition, prediction and sales".[31] And you might add narrative control.

The premise becomes no less challenging for progressive artists and other truth tellers when taking into account who owns and dominates the vast majority of the data, knowledge and resources to run these predictions about our future attention and behaviour. Our current digital infrastructures are either ultimately controlled and regulated by digital authoritarian states—most notably Chinese owned Baidu, Alibaba, Tencent, ByteDance (creator of TikTok that passed two billion app downloads globally last year[32]) and Huawei, or governed by a handful of American owned tech giants like Facebook, Amazon, Alphabet, bordering on monopolies when it comes to the concentration of data, wealth and power, with business models relying on selling citizens attention and data to the highest bidder including actors working against free open democratic societies. The disturbingly close ties between US intelligence services and Alphabet—the parent company of Google and YouTube—as well as the scale of Facebook's Cambridge Analytica scandal and the company's outrageous negligence in regards to its role in the Rohingya genocide, crystallizes the scary challenges of our data-driven predicaments.[33]

The companies' and ultimately their governments' ability, both Chinese and American, to predict and influence our future behaviour is dependent on them gathering more data on us. That ability is currently improving at unimaginable rates. Looking at it from this perspective, the artistic practices described above that so heavily involve giant tech companies' platforms, apps and search engines have thus—despite undoubtedly creating change at local levels—also contributed to strengthening some of the very power structures they are trying to challenge.

This is a new condition for artists and other truth tellers that needs to be taken into account all the way from the individual art performance, to how we organize, communicate and demand change as a creative civil society.

But if there is one thing I have learned from my many encounters with courageous awe-inspiring artists like Badiucao, who is no longer in China, Nika Nikulshina in Russia and Sheema Kermani in Pakistan, on the frontlines of some of our defining struggles of our times, it is that artists will never rest. I have also witnessed how well-organized human rights campaigns have led authoritarian governments to change behaviour—simply because the cost of keeping an artist silenced in jail has increased, as a result of coordinated civil society pressure, to a level that outweighed the benefits of holding her behind bars. So although human rights organizations—many of them founded in the late 70s, early 80s—have been slow to adapt to the fundamental conditions of our data-driven worlds, the core mandate and mission of putting pressure on and holding power structures to account is as important and relevant as ever. I have met artists who have been jailed multiple times and have had their life work and finances dismantled only to start again as soon as the prison doors opened. As F. Scott Fitzgerald has said "the test of a first-rate intelligence is the ability to hold two opposed ideas in the mind at the same time, and still retain the ability to function. One should, for example, be able to see that things are hopeless and yet be determined to make them otherwise".[34] We need this relentless approach from artists and it must be encouraged and empowered by human rights and other support structures so artists can help us reimagine and build alternative digital infrastructures that replace the current market-oriented or authoritarian default approaches to data governance with a common-oriented approach that puts rights, interests and sovereignty of all people in all parts of the world at its centre.

It is no small task and will demand a lot of truth-telling from a multitude of critical approaches about surveillance capitalist companies as well as digital authoritarian states. But thanks to Pablo Picasso, we know where to start, since:

Art is the lie that tells the truth.[35]

Notes

1. CNN Editorial Research, "Tiananmen Square Fast Facts", *CNN.com*, May 20, 2021, https://edition.cnn.com/2013/09/15/world/asia/tiananmen-square-fast-facts/index.html.

2. "Badiucao, "Using Art to Resist: Cartoonist Becomes The Tank Man", *China Change*, June 5, 2016, https://chinachange.org/2016"/06/05/using-art-to-resist-cartoonist-badiucao-becomes-the-tank-man.

3. Lotus Ruan, Jeffrey Knockel, Masashi Crete-Nishihata, "Information control by public punishment: The logic of signalling repression in China", *Sage Journals*, October 13, 2020, https://journals.sagepub.com/doi/full/10.1177/0920203X20963010.

4. "Censored Commemoration", *Citizen Lab*, June 4, 2019, https://citizenlab.ca/2019/06/censored-commemoration-chinese-live-streaming-platform-yy-focuses-censorship-june-4-memorials-activism-hong-kong.

5. "China: Account for Tiananmen Massacre", *HRW*, June 3, 2021, https://www.hrw.org/news/2021/06/03/china-account-tiananmen-massacre.

6. Helen Davidson, "Tiananmen Square massacre marked with Hong Kong vigil", *The Guardian*, June 4, 2019, https://www.theguardian.com/world/2019/jun/04/tiananmen-square-massacre-marked-with-hong-kong-vigil.

7. https://www.facebook.com/agmagnus/posts/10161952797675074.

8. "2019–2020 Hong Kong protests",, *Wikipedia*, accessed June 23, 2021, https://en.wikipedia.org/wiki/2019%E2%80%932020_Hong_Kong_protests#Early_large-scale_demonstrations.

9. Rhoda Kwan, "Hong Kong effectively bans Victoria Park's Tiananmen Massacre vigil again, citing Covid-19 restrictions", *Hong Kong Free Press*, April 28, 2021, https://hongkongfp.com/2021/04/28/hong-kong-bans-victoria-parks-tiananmen-massacre-vigil-again-citing-covid-19-restrictions/; Lilit Marcus, "Hong Kong's Tiananmen Square museum forced to close two days ahead of memorial", *CNN.com*, June 2, 2021, https://edition.cnn.com/travel/article/june-fourth-museum-tiananmen-square-hong-kong-cmd/index.html.

10. "State of Artistic Freedom 2021", *Freemuse*, February 25, 2021, https://freemuse.org/news/the-state-of-artistic-freedom-2021.

11. Nicholas Monaco and Carly Nyst, "State-Sponsored Trolling", *Institute for the Future*, 2018, https://www.iftf.org/statesponsoredtrolling.

12. Ibid.

13. Ibid.

14. Make Everything Great Again, *Wikipedia*, accessed June 23, 2021, https://en.wikipedia.org/wiki/Make_Everything_Great_Again.

15. Third inauguration of Vladimir Putin, *Wikipedia*, accessed June 23, 2021, https://en.wikipedia.org/wiki/Third_inauguration_of_Vladimir_Putin.

16. Magnus Ag, "In Russia, Scared of the Arts then and now", *Freemuse*, October 23, 2017, https://freemuse.org/news/in-russia-scared-of-the-arts-then-and-now.

17. Nika Nikulshina, interview conducted on February 2, 2020 by the author via video call.

18. https://www.instagram.com/protrezvey.

19. Interview with Nika Nikulshina conducted on February 2, 2020 by the author via video call.

20. Magnus Ag, "In Russia, Scared of the Arts then and now", *Freemuse*, October 23, 2017, https://freemuse.org/news/in-russia-scared-of-the-arts-then-and-now.

21. Julie Posetti, Nabeelah Shabbir, Diana Maynard, Kalina Bontcheva, Nermine Aboulez, "The Chilling: Global trends in online violence against women journalists", *UNESCO*, April 2021, https://en.unesco.org/sites/default/files/the-chilling.pdf.

22. Bridge Figures, "Dance for Women's Rights", *bridgefigures.org*, https://bridgefigures.org/sheema.

23. Sheema Kermani, interview conducted in 2018 by the author via video call.

24. YouTube, "she danced and danced, until she and Sehwan became one..." https://www.youtube.com/watch?v=THgM3Y85S2Q.

25. Peter Weibel, *Global Activism, Art and Conflict in the 21st Century*, (The MIT Press, 2015).

26. Magnus Ag, "Inside Hong Kong's Leaderless Uprising", *The Diplomat*, October 24, 2019, https://thediplomat.com/2019/10/inside-hong-kongs-leaderless-uprising.

27. Jamila Raqib, interview conducted in October 2019 by the author via video call.

28. Peter Weibel, *Global Activism, Art and Conflict in the 21st Century*, 2015; Tanya Ravn Ag in *Digital Dynamics in Nordic Contemporary Art*, Intellect 2019.

29. Mark Hansen, *Feed-Forward*, (Chicago and London, The University of Chicago Press, 2015).

30. Ibid., 4.

31. Shoshana Zuboff, *The Age of Surveillance Capitalism*, (New York, PublicAffairs, 2019).

32. Manish Singh, "TikTok tops 2 billion downloads", *TechCrunch*, April 29, 2020, https://techcrunch.com/2020/04/29/tiktok-tops-2-billion-downloads.

33. Zuboff, *The Age*, 112-121; "Facebook–Cambridge Analytica data scandal", *Wikipedia*, accessed June 23. 2021, https://en.wikipedia.org/wiki/Facebook%E2%80%93Cambridge_Analytica_data_scandal.; BBC, "Facebook admits it was used to 'incite offline violence' in Myanmar", *bbc.com*, November 6, 2018, https://www.bbc.com/news/world-asia-46105934.

34. F. Scott Fitzgerald, "The Crack-Up", *Esquire*, 1936, https://www.esquire.com/lifestyle/a4310/the-crack-up.

35. Inspired by Pablo Picasso, to whom several versions of the sentence "Art Is a Lie That Makes Us Realize Truth", have been attributed, *Quote Investigator*, 2019, accessed June 23, 2021, https://quoteinvestigator.com/2019/10/29/lie-truth.

Photo by Dorothy Edwards

OS KEYES

Os Keyes is a researcher and writer at the University of Washington, where they engage with questions of gender, race, disability, technology and power. Their research on facial recognition, the politics of technology and the philosophical underpinnings of "AI ethics" has been published in *Cultural Studies* the *Journal of Sociotechnical Critique* and the Conference on Computer-Human Interaction, amongst other venues. They are an inaugural winner of the Ada Lovelace Fellowship.

OS KEYES

JUSTICE, CHANGE AND TECHNOLOGY
ON THE LIMITS OF WHISTLEBLOWING [1]

THIS CHAPTER is about social change, and the means we go about achieving it. Social change is fundamentally just that: *social*. It is about different ways of relating to each other, and the different kinds of people we might be as a result. Vitally, the work of making this change happen—of working towards a world in which people relate and reflect in different ways—is just as social. It consists of ways of changing or enabling those relations, ways of reflecting on ourselves and each other, and ways of forming and reforming collective movements and identities. Social change is social, and so is the work of producing it.

Confusingly, some of the archetypes and personas we celebrate as representing activism at its purest are fundamentally asocial. One of those is the "truth-teller": the whistleblower, the critic, the iconoclast. In this chapter I argue that the way we frame truth-telling, and the figure who does it ignores the social nature of change, and risks celebrating and mimicking ideals that not only do a poor job of getting us closer to a better world, but in many respects *undermine* efforts for social change through the voices and attitudes they do (or do not) make space for.

Ideas and Ideals of Social Change

The techniques to be used in activism or social movements—what approach makes the most sense given a particular problem or situation—are endlessly contested. To adapt a Yiddishism: if you have three activists, you have nine opinions. But one particular cluster of archetypes and people stands out. I'm thinking specifically of the "whistleblower"; the critical thinker and practitioner of critique; the iconoclast (literally: smasher of false idols).[2] Each of these archetypes is distinct, but what brings them *together* is the idea of a person who tells "dangerous truths",[3] and through doing so, catalyses and generates change in how we see the world—individually, and collectively—and how we behave towards it.

Each of these archetypes are individually valorised—particularly in progressive and leftist spaces. Whistleblowers are described as the "saints of the secular age"; as "extraordinary heroes" of "exceptional courage".[4] Snowden, Ellsberg, Manning—we give them awards, we praise their bravery and impact, we hold them up as a very particular idea of what people should be. And at the risk of assuming my audience: the perceived "purity" of critique, the value of the scholar Rita Felski vividly describes as "suspicious, knowing, self-conscious, hardheaded, tirelessly vigilant",[5] goes almost without saying. For individual activists, this is never one-sided—Snowden or Manning are portrayed as traitors as frequently as they are heroes, if not moreso. But critics portray them as traitors *rather than* whistleblowers; the link between whistleblowing and heroism remains intact.

I don't want to come off as entirely unsympathetic; truth-telling *does* create avenues for change, and there are very good reasons (particularly on the left) to be suspicious, and to value suspicion.[6] More broadly, in a society that centres the pursuits of truth and authenticity (Foucault, Taylor), truth is the currency of the day.[7] If you want to create change, reformist or radical, revealing hidden truths is a familiar way of doing it. The problem is not truth-telling, but the status we give to it and the very odd way we see those who do it—specifically, our failure to attend to the *social relations* of the very methods we're using to seek changes to social relations. I'm thinking of three things, in particular; the vulnerability of truth-telling to existing social inequalities, the way lauding and atomizing "truth-telling" creates unjust and perverse incentives for the forms of activism we value and engage in, and the actual impact that this mentality of suspicion, of unmasking, of taking nobody's word for it, has on the ability of us—activists—to build community. I will unpack each of these in turn.

Whose Truths?

In 2018, Alex Stamos—the Chief Security Officer of Facebook—publicly began disassociating himself from the company, and making plans to leave. The central reason for his departure was misinformation: specifically, the feeling that Facebook had done a poor job in controlling it during the 2016 US presidential election, and the increasing certainty that the changes he felt were necessary would not be tolerated by the company.

Three years later, Doctor Timnit Gebru—a senior researcher at Google—went just as public with concerns, writing a paper that took issue with the societal and ecological consequences of large-scale machine learning systems (including those built by her employer). The two's stories diverge entirely at that point. Alex Stamos, a White man with an undergraduate degree in electrical engineering, is now the director of the Stanford Internet Observatory and a visiting professor at Stanford

University. Doctor Gebru, an Ethiopian woman with a PhD *from* Stanford, is unemployed. The response to her work was to fire her.[8]

These are not unusual injustices: White man is lauded, Black woman is fired. Stamos's complaints were within what the game allowed; Gebru's were her getting above her station, and forgetting her place—a place characterized not only by the gendered and racialized inequalities that are endemic to US society in general, but the specific, additional inequalities and presumptions of ignorance and incompetence that come from the social character of the technology sector. Indeed, as someone who followed along both controversies, I cannot help but notice the ways in which Dr. Gebru's technical skills and brilliance are undercut and belittled precisely in order to delegitimize her experiences of racism and misogyny—and the way that the debate over those experiences has come to overshadow the concerns she first intended to go public about. In technological critique, it seems, Black women can (maybe) speak as Black women. But they better not dare to speak as scientists.

I highlight these disappointing yet unsurprising disparities here to emphasise that one way in which truth-telling is social is that it occurs *in society*: that it is undertaken under the conditions of society as it stands. These conditions include widespread epistemic injustice: inequalities in whose knowledge counts as knowledge, or as truth; inequalities in who is listened to, or permitted to speak without punishment.[9] This goes double for *technological* critique: not only is there the general air of illegitimacy about the knowledge of women, queer people, disabled people and people of colour, there is the particular prominence and history of excluding such people from technology in particular.[10]

If truth-telling is merely one of a sheaf of approaches, and the truth-teller one of many actors, then this is not a *major* limitation: all tactics are flawed and partial. But my worry is that in our rhetoric and imaginaries, truth-telling becomes centred as the primary, or only, way of effecting change. If this is the case, then we are going to end up with imbalanced and *unjust* ideas of social change itself: we will end up prioritising those concerns that are taken up by those who are already listened to, and diminishing the rest. This is inarguably the precise opposite of what injustice-focused activism should be doing.

Collective Truths

Beyond the question of who gets to tell truths, there is also the question of what work goes into doing so—and how our centring of not just truth telling but the truth-teller, singular, obscures much of the labour that social movements depend on to thrive. As an illustration of precisely this, we can look at media portrayals of WikiLeaks, and the figures involved in operating it.

Following the disclosures of Edward Snowden—specifically, the information on NSA surveillance practices—WikiLeaks became practically a household name. Public and media attention rapidly focused on those working at the organisation, one of whom was Sarah Harrison. Originally a journalist, and a researcher for the Centre for Investigative Journalism, Harrison quickly became a vital part of WikiLeaks, playing a central role in the decision to publish the US diplomatic cables and in organising Edward Snowden's escape to Hong Kong, as Angela Richter recounts in her introduction to *Women, Whistleblowing, WikiLeaks*:

> [Harrison] had travelled to Hong Kong for the organization and had helped Edward Snowden escape after his announcement that he was the NSA whistleblower. She intervened as his situation was becoming increasingly difficult. By the time she arrived in Hong Kong, Snowden was on his own…She stayed with him after the successful escape to Moscow, first for weeks in a windowless room in the transit zone of Moscow's Sheremetyevo airport, and then for many more months in the city. She did not leave for her voluntary exile in Berlin until she knew that Snowden was safe.[11]

This "voluntary exile" continues to this day: as a consequence of her work for WikiLeaks, Harrison has been unable to return home since 2014. The centrality of Harrison's work according to those who were actually *involved* in WikiLeaks and its disclosures contrasts strongly with how media coverage discussed her. Harrison, *Der Spiegel* wrote, was simply the "assistant" or "friend" of Julian Assange—and this was the coverage by WikiLeaks media *partners*, nevermind venues more hostile to the disclosures.

What is the point of me telling this story? Is this not just misogyny, already discussed in the last section? No doubt, misogyny plays a massive part of the diminishing of Harrison's role, as highlighted by both Richter and Agostinho & Thylstrup.[12] But I would argue that there is something beyond, or perhaps intertangled with, misogyny, here. Specifically, there is a certain *atomisation* and *individualisation* of WikiLeaks, with a particular focus on (in this case) Snowden and Assange.

Stories of truth-telling heroes, like stories of heroes more broadly, are stories of unusual individuals. Truth-telling comes from the *one* person in a situation be brave enough (or insightful enough, or lucky enough, or mad enough) to say the unspeakable. Truth-telling is an individual practice, and if truth-telling is the idealised mechanism of social change, then social change, too, is an individual practice. Such a perspective makes a lot of sense; not only does it fit the broader individualist narratives of neoliberal society in general, there is a grain of truth to it. Social movements and social change often do begin with individual awakenings, and individual efforts.[13] But the key word, there, is *begin*: even truth-telling often involves multiple parties, and turning those truths into action always does. The *Collateral Murder* video would not be what it was without the editing of Birgitta Jónsdóttir; the escape of Snowden may have failed without the presence of Harrison. But our framings of truth-tellers are so individualised, and so focused on singular heroes, that we ignore these wider networks and the more mundane work required to keep them running.

Writing about the failure conditions of mutual aid networks, Dean Spade warns that one prominent vulnerability is the way in which "we are used to being part of groups that ignore ordinary caring labour, much of which is seen as women's work...while celebrating only the final, outward-looking evidence of production: the big protest march, the finalized legislation, the release of someone from prison, the media coverage...many of us think 'process is boring'. Everyone wants a selfie with Angela Davis at the big event, but many people are less interested in the months of meetings where we coordinate how to pull off that event".[14] The result of this perceived "boringness" is that the work of coordination, of editing, of administration, is devalued, and so are those who do it. Yet this work is also *vital* if groups are to be sustainable, and sustained—if they are to have a shot at making real change, and doing so without being deeply miserable for those participating.

To link this back to our example here: what is telling about the treatment of Harrison is not simply the misogyny that led to her being dismissed as an "assistant" or a "friend", but that classification as an assistant or friend is the same as dismissing the importance of their work. The individualised nature of "the truth-teller" implicitly carries with it a certain *solitary* component; an intentional ignorance of (or, assumed absence of) the communities and networks needed to make truths matter, and the less "heroic", but no less vital, work undertaken by those networks. By individualising change, and associating it only with heroic, public work, we risk kicking the chair out from under ourselves. Change needs communities, collectives, and networks, and organising them rarely involves work that is heroic. But it is work that matters, nonetheless.

After Truth

Finally, there is the issue of how these imageries not only misrepresent the relational nature of change, but sometimes actively *damage our ability to form those relationships*.

This section is personal for me, and is the reason I was first drawn to writing about this topic. Over the last four years, I fell—in some ways accidentally—into the role of the "teller of dangerous truths". I was the critic, the exposer, the whistleblower, the walking, talking stereotype. My work—originally focused on facial recognition and its harms and inequalities[15]—centred on exposing falsehood, in unmasking shallow thinking. By most accounts, it was fairly successful, with publications, press coverage, and growing public awareness. As I write, in fact, a collective of activist groups and individuals are preparing draft legislation to ban the technology I wrote about in the European Union. Presumably I should be rather happy with this; I pointed out that the emperor had no clothes and people are moving pretty fast to get him some underwear.

But the fact of the matter is that I am *not* happy, not now, and certainly not while I was doing the work. What I mostly remember is being miserable, and being exhausted, and being the source of profound hurt for a lot of other people. What I mostly feel is regret—regret for how I behaved, for how I went about my work, for how some of the same phenomena I highlight above (inequalities in who gets to speak, and an ignorance of the work needed to make change *sustainable*) absolutely snookered me. Many people from that time simply no longer talk to me, and while I hold out hope that the few who promised they would return will keep that promise, I consider it entirely understandable if they do not.

The reason for this all is psychic, affective; it is about the *mindset* of truth-telling, the persona and personality of that figure we valorise so much. Critical analysis is (as discussed above) a particular species of truth-telling, and the critic a type of truth-teller. Watkins describes the critic as one whose role is of "heroic resistance to all the social pressures toward conformity, mass culture homogeneity, utilitarian demands and the bureaucratization of knowledge"[16] Felski, as mentioned earlier, articulates the mindset of the critic as "suspicious, knowing, self-conscious, hardheaded, tirelessly vigilant",[17] deploying these attitudes to unmask falsehood and shout truth.

Truth-tellers, as these descriptions make clear, certainly make bad enemies. But they make far more atrocious friends. I was this stereotype, and believed I had to be; I was suspicious, knowing, vigilant, hardheaded (definitely hardheaded). And if truth-telling truly was an individual, heroic practice, maybe this would have been okay. But it is not: it is, as we have discussed, *social*, involving whole networks of people collaborating to shape and endorse and publicise a truth, and even more vitally, ensure that something is *done* with it. And suspicion is a terrible basis on which to build a friendship. It is also, given the implicit and paradoxical dogmatism that comes with it, arguably a terrible basis to build truth.[18]

When truth-telling becomes a mindset and a personality—and when exposing truths becomes the highest value you adhere to—relationships become damaged, and impossible. Damaged, because when the only tools you have are destructive, building things—spaces, hopes, relationships—becomes incredibly hard, and incredibly alien. Impossible, because nobody can truly be that person all the time; we are all riven with contradictions, insecurities, little white lies that slowly blossom and less-white lies that metastasise like a cancer. Hanging your hat entirely on the truth means disappointing and hurting those around you when you fail to live up to that impossible standard—and it means lacking any useful tools for repairing relationships when this inevitably happens. Suspicion does not allow space for vulnerability; vigilance does not allow space for trust.

Perhaps if we treated truth-telling as an activity for anyone, rather than truth-tellers as standalone "heroic" figures, things might be different. We would hold ourselves to more generous standards, we would have greater humility, less paranoia, and less fear; we would build precisely the kinds of relationships within our activism we are hoping for our activism to make possible for *everyone*. Perhaps not. But if we believe that there is a moral duty to aid efforts for social change— to build a better world, of better people, relating in better ways—then we have a duty to undertake this work *prefiguratively*: to embody the very values we wish to see.[19] To trust, though trust is a risk;[20] to offer solidarity, though we might be disappointed. To understand that no one person can lead us to a better world, and that—as Debs put it—if they could lead us in, it would mean someone else could just as easily lead us out. To work collectively, not individually.

As I have learned the hard way, the valorisation of the truth-teller—the truth teller as an individual, as a *heroic* individual, as a *cynical* individual—trips us up in doing just these things. If truth-telling is what matters, then the questions of whose truths are listened to does not fit the frame. If truth-telling is *individual*, the work that scaffolds social change and makes it sustainable is wasted. And if truth-telling is a *mindset*, rather than a *technique*, then we can only be that cynical, paranoid, vigilant person. And frankly, a world of insecure cynicism that dismisses the value of "boring" work and glosses over the silencing of marginalized voices is an odd goal to have. We don't need to go there; we already live there.

What we need is not more iconoclasts, or judgment; what we need is more understanding, more recognition. What we need is more appreciation of the bonds between us, the work that goes into sustaining them, and the need to *prioritise* sustaining them if we are to mirror the values we want to see in the world as a whole. We need well-rounded people, and well-rounded ideals of people, to have well-rounded spaces. As "well-rounded" hopefully makes clear, I am not suggesting that negativity or suspicion are bad, or have no place in our formation and undertaking of collective organizing. Both can be productive, and necessary; there is often much to be angry about. There is often an "aptness of anger",[21] a justified basis of suspicion and unmasking. As Eve Sedgwick notes, the tendency towards "paranoid readings" in segments of activism and academia is often entirely understandable: many of us start from positions in which there is much to be furious about.[22]

What I am suggesting is, perhaps, simply that if we care so much about toppling false idols we should start with those in our midst. The idea of an atomized, suspicious, destructive hero as the sufficient conditions for change is one such idol. If we want a better world, one built by all of us, one for all of us, we cannot fall back on imaginaries about a single person tearing down the old. Such imaginaries preserve as much of the here-and-now as they claim to destroy. We have to learn how to build better ways of relating, and better ideas of what it means to be a good activist—and we have to do so together. Enough people want to be Edward Snowden; we need more people who want to be Sarah Harrison. Whole networks, collectives, communities of Harrisons.

Notes

1. My thanks to Adam Hyland, Kathleen Creel, Claire Hopkins and Shannon Hackett for their support, feedback and kindness. Additional recognition goes to Anna Lauren Hoffmann, for being an exemplar of how essential trust, honesty and radical vulnerability are in social relationships, Kate Crawford, for first introducing me to the work of Eve Kosofsky Sedgwick, David Ribes, for having the courage to remain invested through the personal growth that underpins much of this chapter, and the many, regretted, absent presences who—quite reasonably—chose a different path.

2. Related, more niche archetypes include Lorraine Code's evocative idea of the "epistemic gadfly". See Code, Lorraine. *Epistemic Responsibility.* (SUNY Press, 2020).

3. This framing is a riff on and echo of Foucault's concept of "parrhesia" and the "parrhesiac"; see Foucault, Michel. "*Discourse and Truth" and "Parresia"*, (University of Chicago Press 2019). Without getting too into the weeds, however, the two cluster concepts are very different in their relation to social and communal dynamics, rather than simplistic ideas of the speaker and listener existing in a vacuum together—although they do both suffer from obvious gendered flaws. See Maxwell, Lida. "The politics and gender of truth-telling in Foucault's lectures on parrhesia." in *Contemporary Political Theory* 18.1 (2019), 22-42.

4. See Kenny, Kate, Marianna Fotaki, and Wim Vandekerckhove. "Whistleblower subjectivities: Organization and passionate attachment". in *Organization Studies* 41, no. 3, (2020), 323-343; Grant, Colin. "Whistle blowers: Saints of Secular Culture." *Journal of Business Ethics* 39.4, (2002), 391-399; Mansbach, Abraham. "Whistleblowing as Fearless Speech: The Radical Democratic Effects of Late Modern Parrhesia." *Whistleblowing and Democratic Values*, (2011), 12-26; Brown, A. J. "Whistleblowers as Heroes." *Handbook of Heroism and Heroic Leadership*, (2017).

5. Felski, Rita. *The Limits of Critique.* (University of Chicago Press, 7, 2015).

6. Consider the long history of state government oppression of left-wing movements, in particular. COINTELPRO, the post-WTO crackdowns, and the current hyperfocus of policing resources on movements responding to White supremacy make for good reasons not to trust new people or information. My local and much-beloved anarchist bookstore, Left Bank Books, features a sign to the tune of: talk here as if the FBI is bugging it, because they probably are.

7. See Taylor, Charles. *The Ethics of Authenticity.* (Harvard University Press, 1992) and Williams, Bernard Arthur Owen. *Truth & Truthfulness: An Essay in Genealogy.* (Princeton University Press, 2002).

8. Lyons, Kim, "Timnit Gebru's actual paper may explain why Google ejected her", *The Verge*, 2021, https://www.theverge.com/2020/12/5/22155985/paper-timnit-gebru-fired-google-large-language-models-search-ai.

9. See Code, Lorraine. *What Can She Know?: Feminist Theory and the Construction of Knowledge* (Cornell University Press, 1991); Collins, Patricia Hill. *Black Feminist Thought: Knowledge, Consciousness and the Politics of Empowerment.* (Routledge, 2002); Prescod-Weinstein, Chanda. "Making Black women scientists under white empiricism: the racialization of epistemology in physics." *Signs: Journal of Women in Culture and Society*

45.2 (2020): 421-447 and Dotson, Kristie. "How is this Paper Philosophy?" *Comparative Philosophy* 3 no.1., (2013): 121-122.

10. See Hicks, Mar. *Programmed inequality: Programmed Inequality: How Britain Discarded Women Technologists and Lost Its Edge in Computing.* (MIT Press, 2017); Keyes, Os. "Automating autism: Disability, discourse, and Artificial Intelligence." *The Journal of Sociotechnical Critique* 1 no.1, (2020); Dunbar-Hester, Christina. *Hacking diversity: The Politics of Inclusion in Open Technology Cultures.* Vol. 21, (Princeton University Press, 2019).

11. Avila, Renata, Sarah Harrison, and Angela Richter. *Women, Whistleblowing, WikiLeaks: A Conversation.* (OR Books, 2018), 1-2.

12. Agostinho, Daniela, and Nanna Bonde Thylstrup. "'If Truth Was a Woman: Leaky Infrastructures and the Gender Politics of Truth-telling." *Ephemera* 19, no.4, (2019): 745-775.

13. See, for example, the interviews with organizational founders in Nownes, Anthony J. *Organizing for Transgender Rights: Collective Action, Group Development, and the Rise of a New Social Movement.* (SUNY Press, 2019).

14. Spade, Dean. *Mutual Aid: Building Solidarity during this Crisis (and the Next),* (Verso Books, 2020), 65-6.

15. Keyes, Os. "The Misgendering Machines: Trans/HCI Implications of Automatic Gender Recognition". *Proceedings of the ACM on human-computer interaction* 2, no. CSCW (2018): 1-22.

16. Watkins, Evan. "The Self-Evaluations of Critical Theory." *Boundary 2,* (1984): 359-378, quoted in Anker, Elizabeth S., and Rita Felski, eds. *Critique and Postcritique,* 7, (Duke University Press, 2017).

17. Felski, Rita. "The Limits of Critique", 7, (University of Chicago Press, 2015).

18. See Code, "Epistemic Responsibility", Chapter 1.

19. Drouhard, Margaret, Josephine Hoy and Os Keyes, "Human-Computer Insurrection: Notes on an Anarchist HCI", *Proceedings of the 2019 CHI Conference on Human Factors in Computing Systems,* (2019).

20. Baier, Annette. "Trust and its vulnerabilities." *Moral Prejudices,* (1994): 130-151.

21. Srinivasan, Amia. "The Aptness of Anger" *Journal of Political Philosophy* 26. no. 2, (2018): 123-144.

22. Sedgwick, Eve Kosofsky. "Paranoid Reading and Reparative Reading, or, You're So Paranoid, You Probably Think This Essay Is About You." (1997).

Bibliography

Agostinho, Daniela, and Nanna Bonde Thylstrup. "'If truth was a woman': Leaky infrastructures and the gender politics of truth-telling." *Ephemera,* 19, no.4, (2019): 745-775.

Anker, Elizabeth S., and Rita Felski, eds. *Critique and postcritique.* (Duke University Press, 2017).

Baier, Annette. "Trust and its vulnerabilities." *Moral prejudices* (1994): 130-151.

Brown, A. J. "Whistleblowers as heroes." *Handbook of Heroism and Heroic Leadership* (2017).

Code, Lorraine. *Epistemic responsibility.* (SUNY Press, 2020).

Code, Lorraine. *What can she know?: feminist theory and the construction of knowledge.* (Cornell University Press, 1991).

Collins, Patricia Hill. *Black feminist thought: Knowledge, consciousness, and the politics of empowerment.* (Routledge, 2002).

Dotson, Kristie. "How is this paper philosophy?." *Comparative Philosophy* 3, no.1, (2013): 121-121.

Drouhard, Margaret, Josephine Hoy and Os. "Human-computer insurrection: Notes on an anarchist HCI." *Proceedings of the 2019 CHI Conference on Human Factors in Computing Systems.* (2019).

Dunbar-Hester, Christina. *Hacking diversity: The politics of inclusion in open technology cultures,* Vol. 21 (Princeton University Press, 2019).

Felski, Rita. *The limits of critique.* (University of Chicago Press, 2015).

Foucault, Michel. *Discourse and truth and parresia*. Chicago Foucault Project, (2019): 46.

Grant, Colin. "Whistle blowers: Saints of secular culture." *Journal of Business Ethics* 39 no.4, (2002): 391-399.

Hicks, Mar. *Programmed inequality: How Britain discarded women technologists and lost its edge in computing*. (MIT Press, 2017).

Kenny, Kate, Marianna Fotaki, and Wim Vandekerckhove. "Whistleblower subjectivities: Organization and passionate attachment", *Organization Studies* 41, no. 3, (2020): 323-343.

Keyes, Os. "Automating autism: Disability, discourse, and Artificial Intelligence", *The Journal of Sociotechnical Critique* 1, no.1, (2020): 8.

Mansbach, Abraham. "Whistleblowing as fearless speech: The radical democratic effects of late modern parrhesia." *Whistleblowing and democratic values*, (2011): 12-26.

Maxwell, Lida. "The politics and gender of truth-telling in Foucault's lectures on parrhesia." *Contemporary Political Theory* 18, no.1, (2019): 22-42.

Prescod-Weinstein, Chanda. "Making Black women scientists under white empiricism: the racialization of epistemology in physics." *Signs: Journal of Women in Culture and Society* 45, no. 2, (2020): 421-447.

Sedgwick, Eve Kosofsky. "Paranoid reading and reparative reading, or, You're so paranoid, you probably think this introduction is about you." (1997).

Spade, Dean. *Mutual Aid: Building Solidarity during this Crisis (and the Next)*. (Verso Books, 2020).

Srinivasan, Amia. "*The aptness of anger.*" Journal of Political Philosophy 26, no. 2, (2018): 123-144.

Rose, Nikolas. *Powers of freedom: Reframing political thought*. (Cambridge university press, 1999).

Taylor, Charles. *The ethics of authenticity*. (Harvard University Press, 1992).

Watkins, Evan. "The Self-Evaluations of Critical Theory." *Boundary* 2, (1984): 359-378.

Williams, Bernard Arthur Owen. Truth & truthfulness: *An essay in genealogy*. (Princeton University Press, 2002).

6

SILENCED BY POWER

REPRESSION, ISOLATION & PERSECUTION

DANIEL HALE
SUELETTE DREYFUS
WITH NAOMI COLVIN
ANNA MYERS
DELPHINE HALGAND-MISHRA
BARRETT BROWN

WHAT ARE the implications of speaking out? Which are the personal consequences of revealing classified information? How can we all support whistleblowers? This section brings to public attention important cases of whistleblowers, truth-tellers, and publishers that contributed to making a deep change in society, and that are paying a high price for it.

Daniel Hale, US American Air Force veteran and former intelligence analyst, was convicted on July 27, 2021 under the Espionage Act to serve a prison sentence for leaking information about the US drone programme. To call for a public debate around his case, we publish the court statement he gave on the day of his sentencing that explains his motivations of disclosing human rights violations in Afghanistan. The chapter that follows is of high relevance to denouncing the current persecution of Julian Assange, who has been incarcerated at the Belmarsh high-security prison in the UK since April 2019, and faces extradition to the US and criminal prosecution under the Espionage Act. Suelette Dreyfus and Naomi Colvin trace the story from the early releases of WikiLeaks in 2010 to the present, describing important moments of the life of Julian Assange, including his meeting with Daniel Ellsberg, the whistleblower of the Pentagon Papers. They stress the unjust dimension of the US Espionage Act, and the many cases of whistleblowers that paid the price of having this draconian law still in use.

Anna Myers and Delphine Halgand-Mishra, respectively the executive directors of Whistleblowing International Network and The Signals Network, give an insight of their motivations to work in the field of whistleblowing protection and advocacy, focusing on the necessity of implementing a "whistleblowing policy" at an European and international level.

The journey of this book ends with the text by Barrett Brown, who reflects on the meaning of whistleblowing, tracing his personal story from the foundation of Project PM, his work with Anonymous, and his later arrest in 2012 and sentencing to four years in federal prison. Despite the serious threats posed to whistleblowers, Barrett Brown makes us reflect on the importance of continuing to confront broken institutional power.

DANIEL HALE

Photo by Bob Hayes

Daniel Everette Hale is a 34 year old US American Air Force veteran and former intelligence analyst from Bristol, Tennessee. In July 2021, Daniel was convicted under the World War I-era Espionage Act for leaking information about the US drone program. He is currently serving a 45-month sentence in federal prison. Daniel joined the US military in 2009, seeing it as the only option for pursuing an education, and was sent to Bagram Air Base in Afghanistan in 2012 as a signal intelligence analyst. He then worked as an analyst for the National Security Agency and at the defence contractor Leidos. Because of Daniel's disclosures, the public learned that during a five-month period in Afghanistan, 90 percent of those killed by US airstrikes were not the intended targets. Daniel explained that his actions were driven by a desire to repent for the harm that he had witnessed and been a part of creating. He is an activist who was involved with various anti-war and social justice efforts including About Face: Veterans Against War and Occupy Wall Street. Daniel enjoys cooking, long motorbike rides, reading and spending time with his cat, Leila.

DANIEL HALE
I BELIEVE THAT IT IS WRONG TO KILL

DANIEL HALE DELIVERED THIS 17-MINUTE STATEMENT to a courtroom packed with friends, advocates, and other whistleblowers on July 27, 2021 on the date of his sentencing in Alexandria, Virginia. Because of the nature of the Espionage Act, under which Daniel was convicted, he was unable to explain the motives for his disclosures in his own voice prior to this moment. Daniel hand-wrote this statement while incarcerated before his sentencing at the Alexandria Adult Detention Center.

"YOUR HONOR, my surname, "Everette Hale", was passed down to me by my father, to him by his father's father, and so-on going back to the theologian writer "Edward Everet Hale." Edward was a Massachusetts-born columnist for the Atlantic monthly newspaper writing about issues of abolition and slavery during the Pre-Civil War era. He was the grand nephew of Revolutionary War Hero Captain Nathan Hale. Nathaniel, of course, is well-known for having been executed for his efforts to spy on the British troop movements in support of Gen. Washington's rebel army as they fought to free the States of colonial rule. Denied clergy, he was given only the chance to speak his piece before left to hang three days in a public square as a warning to other would-be saboteurs. It bears mentioning that, under certain circumstances, an act of espionage is still punishable by death in this country today. Nathan was not a very good spy. Nothing of material value on troop movements was provided, though his true contribution was his defiant last moments. I am not as brave as him. There is no shortage of Americans in history who will sacrifice for others so that they may live dignified lives in a just peace under the rule of law. My only regret is that I have but this one life to give in the sacrifice of my country and I can give that from prison as from without. I do not want to go to prison. I want to start a career, work towards my future, and if I'm lucky, be able to start to heal and begin a family.

The day after I pleaded guilty to a violation of the Espionage Act, I took a lonely bicycle ride towards the Capitol to clear my head, in search of the statue honoring Capt. Hale's sacrifice. I wish I could say that I wasn't surprised to find it located next to the John F. Kennedy Department of Justice building. But there it was, exactly where it belonged. I asked a reluctant security guard to take my photo with the statue of Nathan behind me, told him thank you, to which he responded with a shrug and went about his day. A short way from there, I came to be at the Lincoln War Memorial Park. The park was alive and bustling with people speaking different languages, coming to and fro, from across the country and around the world. Of the many awe-inspiring commemorative monuments surrounding the reflective pool, I believe the Vietnam War Memorial to be the most striking because of its straightforward simplicity. The more than 58,000 names of every American killed in action etched into a 400ft granite wall stands as a testament to the completion of the war and our nation's commitment to never forget the fallen. By contrast, were it also to include the names of every Viet person killed would require it to be another 4 miles long. Curiously, there is still no monument to commemorate the formal end of the Iraq war. I often wonder how we'll remember it. And with the withdrawal of troops in Afghanistan looming, I wonder how we'll remember it as well; or if we intend to at all. What I remember best about Afghanistan is the enduring spirit of its people. I think of the farmers in their poppy fields whose daily harvest will gain them safe passage from the warlords. Who will, in turn, trade it for weapons before it is synthesized, repackaged, and re-sold dozens of times before it finds its way into this country and into the broken veins of our nation's next opioid victim. I think of the women who, despite living their entire lives never once allowed to make so much as a choice for themselves, are treated as pawns in a ruthless game politicians play when they need a justification to further the killing of their sons & husbands. And I think of the children, whose bright-eyed, dirty faces look to the sky and hope to see clouds of gray, afraid of the clear blue days that beckon drones to come carrying eager death notes for their fathers.

Your Honor, I oppose drone warfare for the same reasons I oppose the death penalty. I beleive capital punishment to be an abomination and an all-out assault on common human decency. I believe that it is wrong to kil" no matter the circumstances, yet I believe it is especially wrong to kill the defenseless. And, in spite of what the Supreme Court has ruled, I believe there is simply no way in which a person can be killed that is not cruel and unusual. If anyone here is still not convinced of this, then they must ask themselves if they believe that the 4% of death row inmates exonerated after the fact is an acceptable price to pay. I don't. No person should have to die for a crime that they did not commit. Just as no person should have to live with the burden of having taken a poor, defenseless innocent life. Not a soldier carrying out his duties, nor a judge theirs.

When it comes to the drone assassination program, the disparity between the guilty and the innocent killed is incalculably higher. In some cases, as many as 9 out of 10 individuals killed are not identifiable. In one particular instance, the American-born son of a radical American Imam was assigned a Terrorist Identities Datamark Environment or TIDE pin number, tracked and killed in a drone strike along with 8 members of his family while they ate lunch together a full 2 weeks after his father was killed. Asked about why the 16 year old Abdul Rahman TPN26350617 needed to die, one White House official said, "He should have had a better father."

While deployed to Afghanistan, I was exposed to similar ways of thinking to distract myself from the true nature of my actions. As one drone operator put it, "Do you ever step on ants and never give it another thought? That's what you're made to think of the targets. They deserved it, they chose their side. You had to kill a part of your conscience to keep doing your job—ignoring the voice inside telling you this wasn't right." I too ignored the voice inside as I continued walking blindly towards the edge of an abyss. And when I found myself at the brink, ready to give in, the voice said to me, "You who had been a hunter of men, are no longer. By the grace of God you've been saved. Now go forth and be a fisher of men so that others might know the truth."

So I ran to the press with documents in hand, not one more nor one less than necessary, to dispel the demonstrable lie that said drone warfare kept us safe, that our lives are worth more than theirs, and that only more killing would bring about certain victory. Simply put: It is wrong to kill, it is especially wrong to kill the defenseless, and it is an abdication of the Bill of Rights to kill without due process of law.

Your Honor, much has been said about the potential that "serious" or "exceptionally grave" harm was brought about due to my actions. But since no evidence of this fact has materialized in all the years since my criminal investigation began, it might appear to an outsider looking in that such claims are yet another example of a "boy crying 'wolf'." But in wishing to settle the matter myself, I might have uncovered one instance where my actions did contribute towards one of the most grave attacks in our Nation's history.

At 2 a.m. July 22nd 2016, a lone gunman entered an Orlando nightclub and proceeded to kill 49 people in what became the most deadly mass shooting in American history at the time. In a 911 call the gunman stated, "They need to stop the US Airstrikes, ok? This went down because a lot of women & children are getting killed in Syria, Iraq, and Afghanistan." The gunman, Omar Mateen, was killed by police 3 hours after his bloody, homicidal rampage began. It goes without saying, Omar Mateen was a deranged homicidal lunatic who could in no way justify the killing of 49 innocent people that night. Tragically, this is a story all too common in American life today: A maniac believes himself aggrieved and unheard, with easy access to a gun. What is unique to this case is the gunman's stated motives. Though it in no way excuses his heinous crimes, it is impossible to deny that airstrikes in the middle east have often dismissed innocent people as "collateral damage." When I consider my own participation in the drone program, I worry that my past actions have given provocation to would-be terrorist Omar Mateen to carry out his vengeful fantasies. In that sense my actions have contributed greatly towards the potential harm, or to use the CIA's term—"blowback." I'm left to wonder if only I'd had the courage to come forward sooner with my disclosures, could I have prevented such a tragic loss of life? Of course there's no way to be absolutely certain of anything, but I sometimes wonder if Omar Mateen had seen someone accept responsibility and show remorse for their part in the way, would it have reached the part of his heart that still held onto a shred of humanity? If so, maybe he and his 49 defenseless, innocent victims would be alive today. Best rule: To prevent terror on us we must stop the terror on them.

Nevertheless, I am here to answer for my own crimes and not that of another person. And it would appear that I am here today to answer for the crime of stealing papers. For which I expect to spend some portion of my life in prison. But what I am really here for is having stolen something that was never mine to take: precious human life. For which I was well-compensated and given a medal. I couldn't keep living in a world in which people pretended things weren't happening that were. My consequential decision to share classified information about the drone program with the public was a gesture not taken lightly, nor one I would have taken at all if I believed such a decision had the possibility of harming anyone but myself. I acted not for the sake of self-aggrandizement, but that I might some day humbly ask forgiveness:

Please, I beg you, forgive me, your honor, for taking papers as opposed to the lives of others. I could not, God so help me, have done otherwise.

aniel Hale in the documentary
ational Bird by Sonia Kennebeck,
16. Photo by Torsten Lapp.

SUELETTE DREYFUS

Suelette Dreyfus is an academic in the School of Computing and Information Systems at the University of Melbourne. She is also the Executive Director of Blueprint for Free Speech, an international NGO dedicated to supporting freedom of expression. Her fields of research includes information systems, digital security and privacy, the impact of technology on whistleblowing, health informatics and e-Education. She is a specialist in cybersecurity technologies and in integrity systems that work as corrective mechanisms in society. She co-wrote the first mainstream book about computer hacking in Australia, *Underground*, with Julian Assange.

NAOMI COLVIN

Naomi Colvin is UK/Ireland/Belgium Program Director at Blueprint for Free Speech. She has a particular interest in whistleblowing as a freedom of expression issue and the intersection of digitally-mediated whistleblowing with the criminal law. She occasionally writes for *Byline Times*.

SUELETTE DREYFUS
WITH NAOMI COLVIN

DIFFICULT ACTS
OF COURAGE

DANIEL ELLSBERG, the whistleblower whose revelations helped turn the US away from its disastrous war in Vietnam, and helped the US media adopt an authority-defying pose for a time, has a searing stare. It's unnerving. He doesn't blink or look away. It's not hostile. There is just deep concentration, a sort of laser-like watching and reading of the person he is speaking to.

His eyes felt grey-blue, but now, a decade on, it's hard to be sure.

Ellsberg had travelled to London in October 2010. He was going to give the Sam Adams Award to WikiLeaks publisher Julian Assange, and to introduce the publisher and journalist at a major media event. It was the first time both men were going to meet in person, and I (Suelette) accidentally found myself at this historic meeting between perhaps the world's most famous whistleblower and the most famous publisher of whistleblowers' stories and data.

The winner of this award is determined by the Sam Adams Associates for Integrity in Intelligence—a group of retired intelligence officers and related professionals present the award to "a member of the intelligence community or related professions who exemplifies Sam Adam's courage, persistence, and devotion to truth—no matter the consequences".[1]

The prize is named after Samuel Alexander Adams, another Vietnam war-era whistleblower. Adams had been working at the CIA when he realised that estimates of enemy troop numbers were completely wrong, but it was too politically inconvenient to say so. Adams ended up being a defence witness for Ellsberg at his trial in 1973. He left the CIA after that.

I've met many of the winners of the Sam Adams Award one on one over the years and it's a special club. If I had endless money, my idea of fun would actually be to get all of them around a large dinner table, let the alcohol flow, and listen.

Together, the Sam Adams Award alumni form a pool of training from some of the best intelligence and law enforcement agencies in the world. They come from the CIA, NSA, various parts of US military intelligence, the State Department, the British domestic intelligence agency MI5 and its outward looking counterpart

M16, the British diplomatic corps, and some more exotic places such as the Danish military. There is a certain rigor of thinking, an eye for detail, a way of modelling a problem where their thought processes look like a Rubik's Cube being manipulated this way and that. It's a cross between training so deep that it's become ingrained, combined with an agility at problem solving so light it would put Jason Bourne to shame.

This training isn't that unusual; after all, the US has more than four million people with security clearances. What's unusual about the Sam Adams associates is that all the rigor of this state-based training sits beside some pretty nonconformist personality traits. To a person, they have all had some sort of Dorian Gray moment where actions in their professional life threaten to distort their sense of who they really are.

A fork appears in the road before them. To do the right thing would be hard. Would they acquiesce, go along the path of least resistance, even though every moral fibre shouted out "No! This is wrong!" Or would they take the harder route?

I'm told most spies hit this moment in their career if they stick around long enough. And most take the low road, the easy path. It is the moment when the painting of their likeness in the attic takes on a grey tinge, when warts begin to appear on the painting's visage.

To meet Ellsberg, I travelled across London to the Pimlico townhouse of Gavin McFadyen, an American investigative journalist and documentary maker who had shifted his reporting from the US to the UK some years earlier. Gavin took the concept of adversarial, public interest journalism to heart. There was power, and the role of the investigative journalist was to call that power to account when it stepped out of line.

Gavin graduated from what is now the London Film School, and went on to produce documentaries for the BBC, *Granada TV*, *ABC-TV* and *Frontline* on *PBS*. He covered anti-Vietnam war protests, race riots and demonstrations at the famous 1968 Democratic National Convention in Chicago. He covered the CIA's dirty war in Nicaragua in the 1980s where they were training the contra rebels to dislodge the duly elected left-leaning government of the Marxist Sandinistas. His documentaries tackled nuclear proliferation, child labour and neo-Nazi violence.

When Julian and Gavin came to find each other, after Gavin reached out to him upon learning what WikiLeaks did as an online publisher, it was a hand-in-glove fit. Gavin soon became a journalistic mentor to Julian Assange.

It was no surprise then that Ellsberg would be staying with Gavin McFadyen in London, nor that the visit should happen in October 2010, for it was in this window of time that WikiLeaks had planned its as yet then biggest ever publications. There was a frenetic pace as staff organised the ballroom of the Park Plaza hotel near the banks of the Thames for the event. The ballroom seemed an extravagance—a whole ballroom? When the day came, that decision was proven right.

In April that year, WikiLeaks had published *Collateral Murder*, the video and audio recording from an Apache helicopter that shows US military personnel gunning down unarmed civilians, *Reuters'* media staff and even children, in Baghdad. If you are around 20 years old as you read this, it's quite possible you've never seen or even heard of *Collateral Murder*. Go watch it.[2]

Julian Assange had released the video at the National Press Club in Washington DC and the world had suddenly gone berserk around him. The video clip was being compared to Associated Press photographer Nick Ut's iconic photo of Phan Thi Kim Phúc, the naked Vietnamese child running in terror with her body burning from the napalm dropped on her village by South Vietnamese planes in June 1972. The image won Ut a Pulitzer, and helped to turn the tide on the Vietnam War.

The frenzy around *Collateral Murder* meant Julian was getting media requests from around the world. Even then the knives of professional jealousy were starting to come out, with a small number of traditional media types sniffing that what WikiLeaks was doing was somehow "not journalism".

Which, of course, totally missed the point. Julian's work was adding another dimension to the journalistic process and what could result from journalistic partnerships was very powerful. He and his team interviewed people, wrote stories, edited copy, and picked news headlines. Award-winning Icelandic investigative reporter Kristinn Hrafnsson was working for Iceland's public broadcaster RUV when the *Collateral Murder* video was being prepared for release in early 2010. He hired a fixer in Baghdad in order to track down the individuals in the video and those who had been affected. They managed to track down the widow of Sale Matasher Tomal, the minivan driver, and their children Sayd and Do'ha.

Julian agreed to WikiLeaks co-financing the trip to Baghdad where Hrafnsson and a colleague, Ingi Ragnar Ingason, interviewed witnesses, victims, everyone they could in and around the story on the day. Even though two of the dead were *Reuters* journalists, Hrafnsson and Ingason were told by locals that they were the first journalists who had gone to investigate on the ground at the site where *Collateral Murder* took place in south-eastern Baghdad. It was not just the acquisition of newsworthy material, but the thought that went into its presentation and the mechanics of organising secure collaboration protocols and a common embargo date that made it possible.

The partnership between two journalist organisations, which was the first of many such journalism partnerships with the biggest media organisations in the world, meant that the *Collateral Murder* footage was backed up with supporting data when it was released to the world at large. The story could be reported in full. It meant that, when the findings were published by RUV and WikiLeaks at the same time as the video itself on April 5, 2020, the dead were named and the voices of those directly affected by their loss were heard loud and clear.

Hrafnsson went on to join WikiLeaks in summer 2010.

By early May, Julian had come home to Melbourne, Australia for a visit. He agreed to give a talk downtown one evening about *Collateral Murder* in a large university lecture hall. I knew the organisers, so we met up and went into the city together. When we walked in together, we couldn't believe our eyes. Every available square inch of the hall was taken up by human beings. We could barely walk down the steps of the lecture hall, from the elevated back entry to the speaking dais. It was a ballerina's toe-step amid people sitting on the stairs, and then at the bottom, across the floor of the front of the lecture hall. It seemed to me that about ninety per cent of the audience was under the age of 25.

Someone had kindly saved a small number of seats in the front row, so I sat down, still reeling at what I was seeing. Julian introduced the video footage to some 400 people, and explained what people were about to see, which was an armed assault by the US military on young children and the murder of their father, who had stopped to help the dying *Reuters* news staff, who had also been killed by the US Apache soldiers. Then Julian sat down while the video played. When the lights came up, the audience was speechless. People were truly shocked. Except I remember a small handful of middle-aged men in the back left hand side. They were definitely not students—too old and too well-dressed. They stared daggers at Julian from across the lecture theatre.

This was just the start of the global interest in WikiLeaks and Julian Assange.

He returned to Europe and on July 25, WikiLeaks published the Afghan War Diary in London.

This was the most extraordinary collection of US modern military reports ever published in raw form. WikiLeaks wrote and published the news story—and then backed up that story with 75,000 reports from the field in Afghanistan. Many were day to day reports of incidents by soldiers and intelligence officers listening to reports sent via radio from the front lines. The reports were submitted from 2004 to 2010. WikiLeaks redacted about 15,000 reports as it did not feel they could be safely published at that time.

There's a lot you can learn from this material. The reports become heavier and more serious as the datelines progress. The reading becomes more depressing the longer on it goes. Rockets and mortars are located, an RPG is found in a pile of sawdust shavings, then it's hand grenades... By 2009 the data shows IED "find events" happening all over the place. And then there were the kidnappings.

It would be interesting to track the trends over time in these "honest" reports and compare them to the tone adopted in public statements by the US administration in the same time frame. It wouldn't take forensic analysis to discern that what was being sold—not just to Americans, but also Australians, Britons, Canadians and others—as "we're winning the war" did not stand up against the reports being made by soldiers on the spot. The public knew something was wrong, but it had not had large scale, real proof—until WikiLeaks broke the story with its accompanying data.

It took another decade for the US presence in Afghanistan to be drawn to a close. After two trillion dollars spent and tens of thousands dead—an estimated 50,000 of them civilians—more of the country was left under Taliban control than had been the case before the intervention. The images of chaos at Hamid Karzai International Airport in Kabul in August 2021 bore a strong similarity to photographer Hubert van Es' 1975 photographs of people rushing to board a US helicopter during the evacuation from Saigon, then the capital of South Vietnam.

WikiLeaks' reporting in 2010 foreshadowed the diabolic situation of the Afghan war as well as showing the *Collateral Murder* nature of the Iraq War. Yet there was still much more to come that same year. And so it was that WikiLeaks was soon to launch its third big tranche of data; the Iraq War Logs in October 2010. Daniel Ellsberg had flown to London, at Julian's invitation, to be part of this history-making event—and to hand Julian his Sam Adams Award in person—a wrought iron candle stick holder for holding the light of truth. The whistleblower and the publisher would finally get to meet each other face to face.

German publication *Spiegel Online*, called the Iraq War Logs "the greatest leak in the history of the United States military".[3] Like *Der Spiegel*, *The Guardian*, *The New York Times*, *Al Jazeera* and *Le Monde* were co-publishing material at WikiLeaks' invitation, along with the not-for-profit civil society group, Iraq Body Count which had done detailed analysis of the data in the logs. Daniel would attend what was now the main game: the packed ballroom holding hundreds of journalists from around the world who were waiting for the Iraq War Logs. At the event, WikiLeaks would reveal that the Iraq War had caused some 15,000 civilian deaths[4] that had never been disclosed anywhere before.[5] "Iraq was a bloodbath on every corner", Julian told *The New York Times*.[6]

And then Julian Assange and Daniel Ellsberg would go on to slam the Obama administration's "aggressive pursuit of whistleblowers"—including those responsible for the release of the Iraq War Logs.

Through the Window, Down to the Street Below

When Julian and Daniel met each other, they were both surprisingly slightly shy with the other. It was in the Green Room, before Julian was due to lead the press event downstairs in the ballroom. There were just a handful of us there at the time.

Neither Julian nor Daniel are fawners. Julian started by saying what an honour it was to meet Daniel. His voice faded slightly, dropping lower in tone and audibility as it does from time to time when he is slightly embarrassed but doesn't want to show it. He was unsure what to do with his hands, and they moved in front of him as if detached from his body. Daniel was nearly twice his age, and so more assured, but he too was clearly affected by the meeting. There was a kind of awkward joy in the room.

"Hero" seems like a word that wouldn't fit in either of their vocabularies comfortably. Both take a critical eye to everything around them such that it would be impossible for anyone to survive to the perfection of hero-dom. But there is courage, and maybe there is heroism.

The British historian Timothy Garton Ash studied the once hidden files of the intelligence agencies of Eastern Europe after the fall of the Berlin Wall. The primary documents revealed how people traded their neighbours, friends and family in to the secret police, among other things, when living in a repressive state. Speaking informally at the Melbourne Writers' Festival in August 2000, he observed, "I don't believe in heroes anymore: only acts of heroism".

Perhaps so it was with Daniel Ellsberg and Julian Assange. When courage faces a 60-foot tsunami of revenge by state or corporate power, it morphs into heroism. In the minutes before Julian strode out on stage in front of hundreds of media, with the glare of TV lights beaming in on his face, in a packed ballroom in London to talk about the Iraq War Logs, both Daniel and Julian had met someone else who had, in their eyes, engaged in important acts of heroism.

Daniel told the media that the WikiLeaks founder had been "pursued across three continents" by Western intelligence services.[7] The Obama administration's threat to prosecute Julian was similar to former US President Richard Nixon's treatment of Ellsberg, he said.

After the event, when things quieted down, and I finally had a chance to interview Daniel Ellsberg alone, in the quiet of Gavin's home, I asked him what was important for whistleblowers to know before their started their journey.

He said he had given support to many whistleblowers over the years, some of whom were in the national security and intelligence area.

Whistleblowing is hard on the spouse, he said. The marriages that last tended to be the ones where the whistleblower tells his or her partner early on what is really happening. When the job goes away, when the mortgage payments come due, and the kids get teased at school, or worse have to leave their school, when armed FBI agents break in the front door of the family home at 6 am in the otherwise quiet suburban neighbourhood, the spouse is going to handle the upheaval better if they know that it's coming.

If you can take your partner on the journey with you—and that does take a very special type of partnership—then that is worth fighting for, he said. If you both come out the other end of the dark tunnel, the relationship can actually get stronger.

What makes a whistleblower? What is different about those very particular people? Daniel paused and thought about it a little bit. Then he said, that the whistleblower was the person who, sitting at his desk amid all the other people in his office, could see how what he was doing would impact not only himself, and the people on his floor at work, across the organisation, but looking outside, through the window, down to the street below, to the city beyond, the people beyond. The ability to see that impact there, not only to see, to understand that, but to act on it, to do the right thing, exactly because it would reverberate... that ability to see is what a whistleblower often has.

It seemed to me the compartmentalisation of the intelligence world discourages this kind of imaginative empathy.

Looking through this lens at the unusual club of Sam Adams Prize winners, somehow it makes sense what might unify this diverse group. I don't know if they are all heroes. Being a hero is a big mantle of perfection to carry around all the time. But they've engaged in acts of courage and heroism. In a world of greed, self-interest, power-grabbing and fame-seeking, genuine acts of heroism are spectacular, particularly when they come with a high personal price tag.

This makes it sound a bit like the biggest problems whistleblowers like the Sam Adams Associates have to worry about are their income and personal relationships. That would be bad enough, but unfortunately, the US security state doesn't take acts of conscience informed by non-compartmentalised empathy lying down.

Sam Adams, for whom the award is named, sounds like a pseudonym, borrowed from one of the Founding Fathers of the United States. A graduate of Harvard College, the original 18th century Sam Adams played a pivotal role in the American Revolution. He helped draft and pass the Declaration of Independence, the Articles of Confederation and the Constitution of Massachusetts, the state where he was eventually elected governor. In the US, it is standard for every year 11 high school student to take a year of American History; most textbooks in this subject would describe the contributions of Sam Adams to the American Revolution. In Boston, the birthplace of that revolution, the Adams family name is one of the oldest, and most revered in the history of this era of American cities.

But the award is named for another Sam Adams.[8]

That Samuel Adams, the modern-day CIA officer, was born into privilege, a descendent of that same prestigious Adams family. It also produced a President (John Adams). His father, Pierrepont Adams, had a seat on the New York Stock Exchange and was an ambassador to South Vietnam. Samuel attended St Mark's, an elite New England boarding school. It is a place where the boys played Saturday morning sports on manicured fields fringed by maple trees and beautifully preserved 19th century white colonial salt-box faculty homes. From St Mark's, Samuel went on to Harvard, less than an hour's drive away, then the Navy and a stint at Harvard Law School. He joined the CIA, launching a promising career.

With so much privilege enveloping such a rising star, it would have been easy for Samuel Adams to look the other way when he transferred to the agency's Vietnam desk in 1965. Instead, there he discovered the US military had grossly underestimated the number of Viet Cong guerrillas fighting for North Vietnamese victory, and the CIA had acquiesced in this lie. This was not a small error. There were hundreds of thousands of uncounted Viet Cong fighters.

His finding was catastrophic: it meant the US-backed South Vietnamese were much less likely to win the war. It called into question the American Government's claims of successful advancement in the war. It raised the likelihood that, in fact, US troops were on a treadmill of death heading to defeat.

In war, data matters. Samuel launched an internal whistleblower's war against the CIA. Samuel wrote a memorandum calling the agreement the CIA had made to accept the US military's false numbers "a monument of deceit".

At one stage, Adams was so worried his agency opponents would try to destroy the evidence, he spirited CIA files away and reportedly buried them in the woods on his farm in rural Virginia. In addition to his own fight, Samuel stepped up to give evidence in defence of Daniel Ellsberg and Anthony Russo, who were themselves charged under the draconian 1917 Espionage Act for their whistleblowing.

The US Government had produced a secret history on the Vietnam War—in 47 volumes. Ellsberg and Russo made sure that key parts of that history made it into the hands of the media.

The US security state tried to come after Daniel Ellsberg, who had served as a high-ranking staffer in the Defense and State Departments, but its legal case ended up collapsing due to malfeasance. There had been malfeasance from the prosecution, via concealing exculpatory material and particularly hiding the existence of wiretaps on which Ellsberg was heard. But it was the crimes committed by the *White House* itself against Ellsberg in its effort to keep him from revealing the Nixon Administration's dirty secrets about Vietnam that captured the judge's attention. Those acts included an attempt to seize documents from Ellsberg's psychiatrist's office. The judge dismissed all charges against the two men, citing the "totality of circumstances...that offends a sense of justice"

Fifty years on from the publication of the Pentagon Papers, Ellsberg is currently attempting to provoke a second Espionage Act prosecution to resolve long-standing questions about the law's compatibility with the US constitution. In May 2021, Ellsberg spoke to an online conference of whistleblowing experts—NGOs, researchers, activists, academics, thinkers from around the globe.[9] He said that getting the US' Espionage Act changed was the last thing he wanted to achieve before he died.

How would he do this? By committing an act of unauthorised disclosure that would force the US attorney's office to indict him. "It won't be easy", he said.

That was an understatement. So much of what Ellsberg revealed turned out to be true—and the public knew it. The politicians, the military and the intelligence agencies had all colluded to lie to the public in ways that made the citizenry pay a terrible price, losing sons and husbands and breaking the physical and mental health of many in that Vietnam Vet generation. These same venal and pernicious lies were repeated for wars that came after Vietnam. Ellsberg represents truth-telling in the face of those lies to an entire generation of Americans. To go after him, was to attack an act of heroism.

Ellsberg has said that, if he was prosecuted for the latest leak, he would mount a First Amendment defence. He would want to live long enough to see the case go all the way to the Supreme Court, he told the conference. Yes, the court is a conservative one, that would probably rule badly. But in doing so, it would force the issue, and the Congress and White House would be shown as running from the deep-seeded problem of the Act: the accused can offer no defence.

Ellsberg says that since his case, there have been almost a score of other such cases, all of which were against sources—until Julian's indictment. Why had no journalist or publisher been prosecuted before under the Act? According to Ellsberg, it is because applying the Espionage Act that way would be a *blatant and unmistakable* violation of the First Amendment's guarantee of freedom of the press. The wording of the Act permits indicting journalist or, according to Ellsberg, even unauthorised readers.

In his view, the Biden Administration's Department of Justice is experimenting with a prosecution that has never been tried before for that very reason, clearly in hopes that the current Supreme Court will not notice the blatant unconstitutionality.

Ellsberg is elderly, and increasingly frail. But his brain is as sharp and feisty as ever.

All in All, Bad Odds for a Prosecutor

A few weeks after Ellsberg told us all this, *The New York Times* published a story drawing attention to another unauthorised disclosure by Ellsberg, of a top-secret study of the 1958 Taiwan Strait crisis, revealing that the US had considered a nuclear strike against the People's Republic of China.[10] A declassified summary version of the study had omitted pages where the likelihood of a second strike by the Soviet Union and the deaths of hundreds of thousands of people was discussed.

Ellsberg had copied the full study at the same time he made copies of the classified history of the Vietnam War that became known as the Pentagon Papers and had published it online quietly in 2017. That additional pages from the study were available online was mentioned in the footnotes of Ellsberg's book *Doomsday Machine*, published the same year, but they had not quoted from it directly as his publishers were concerned about the potential legal liability.

Ellsberg's desire to become an Espionage Act test case (again) is not as quixotic as it might seem; in many ways, it all ties back to that meeting at the London Park Plaza in 2010. Espionage cases against journalistic sources were an anomaly in Ellsberg's day, but no longer. The Obama administration notoriously launched more of these cases against whistleblowers than all previous presidencies combined. Then Trump equalled that number of indictments in half the time.

Fighting these cases is extraordinarily difficult and carries the risk of decades long prison sentences. Evidence of imaginative empathy is generally not admitted; in recent years judges have told a series of defendants that their motivation, and the positive impact of their disclosure is not relevant to the case against them.

The only permissible defence is "it didn't happen". The Act's strict liability character permits no mitigating circumstance. No context is allowed to be given or considered, no examination of the full facts—or of any lies—may be had. The US Espionage Act is one of the most unjust laws still in use federally in the United States. The difficulty of defending these cases means that defendants invariably take a plea deal.

And it is no accident that many of the winners of the Sam Adams Award—those men and women who have committed acts of heroism in the public interest—have been threatened with, charged with or convicted of this heinous law.

These include former CIA officer John Kiriakou, who remains the only former US federal employee to have been prosecuted for his actions in the post-2001 rendition and torture programme—he, of course, was the one who blew the whistle on it. Thomas Drake, who was a senior executive at the NSA, was betrayed by the internal channels he was supposed to be able to report his concerns about population-scale surveillance to. Edward Snowden, another Sam Adams Award winner, has said that he studied what happened to Drake when contemplating his own disclosures.

The difficulty of mounting a challenge to charges laid under the Espionage Act means that the compatibility of the law with the US Constitution has never been fully tested. Many legal scholars think that the use of the Espionage Act as a kind of unofficial Official Secrets Act against journalistic sources is a violation of the First Amendment and its free speech protections.

Ellsberg's act of provocation, with 50 year-old material that is still "top secret" in the eyes of the state, has a bell-like clarity to the logic. *The New York Times* bylined writer Charlie Savage wrote up Ellsberg's unauthorised disclosure and the paper published it on May 22, 2021.[11]

Now Ellsberg asks, "Why is Julian indicted for doing exactly what Charlie Savage and *The Times* did with the classified material I gave them?"

With 90 years of hindsight vision spanning two centuries of American wars, Ellsberg has distilled the complicated problem of protecting national security whistleblowers into one simple action: fix this bad law.

Falling Through the Gaps

In May 2020, Julian Assange became the first journalist, the first editor, the first publisher, to be charged under the 1917 Espionage Act. Human rights organisations, press freedom associations and media entities across the English-speaking world and beyond were aghast. If the use of the Espionage Act against whistleblowers was dubious in constitutional terms, this was a brutal attack on the freedom of the press.

The US Department of Justice is currently seeking Julian's extradition from the United Kingdom on 17 Espionage Act charges relating directly to the 2010 publications. A further charge of computer misuse has been recently discredited by one of the key prosecution witnesses disowning his statements in public. No one from *Der Spiegel*, *The New York Times*, *Le Monde*, *The Guardian* or any other media partner of WikiLeaks which published leaked material has been charged.

Though the mainstream media was often determined not to see this in what could only be described as acts of wilful blindness, Julian always had good reason to fear reprisal from the US authorities. The treatment meted out to the source of the 2011 publications (as well as 2012's Guantanamo Files) Chelsea Manning should have been proof enough of that.

Manning had been working as an intelligence analyst in the US military in Iraq. She had reached that fork in the road moment familiar to Sam Adams Award winners. (Manning was herself honoured in 2014). After unsuccessfully trying to reach journalists at the *The New York Times* and *The Washington Post*, she had turned to WikiLeaks, which accepted information disclosed anonymously. Manning's covering note said the disclosures were "significant documents... removing the fog of war and revealing the true nature of 21st century asymmetric warfare". Later she said she wanted the documents to produce "worldwide discussion, debates, and reforms". She was looking through the window down on to the street below.

Chelsea Manning was arrested in Iraq at the end of May 2010, in between the publication of *Collateral Murder* and the Afghan War Diary. The series of publications based on Manning's disclosures continued; after the Afghan War Diary came the Iraq War Logs and the State Department cables. As far as public information about what was happening to the whistleblower herself went, everything went dark for the rest of that year.

What happened next would be the subject of censure from the UN Special Rapporteur on Torture, Juan Mendez. The US authorities never allowed Mendez to speak to Manning—they insisted guards be present at any meeting, which is not how the Special Rapporteur office operates—but based on the information available, Mendez concluded that at the very least Manning had been subjected to cruel and inhumane treatment, which might rise to the level of torture.

Manning had spent her first two months of incarceration in a Guantanamo-style cage at a US military installation in Kuwait. Her lawyers managed to get her brought back to the US mainland in order to receive a mental health assessment.

For the next nine months, Manning was incarcerated at the Marine Brig in Quantico, Virginia. She was kept in virtual solitary confinement, frequently deprived of sleep, her glasses and, for a period, her clothing. The ostensible rationale for this treatment was a "prevention of injury watch" that was renewed several times against the explicit recommendation of in-house psychiatrists. This was the excuse of medical treatment used to justify no-touch torture.

It wasn't until the end of December 2010 that any of this found its way into the public domain. After a domestic and international outcry, Manning was moved to the mainstream US military prison at Fort Leavenworth four months later. Eventually the military judge overseeing Manning's court martial awarded 112 days of credit for the wrongs done to Manning at Quantico, not a huge amount when set against her unprecedented 35-year sentence. Manning was released after seven years in prison in one of President Obama's last acts in office (he recognised that her punishment was "disproportionate").

Despite everything she has gone through, she ended up spending another year in prison under Trump for not cooperating with the grand jury investigating WikiLeaks.

Accountability for torture is hard to come by. Key to the value of WikiLeaks' publications sourced from Manning is that they allowed the balance to swing a little in favour of the victims.

One of the most powerful pieces of evidence brought in Julian's defence in the UK when he was fighting extradition to the United States in September 2020 was the testimony of Khaled El-Masri. El-Masri is a German citizen who was seized from Europe under the US extraordinary rendition program and tortured at a CIA black site. Extraordinary rendition is the technical term for "kidnapping". The CIA had belatedly realised that his was a case of mistaken identity and dumped him in rural North Macedonia, threatening him to keep quiet.

When El-Masri had got back to Germany and tried to tell his story, no one had believed him. Bringing the story into the light had taken the assistance of investigative journalist John Goetz, who had helped El-Masri make, and back up, his case. Later, WikiLeaks' November 2010 release of cables from the US State Department had shown the degree of diplomatic pressure applied by the US to stop German prosecutors seeking accountability from El-Masri's torturers for a German citizen. A number of journalists and legal experts had told the extradition hearing about the difference WikiLeaks' publications had made, but El-Masri was an actual victim of torture who addressed the London court.

It might be more accurate to say he almost addressed the court: a summary of his testimony was read out in court by one of Julian's lawyers and the full written version entered into the official record. As if to illustrate how hard it is for voices like El-Masri's to be heard, he was ready and waiting on a video-link in order to address the court himself, through an interpreter. The US side's legal team then announced they would not be challenging the evidence, meaning that El-Masri did not need to be asked questions and so his voice did not have to be heard in court. This was one of only a handful of instances during the extradition hearing when Julian intervened from the dock. He was determined that El-Masri should not be silenced.

In 2012 Julian had sought asylum at the Ecuadorian Embassy in London, where he was unable to leave because of the threat from the US of extradition. He was expelled from the Embassy and arrested in April 2019. He has been in the high security Belmarsh prison ever since. In May 2019, Julian was put on the healthcare wing of Belmarsh, imprisoned in virtual isolation for the rest of the year. Evidence presented to the September 2020 extradition hearings showed that his mental health and cognitive abilities declined significantly during this time. The UN Special Rapporteur on Torture and two psychiatrists said he showed signs of psychological torture and his life was at risk.

In January 2021, the British judge who heard that evidence ruled that the near certainly of Julian being held in solitary confinement in the United States, and the equally certain impact that would have on his welfare, meant that the extradition would be "oppressive" and should not happen. Defence arguments and expert evidence said his likely sentence will cause him to spend the rest of his days in prison. The judge's reasoning left open the possibility that journalists could still face the threat of extradition for their work in the future.

The US appealed the decision against extradition and, at the time of writing, it's not clear how that's going to turn out. A recent decision allowing the US to challenge the medical evidence makes a successful US appeal a much more realistic possibility. If Julian Assange is shipped to the US, he will end up in an American prison for at least a decade or more just fighting his case under the draconian Espionage Act. If convicted, he would be facing years if not decades of prison time, with a possible maximum sentence of 175 years. Julian's case would be unique as the only Australian citizen and publisher awaiting trial for espionage in the US. The precedent will then be set: any non-American publisher can be kidnapped off the street like El-Masri, forced into extradition like Julian Assange, and made to suffer no-touch torture like Chelsea Manning.

If Julian is extradited, other cases will follow. Extradition is increasingly being used as a political tool in whistleblowing cases. Since 2001, there has been a tendency for extradition processes to be streamlined between countries that have decided to put trust in each other's legal systems. In these systems, like the arrangements between the US and the UK or between the countries of the EU, old defences against politically motivated prosecutions have been deprecated or withdrawn. We're now seeing the consequences of that misplaced trust. Even as countries introduce their own whistle-blower protection laws, the lack of protections in extradition processes mean that the "gap" between national jurisdictions is a weak spot that can easily be exploited.

One such case is that of Jonathan Taylor, a British oil industry whistleblower who Monaco has sought to extradite from Croatia.[12] Taylor had lifted the lid on bribery at his former employer, Dutch resources firm SBM Offshore. Years after Taylor's revelations, SBM Offshore had made a criminal complaint in Monaco and Monaco had duly got Interpol to issue a Red Notice, obliging authorities to arrest Taylor. Red Notices are unusual and generally reserved for the most severe crimi-nals, not whistleblowers.

Jonathan Taylor was only in Croatia for a family holiday, but he ended up trapped in the country for the best part of a year. A first instance court and an appeal court in Croatia both ruled that he should be extradited. British MPs raised questions in Parliament and the UK Government repeatedly said it had no powers to get involved. It took the political intervention of the Croatian Foreign Minister for Taylor to be able to leave the country in summer 2021.

The world's understanding—and acceptance—of whistleblowing has dra-matically changed in just one decade. Governments and lawmakers are still playing catch up to meet the shift in public attitudes here.

That may take a while yet. The acts of imaginative empathy and courage that lead individuals to blow the whistle are inimical to unaccountable hierarchies and impunity for the powerful. We've lost important fighters in this battle along the way; Gavin McFadyen passed away in 2016. Yet a raft of civil society groups, un-ions and legal firms have stepped in to grow support for fundamental change.

It is the nature of power threatened to find ways to single out and isolate those who take risks in the public interest. At present, unfortunately, there are too many gaps to exploit: the conflation of public interest journalism with espionage, the lack of individual protections in cross border proceedings and the utter absence of accountability for the most serious human rights abuses among them. Chang-ing this situation is going to be a challenge, but the distance we've travelled so far shows it is possible to get this change.

We can fight for individual cases, and advocate for fundamental change—both of which have seen successes since Julian Assange and Daniel Ellsberg met each other in London in 2010.

We just need enough people, with enough courage.

Notes

1. *Sam Adams Associates for Integrity in Intelligence*, http://samadamsaward.ch.

2. "Collateral Murder", *WikiLeaks*, April 5, 2010, https://collateralmurder.wikileaks.org/.

3   "The WikiLeaks Iraq War Logs—Greatest Data Leak in US Military History", *Spiegel Online International*, October 22, 2010, https://web.archive.org/web/20101023194129/http://www.spiegel.de/international/world/0,1518,724845,00.html.

4   Croft, A. "WikiLeaks says logs show 15,000 more Iraq deaths", *Reuters*, October 24, 2010, https://www.reuters.com/article/idUSTRE69L54J20101024.

5. Tavernise, S. & Lehren, A.W. "A Grim Portrait of civilian deaths in Iraq", *The New York Times*, October 22, 2010, https://www.nytimes.com/2010/10/23/world/middleeast/23casualties.html.

6   Burns, J.F. & Somaiya, R. "WikiLeaks Founder Gets Support in Rebuking US on Whistle-Blowers." *The New York Times*, October 23, 2010, https://www.nytimes.com/2010/10/24/world/24london.html.

7. Ibid.

8. Krebs, A. "Samuel Adams, ex C.I.A. Officer and Libel Case Figure, Dies at 54", *New York Times*, October 11, 1988, https://www.nytimes.com/1988/10/11/obituaries/samuel-adams-ex-cia-officer-and-libel-case-figure-dies-at-54.html.

9. "The International Festival of whistleblowing, Dissent and Accountability", held online May 8, 2021, organised by the Centre for Global Justice, Peace and Accountability. Retrieved from: https://www.blueprintforfreespeech.net/en/news/international-festival-of-whistleblowing-dissent-and-accountability-may-8-2021.

10. Savage, C. "Risk of Nuclear War Over Taiwan in 1958 Said to Be Greater Than Publicly Known", *The New York Times*, May 22, 2021, https://www.nytimes.com/2021/05/22/us/politics/nuclear-war-risk-1958-us-china.html.

11. Ibid.

12. "Jonathan Taylor: Oil whistleblower 'coming home' from Croatia", *BBC Online*, 2021, July 8, https://www.bbc.com/news/uk-england-hampshire-57760128.

ANNA MYERS

Anna Myers is the founding Executive Director of Whistleblowing International Network, UK. She has worked in the field of whistleblowing for 20 years—advising individual whistleblowers, employers of all sizes and sectors, and national and international policy makers. Anna is originally from Canada and prior to getting her law degree at Dalhousie University in Nova Scotia, completed her history degree (BA) at the Université de Montréal in Québec. Anna was Deputy Director of Public Concern at Work (now called Protect) for 9 years, and has worked at Group of States against Corruption (GRECO) and at the Government Accountability Project in Washington DC. Anna is a Member of the Law Society of England and Wales, and

ANNA MYERS

ALL I EVER WANTED TO KNOW ABOUT WHISTLEBLOWING...

I HAD NEVER heard of whistleblowing until I applied for the job of Legal Officer at Public Concern at Work (now called Protect) in London, nearly 22 years ago. As I researched what the charity did to advise whistleblowers and educate employers, and read one of the few legal academic articles I could find about what this new UK law, the Public Interest Disclosure Act (1998), was trying to achieve, it all made perfect sense to me—people who come across wrongdoing, or anything that could harm others, should not be fired or punished for speaking up about it.[1] Those working within organisations are often the first to notice something is going wrong and so people should, in fact, be encouraged to raise any concerns they have. None of this seemed very controversial to me. In some ways, it was hard to see what the problem was, or how anyone could argue against it. Put in these terms, in fairness, very few people do argue against it.

I was a newly minted lawyer when I got the job in London, but it had taken me a while to get there. I grew up in Ontario and Nova Scotia in Canada. I learned French in Québec, and eventually studied history at the Université de Montréal. I come from a country of many identities, which was also a former British colony, and was always fascinated by the different histories of Canada. I grew up during a period of intense debate about the very idea of Canada—as a federation or a divided land—which focused on Québec's desire for self-determination. It was essentially an argument between the two former colonising groups, and it was as much about power as it was about culture. The debates barely recognised the true cost of the French and British arrivals in North America, or how to make peace and reparations with the First Nations people and work with them as full participants in Canada's future. I think my interest in law and then in whistleblowing comes from some of this background.

I took my LLB at Dalhousie University, and qualified before moving with my husband to London. There I had to requalify and, despite my training in a common law jurisdiction, at times I felt truly baffled by the English legal system. The differences of history, culture and power affect how law develops and is applied—even in jurisdictions with common roots.[2] This is also true for laws to protect whistleblowers; similar legal provisions may not be applied in the same way around the world.

At Public Concern at Work I quickly learned that, in order to advise people, it was not enough to understand what the law said—you had to understand how power worked to help individuals be strategic in how they blew the whistle. It was about helping people to mitigate the risk to themselves, while maximising their chances to make a difference. The law certainly helped guide the advice, but is only formally triggered after the fact, when making a claim to remedy a wrong done to a whistleblower. Therefore, early advice had to be practical, geared towards making it very difficult for an employer to take action against a whistleblower, and if the worst happened, helping ensure that the whistleblower was in a strong enough position to take a claim and be successful.

The difficulty is that few individuals seek independent advice *before* they blow the whistle. Understandably, people look for help when something goes wrong, and when they are already suffering for trying to do the right thing. Most whistleblowers are people just doing their job. It is only when the response they get is not right—whether dismissive, negative or hostile—that they start to realise something may be seriously wrong, or that whatever is wrong may not get fixed. This explains why so many of the NGOs I work with now and who advise and support whistleblowers end up actively seeking to raise awareness. They all work hard to educate the public, employers, government, media, and other key social stakeholders in their countries about whistleblowing in order help everyone identify it and be better prepared to address it. Once it starts to go wrong, the advice necessarily shifts to trying to reduce the damage and to rehabilitate the whistleblower, or to sue the employer, on top of working to protect the public interest. Much depends on the advisors' understanding of the institutional, political, and media landscape in which the whistleblower is operating. Ultimately, a whistleblower is a voluntary defender of the public interest and the risks to them can be very high, both professionally and personally; decisions *must be* determined with them, and actions only taken only with their consent and, if they wish, their participation.

Whistleblowing Directly Connects Communicating Information to Accountability

Back to basics. My first premise, posited naively perhaps, is that the concept of whistleblowing is straightforward: speaking up to stop wrongdoing. My second premise is also fairly simple: the activities of *all* organisations—whether public, private or non-profit (voluntary)—affect people and communities in real and direct ways: in the resources they use, the services they provide and the products they sell. Corporations, governments and NGOs *all* have a public and social impact of some kind, and each runs the risk of harbouring wrongdoing and causing harm.

And finally, a third premise: no matter what systems we put in place to try to do things properly and safely, whether they are human systems or technological ones, they do not always work as intended. They can be corrupted or by-passed in some way, and things can still go wrong.

Keeping hold of the simple notion of whistleblowing, then, clearly the act of blowing the whistle means communicating information about potential wrongdoing or harm to someone who can or *should do something about it*. As my esteemed colleagues at the Government Accountability Project in Washington DC put it, the aim of whistleblower protection is "to assure the free flow of information necessary for the responsible exercise of institutional authority."

Organisations are not just beholden morally to do the right thing, but they are often liable if they do not, particularly for any harm caused by their failures. Inside organisations, then, whistleblowing can act as an early warning system. For many employers, this is where they would like it to stop. But, as I have set out above, because *all* organisations have a social, ecological and public impact of some sort, whistleblowing is not just about internal reporting and the interests of employers to run their organisations as they see fit; whistleblowing cannot be divorced from an organisation's wider public responsibilities. This is why most countries have systems to regulate the conduct of business and to provide some sort of check on the powers of government—to hold decisions-makers to account.

The only way such checks and balances, including regulators and law enforcement, can work is if they have the information they need to properly exercise their powers. Again, if these institutions and their systems worked perfectly, all would be well. But they do not. So we return to whistleblowing, and the final premise; *whistleblowing is essential to protecting freedom of expression and the public's right to know.*

Whistleblowing is citizen action at its finest—our back-up alarm when our societies' systems of oversight fail or are corrupted. In my experience, while each individual case reveals specific organisational or regulatory failures, by the time someone determines that they have to go outside their organisation or go public with their concern, they are signalling a more serious, longer and deeper failure in accountability. Edward Snowden was not the first US national security whistleblower, for example. In fact, his whistleblowing was the culmination of a long line of national security whistleblowers raising the alarm about similar issues, although most did so inside the system and were punished or fired as a result.

However, in some regions, institutional mechanisms do not exist at all or, where they do, they are so poorly resourced and lack independence to such a degree they are not trusted by those they are meant to serve—whether it is the judiciary, law enforcement, parliament or media. Seen in this light, one can understand why whistleblowing is increasingly understood as a vital democratic accountability mechanism and as a catalyst for democratic change.

Good Governance or Freedom of Expression? Both?

Despite my insistence that we must return regularly to the simplicity of whistleblowing, it is obviously complicated by power and the dynamics of power. It is very important to distinguish between whistleblowing and *information control*, and to be aware of how easily the two are conflated.

Sure, "good" organisations will want the opportunity to address problems before they get out of hand and, one hopes, work hard to encourage communication throughout their operations. But even the most responsible organisation runs the risk of things going wrong. It is always possible that warnings are missed and that problems escalate seriously before they are addressed. This is nothing new. Management consultants have made significant money over the decades, advising organisations in all sectors how information *should* flow and be managed. Rarely, however, do these consultants tell their clients to ensure that people can by-pass all the systems and let the right person at the right time know what is happening—especially if it means encouraging people to disclose information outside the management hierarchy, or to someone outside the organisation entirely.

In those early days, as I got to grips with advising people on Public Concern at Work's advice line—people working in care homes, local government, credit rating agencies, banks, hospitals, animal shelters, supermarkets and on construction sites—they were teaching me how to educate employers about what encouraging and protecting whistleblowing in the workplace really meant. This was not theory, but guidance informed by real experience and practice.

At the time, there was a lot of resistance to the very notion of implementing a "whistleblowing policy" to provide options and reassurance to staff if they came across suspected wrongdoing and were worried about telling their manager in the normal way. Resistance was often strongest at board level, but not always. Middle management felt threatened about promoting an arrangement that allowed staff to skip them; a human tendency to control information, if for no other reason than to save oneself the embarrassment of having one's actions questioned. Of course, corrupt managers do all they can to discourage anyone from speaking up about anything—hence the importance of reinforcing alternative channels of communication.

Certainly, the term whistleblowing, in the UK as in many countries, was strongly and negatively associated with the notion of "breaking rank"—the focus then (and often still) was on the messenger and not the message. Whistleblowers were "snitches" or "tattle-tales", disloyal or disgruntled employees, or all of the above.[3] In some sectors, like in defence or policing, insiders who blew the whistle were considered traitors. These views will be familiar to most, no matter the country or language. Yet, by focusing these early employer workshops on the human cost of failing to heed the warnings of staff, and the reality of the dilemmas people face when confronted with wrongdoing—worries that can stop them even when they suspect serious wrongdoing or harm—serious minds turned to finding solutions.[4] We were often asked back to help map out whistleblowing arrangements, or provide extended training to those with the responsibility for implementing them.

And yet here lies the tension that anyone working with whistleblowers and advocating for whistleblower protections must face. No matter how much positive work is done with employers to encourage them to see it in their organisational interest to set up whistleblowing arrangements that allow staff to bypass management hierarchy and to report right to the top, it will not work if those organisations are not in fact properly accountable to the public. Without having to explain one's conduct—which is what accountability means—complacency and the potential for the abuse of power is built right into the system. Having to explain one's conduct, knowing that those seeking the explanation have only partial information at best, means that there is little pressure to provide a complete answer. In the wider context of seeking the truth, an incomplete answer often provides a false picture.

Organisations must be put on notice that that they will be held legally liable for any failures to protect those who disclose public interest information to any relevant accountable body, in or outside the employer (regulators, MPs, law enforcement, etc.) and to the public (typically via the media) when the information is in the public interest.

Consider for a moment the case of BP (originally known as British Petroleum). BP and other emerging global companies had basic whistleblowing systems as early as 2002, although typically limited to outsourced hotline providers.[5] This surprised me only because the idea of whistleblowing was still so new in the UK and completely unknown elsewhere. These hotlines were part of the corporate response (i.e. public facing "corporate social responsibility" programmes) to concerns raised about the harms of globalised business, but were not singled out for any particular scrutiny or public endorsement.

I remember wondering to whom BP, or any other multinational, was accountable if these systems failed—either for failing to address the concern reported via the hotline, or for failing to protect the worker who used them. Sure, UK workers might have some protection in the UK through the Public Interest Disclosure Act (if they knew about it), but BP was under no obligation to extend these protections to anyone working anywhere else. What about the workers in all of the other countries in which they operated, in China, Colombia, Angola or Azerbaijan? Could workers in those countries go to their national regulators if BP did not respond to their concerns? What would happen to BP in the UK if it failed to protect workers or deal with problems elsewhere? Who was responsible?

In March 2005, an explosion and fire at BP's Texas City Refinery killed 15 people and injured 180 people. It was one of the most serious workplace disasters in the US. Subsequent compensation settlements exceeded $1.5 billion.[6] In addition, BP had to pay various criminal penalties and fines for health and safety violations, despite having reportable safety incidents systems in place and, presumably, a global hotline. This tragedy was closely followed by an even greater disaster. The explosion of BP's Deepwater Horizon oil rig in the Gulf of Mexico on April 20, 2010 killed 11 workers and injured 17, and the resulting ecological devastation reverberates to this day. After the rig capsized and sank, oil began to discharge into the gulf. Estimated to have peaked at more than 60,000 barrels per day, the leak was not stopped until nearly five months after the explosion.[7] The spill and the toxic clean up has had heartbreakingly severe and ongoing environmental consequences on the water, fish, plants and wildlife of the gulf and the health and economic well-being of the people along its coast.[8] In June 2016, BP issued an estimate of the cost of the spill, the largest in US history, as $61.6 billion.[9]

An examination of the various investigations into both disasters, summarised in a paper presented in 2015, concluded that by "failing to listen to—[and] protect whistleblowers and by having an executive bonus scheme that focused on financial consideration above safety—BP—was unable to see what impact their tight *costs* controls were having on low frequency high impact incidents." In other words, people were speaking up regularly about serious safety issues, but the culture and systems of the company itself disconnected local concerns from executive policies and, by linking executive bonuses to financial performance (70%) rather than safety (15%), the company put profit well ahead of its public responsibilities.[10]

This disaster, as well as the global financial meltdown in 2008, among many other man-made tragedies, revealed how ineffective national regulators and legal systems were becoming in regulating corporate conduct globally; partly because of their own market-driven priorities, and because of the size and complexity of the companies they were meant to control. BP's disasters also demonstrate, in my opinion, the key difference between a company's internal risk management systems to control information from a whistleblowing arrangement that recognises the necessity of protecting those who raise the alarm inside or outside the company. There is absolutely no point in *only* being allowed to tell the people within a burning building that the house is on fire.

Law and Culture

When I started working at Public Concern at Work, we had the new Public Interest Disclosure Act as a hook to talk to employers. While there was no positive obligation on them to do anything, employers could face legal action if they failed to protect staff, and the public fall-out could be high in terms of cost and reputational damage. Because the Act is part of the UK's broad employment protection framework (covering all sectors), it caught the interest of human resources first. While we talked about the rights of workers, we used the opportunity to reinforce the wider accountabilities of UK employers. For example, we explained that it was not in the interests of an employer to try to shut down whistleblowing, or do anything to stop someone from going to a regulator, because any attempt to stop someone from disclosing information about potential wrongdoing via a legally protected channel, including to a regulatory authority, was a key trigger under the new law for protecting someone who goes public with their concern.[11]

Changing culture is a long, slow process and, while the law is a helpful, there are always other factors at play. Certainly, in the eight years I worked at Public Concern at Work, strong regulatory and inspection bodies were being dismantled altogether or replaced with "light touch" regulation and self-reporting systems. The neoliberal capitalist agenda was in full operation; government intervention was "bad", markets and competition were "good." The rolling back of unions was already well underway, and the pressure on those that survived to work "with" business seemed to reduce their capacity to support workers raising public interest issues, as well as their ability to hold business and government to account for some of the structural and exploitation problems we are experiencing today.

While the new law to protect whistleblowers was starting to embed, the avenues for whistleblowers to safely report issues outside the workplace, and the effectiveness of their responses, were significantly reducing. This was certainly the case in the financial sector. For example, take the experience of Martin Woods, an 18-year veteran police officer and detective, who joined the London branch of Wachovia Bank as a senior anti-money laundering officer (AML) in March 2005. Martin soon became suspicious of transactions involving Mexican currency-exchange outfits known as Casa de Cambios (CDC). Unusually large amounts of sequentially-numbered traveller's cheques lacking adequate identifying information were being deposited in CDCs and transferred to Wachovia accounts.

Martin issued a "suspicious activity report" and requested that the cheques be temporarily blocked, pending further investigation. His actions were reported to Wachovia in the US and followed best-practice AML procedures and US law. Nevertheless, their reaction was swift and shocking. Senior management harshly criticised Martin's actions and began undermining his work and credibility; he was disciplined, marginalised, and isolated. Despite the pressure, Martin persevered and subsequent investigations by the FBI and US Drug Enforcement Agency confirmed his suspicions: Wachovia had been laundering money for some of the most dangerous and violent drug cartels in Mexico for years—an estimated $378 billion, netting the bank $12.3 billion in profit.

Martin eventually filed and settled a whistleblower claim against Wachovia in London. The US Department of Justice opted not to criminally prosecute Wachovia executives, allowing them instead to plead guilty in order to drastically reduce civil charges and pay a $160 million fine—less than two percent of the bank's drug money profit. The bank was then sold to Wells Fargo, which received $25 billion in US government support during the financial crisis.

Martin Woods raised the alarm because it was his *job* to do so. His employer tried to shut him down and, while US authorities did eventually act, the UK Financial Services Authority (now the Financial Conduct Authority) did little to investigate. After leaving Wachovia, Martin applied for many jobs but was unsuccessful. He found out later the FSA had internal conversations about whether, in speaking about his experiences as a whistleblower, Martin might be critical of the FSA. They reasoned that it was likely, and if he had signed a confidentiality agreement with Wachovia, he would be in breach of it. Without confirmation of such an agreement, they recorded Martin as "non-routine" in relation to his status as a "fit and proper person", making it more difficult to obtain FSA approved status in future. Martin only found this out when he found employment three years later, when his prospective employer informed him that the process of seeking approval would take much longer than usual. He discovered the sequence of events via a subject access request under the Data Protection Act.[12]

Whistleblowing and Civil Society: The First, the Next, and the Only Frontier

Whistleblowing is no longer a niche topic of conversation. It comes up in relation to all sorts of issues—whether it is doping in sports, or the excesses and exploitation of global tech companies. In the 20 years I have worked in the field, the last 10 have seen a marked shift in how the wider civil society community views whistleblowers; from being limited and problematic players in the quest to hold power to account, to being valuable partners who must be supported in their efforts.

I chose to write about some of the issues that affect the support and protection of whistleblowers through my experiences working at a national NGO to help explain the foundations of the Whistleblowing International Network (WIN) which I now run.[13] Part of WIN's goal is to help build the local civil society capacity to make the collective case quickly in individual cases, to ensure that the whistleblower is not the only messenger of the public interest message they have delivered. It is much easier to shut down and discredit a single whistleblower than it is if a whole community agrees with them.

It was also while working nationally that I realised the importance of sharing hard-won expertise across borders.[14] Alongside its core legal advice members, WIN has 30+ associates. These are all are non-profit organisations that share a long-term commitment to protecting whistleblowers, whether working on access to information, fighting corruption, protecting journalists, or defending human rights. Our associates include organisations like Xnet, The Signals Network and Blueprint for Free Speech—all contributors to this book. While we hope to encourage many more lawyers and unions to provide direct and specialised advice to whistleblowers around the world, we know from experience that whistleblowers need a wider community to understand what is at stake and to ensure that their disclosures reach the right places to make change happen.

In the three years since WIN was formally established, our website has become the centre of global whistleblowing information, news and events. We launched a podcast, *Whistleblowing Now and Then*, and held our first international practitioners conference in Glasgow. WIN has been a key player in the civil society coalition that successfully advocated for an EU Directive to protect whistleblowers, and we are currently tracking its transposition across 27 EU Member States.[15] WIN works across the NGO space to support efforts like the Coalition Against SLAPPs in Europe (CASE) to protect freedom of expression and the rights of public interest watchdogs around the world, including whistleblowers. Importantly, we work in collaboration to support cross-border whistleblowing cases, for whom protection is rare, and to share that learning with our membership so that, collectively, we can do more.[16]

I helped to establish WIN because I believe it is vital that civil society supports each other's work and that we have the space to reflect and learn from our practice and to adapt our methods in a changing world. People do not act just because someone tells them it is safe to do so; people act when they think it will make a real difference. I want more of us to be there with whistleblowers, helping them to make that difference.

Notes

1. Gobert, James and Maurice Punch, "Whistleblowers, the Public Interest, and the Public Interest Disclosure Act 1998", *Modern Law Review* 63, no. 1 (United Kingdom: 2000).

2. Canada did not have a fully independent Supreme Court until 1949. Until then, Supreme Court decisions could be appealed to the Judicial Committee of the Privy Council of the House of Lords in Westminster. Canada passed its own Constitution Act in 1982, including a Charter of Rights and Freedoms, but Canadian constitutional still includes the former

British North America Act (1867) and a number of pre-Confederation laws and common law principles as well.

3. Such views are often inculcated from early childhood—and the unwritten rules of the school playground not to "tell the teacher."

4. We trained on the widest range of failures to help people understand how whistleblowing could help protect their own families and well-being, not just their business or profit margins. Examples included: inquiries set up to examine the deaths of 8 school children attending St Albans Outdoor Centre on a kayak trip across Lyme Bay, Wales; the Piper Alpha oil rig explosion that killed 167 workers off the east coast of Scotland; the scandal of high mortality rate of babies at the cardiac unit of the Bristol Royal Infirmary Hospital.

5. Christiansen, Atle Christer, "Beyond Petroleum: Can BP Deliver?", *Fridtjtof Nansens Institut*, (Norway: June 2002), https://www.files.ethz.ch/isn/100209/FNI-R0602.pdf.

6. US Chemical Safety and Hazard Investigation Board (March 2007), Investigation Report, Refinery and Explosion Fire, BP Texas. Report No.2005-04-I-Tx, 17, https://www.csb.gov/bp-america-refinery-explosion.

7. Pallardy, Richard, "Deepwater Horizon oil spill", *Encyclopedia Britannica*, April 13, 2021, https://www.britannica.com/event/Deepwater-Horizon-oil-spill.

8. See the long standing investigative work carried out by the Government Accountability Project's Environment, Energy and Climate Change programme into the impact of BPs Deepwater Horizon oil spill including its 10-Year Anniversary Report, "Ten Years After Deepwater Horizon, Whistleblowers Continue to Suffer an Unending Medical Nightmare Triggered by Corexit", (2010), https://whistleblower.org/wp-content/uploads/2020/04/Ten-Years-After-Deepwater-Horizon.pdf.

9. See The Arthur W. Page Center, Public Relations Ethics Module 9, "Ethics in Crisis Management—Case Study: BP Oil Spill", https://www.pagecentertraining.psu.edu/public-relations-ethics/ethics-in-crisis-management/lesson-1-prominent-ethical-issues-in-crisis-situations/case-study-tbd.

10. James, Cathy, and Keith Plumb, "Whistleblowing–Avoiding the Hazards", *IChemE Symposium Series*, Paper for Hazards 25, Edinburgh: May 2015, https://www.icheme.org/membership/communities/special-interest-groups/safety-and-loss-prevention/resources/hazards-archive/hazards-25.

11. Public Interest Disclosure Act (1998), Section 43G (2)(a). For further explanation and guidance, https://protect-advice.org.uk/pida.

12. Public Concern at Work, "Time for Change: A 5 Year Review" (London: 2016), https://s3-eu-west-1.amazonaws.com/public-concern-at-work/wp-content/uploads/images/2019/12/18171747/PCAW_5yr-review_Time-for-a-Change.pdf.

13. WIN began informally on the margins of an academic conference on whistleblowing at Middlesex University in 2011, and formally registered as a charitable organisation in Scotland in 2018.

14. Prior to setting up Public Concern at Work (now Protect) in 1993, its founders visited and studied the approach of the Government Accountability Project in Washington DC, in operation since 1979. The Open Democracy and Advice Centre in Cape Town looked to the work of Public Concern at Work as a model, as South Africa's new democracy was taking root in 2000. Similarly, the journalist-founders of Serbia's Pištaljka ("The Whistle") consulted both the Government Accountability and Protect before setting up their organisation in 2010 to investigate whistleblowers' concerns and provide legal advice.

15. See our online EU Whistleblowing Monitor: https://www.whistleblowingmonitor.eu.

16. See our work on the case of oil industry corruption whistleblower Jonathan Taylor: https://whistleblowingnetwork.org/News-Events/News/News-Archive/UK-whistleblower-Jonathan-Taylor-finally-freed-fro and World Health Organisation and COVID-19 whistleblower Francesco Zambon: https://whistleblowingnetwork.org/News-Events/News/News-Archive/Open-Letter-for-Ms-Wangmo-President-of-WHO-Supp.

HALGAND

DELPHINE HALGAND-MISHRA

Delphine Halgand-Mishra is the Executive Director of The Signals Network, a non-profit organisation that supports whistleblowers who have shared major public interest information with the press. She previously served as Reporters Without Borders' North America Director, advocating for journalists, bloggers and media rights worldwide. She is a CIGI senior fellow and an expert on press freedom and regulatory frameworks for platforms. In May 2017, she received the 2017 James W. Foley American Hostage Freedom Award for her work assisting American journalists detained abroad.

DELPHINE HALGAND-MISHRA

HOW TO SUPPORT WHISTLEBLOWERS?

THE SIGNALS NETWORK EXPERIENCE

"DECIDING what to tell and to whom can be paralyzing, and whistleblowers should not have to navigate these decisions in a vacuum. You need someone you can trust, who can connect you to resources, and who can help navigate through the legal, ethical, and personal issues associated with whistleblowing. I wish The Signals Network existed back in 2014."

Tyler Shultz, Theranos whistleblower

There isn't one universally applicable roadmap to blowing the whistle, even less to supporting and empowering whistleblowers. There are as many as there are whistleblowers. People who have taken the whistleblowing path before can share knowledge from their own experience, but each whistleblower has to navigate their own unique path.

Here is how I started my path, trying to support and empower whistleblowers. During my time as the US Director of Reporters Without Borders (RSF), I worked to advocate for press freedom rights worldwide, and for the release of journalists imprisoned or held hostage. From this perspective I observed the increasing crackdown on whistleblowers in the US and around the world. I witnessed the lack of support that whistleblowers face in comparison to the journalists they work with.

When *The New York Times* journalist James Risen was threatened with jail because the US Department of Justice (DOJ) wanted to force him to reveal who his source was in an embarrassing CIA failed operation he revealed, all the press freedom community (me included) worked hard to pressure the DOJ to drop their attempt to send him to jail. The DOJ finally gave up. In contrast, when James Risen's alleged source, the CIA whistleblower Jeffrey Sterling, was sentenced to 3.5 years in prison just for being in touch with him, the press freedom community disappeared almost completely. This shocked me and marked me deeply. Press freedom is not only about defending the rights of journalists; press freedom is about the rights of all of us to know and our duty to tell. I started campaigning to obtain Jeffrey's release along his wife and other courageous advocates like Norman Solomon and Dr. Cornel West. My journey supporting whistleblowers started with Jeffrey Sterling. This opened my eyes, and then I was outraged by the retaliation faced by Chelsea Manning, Edward Snowden, Reality Winner and many more.

These citizens have brought to light the most significant information of our time and still they face unprecedented retaliation. I realized that whistleblowers are key players in holding powerful interests accountable. We need more whistleblowers to come forward, we need more wrongdoings to be revealed if we want them to be corrected, and so we need to offer whistleblowers stronger safety nets.

That's why I—with the support of an extraordinary board—founded the French-American non-profit organization The Signals Network in 2017, to enable whistleblowers and international media investigations to work together to hold powerful interests accountable. We are now operational in 12 countries, in the US and 11 European countries, where we support three dozen whistleblowers who have provided information on the biggest media stories of our time, from COVID-19, #MeToo, corruption, crimes committed by governments and tech companies, political propaganda online and health hazards to media outlets ranging from *The New York Times*, *The Guardian*, *BBC* and *NPR* to *Der Spiegel* and *Mediapart*.

I remember the first few months after we created The Signals Network. The founding chairman Gilles Raymond and I were traveling the capitals of Europe and the US, from Berlin to London and Washington DC to convince the biggest media outlets to work with us, and to make a pledge to put the protection of sources at the core of collaborative investigations. Some said yes in 20 minutes, some in a few weeks, some never and some, finally, a few years later. The Signals Network now manages collaborative efforts on international investigations with more than 15 major media outlets on a regular basis. And thanks to The Signals Network, the whistleblowers who shared with them public interest information can access the advice of a trusted lawyer, temporary safe housing, sessions with a therapist to deal with acute stress, an online security expert to protect their online accounts, etc. The Signals Network also connects its media partners with a network of lawyers to which they can refer possible future whistleblowers who are in need of legal guidance.

The Signals Network affords customized support services to a selected number of whistleblowers who have contributed to published reports of significant wrongdoing. The types of services The Signals Network can provide to selected whistleblowers in appropriate cases are: Access to Legal Representation/Counsel, Information Security, Media Relations Management, Advocacy, Psychological Support, and Safe-Housing. Each situation is unique, and each whistleblower has unique needs. Whistleblowers can face legal, physical, psychological, and economic consequences. That is why The Signals Network customizes the support services it can provide to each selected whistleblower. Because each whistleblower's circumstances are evaluated on a case-by-case basis, no whistleblower can reasonably rely on the availability of any support services in advance. The Signals Network does not request, encourage or counsel potential whistleblowers to act unlawfully. In addition, The Signals Network does not receive the public interest information from whistleblowers; rather, this information provided by whistleblowers is shared only with The Signals Network's partner media organizations.

We support media committed to protecting their sources and to working on collaborative investigations based on information shared by whistleblowers. We have already coordinated the publication of four major investigations through media in the US and across Europe (*Die Zeit, El Mundo, Mediapart,* and *Radio France*) reaching hundreds of millions of readers. One was related to blood donations, another to the Chinese company Huawei and the latest one to tax practices in Luxembourg. In May 2019, the investigation we coordinated exposed previously unreported connections between the heart of Russia's internet disinformation campaign and a Spanish company. In July 2020, our media partners published the Plasma Files investigation related to plasma collection devices manufactured by the US company Haemonetics. Some of these machines have been shelved in France since 2018 following a decision by the French authorities. However, they are still in use in the rest of the world. Our media partners raised questions about mysterious particles found in collected materials.

This investigation was the result of months of research on hundreds of documents provided by whistleblowers to the media partners of The Signals Network, including *Bastamag* (France), *Die Zeit* (Germany), *El Mundo* (Spain), *Il Fatto Quotidiano* (Italy), *Mediapart* (France), *McClatchy/Miami Herald* (US), *NRC Handelsblad* (Netherlands) and *Radio France* (France).[1]

Our media partners for the Plasma Files represented a cumulative audience of 165 million readers in six languages. After whistleblowers provided information to the media partners, The Signals Network coordinated the logistics of their collaboration and connected legal support to some of the whistleblowers. The media groups worked together to maximize the impact of their reports, tied to the larger public interest. They shared the received information, investigated the leads as a team, coordinated with each other as they decided their respective formats and angles of the stories, and published under a common embargo.

In January 2021, another group of media partners published an investigation into work conditions at the Chinese technology company Huawei. Our media partners reviewed internal documents and interviewed many former employees of the company across Europe. This investigation was the result of months of research by our media partners, including *El Mundo* (Spain), *The Daily Telegraph* (UK), *Netzpolitik.org* (Germany) and *Republik* (Switzerland).[2] Now, The Signals Network manages the collaborative efforts of different investigations simultaneously and with different and increasing groups of media partners.

In July 2021, a coalition of new media partners (*Sueddeutsche Zeitung, Le Monde, Woxx, El Mundo, IRPI*) published the Luxletters investigation related to the possible existence of secret tax practices in Luxembourg for designated multinational corporations that likely breach EU transparency rules, according to our partner Tax Justice Network.

Whistleblowing Is about the Public Interest, not About the Individual Who Speaks Up

Whistleblower in English, lanceur d'alerte ("alert thrower") in French, and denunciante or informante in Spanish. The concept of whistleblowing might be so intangible that the word itself doesn't exist in many languages. Whistleblower is translated by words which carry a whole unique history and connotation in each country. Sometimes linked to wars, to unions, or to the mafia. Whistleblowers can be perceived as troublemakers, looking for their own prestige, as traitors to their companies, and sometimes even as snitches. For some obscure reason that I cannot understand, whistleblowers can suffer from a negative aura; often to the extreme extent that other people want to stay away from them.

In addition to the multiplicity of words and translations, the definition evolves over time as well. My favorite definition is from the Council of Europe, because it is the most inclusive: "The term whistleblower must be broadly defined so as to cover any individual or legal entity that reveals or reports, in good faith, a crime or lesser offence, a breach of the law or a threat or harm to the public interest of which they have become aware either directly or indirectly."

This definition of whistleblower focuses on the public interest, not the individual and its characteristics. What matters is that someone speaks up in the public interest.

Whistleblowing is About Us All

The COVID-19 crisis has made it clearer than ever that we need whistleblowers, and shown why we must protect them everywhere—not just for their sake, but for ours. Indeed, the COVID-19 crisis made more obvious than ever before how the lack of freedom of information and whistleblower protection in China (to start with) impacts directly on the lives of citizens across the world.

The COVID-19 outbreak has taught us this lesson the hard way. A countless number of COVID-19 whistleblowers have exposed global health hazards, health policy failures, market abuses, privacy concerns and much more. We might not know their names, but we read and heard their revelations in the news almost every day since the beginning of the pandemic. We should be grateful to them all for taking the risk to share information of public concern. We need to protect them now more than ever. Health workers, scientists, politicians, business owners, school teachers, parents and frankly everyone needs to know how the pandemic evolves in order to act appropriately. We need to know about the reliability of tests, treatments, vaccines, and safety protocols across the world in order for us all to return to normalcy as soon as possible.

Whistleblowing is a Long Life-Defining Journey

"Whistleblowing is inherently trouble", Ben Wizner told me recently. All whistleblowers have a different level of risk tolerance, a unique personal situation and their own impact goals. Whistleblowing can be a life-defining journey, and it is crucial for whistleblowers to know what their life may hold in the coming months and years.

Usually when we are put in touch with a whistleblower, the first few weeks are time intensive. For a couple of weeks, we can talk every day to the whistleblower. Then, it generally spaces out to once a week. Over time, this becomes once a month and then, maybe, once a year. But the bond will always exist.

After assessing the case, typically with the assistance of the media partner that referred them, I'll recommend to The Signals Network Board Engagement Committee appropriate types and levels of support services (nature and duration) based on the whistleblower's profile, needs, and expectations. The Signals Network Board Engagement Committee is composed of six members drawn from the Board of Directors and Board of Advisors, each serving a 1-year term: three members review requests from North America, and three members review requests from Europe. In each case, the Board Engagement Committee will review and act at its own discretion, and on the Executive Director's recommendation, taking into consideration the global, human, financial and public interest impact of the information provided to a media organization. No whistleblower can reasonably rely on the availability of any support service before a request is acted on by the Board Engagement Committee.

During the first few weeks, we try to guide the whistleblower towards a personal assessment. The whistleblower needs to ask themselves some hard questions. Nobody will judge them if they change their minds.

Over the years, we summarized the key questions that whistleblowers should seriously consider:

- Would I be okay if the disclosure does not have the impact I wished for? If nobody cares?
- Am I ready for a years-long process?
- What are my goals? What do I want to achieve? Is this realistic?
- What is my level of risk tolerance (professional, financial, legal, personal, etc.)?

- What is my emotional support system? Are my close ones supporting me?
- Should I try to find another job?
- What is my financial situation?
- Do I want to stay anonymous, or should I go public?
- What would I like my post-whistleblowing life to look like? How do I get there?

99% of whistleblowers do not expect such a long journey. It generally takes months for journalists to investigate and eventually publish a strong investigation. Then, it takes years to hold the wrongdoers accountable. I like the way that Pinterest whistleblower Ifeoma Ozoma summarized it: "Do not focus only on whistleblowing, it takes years to see concrete outcomes. Manage your expectations regarding the outcomes. You won't get your job back. It takes years to correct wrongdoings, look at Theranos." (Ifeoma Ozoma, Pinterest whistleblower).

Ifeoma Ozoma filed complaints about wage discrimination and retaliation at the tech company, and finally decided to come forward publicly despite her NDA (non-disclosure agreement). She now fights for the adoption of the Silenced No More Act along with the California Employment Lawyers Association and Equal Rights Advocates.[3] If passed, the measure will allow victims of any type of workplace discrimination—on the basis of categories such as race, religion, age, disability and sexual orientation—to speak honestly and openly about what they have faced, regardless of the language in a non-disclosure or non-disparagement agreement."[4] At The Signals Network, we work closely with Ifeoma Ozoma to share knowledge among tech workers about their options if they see something wrong at their company.

Usually when a media partner reaches out for a source who is requiring support, in 95% of cases, the whistleblower would like to be connected and advised by a trusted expert lawyer. Our network of on-call lawyers continues to expand as cases require new specialties, from California employment lawyers to European human rights lawyers. Only once (in three years) was the initial request of support for a temporary safe house. We provided this for a couple of months in a safe European country. Very regularly, online security consultancy is required to help protect the whistleblower's online accounts. In the next phase of our development,

I want to focus on the advocacy and campaigning work needed for the whistle-blowers' revelations to turn into real change after the public disclosures happen.

All whistleblowers need pastoral care, and sustained psychological support. They face acute stress, intense emotions, a sense of loneliness, and a lot of pressure; they are often not used to expressing such feelings, nor used to asking for help. Very few ask about getting professional psychological support, although most probably need it.

"80% of the support you need is not legal support, but psychological support, career support…", according to Cambridge Analytica whistleblower Chris Wylie, who expressed his frustration to me that the focus is mostly on the legal issues, when whistleblowing is a whole life-defining journey. Whistleblowers need to know how they will pay their rent if they lose their job and who will support them emotionally during this years-long journey.

We Can All Support Whistleblowers

As citizens, we can all support whistleblowers in different and concrete ways. First, we can keep our eyes open, pay attention to the news, and subscribe to media outlets we respect for their investigations. We can also support groups that advocate for the change that whistleblowers have revealed, by becoming a member of such organizations. There is nothing worse for a whistleblower than to think that all of their efforts were in vain. We can all be a part of correcting the wrongdoing and holding powerful interests accountable.

If we are concerned or if we support a new law related to the better protection of whistleblowers, reaching out to our Parliamentary representatives is also an efficient method. The coming months (2021-2022) will be crucial in Europe, as the country members of the European Union are adopting the new EU Directive which should guarantee a stronger protection to whistleblowers. We should all remain careful that this represents a step forward and keep an eye on the legislative process to ensure the national implementation provides the protection needed.[5]

As a lawyer, or a licensed psychotherapist, a website designer, or perhaps the owner of a safe house, you can reach out to organizations like The Signals Network to offer your expertise and help us to continue to support whistleblowers. It is our duty to make sure that freedom of information, transparency, accountability and whistleblowers' protections are not stifled. Whistleblowing is about us all; our rights and our duties.

Notes

1. Simon Gouin, "Plasmafiles: une enquête internationale révèle d'éventuels dangers pour des donneurs et receveurs de plasma", *Bastamag*, July 1, 2020, https://www.bastamag.net/plasmafiles-machines-haemonetics-donneurs-risques-plasma-particules-PCS2; Eva Hoffmann, Luisa Hommerich, Yassin Musharbash, Florian Schumann and Sascha Venohr, "The Machine and the Blood", *Zeit Online*, July 1, 2020, https://www.zeit.de/wissen/gesundheit/2020-07/blood-plasma-donations-health-risk-haemonetics-english; Pablo Herraiz, "Una filtración de la mayor empresa de transfusiones desvela 36.000 percances en 40 países", *El Mundo*, July 1, 2020, https://www.elmundo.es/ciencia-y-salud/salud/2020/07/01/5efc8c1ffdddff3e5e8b45c9.html; Stefania Maurizi, "Plasma Files (esclusivo): tutti i rischi della tecnologia Haemonetics", *Il Fatto Quotidiano*, July 1, 2020, https://www.ilfattoquotidiano.it/in-edicola/articoli/2020/07/01/plasma-files-esclusivo-tutti-i-rischi-della-tecnologia-haemonetics-per-la-donazione-del-plasma/5853682/; Simon Gouin, "Dons de plasma: des incidents sur des machines révélés dans plus de 20 pays", *Mediapart*, July 1, 2020, https://www.mediapart.fr/journal/international/010720/dons-de-plasma-des-incidents-sur-des-machines-reveles-dans-plus-de-20-pays; Ben Wieder, "Plasma Files: How a device shelved for health reasons in France remained in use in U.S.", *Miami Herald*, July 1, 2020, https://www.miamiherald.com/news/health-care/article243792007.html; Lisa van Lonkhuyzen and Jeroen Wester, "Groot alarm bij de bloedbank: alweer een zak vol zwarte deeltjes", *NRC Handelsblad*, July 1, 2020, https://www.nrc.nl/nieuws/2020/07/01/groot-alarm-bij-de-bloedbank-alweer-een-zak-vol-zwarte-deeltjes-a4004647; Sylvain Tronchet, "Don de plasma : une enquête internationale soulève de nouveau des interrogations autour d'une multinationale", *France Culture*, July 1, 2020, https://www.franceculture.fr/societe/don-de-plasma-une-enquete-internationale-souleve-de-nouveau-des-interrogations-autour-dune.

2. Pablo Herraiz, "Exclusiva: Una investigación internacional desvela que Huawei penaliza a sus empleados chinos por relacionarse con occidentales", *El Mundo*, January 13, 2021, https://www.elmundo.es/economia/2021/01/13/5ffe1f39fc6c83b1588b463e.html; Sophie Barnes, "A Chinese former expat employee said that marrying a local in Europe is informally viewed within the company as an act of betrayal", *The Daily Telegraph*, January 13, 2021, https://www.telegraph.co.uk/news/2021/01/13/huawei-expat-employees-marry-westerners-faced-forced-leave-europe/; Daniel Laufer and Alexander Fanta, "How Huawei controls its employees in Europe", *Netzpolitik.org*, January 13, 2021, https://netzpolitik.org/2021/wolf-culture-how-huawei-controls-its-employees-in-europe/; Sylke Gruhnwald, "Inside Huawei", *Republik*, January 13, 2021, https://www.republik.ch/2021/01/13/inside-huawei.

3. Nitasha Tiku, "Black women say Pinterest created a den of discrimination — despite its image as the nicest company in tech", *The Washington Post*, July 4, 2020, https://www.washingtonpost.com/technology/2020/07/03/pinterest-race-bias-black-employees/; Paulina Villegas, "NDAs have long been used to silence the abused, advocates say. A new law may change that", *The Washington Post*, February 9, 2021, https://www.washingtonpost.com/business/2021/02/08/california-silenced-no-more-act/.

4. Ifeoma Ozoma, "An NDA was designed to keep me quiet", *The New York Times*, April 13, 2021, https://www.nytimes.com/2021/04/13/opinion/nda-work-discrimination.html.

5. EU Whistleblowing Monitor, Accessed July 5, 2021, https://www.whistleblowingmonitor.eu/.

BARRETT BROWN

Barrett Brown is a writer and activist. His work has appeared in *Vanity Fair*, *The Guardian*, *The Intercept*, *Huffington Post*, *New York Press*, *Skeptic*, *The Daily Beast*, *Al Jazeera*, and other outlets. In 2009, he founded Project PM (projectpm.wiki), a "distributed think tank" later repurposed to oversee a crowdsourced investigation into private intelligence contractors and little-known surveillance/disinformation methodologies. In 2011 and 2012, he worked with Anonymous on campaigns involving the Tunisian revolution, state misconduct, and other issues. In 2012, Brown was arrested and later sentenced to four years in federal prison on charges stemming from his investigations into HBGary, Stratfor, Palantir, Archimedes, and other firms that would later be implicated in election interference operations in the US and UK. While imprisoned, he won the National Magazine Award and other journalism and writing honours for his column, "The Barrett Brown Review of Arts and Letters and Prison." Upon his release in late 2016, he established the non-profit Pursuance to develop a platform for mass civic engagement and to promote his doctrine of non-institutional "process democracy." His third book, *My Glorious Defeats*, is available for pre-order from

BARRET BROWN
THE WAR FORWARD

"I SHOWED HIM *my press card and a few letters from several influential persons. I had already got into the humiliating habit of carrying them on me."*

Arthur Koestler, Scum of the Earth, 1941

The easiest part of being a whistleblower is blowing the whistle. The most difficult part of being a whistleblower is ensuring that the results are worthwhile. Those who support the practice of whistleblowing can do little or nothing to help with the initial act of making public that which was intended to be secret. But there is a great deal they can do to assist with that which comes afterwards—and on which everything ultimately depends. A decade after the current wave of highly public whistleblowing kicked off in earnest, in tandem with the rise of WikiLeaks, we have enough information to start systematizing this, just as the adversary has systematized its own response.

The essence of whistleblowing is narrative. There is no use simply releasing data if it is not publicized and placed in its proper context. This is understood on some level by those parties who wish to suppress, ignore, and otherwise divorce information from its proper context—and who in many cases are specially trained and equipped with this end in mind. This is unlike most parties on our own side, who must generally rely upon other advantages to achieve success in the information war that follows every act of whistleblowing.

Before we look further into the nature of such conflicts, we should determine what we mean when we speak of "whistleblowing", as its definition varies among dictionaries just as it does among observers. It is defined separately in an assortment of laws and policies (indeed, largely arbitrary attempts to redefine the term so as to alternatively encompass or exclude particular acts serves as one common front of the subsequent conflicts, which often extend to courtrooms). For our purposes, we may define whistleblowing as the act of exposing alleged wrongdoing. This will serve our inquiry nicely so long as we keep in mind that its use will invariably depend on how one also defines the words, "act", "exposing", "alleged", and "wrongdoing", and how these definitions change in accordance with the semi-conscious, obscurantist ballet that is public political disputation in the 21st Century. At any rate, this definition is similar to those presented by English dictionaries, while summing up popular usage as well. It will allow us to cite and draw useful lessons from cases as diverse as those of Julian Assange, Edward Snowden, Chelsea Manning, John Kiriakou, Thomas Drake, Jeremy Hammond, Aaron Swartz, Daniel Ellsberg, Emma Best, Lauri Love, Reality Winner, and myself, to name some of the better-documented cases.

Whistleblowing can vary dramatically in terms of its motivations, scope, subject matter, consequences for the practitioner versus those suffered by the alleged wrongdoing party, format, public perception, and extent to which public ideology informs the degree of support and attention. It includes actions taken by military and intelligence staffers who use their positions to leak data sets (Snowden, Drake, Manning, Ellsberg, Winner); by those who seek to relay information directly to the press for the public good (Kiriakou); by those subsequently pursued by states for allegedly obtaining similar information via means of hacking (Hammond, Love); and those who more typically seek out and curate the fruits of all of the above (Assange, Best, myself). Those of us who are primarily curators of data provided by others are, of course, better understood as facilitators of whistleblowing than whistleblowers ourselves, but often share the label with our more traditional counterparts—along with such other labels as "journalist", "activist", "hero", and "traitor".

The most important commonality among these cases is that the limiting factor of the effectiveness of our work has been the extent to which the subsequent narrative succeeded; the extent to which the information at stake was successfully and contextually inserted into the civic consciousness in a manner that prompted substantive change. Naturally, many factors contribute to the end result, beginning with the nature of the information—for instance, whether it consists of a few key smoking-gun leaked memos that lend themselves to effective action or, alternatively, a vast trove of documents detailing an array of misconduct but requiring intense analysis along with a successful bid to bring sufficient attention to the results. Other factors are better categorized in accordance with whether they tend to serve the ends of our side or the other; they are also worth listing to provide a better picture of how the ensuing information war is fought, and on what fronts.

The advantages of the adversary—states, institutions, and individuals who are more or less consciously dedicated to suppressing the whistleblower and, more importantly, the whistleblower's narrative—include access to the law enforcement apparatus of assorted states; use of relatively amoral and unaccountable collaborators such as the loose networks of FBI co-operators that have historically been successful in disrupting various strains of activism in and out of the US; bipartisan support for anti-whistleblower measures; the existence of whistleblower protections that are too insufficient or too narrowly or consistently applied to perform their stated functions, but which by simply existing may lead observers to conclude that whistleblowing conducted outside of their confines is unnecessary and illicit; credulity and reverence for establishment institutions on the part of elements of the press; the use of quasi-official channels to put out damaging misinformation (and occasionally accurate information that happens to serve the state narrative); some unknown but evidenced degree of state infiltration of media; and the varying degree to which states are comfortable acting outside of the law while possessing the sole effective agency by which to determine what it is and who has and has not violated it.

The advantages of those of us among whistleblowers, curators, assorted activists, and a small portion of the press and wider establishment who might be collectively termed the "transparency activism community" (TAC) include the fact that our apparatus works mostly for free, that the movement attracts philanthropic funding and resources, access to a helpfully eccentric array of participants, flexibility, relative freedom to speak freely and candidly to the media, and the ability to present novel narratives that the media finds more compelling than the static output on which the state tends to rely.

There are also a handful of factors that are best categorized as double-edged swords, variously serving the interests of both sides depending on which is better able to capitalize on each. Chief among these is the tendency for much of the press and public—supporters and detractors alike—to focus on the personality of the whistleblower above the data the whistleblower makes public, and the implications thereof. There is a limited extent to which this preoccupation can serve the public interest, which is just as well given that it is largely inevitable. To humanize and justify the whistleblower is to partially insulate them from state retaliation—to make it less viable due to public response, and to promote fundraising for legal fees and so on. Retaliation will most often entail some degree of scrutiny towards whistleblowers themselves—and thus also the impetus to discredit them in the course of obtaining warrants and convincing juries.

As with much else, though, focus by supporters on the whistleblower themselves soon reaches a point of diminishing returns. It is also the easiest sort of support to drum up, and thus always more in evidence than the other basic form of support—the form which entails capitalizing on the information at hand, or in assisting to bring about the conditions wherein this may occur via existing processes. It is this latter kind of support that must be advanced above all else if any of our sacrifices are ultimately to matter.

The modern whistleblower loses control of the narrative they set in motion, often at the very time in which a full and accurate accounting is most crucial for the public good. In some sense, anyone who presents information of any sort can expect to lose control of the narrative as it as proceeds into the world and becomes a part of the culture, to be interpreted and misinterpreted by others. But to the extent that the whistleblower's narrative is perceived as a threat to some combination of powerful entities, the whistleblower in question is confronted with the added difficulty of sitting at the apex of a partially covert struggle involving significant global interests who will seek to advance some contradictory counter-narrative—and are often well-practiced in doing so. Along with more mundane, but often more consequential, factors such as the reluctance of the citizenry to pay sufficient attention to matters they are duty-bound to assess and act upon—even in the face of existential and increasingly obvious threats to democracy, and civilization itself—the scope for failure is broad.

My own story is illustrative because it involves several sorts of whistleblowing from a variety of angles; extensively documented via state surveillance and the discovery process by which evidence to be used in federal court must also be provided to my legal defense team and made more or less public (along with a variety of leaks that have occurred since, including correspondence among law enforcement personnel and their collaborators). Also, because it is partially intertwined with the stories of other whistleblowers and, most of all, because of how difficult it is to obtain an accurate account of it given the vastly contradictory accounts one finds in assorted books, documentary films, and press articles.

In 2009, I founded an entity called Project PM with the initial intent of developing a framework for press reform. I soon realized that the same framework could be applied to a much broader array of pursuits that I began to term "crowd-sourced civics"; pilot programs including an effort to improve science journalism by linking scientists with reporters, and a separate program to use defunct patents in assorted sub-Saharan African development efforts. I recruited for this effort via my columns in outlets like *The Huffington Post, Vanity Fair,* and *Skeptical Inquirer.* At the same time, my interest in weaponizing internet phenomena such as the nascent Anonymous activist movement prompted my recruitment by individuals associated with the Anonops internet relay chat server, which in late 2010 was used as a staging ground for Tunisian revolutionaries such as "Slim" Amamou, who would soon become the first Anon to join a provisional government (after the Ben Ali regime was successfully removed from office). Within a month, my focus shifted from the movement for Arab democracy to organizing legal defense for other Anonymous activists in the wake of a mass US-UK roundup of alleged participants. Shortly after, revelations that a former US Navy intelligence officer named Aaron Barr—then CEO of an "intelligence contracting" firm called HBGary Federal—had been spying on our server in a bid to promote his work with the FBI and Pentagon prompted several of my more technically-inclined colleagues to conduct a raid on the servers of his firm and its parent company, which I was told of in advance so that I'd be prepared to handle any media operations that might follow. This hack resulted in the theft of 70,000 of the firm's emails, covering several years of work with various US intelligence agencies, the Department of Justice (DOJ), and Palantir—a far more substantial firm.

Palantir turned out to have been leading a corporate black ops network for the purpose of targeting activists and the press on behalf of entities like Bank of America, and with the covert assistance of the DOJ itself. Over the following months, as it became clear that neither the traditional press nor Congress was inclined to use these materials sufficiently or appropriately, I converted Project PM into a crowd-sourced research apparatus for the purpose of investigating these and other troves of leaked documents, supplementing the data with additional inquiries, and presenting our findings on a Wiki we set up to this end, as well as via my ongoing articles for *The Guardian*. Occasionally, we provided better-positioned reporters at outlets such as *Bloomberg* with tips that led to articles exposing similar digital misconduct.

Even to the extent that we took pains to put out materials via other sources, the adversary knew quite well where this was coming from. The FBI sought and obtained the first of several secret grand jury search warrants for ongoing access to my communications in April 2011, on the basis of my alleged criminal conduct against Palantir in the prior two months. This was supplemented a year later with armed raids on my apartment and mother's home, citing HBGary Federal and Endgame Systems as my chief targets, along with Project PM, our website, Anonymous, and LulzSec as subjects for search. Within a few days, the prosecution made it known to me that they would be prosecuting my mother for her role in hiding my laptops from the FBI agents before they had even obtained a warrant for her house. Towards the end of 2012, I threatened to retaliate against the lead FBI agent using the same methods that HBGary and Palantir had proposed using on activists; a few days later, I was arrested and charged with threatening a federal agent; denied bond and further indicted on a century's worth of charges relating to the hack of Stratfor, another intelligence contracting firm with ties to the State Department and CIA. Over the next two years, the DOJ would attempt to gain my co-operation via additional threats to prosecute my mother (which were carried out when I refused), as well as an offering to drop 20 years of mandatory sentencing charges were I to plead to one of the eleven counts involving my copying and pasting a link to stolen materials from Stratfor, which I refused on the grounds that this would set a dangerous precedent.

Eventually, the prosecution dropped the linking charges and I plead to three other charges: interference with a search warrant, threatening a federal agent, and accessory after the fact to the Stratfor hack. Along the way, it also transpired that the DOJ had illegally sought and obtained the identities of everyone who contributed to Project PM—even those who had simply donated to my legal defense fund. After four years behind bars (including a total of six months in segregation cells for "disciplinary" and "investigative" reasons), I emerged from a medium security Texas prison in the wake of the 2016 US presidential election, and began the depressing process of discovering the degree to which so many sacrifices on the part of so many people had ultimately come to nothing.

Palantir, Archimedes Global, and White Canvas Group—three of the firms whose projects and personnel had come under our particular scrutiny as the subjects of our most constant public warnings, including in my last article for *The Guardian* (which the DOJ cited in the course of having me placed under a gag order, after I wrote it from prison in 2013)—had not only managed to expand their operations in the interim, but played key roles in the Cambridge Analytica/Facebook data mining operations. This had almost certainly tipped the election to Trump; Archimedes also shared executives with Cambridge, including one who went on to join the Trump administration. Furthermore, even these revelations which came out in 2017, in the course of various Congressional and law enforcement investigations in tandem with the testimony of additional whistleblowers, were quickly forgotten—including by the FBI, which leaked information about White Canvas Group's longstanding ties with General Flynn to *The Washington Post* and then never mentioned it again in any filings.

Today, the mainstream English-speaking press routinely reports on Palantir's advancing strategic hegemony over the world's intelligence, governmental, and even political apparatus (a search of the Podesta emails on WikiLeaks reveals the Clinton campaign also sought its aid, perhaps failing to realize that co-founder Peter Thiel's professed vision of an obscurantist and neo-fascist "Dark Enlightenment" was more aligned with the Trump campaign, which it opted to assist instead). Almost none of these articles mention Palantir's 2016 role in subverting what is left of Western democracy; even fewer make mention of the fact that this scandal could have been averted had its 2011 plot to do likewise—considered serious enough by the US House of Representatives that more than a dozen Congressmen called for an investigation—received more than a few weeks of sporadic and incomplete press coverage. This is true even for outlets like *The New York Times*, which provided coverage of both incidents; some of which directly contradicts other *Times* articles on the very same scandals on the occasion they're mentioned at all.

A similar dynamic can be seen vis-à-vis Aaron Swartz, who aside from his more celebrated accomplishments also assisted our research into the Pentagon's use of automated social media bots of the sort that the public belatedly began to recognize as a threat to democracy in 2016, and who also warned the public about the danger of the Stratfor-affiliated Trapwire facial recognition program and its potential implications. His prophetic utterances on these matters, however, were drowned out by a handful of media figures who have themselves only increased in influence. This is merely one example of a dozen I could cite in which our efforts as whistleblowers and activists have come to nothing when they might otherwise have spared the world much of what has happened in the years that have followed. This is on top of the far more profound waste that has been made of the millions of documents hosted in accessible, searchable form on WikiLeaks that have nonetheless gone unused, despite ongoing instances in which searches for newly-relevant keywords—like "General Flynn" or "Wikistrat", for instance, have yielded information central to understanding the most reported-on stories of our time.

The particular threat posed by media failure, incidentally, does not simply entail that misinformation will spread to the detriment of the public at the time it occurs, but also that it leads to a situation wherein each individual reporter who weighed in wrongly at the time of "the story" now has a pragmatic interest in suppressing or at least ignoring the truth. To a much lesser, but still noticeable, extent, this same pragmatic interest applies to colleagues who simply missed the story. The threat that this may become the story—and it should, if it matters whether our collective system for discovering and assessing the world has considerable, trenchant flaws due to a lack of viable means of making this known, much less correcting it—means that the original information is even less likely to be conveyed to the public, even when it directly applies to issues that the media itself has deemed significant.

Along with a broken press infrastructure, the whistleblower's narrative—and ability to shepherd that narrative through the critical early days of its presentation, when misunderstandings and disinformation can do the most damage to the public awareness—is also under perpetual threat from those portions of the law enforcement apparatus that target, identify, discredit, and disrupt parties engaged in whistleblowing and activism, as well as those who work directly or indirectly on their behalf. The best known among the latter sort include figures such as the late Adrian Lamo, a hacker who won Chelsea Manning's trust before turning her in to the US authorities, and who went on to play an even more baroque role in my own prosecution. Other useful examples include the figure known as th3j35t3r—allegedly a US military veteran and hacker who's now known to have been a persona operated by at least two or three people—along with the loose network of largely ideologically-motivated parties who worked with "him" out of another IRC server, in an emergent collaborative effort not dissimilar to Anonymous itself.

Thanks to an ongoing series of conflicts among those involved in such things, along with the propensity among some of them to brag and even publicly fight for credit, we have an irritatingly large amount of raw information about many of the participants, as well as records indicating how they operate, what sorts of personal issues tended to motivate them other than ideology, and so on. Although confusion remains over some of what occurred when these networks were at the height of their activity, it's clear enough that these networks often proved decisive in derailing our work at key moments, sometimes with significant consequences. In at least a few cases, some of those involved were found to have been working with individual FBI agents who served as their handlers—sometimes with the firms we were pursuing, and separately with some of the more credulous elements of the press.

We have enough documentation on this that we are today in a position to create a very different environment for anyone who may choose to follow in the footsteps of the whistleblowers of a decade ago, or in those of the activists who worked diligently to support their mission. Aside from an apparatus called Pursuance—an enhanced framework for civic collaboration, crowd-sourced research, and emergent activism that builds on the lessons we've learned and the dynamics we've observed so as to make this kind of activity more effective and secure going forward—my colleagues and I have recently relaunched the long-defunct Project PM initiative, restoring its old website and once again making it available for curated editing and new additions. Information on Pursuance can be found in articles and lectures that have appeared on the subject since my release in 2016. Project PM strives to once again present a compelling public dossier of the illicit state-corporate intelligence axis that continues to threaten democratic institutions across the world.

Lest these efforts once again be neutralized by the very same kinds of dynamics that have thwarted us in the past, we've also launched two similar crowd-sourced research entities to publicly document what is otherwise privately endured. ProjSwartz, named for Aaron Swartz, presents raw data on law enforcement and affiliated parties who target activists, compiled into individual pages that in most cases will come up first on any search engine query for the individuals involved. This means, among other things, that activists who find themselves engaged by any of these parties and who do even a cursory search for information on them will find it, and thereby also become aware of the assortment of relevant resources and assistance that we're in a position to provide on these issues. ProjHastings, named for the late American journalist and Project PM participant Michael Hastings, will use similar means to document press failure, using narrow and unambiguous parameters that focus on whether an outlet or individual reporter have prevented contradictory versions of the same events in two or more stories without addressing the discrepancy (sadly, even this refined definition of what constitutes such failures allows for enough examples that the project's Wiki is launching with a good portion of material on hand, even before our call for tips and curated contributions goes out).

Ultimately, these two projects will serve to paint an unprecedented picture of how incompetence on the one hand and malice on the other have strangled reform efforts in the crib, while also providing an increasing modicum of edifying accountability to those found to be guilty of either. Both projects, and others like them, are designed to gradually and effectively incorporate the efforts of the untold thousands who wish to support this movement and compatible causes, but who have so far been left without good options in doing so. The end result will be a world in which the necessary business of activism, journalism, and reform may proceed and prosper without being quite so constrained by the same broken institutions that they're intended to address.

There is a concept born of ancient Judaism, Tikkun Olam, that translates loosely to "repair of the world". Coupled with new forms of democratic self-organization that have become increasingly viable with the advent of the information age, such a concept can (and should) come to form the organizing principle by which this movement, so long in retreat and disarray in the face of an enemy we have failed to truly fight, can re-emerge in the years ahead. It has the potential to spark a global, empirical, and principled reform movement, capable of confronting criminalized institutional power. The alternative is tragedy beyond imagination.

TATIANA BAZZICHELLI

Photo by Felicia Scheurecker

Tatiana Bazzichelli is founder, board member, and programme director of the Disruption Network Lab. Her focus of work is hacktivism, network culture, art, and whistleblowing. A longer version of her biography can be found on page 10.

LIEKE PLOEGER

Lieke Ploeger is the community director and administration officer of the Disruption Network Lab since 2019. She also serves as board member of the Disruption Network Lab e. V.. She is the co-founder of the independent project space SPEKTRUM art science community in Berlin, where she worked as community builder from 2014 to 2018. Her core interest lies in building and developing both online and offline communities of interest, with a focus on sharing knowledge and expertise in an open way. In 2018 she published the manual "How we can all make it to the future: A guide to offline community building in art & science" on the community building process of SPEKTRUM art science community. She previously worked for the Open Knowledge Foundation, a global non-profit organisation focused on realising open data's value to society by helping civil society groups access and use data to take action on social problems. She also worked for the National Library of the Netherlands. She has a double Master of Arts from the University of Utrecht, the Netherlands, and has been involved in various European research projects in the

CONCLUSION

TATIANA BAZZICHELLI &
LIEKE PLOEGER
BUILDING NETWORKS OF TRUST

Before and After Blowing the Whistle

WHISTLEBLOWING is an act of social justice that is often performed individually and in isolation from peers, but it cannot be fully understood without considering it as strictly embedded in social, political and cultural dynamics. The social structure of friends, advocates, supporters and colleagues becomes extremely crucial before and after blowing the whistle. It is a resource for whistleblowers and people working on whistleblowing that needs to be considered as central in order to be able to contain the pressure of whistleblowing and to give a sense of belonging to a larger community. Isolation is also one of the multiple facets of persecution towards whistleblowers, and it is the responsibility of all of us engaged with this subject to provide a context for sharing, discussion and mutual trust among different actors in this field. Furthermore, acts of whistleblowing are usually based on the witnessing of events that happen inside a specific sector, which implies relations with colleagues and other people, and therefore possible consequences for these colleagues, as well as society at large. Working in this field, either as an advocate, or as a curator, activist, journalist, filmmaker, writer, etc., requires establishing an intensely sharing and close relationship with the people that blew the whistle. Acts of whistleblowing are often made possible thanks to a mutual network of trust that gave the whistleblower the right courage. At the Disruption Network Lab, we believe that the organisation of our events on the topics of whistleblowing and social justice is only the final stage of a longer journey, one that is based on closer research and scrutiny of the given subjects, but also on the careful development of personal relationships with the invited speakers that share their stories with our audience. We consider what happens before and after our events to be the central part of our work and the most relevant, because it is through the establishment of networks of trust that we can work collectively to provide literacy and, in the best cases, societal and cultural changes.

The core of our work is to connect people, and to offer them the opportunity to exchange perspectives from different fields of work and investigation. Since 2014, we organised participatory, interdisciplinary, international events at the intersection of human rights and technology with the objective of strengthening freedom of speech.

For each topic we analyse at the Disruption Network Lab, our central focus is to expose systems of power and injustice. How do we explain the systems of power related to a specific topic, and how can we find countermeasures to forms of injustice? Our approach is critical, stemming from within the subject, but also open to different expertise and to further investigation.

In our events, we seek to combine people and groups with different backgrounds and knowledge, and to create a network based on the analysis of multiple points of view. This chapter illustrates how the Disruption Network Lab works on building networks of trust through both the conference and community programme.

Disruption Network Lab: Sharing a Common Mindset for a Radical Change—Tatiana Bazzichelli

In April 2014, drawing upon my previous experiences as curator, researcher, and networker in the field of art, hacking and activism, I decided to start a new project, which I called Disruption Network Lab. The initial idea was to bring together three areas of work: Disruption, as an interference of closed political and technological systems; Networking, as the creation of open contexts for sharing and social exchange; and the format of an experimental Laboratory for generating public awareness, investigating, and denouncing injustices. The main focus, learning from the experience of whistleblowers, truth-tellers, activists and hackers, was to identify hidden systems of power, and how to expose them. From 2015, our programme took shape through a series of conference events in Berlin at Studio 1 of Kunstquartier Bethanien, which is a lively space for artistic and cultural institutions of the city since the 1970s. To date, we are a team of eight people, but more colleagues in the past contributed to the development of our programme.[1]

In 2016, we became a registered Berlin-based nonprofit organisation in Germany (Disruption Network Lab e. V.), and since 2019, Lieke Ploeger joined me in the organisation as director of our Activation community programme. Since the foundation of the Lab, the scope was to introduce disruption as a multi-faceted concept, to research whistleblowing and truth-telling, and to understand how whistleblowing could be seen as a source of inspiration for creating a difference in society. However, the Disruption Network Lab has not only been focusing on whistleblowing. The experimental approach in curating the programme involved a larger set of practices in connection with whistleblowing—as we have also seen throughout this anthology.

To better understand the notion and practice of whistleblowing, I proposed to link it with other topics, from social criticism, technological experimentation, to tactical media practices as a mix between art and activism. The purpose of the broad scope was to encourage a critical mindset shared by a variety of people, rather than only focusing on the presentation of specific facts.

Following my theoretical approach described in the introduction of this book, the Disruption Network Lab has made public the projects that disrupt the field of information technology in an unexpected way, in order to present interventions fostering political and social change. Since the early 2000s, my curatorial methodology has brought together a montage of methods and practices, as well as fieldworks, to create a network of experiences that can be understood in their full potential only if combined together. The first series of our conference events (April-December 2015) focused on media practices at the border of hacking, art and activism covering a wide spectrum of contemporary political, cultural and economic issues: from the use of drones in political conflicts, to the emergence of social media practices causing critical consequence on our privacy; from the critical reflection on gender, identity and sexuality in post-digital contexts, to the upcoming frontiers of bio-hacking; from the practice of whistleblowing as a way of exposing sensitive facts and information, to political stunts and tactics of disruption that reveal the bugs of economic and business systems from within.

Merging digital culture with other practices, e.g., hacking, activism, politics, sexuality, investigative journalism, whistleblowing, and popular culture, the aim is to create new forms of imagination, social awareness, and to provide literacy. This "montage method" (inspired by Walter Benjamin, 1928) is at the core of the conference events at the Disruption Network Lab, where different experts meet and collaboratively investigate the matters at hand. The event series unfolds a variety of issues through the years, which only appear to have no direct connection to each other. By keeping such thematic and practical connections open without necessarily reaching a curatorial synthesis, we invite the public to get inspired by the in-depth analysis of subjects that are often difficult to fully access.

In the framework of the Disruption Network Lab, the dialogue between disciplines is crucial for enabling the adoption of multiple points of view, and this approach is the basis for an experimental theoretical—and empirical—perspective. In the 1980s, James Clifford described the methodology of ethnographic surrealism as a means of dismantling culture's hierarchies and holistic truths. Cultural order had to be substituted with unusual juxtapositions, fragments and unexpected combinations, taking inspiration from Avant-garde practices of the 1920s and 30s. The goal of the ethnographic research was no longer seen as rendering the unfamiliar comprehensible as the previous tradition had required, but making the familiar strange "by a continuous play of the familiar and the strange, of which ethnography and surrealism are two elements" (Clifford, 1981).

This perspective of generating unusual juxtapositions and unexpected connections is applied within the event series of the Disruption Network Lab, by adopting a curatorial methodology that creates multiple contradictions without actually solving them. The idea is to keep the thematic frameworks open to new interpretations as a form of cultural criticism and as a way to experience crucial issues of society and politics from within.

This method, which works on the creation of networks of affinities as well as the interconnection of diverse subjectivities, becomes a mode of thinking about tactical strategies in the field of art, politics, and media. The methodology applied onto our curatorial series is to put the network configurations under investigation, and analyse their inner logics.

A comparative approach becomes of central importance, by creating a dialogue of practices in the field of whistleblowing, art, digital culture, politics and hacking. The goal is to encourage the creation of networks of trust, as a dialogue among the organisers and the speakers, among the participants of the programme and the audience, and among those and the broader scene of whistleblowing, media, art and technology in Berlin and internationally.

The creation of such conceptual and practical juxtapositions is often experienced as a surprise for our speakers, when for example whistleblowers are called to share ideas and methods with artists and activists. And more than once, we found ourselves in a situation where we needed to explain to either funders or the audience, who normally are confronted with programmes that deal with one specific field of expertise, how and why corporate wrongdoing, whistleblowing, the financial crisis, social hacking, and the critical reflection on identity and sexuality are connected.

This common effort results in the revealing and studying of the inner structures and logics of political, economic and technological systems, in order to encourage debate on sensitive issues, and to shed light on the hidden reasons of decision-making and their consequence on broader society.

Furthermore, at the Disruption Network Lab, we work on interconnecting various formats; on one hand we organise international conferences, both physical and digital events, and on the other hand, we organise local meetups and workshops through our community programme, as described later by Lieke Ploeger. So far, we realised more than twenty conference events[2].

The first conference we organised was "Drones: Eyes From A Distance", in April 2015, and our first keynote speaker was Brandon Bryant, a very important encounter for us. He describes his story by himself in the first chapter of this book, but nevertheless, I want to mention my personal experience in meeting him to explain the idea of building networks of trust more in depth. From 2006 to 2011 Brandon Bryant was a sensor operator of the drone programme in the US Air Force. After he left the programme, he tried to discuss and share what he experienced, making people understand that even if you were part of the military, you still had the possibility to create an impact by radically changing your point of view. He also showed how, as a drone operator, you could still experience forms of mental abuse that members of the military on the ground also go through.

Coming from an activist background, and witnessing events of police and paramilitary brutality in Italy as I described in my introduction of this book, I generally perceived the military forces as the enemy. Yet, when I met Brandon Bryant, and he shared with us his difficult experience of changing his opinion to open up a radical transformation in society, I understood that in that moment we shared an important mindset. I realised that both of us were seeking to investigate (almost hopelessly) powerful systems, trying to understand how to enact a change by exposing abuses and injustices. This was both shocking and revelatory for me, and it was a moment of deep reflection that informed a big part of the future programme I curated at the Disruption Network Lab, as well as a big part of my research on whistleblowing. The personal stories of all the whistleblowers that I met in the past years have been teaching me a different way of looking at my everyday life. Especially because the act of blowing the whistle—which is a radical gesture of changing opinion—is often followed by a consequent isolation and repression.

After blowing the whistle and deciding to leave the previous institutional structures, some whistleblowers gain quite a lot of popularity. But it is generally impossible to become completely free from a previous life, to avoid repercussions and persecution—as we also read in some contributions in this book. Whistleblowers are very important in that sense, in order to inform on abuses and wrongdoing, or to help people understand which forms of social and political control become pervasive without the public's knowledge. Establishing a network of trust is our responsibility not only as advocates, curators and organisers of a public programme, but also as members of a civic society.

Reading the stories of whistleblowers and speaking with them also teaches us the importance of a dialogical perspective, one that does not refuse those who appear to be very different from us because they come from opposing ideological backgrounds. In September 2018, I curated our conference "Infiltration: Challenging Supremacism". We were trying to understand how we could challenge forms of White supremacy and right-wing ideology to better understand the Alt Right and the far-right phenomena. At the conference we invited speakers who were enacting disruption by infiltrating these groups—among them, anti-racist

Daryl Davis at the Disruption Network Lab conference *Infiltration: Challenging Supremacism*, September 7, 2018. Photo by Maria Silvano.

activist Patrik Hermansson, and terrorism and extremism researcher Julia Ebner. As usual in our programme, the goal was not to confront such systems from the outside, operating a frontal opposition, but reflecting on pervasive tactics of disruption, trying to understand how these systems worked and later turning the inner logic of these systems to our advantage, to dismantle their structures.

At this event, we invited as keynote speaker African-American R&B and blues musician Daryl Davis to share his impressive story, and the fact that he has befriended several members of the Ku Klux Klan (KKK) since the 1980s. Hearing his story of improving race relations by trying to change the Klan's members' mindsets and by having a dialogue with them was also revelatory for me, and made me understood that personal experiences and encounters with people from opposing backgrounds have a very strong potential for societal change, and once again, it made me understand that opposition alone isn't enough for effective criticism. Furthermore, it became clear that we need to give attention to the collective role of citizens in exposing the abuses of governments, institutions and corporations, as well as the work of practitioners to build up shared tools to facilitate this process.

During our conference "Citizens of Evidence: Independent Investigations for Change" in September 2019, we tried to understand how we could mobilise in a way that seeks to expose misconduct and wrongdoing more as a collective activity than as a single whistleblower. The objective was to work on the power of citizens and grassroots movements to expose facts, focusing on the ability of collective action to reveal wrongdoing, and the collaborative production of social justice.

Speakers like Matthew Caruana Galizia, Melissa Segura, Samuel Sinyangwe, Robert Trafford, Crina Boros, Emmanuel Freudenthal, Brennan Novak and M.C. McGrath, Wu Ming 1, Michael Hornsby, Laurie Treffers, to mention a few, experts operating between anticorruption, investigative journalism, data policy, political activism, open-source intelligence, story-telling, whistleblowing and truth-telling, shared community-based stories to increase awareness on sensitive subjects.

This event taught us that we need to work on different levels, highlighting both local and international stories, contributing to the creation of social change through grassroots investigations. The collective sharing and development of tools and tactics becomes crucial for this scope, as we can read in the following reflections by Lieke Ploeger, where she describes her work in developing our Activation community programme.

Activation: Community Building in the Fight Against Injustice—Lieke Ploeger

An essential part of the work of the Disruption Network Lab focuses on creating space for different people and groups to connect to each other, share their knowledge and gain new skills. While from 2015 onwards this has happened through the main Disruption Network Lab conferences, as well as in smaller side events such as discussion nights, workshops or film screenings, since 2019 the Activation programme started adding regular community meetups and workshops to the conference stream. These provide space for Berlin-based initiatives and activists to interact with the conference topics and connect to each other, strengthening the community around the Disruption Network Lab.

Community building and creating networks among different groups is an ongoing and open-ended process, which is also for a major part shaped by the people involved in it. The way Tatiana Bazzichelli and I work on building networks of trust at the Disruption Network Lab, both within the conference and community programme, grew organically out of both our backgrounds, and is likely to continue to evolve in the future based on experiences along the way. You need both openness and flexibility to build up a sense of community, as well as to sustain it and help it grow. Reflecting on our current way of working with community, these are some of the guiding principles, as well as the inspiration that made our working method at the Disruption Network Lab into what it is today.

First and foremost, I believe in the value of mixing different groups that would not otherwise meet. Before joining the Disruption Network Lab, I co-founded an art and community space in Berlin called SPEKTRUM art science community. In a former industrial bakery turned performance venue and bar, we experimented with bringing together a diverse mix of artists, hackers, scientists, activists, and makers in an atmosphere of creative and collaborative exchange and experimentation. We invited and stimulated people to use our space for meetups on weeknights, to share their knowledge openly, form collaborations and create artistic outputs together, which they in turn could show at performance nights and exhibitions at SPEKTRUM itself.

It was inspiring to see how fruitful such a mixture of crowds could be: over a period of four years many communities were established, ranging from the AAARTGAMES community interested in the use of games as audiovisual interactive art, to the XenoEntities Network focusing on intersections of queer, gender, and feminist studies with digital technologies. Out of one of the encounters between a researcher and a sound artist at SPEKTRUM, a cross-disciplinary research project called Sentire was established, which brings together artists, scientists, therapists, and developers to work on cognition and on human-technology interaction, particularly in relation to movement and sound.[3] After four years, we combined our learning from this community building process in a collectively written guide with tips and tricks.[4]

When bringing together different groups and people, the value lies not only in learning from each other's experiences and skills, but in a space opening up for something new. In permaculture, which is a nature-inspired approach to both agriculture and culture as a whole which aims to establish self-sufficient and sustainable (eco)systems, this is described as the 'edge effect'. Where two ecosystems overlap, for example at the edge of a forest, you can find a greater diversity of life: there will be species from each ecosystem there, but also unique species which can only be found in these transition zones.[5] Creating such transition zones for fresh inspiration and ideas is at the core of community building work.

With the community meetups and workshops we host at the Disruption Network Lab, we work to create such an environment where different groups can meet, present their work, interact with each other, and discover new points of connection. The interdisciplinary nature of these events follows that of the conferences, where we offer a platform for discussion for whistleblowers, human rights advocates, artists, hackers, journalists, lawyers and activists, as previously described. In the community events, we offer people an opportunity to connect in a more intimate setting, usually with up to 30 people, and to work in a hands-on format on the conference topic.

This can lead to fruitful points of contact: in connection to our "Evicted by Greed: Global Finance, Housing and Resistance" conference in May 2020, we connected local housing activist groups with the researcher Christoph Trautvetter, who works to collect data on housing ownership structures in Berlin. They are now in contact for future collaborations: his data can greatly enhance the activist work, and their local knowledge provides him in turn with more background information on which data could be relevant for their activism. Seeing such overlaps play out provides us inspiration for combining different fields of work into our events.

A second principle at the core of our work is to open up knowledge and allow it to be more widely used, especially to expose systems of power and injustice. Having previously worked for the Open Knowledge Foundation, a global non-profit organisation focused on realising open data's value to society, I am especially keen on finding ways to give people more skills to understand how to work with data and technology. Open data can often help give insight into problems that our conferences address: data on company ownership can for example shed light on corruption cases.

Our meetups and workshops are open to anyone who wants to join, and we undertake effort to advertise and promote the event in a way that it is accessible for everyone, not just experts on the topic. What unites our audience, speakers and team is a critical and investigative attitude towards political, economic and technological developments in society, and a belief that we can contribute to exposing, as well as improving, these in the future. We want our audience to leave with a feeling that alternative ways of intervening in society are possible and accessible for everyone interested in joining.

Openness is important for the event formats as well: though we often host discussion nights or workshops, we develop each event together with the specific community involved, and are open to experiment with different set-ups. For one of the meetups connected to our "Borders of Fear: Migration, Security and Control" conference in November 2020, we worked with the Migrant Media Network to develop the immersive journey "Facing Invisible Borders". In the meetup, the participants took on the fictional identity of a migrant and had to go through the process of applying for a visa through a visa office set up in the meeting space, with members of the Migrant Media Network playing the role of visa officers conducting the interviews. The design thinking method used for this immersive and playful journey greatly helped make people understand the process of applying for a visa coming from a developing country, brought up food for discussion afterwards, and made the invisible border visible.

Then there is of course the interpersonal dimension. One of the most rewarding aspects of community work is when you are able to create contexts of sharing, and stimulate ongoing connections between individuals. With our regular meetups we now offer our network more opportunities to connect throughout the year, but this also gives us new energy and insights each time we meet with the people interested in our conference topics. We see people returning to our events: while starting up the discussion around a topic at one of the meetups, we continue and deepen the conversation with our audience during the main conference. It has also happened that we met people at a meetup, got to know their work, and then invited them to speak at one of our conferences where their work intersected with our topic. This all contributes to a sense of community.

Last, but definitely not least, there is what I would call unexpected benefits of community work. You never know exactly what will come out of the shared space that is created, and some connections may surprise you. Connected to the previously mentioned "Citizens of Evidence" conference, we hosted two community workshops. Danja Vasiliev and Sarah Grant, part of the Radical Networks conference organising team, taught people how to set up a self-hosted secure file sharing system, using a Raspberry Pi as a web server and wireless access point combined with a self-hosted installation of the open-source NextCloud software. In the other workshop, Hadi Al Khatib of the Syrian Archive explained their workflow for collecting and verifying information about human rights violations through video material, and taught participants specific OSINT skills such as geolocation techniques. Interestingly, the secure file sharing system as explained in the first workshop would be a valuable tool for exchanging the type of video content that the Syrian Archive uses for their work, where content is often taken down by social media platforms such as YouTube. It is exciting to see such connections between groups and communities occur as a result of our community events, and exactly the type of networking that we hope we can encourage more of.

Taking time to build up community around your work and get to know the networks surrounding your fields brings more benefits than can be imagined when you plan for it. This is the essence of the community work for the Disruption Network Lab, creating an atmosphere on the edges of where different ecosystems meet, and being open to what arises.

This is also the essence of building networks of trust, a central premise for this book.

We are open to experience what arises from this common journey.

Notes

1. The profiles of the present and past Disruption Network Lab team members are visible at: https://www.disruptionlab.org/team.

2. The full list and content details of the conference programme by the Disruption Network Lab is visible at: https://www.disruptionlab.org/conferences. The full list of the meetup events is visible at: https://www.disruptionlab.org/meet-ups. Additionally, since the start of the COVID-19 pandemic, we have been hosting regular online dialogues happening every Friday (Disruptive Fridays) since April 2020, visible at: https://www.disruptionlab.org/fridays.

3. *Sentire*, https://sentire.me.

4. Lieke Ploeger, with contributions by Michael Ang, Valeria Barvinska, Troy Duguid, Claire Fristot, Arthur Gib, Magdalena Klein, Felix Klee, Olga Kozmanidze, Merle Leufgen, Byrke Lou and Vladimir Storm, "How we can all make it to the future: A guide to offline community building in art & science". *Re-Imagine Europe* report, October 2018, https://tinyurl.com/spektrumberlin.

5. "Permaculture Design Principle 10 – Edge Effect", *Deep Green Permaculture*, accessed August 17, 2021 https://deepgreenpermaculture.com/permaculture/permaculture-design-principles/10-edge-effect/.

THERESA ZÜGER

Photo by Je

Theresa Züger is head of the Public Interest AI research group funded by the German Federal
Education and Research (BMBF). The group is concerned with the question of how AI can serv
interest and which technical and social criteria must be fulfilled for this to happen. She is als
the AI & Society Lab. In 2017, Theresa received her PhD in Media Studies from the Humboldt U
Berlin. Her PhD, *Reload Disobedience*, focuses on digital forms of civil disobedience. In 2016,
and moderated for transmediale, a festival for media art and digital culture, on the thematic f
rity politics and culture. Theresa's research focuses on the political dimensions of digital techn

AFTERWORD

THERESA ZÜGER

THE WORLD WE THINK IS THE WORLD WE GET

THIS BOOK can be understood as an artifact that exhibits its key messages. It is a literary assembly of actors, each standing for a different perspective, all connected by a collective discourse about the political and societal meaning of truth-telling. In her work of the past years, curator Tatianna Bazzichelli and her Berlin based team have tied the knots of this unique network, and, with the help of the individuals who speak up in this work, shed light on many dark corners of today's society. Tatiana's exceptional curatorial work allowed all participants of the Disruption Network Lab to connect to a community. This book portrays a part of this extraordinary community and the political as well as cultural discourse it represents. It also expands the network to its readers and amplifies the voices that herein speak, analyse, and think loudly and collectively.

The book itself thereby becomes a piece of art and evidence, in the meaning established here. As such a piece of evidence, it captures the ongoing reflection of investigating and exposing truths, which are either hidden, obscured, or collectively suppressed. It also allows us to reflect on this practice of exposing painful and devastating truths as a political act in our societies and specifically as a truly democratic act. This reading can therefore be seen as an act of empowerment for speakers, writers, as well as readers, who share their knowledge and thoughts and thereby extend the discourse and community building which happened over the past years in Berlin.[1]

This editorial selection displays the stories and thoughts of people who in one way or another engaged with painful truths, be it as a whistleblower or another type of truth-teller, artist, activist, journalist, or academic. It allows us to understand the topic of truth-telling from multiple perspectives: through the eyes of a whistleblower, from a close by, but nonetheless outside perspective reflecting on the effects of whistleblowing and artistic practices of truth-telling, as well as by shedding light on the surveillance that is the background against which whistle-blowing has to act in a digital society. Some contributions go on by representing acts of truth-telling in themselves. They allow us to lift the curtain on dark realities, exploring repression, isolation, and persecution, investigating the systematic misconduct and corruption that occurs in front of our eyes, and finally bringing the daily injustices and discriminations of a technology dependent society to our attention.

The truth, it seems, hasn't aged well. Were there times in history, where rationality and logic were (believed to be) stable routes to get to the truth, it seems that today these paths are overgrown and deserted. Postmodern thinkers question the truth's universal existence and stress its relational nature (see Caputo 2013). As everything is mobile and relational today, so too has the truth become a moving target. One that has to be fought for and that has to be collectively rediscovered. The truth is a good that is determined and secured in shared experiences and dialogue. This book—in combination with the events that preceded it—provides such a dialogue and with every chapter offers a search for a truth.

What this book displays are the struggles of becoming a truth-teller and how unwelcome some truths are. For the outsiders of an act of truth-telling they are unwelcome because they shake up our world to an extent that is unbearable for many. There is a limit to the unease that even postmodern minds can bear, and that which extends this limit is muted by the power of denial. Collective denial, it seems, has become the truth's new offspring. This is not to say that past generations didn't live in denial, but it is shocking how widespread and accepted the force of denial has become, as well as how easy conspiracy theories and contesting ideas are to find. It almost seems as if denial has become a fashionable life choice that is deliberately chosen and that searching for truth is out of style.

The stories and thoughts this book speaks about are reports of attempts to describe this vanishing truth in a world that is constantly shaking. But as Barret Brown highlighted in a previous chapter, truths don't make it on their own, they need the be portraited as a narrative and follow the rules of our attention economy. Nevertheless, some of these truths that are told are reminders of the world's instability, its unreliability and its corruption. In a world that is facing challenges that threaten its future wellbeing, like the climate crisis, and that display its conflicts, inequalities and injustices in an ubiquitous media flow (and lived experiences) every day, humans, as psychological beings, desperately need a different kind of truth. We want truth to reveal itself as a lasting pure and good core of our existence. But oftentimes all we get is the disappointment, that those who are supposed to keep us safe are the ones ignoring human rights, and those who act on our behalf are abusing their positions for their own advantage. The truth sometimes is more than we can bear, and the more the ubiquitous media flow is delivering news about the world, the harder it seems to account for all the painful truths that we learn about.

Nevertheless, we should be thankful to those who risk and sacrifice so much to reveal the truth. Instead, we often punish them and deem them suspicious. Whistleblowers, as well as other truth-tellers, often experience a stigma as a troublemaker or traitor. Truth-tellers, to become who they are, often break with community and its insider conventions and convictions. They refuse to tune in with a common need for harmony and trust in our system. They play the dissonant note that our ears can't stand to hear over and over. There are only two ways to avoid the dissonance, to mute the disruptor or to completely change the tune. The question I want to investigate here is, what we would need to do as societies to achieve this change. I believe the answer lies on many—or at least three—levels.

How we see these truth-tellers is a choice that does not only concern them—it concerns us too, and also informs the society which we choose to live in. If we choose to see them as the exemption, the hero or traitor, the extreme in a herd of 'normals', we choose to distance ourselves from them and to live in a society that deems truth-telling extraordinary. As Os Keyes rightly spells out in a previous chapter, the narrative figure assigned to the whistleblower, as the individual hero or traitor, ignores the inherently social situation whistleblowing always takes place in. This narrative leaves no room to pay attention to the social inequalities the whistleblowing occurs (or can't occur) in, and the social relations and collective efforts that most often surround it.

We can choose differently, and see truth-telling as an admirable but *ordinary* act, as ourselves in a different position. This shift in our perception would have consequences on three major levels: Firstly, the societal level, which I will turn to next, secondly, the meso-level of associations, and thirdly, the micro level of the individual.

On a societal level, the shift in our perception of truth-tellers would touch upon our understanding of politics and democracy. If we understand democracy and politics as a system of representation, as a system ruled by a majority and by experts and bureaucrats, we will find little space for active intervention into political affairs by citizens (which whistleblowing represents). If instead we understand democracies as never finished dynamic political constructs, as an organized form of collective self-governance of the people that allows for conflict, scrutiny and rehabilitation, for change, disruption and intervention by citizens in their capacities as political subjects, then we start to think of whistleblowing as an act of fruitful political progress, along the line of other acts of civil disobedience and acts of democratic protest. We would need to accept that democratic structures are not designed to be immutable, but that they are to be re-thought and re-built as soon as they take shape. The practice of speaking truth to power goes to the heart of democracies. It re-negotiates the roles and qualities of democratic institutions and questions systemic democratic deficits. It connects well to the democratic understanding of philosopher John Dewey (1927). He envisioned a transformative democracy and understood democracy not as a static system, but as a collective and deliberative governance. A collective "effort in the first place to counteract the forces that have so largely determined the possession of the rule by accidental or irrelevant factors, and in the second place an effort to counteract the tendency to employ political power to serve private instead of public ends" (Dewey 1927: 32f). In regard to this vision of a transformative democracy by Dewey, our societies seem to be in a state of tension, stuck halfway between attempts to change and the persistence of the status quo.

One important landmark for societal change is the law. In 2019, the European Union released a directive to its member states to implement new laws that protect whistleblowers to a new extent (EU 2019). The implementation on national levels in the EU will (at least in many cases) protect those taking the risk of bringing misconduct to light. The ongoing discourse on the exact enactment of a national whistleblower protection in Germany thus exemplifies how deeply situated resistance against a general protection of whistleblowers is. It is still a point of debate, for instance, if whistleblowers in matters that touch upon national law (instead of Union law), national security, or classified information will enjoy protection (see Positionspapier des Whistleblower Netzwerk e. V.).[2] To leave such matters excluded for protected truth-telling means to define spaces of governance that are untouchable and unscrutinised by the public. The struggle for the implementation of this regulation demonstrates the persistence of organizational and administrative power and its unwillingness to change and allow scrutiny and accountability.

Most chapters of this book exemplify an asymmetry of power that is manifested in state and private institutions. They exemplify that in most cases of truth-telling, it is David challenging Goliath. Laws and regulation, due process, transparency and the rule of law are institutional counter-measures to ensure that no Goliath goes unchecked. The upcoming regulation hopefully allows for a new procedure for whistleblowers to come forth and not risk their societal and financial standing. Nevertheless, this does not mean that extra institutional political direct action is unnecessary or superfluous. Instead, acts of civil disobedience and citizens' interventions are a constantly needed correction that philosopher Hannah Arendt saw as the actual core of democracy itself (see Arendt 2000; Balibar 2014). In the revolutionary spirit of civil disobedience she saw the true democratic root.

Of course, much has changed since Arendt's time and the democracy we live in today is dependent on technological infrastructure to a new extent. The ubiquity of digital technology not only changes our private lives, it also deeply changes politics—understood as the practice of freedom and democracy acted out by humans. Truth-telling under these new conditions still has the same relevance as in earlier decades, thinking of Daniel Ellsberg for instance, but the practices that allow citizens to tell the truth in a meaningful way to our society have changed radically. While Ellsberg copied hundreds of documents in copy shop night shifts, today's whistleblowers can download and transmit massive amounts of data, like for instance Edward Snowden, whose leaks to this day are not captured and interpreted in full. Today's whistleblowers often depend on cryptography to secure their communication, since surveillance on many levels has become an omnipresent countermeasure to secret communication.

Another major change of our public is introduced through powerful intermediaries that operate as new gatekeepers for political information and gather massive amounts of data about citizens around the world. We have new ways to learn about the world, from online news and influencers, to YouTube channels and imageboards. Who and what gets attention in social media has turned into an ongoing struggle for 'eyeballs' in which the predicate of truthfulness is a rather low selling point by itself.

The power of art in this context is an important issue that is reflected on in the concept of art as evidence by Laura Poitras and Tatiana Bazzichelli. Especially in a time where universal truths are out of fashion, art represents a well-established alternative route for gaining deeper insights about a society's truths. Since its beginning, art has depicted truth through the subjective eyes of an artist, never claiming to be rational or accurate, but undoubtedly reaching the roots of societal truths nevertheless. Oftentimes art is able to present a repressed truth more clearly than any report, any bureaucratic document or any eyewitness account could ever do. Art as evidence, as an "act of revealing facts, exposing misconduct and wrongdoings, and promoting awareness about social, political and technological matters" in artistic forms, reminds us that the truth is never only a matter of facts. It is also a matter of interpretation, of reflection and context. Truth is only that which is allowed to think and say, and art has a long standing tradition of expanding this realm of speakable and thinkable things like no other realm of society.

This brings us to a second level of a possible shift we can choose to make when we think about whistleblowers as potentially ourselves, and as whistleblowing not as the extraordinary, but as a normal act of political intervention. This second shift takes place in all the associations that we are part of which are important structures of our society. Associations, such as cultural communities, religions, and organizations, all have more or less binding conventions and normative rules that we are often implicitly or explicitly supposed to follow (see Walzer 1970). Associations are a way for humans to create stability in our subjective and collective world, by creating a feeling of familiarity and belonging. The organizations we work in are often no different in that regard. We identify with what we do, who we consider colleagues, and what we achieve or contribute to as an organization or as a whole. Organizational change is on its own a profession and an area of research. Organizations often work well, if they have clear structures, habits and conventions. They tend to achieve stability in themselves rather than to transform themselves too quickly and often have a status quo bias—so a tendency to prefer the known (even if deeply flawed) over the new. For those inside the association, a hidden truth often connects to the loyalty inside the association. Things that each individual by herself would deem wrong, might become acceptable in the loyalty of an association. Loyalty is the last reliable force that many will choose over justice in a setting where whistleblowing is the only way to get the truth to light (see Dugan et al. 2015).

A whistleblower in this type of setting is often not only in conflict with labour law (or at least status quo) but also acting in contradiction to loyalties and unwritten conventions, that sometimes even incorporate shared secrets about wrongdoings. She is often the breaker of a perceived stability, harmony and trust in an organization's system, sometimes in actual economic terms, but most often in social terms. Whistleblowing—no matter how morally valid and honourable—might risk other people's jobs, social harmony and threaten their psychological model of the world. To understand why whistleblowing is such a contested political act, we need to take into account the social nature of humans; that is at least as important as our moral and political being—and maybe often more powerful.

To normalize whistleblowing, we will need to do a balancing act to stay true to social loyalties and relationships, as they are crucial for our social survival, but also have a higher rule of morality and democratically shared principles that prevails over any type of collective pressure or bond. Every individual who is part of an association needs to feel part of an even higher ranking association—the democratic society we live in. To overcome the stigma of the truth-teller, we need to reach a new level of political reflection in our societies that values loyalty to human rights and democracy higher than loyalty to any in-group.

We need to come to a point where we allow ourselves to think (self-)critically about the networks we are part of and the associations we feel belonging to (even the activist networks surrounding the Disruption Network Lab). To support their goals does not necessarily mean that we support every part of the means they use to achieve them, or that we identify with every convention or person in the organization. It is a hard and brave endeavour to choose justice over loyalty and to scrutinize from within even if this means questioning the existing order of things and oftentimes questioning those in power, be it institutional or psychological. No community, no association, no matter how honourable its goals and intentions may be, is immune to abuse of power, to internal injustices and dynamics of discrimination.

One important option that Keyes also highlights is that we could aim for more collective forms of resistance and go beyond the idealization of heroic individuals.

There is strength not only in numbers, but in a shared cause and shared efforts. Whistleblowing is a practice of the lonely. It shouldn't stay that way.

Lastly, the third shift will happen on the level of the individual. What would it mean to consider the possibility for all of us to step into the role of a whistleblower when the situation calls for it? To normalize this idea also means to deconstruct the image of the whistleblower that we know. We should not see a hero or a traitor; we should be able to see their personalities, their weaknesses and flaws, as well as their strengths and arguments.[3] The important step, though, is to look at whistleblowers' personal story *separately* from their political act. The act of whistleblowing should stand for itself and be accounted for in its value to democracy and not the story of an individual hero or traitor. Its evaluation should not depend on sympathy, empathy, or any media narrative that plays on our emotions. It should depend on our democratic principles and our loyalty to these higher values, beyond personal bonds (be they to the whistleblower *or* to the organization concerned).

Only if our societies, the associations they are built on, and we as individuals start thinking about whistleblowing and truth-telling as an act possible for anyone, can we overcome the blind spots and democratic deficits or injustices our societies maintain.

The reading of this book might provoke pessimism: it demasks deep-rooted corruption and wrongdoing, and it might be a challenge to not feel hopeless as a result. But I believe it can also be read as an important source for hope: it exemplifies the resistance that exists despite all the wrongdoings it describes. Every chapter represents a successful act of uncovering and deepening our understanding of the specific type of resistance that is truth-telling and whistleblowing. It displays a belief in politics and citizens as political subjects that can make a huge difference, even though the struggle never ends.

Notes

1. See https://www.disruptionlab.org.

2. https://www.whistleblower-net.de/wp-content/uploads/2021/03/Positionspapier_Umsetzung_EU_Richtlinie_Hinweisgeberschutz_26.02.2021.pdf

3. Again, I would like to point to the chapter written by Os Keyes that illustrates in a very personal description, how the stereotype of the truth-teller society currently perpetrates is hurtful not only to society and the social contexts of whistleblowing but particularly to the truth-tellers themselves.

Bibliography

Arendt, Hannah, *Zwischen Vergangenheit und Zukunft. Übungen im politischen Denken I*, edited by Ursula Ludz. (1970, reis., München: Piper 2000).

Balibar, Etienne, *Equaliberty: Political Essays* (Durham: Duke University Press, 2014).

Caputo John. D., "Truth". *The Search for Wisdom in the Postmodern Age* (UK: Penguin Books, Random House, 2013).

Dewey, John, The Public and Its Problems: An Essay in Political Inquiry, Reissue Edition, (1927, reis., Athens, Ohio: Swallow Press, 2016).

Dugan, James et al. "The Psychology of Whistleblowing", Current Opinion in Psychology, 6, (2015): 129-133.

"Directive (EU) 2019/1937 of the European Parliament and of the Council of 23 October 2019 on the protection of persons who report breaches of Union law", *Official Journal of the European Union*, https://eur-lex.europa.eu/legal-content/EN/TXT/HTML/?uri=CELEX:32019L1937.

Walzer, Michael, 1970, "Obligations". *Essays on Disobedience, War, and Citizenship*, (Harvard: Harvard University Press, 1970).

Whistleblower Netzwerk e.V., Positionspapier: Umsetzung der EU-Richtlinie zum Hinweisgeberschutz, https://www.whistleblower-net.de/wp-content/uploads/2021/03/Positionspapier_Umsetzung_EU_Richtlinie_Hinweisgeberschutz_26.02.2021.pdf.